E G L I

Date Dr

[

The
Nature
of
Human
Conflict

A publication from the
Center for Research on Conflict Resolution,
The University of Michigan

The
Nature
of
Human
Conflict

Edited by

ELTON B. McNEIL
The University of Michigan

PRENTICE-HALL, INC.   *Englewood Cliffs, N.J.*

PRENTICE-HALL INTERNATIONAL, INC., *London*
PRENTICE-HALL OF AUSTRALIA, PTY., LTD., *Sydney*
PRENTICE-HALL OF CANADA, LTD., *Toronto*
PRENTICE-HALL OF INDIA (PRIVATE) LTD., *New Delhi*
PRENTICE-HALL OF JAPAN, INC., *Tokyo*

Library of Congress Catalog Card No.: 65-13635

PRINTED IN THE UNITED STATES OF AMERICA
22180–C

Preface

FIRST SERVANT: Why then we shall have a stirring world again. This peace is nothing, but to rust iron, increase tailors, and breed ballad makers.

SECOND SERVANT: Let me have war, say I; it exceeds peace as far as day does night; it's spritely, awaking, audible, and full of vent. Peace is a very apoplexy, lethargy; mulled, death, sleepy, insensible. . . .

Coriolanus—Shakespeare

For the young, life needs to be defined in terms of the strenuous, the vivid, the intense. Life is to be conceived in such heroic terms that, in comparison with it, the heroism of war will offer no charms. It is doubtful whether a peaceful way of living will be achieved for modern man in terms of the traditional hymn writers' conception of peace as a region of lilies in the green pastures beside a murmuring brook. The old, the sick, the tired can be charmed by such visions; the young, the tough, and the resolute cannot. They *will* have their danger; they *will* have their struggle against obstacles.

Memories and Studies—William James

If war were only the simple and direct expression of human restlessness and instinctive need for conflict, it might well have been solved by man's reason and social regulation before this time. As the nature and art of war evolved into the stage of instant cataclysm, modern man began desperately to cast about for an answer suited to the peril of the times. It has been with some reluctance that decision makers as well as the general public have come to realize that the violent affairs of man can only be understood, in a systematic way, through the methods and techniques of the social sciences. It is interesting to speculate about the eventual outcome of the atomic age had it been ushered in during any one of the preceding centuries. How would man have fared, had he been "gifted" with current technology, in the middle of any of the past hundreds of years? Difficult as these times may be, they contain greater promise for the salvation of man, because this era is unique in its systematic study of the condition of man.

The social disciplines were tardy in comprehending the size of the responsibility with which they were charged. History will note that their first efforts were fumbling, inept, and more enthusiastic than concise. Hopefully history will also record that the social sciences matured to meet a challenge that ended their adolescence suddenly, and ahead of its natural time. Maturation is a slow process and one marked by an embarrassing awkwardness, but these growing pains mark the beginning of an explosive age in which the scientific knowledge of man's estate may become the social invention necessary to his survival. In this respect, we of this generation will be witness to the success or failure of man's study of his fellow man and of his ability to apply the results of this study in a practical plan to end, for the years ahead, the more deadly aspects of human interaction.

Two events are clear, and this book attempts to reflect and sample both. Each of the social and behavioral sciences has given birth to a number of members who feel a sense of international concern for the welfare of mankind. From the minds of these few has sprung the application of the discipline to problems on a world scale. Fewer yet of these have burst the boundaries of their discipline and ventured along paths not previously charted by their fellows. These social scientists felt less like explorers and more like persons who travelled where curiosity forced them to stray; they travelled without the sense of the pioneer aware of his venture. In some respects, this breed of scientist could be called mutant. He selected from his warehouse of knowledge those facts and insights necessary to his task, and he adapted what techniques and methods the problem demanded. From this, in time, he grew a new and startling system of viewing man—a system that holds the potential for redivision of the social sciences and, perhaps, their unification into a single perception of the nature of man.

This book has as its aim a "posting of accounts" for the existing social sciences and a "summing up" of the mutant disciplines. The thread chosen to bind them together is the issue of war and international relations, for it is in this issue that the test of worth is most likely to be found. The contributions are intended to be both an inventory of past and current viewpoints and an indication of future directions for the study of man. To date, no systematic account of social science and war has been presented. This work is intended to remedy this condition and to be a first approach to what probably will become a tidal wave of observation and comment about the study of man. Let us hope that this effort will be the precursor of a growing refinement of theory and application of social science in the affairs of man.

E.B.M.

Contents

Contributors

CHADWICK F. ALGER

Although based at Northwestern University since 1958, Chadwick F. Alger's most recent experience was as visiting professor of international relations at New York University. He holds a M.A. from Johns Hopkins' School of Advanced International Studies and a Ph.D. in political science from Princeton. For the period from 1950–1954 Dr. Alger was a foreign affairs analyst with the Department of the Navy in Washington, D.C. He is the author of a book entitled *The United States in the United Nations* (1963) and has written a number of articles on political science and international relations.

ROBERT C. ANGELL

Robert C. Angell is currently professor of sociology and former chairman at the University of Michigan and co-director of the Center for Research on Conflict Resolution. In the course of his distinguished career he has received a host of honors and is a past president of the American Sociological Association and the International Sociological Association. He was director of the Tensions Project of UNESCO in Paris from 1940 through 1950 and was acting director of the social science department of UNESCO. He is the author of *The Campus* (1928), *A Study in Undergraduate Adjustment* (1930), *The Integration of American Society* (1941), and *Free Society and Moral Crisis* (1958).

KENNETH E. BOULDING Professor Boulding has been in the economics department of the University of Michigan since 1949 and co-director of the Center for Research on Conflict Resolution since 1961. He is a former fellow of the Center for Advanced Study in Behavioral Sciences, past vice-president of the American Economic Association and president of the Society for General Systems Research. He was awarded the John Bates Clark Medal by the American Economic Association and the American Council of Learned Societies Prize for Distinguished Scholarship. Since his first publication over thirty years ago, he has written extensively on a variety of topics. His most recent books have been *Conflict and Defense* (1962), *Linear Programming and the Theory of the Firm* (1960), *Principles of Economic Policy* (1959), *The Skills of the Economist* (1958), and *The Image* (1956).

RICHARD A. FALK After acquiring a B.S. in economics at the University of Pennsylvania, an LL.B. at Yale Law School, and a J.S.D. at Harvard Law School, Falk was associate professor at the College of Law at Ohio State University and is now associate professor of international law in Princeton's Woodrow Wilson School of Public and International Affairs as well as research associate with the Center of International Studies. He is, in addition, a consultant to the United States Arms Control and Disarmament Agency and a member of the executive council of the American Society of International Law. He is the author of *Law, Morality, and War in the Contemporary World* and has been the editor and contributor of a number of articles covering a wide range of international topics.

OLE R. HOLSTI Born in Switzerland and since 1940 a permanent resident of the United States, Ole Holsti is research coordinator with the Stanford Studies in International Conflict and Integration and acting assistant professor of political science at Stanford. He has concentrated on content analysis of documents in his recent work, and he has presented papers in both national and international scientific meetings on a variety of topics including international tension measurement.

DANIEL KATZ

Daniel Katz is professor of psychology at the University of Michigan, program director in the University's Survey Research Center, and editor of the *Journal of Abnormal and Social Psychology*. In addition to a series of professional honors, he has served as president of two divisions of the American Psychological Association and has been a member of its board of directors. He was co-editor of the volume *Research Methods in the Behavioral Sciences* and has an extended list of publications dealing with organizational theory and behavior and public opinion and political behavior. During World War II he served as research director of the Survey's Division of the Office of War Information.

DONALD F. KEYS

Donald F. Keys served as executive director of SANE from 1958 to 1960 and is currently program director of the National Committee for a Sane Nuclear Policy. He entered organizational work as a field representative for United World Federalists and has been active in the American Association for the United Nations and with Americans for Democratic Action. He is editor of the book *God and the H-Bomb*, a group of essays by religious leaders regarding the response of organized religion to the challenge of the nuclear age.

CHARLES A. McCLELLAND

Charles A. McClelland is professor of history and international relations at San Francisco State College as well as a visiting professor in the department of political science of Stanford University. He is past president of the Society for General Systems Research, vice-president of the International Studies Association, and is editor of the journal *Background*. He is the author of numerous publications on general-systems theory as well as other topics relevant to international relations.

ELTON B. McNEIL

Professor McNeil has been in the psychology department of the University of

Michigan since 1952. He earned his A.B. (cum laude) at Harvard University and his Ph.D. in clinical psychology at the University of Michigan. He is a staff member of the Center for Research on Conflict Resolution and directed the Faculty Seminar on Conflict Resolution and the Faculty Seminar on Arms Control and Disarmament. He has been a consultant in arms control and disarmament research and has taught psychology and international relations. He has published a number of articles focused on the problems of psychology and aggression in man.

MARGARET MEAD

Although Margaret Mead is currently associate curator of ethnology at the American Museum of Natural History in New York, this hardly describes the breadth and depth of her professional contributions. She is the recipient of nearly a dozen honorary degrees, an equal number of national awards, and has authored a host of books and monographs. She is an internationally famous anthropologist who is as well known to the general public as she is professionally. She has been one of the most important voices of anthropology.

RHODA METRAUX

Rhoda Metraux has conducted anthropological field work in Haiti, Mexico, and a number of South American countries and has lectured and written extensively on a wide variety of anthropological topics. In collaboration with Margaret Mead, she has examined human nature in a number of cultures. Her interest in mental health and deviant human behavior has led her to explore the nature of human conflict at individual, national, and international levels.

ROBERT C. NORTH

Robert C. North is professor of political science at Stanford University and director of Studies in International Conflict and Integration. His academic background includes the study of language, international relations, and political science. He has published extensively, and his most recent works include co-authorship of *M. N. Roy's Mission to China* (1963), *Moscow and Chinese Communists* (1963), and *Content*

Analysis: A Handbook with Application for the Study of International Crisis. He is an expert on Sino-Soviet Relations.

ANATOL RAPOPORT

Anatol Rapoport holds a Ph.D. in mathematics from the University of Chicago, but from 1927 through 1937 he engaged in his greatest interest, music. He was a research associate in mathematical biology for eight years, a fellow at the Center for Advanced Study in the Behavioral Sciences, and a professor and senior research mathematician at the University of Michigan's Mental Health Research Institute. His editorial responsibilities have included *General Systems, Etc., Bulletin of Mathematical Biophysics, Behavioral Science, Conflict Resolution,* and *Information and Control.* In addition to an unusually extensive set of journal publications, he has authored *Science and the Goals of Man, Operational Philosophy,* and *Fights, Games, and Debates.*

J. DAVID SINGER

J. David Singer holds the unusual position of research political scientist at the Mental Health Research Institute of the University of Michigan. He has had varied academic experience at New York University, Vassar College, Harvard University, and at the United States Naval War College as a consultant in international relations. Interestingly enough, his experience at Harvard was as a visiting fellow in the department of social relations. He holds a B.A. from Duke and a Ph.D. from New York University and has received a variety of academic honors and grants. He has published a number of articles on international relations and has written several books including *Financing International Organization: The United Nations Budget Process* and *Deterrence, Arms Control, and Disarmament: Toward a Synthesis in National Security Policy.*

ROSS STAGNER

Ross Stagner is currently chairman of the department of psychology at Wayne State University in Detroit, Michigan, and a member of the executive board of its Institute of Labor and Industrial Relations. He was formerly a professor at the University of Illinois and Dartmouth College. He has held national office in a variety of psychological associations. He received his B.A. from Washington University in St. Louis and his M.A. and Ph.D. from Wisconsin. Among the books he has authored are *Psychology of Industrial Conflict, Psychology of Personality, Psychology,* and *Labor and Industrial Relations.* He has been since 1931 a prolific contributor to a number of scientific journals.

STEPHEN WITHEY

Stephen Withey is professor of psychology at the University of Michigan and research program director in that university's Survey Research Center. He received his Ph.D. in psychology from the University of Michigan, but studied and held appointments also at the University of Washington and Northwestern University.

Dr. Withey's work on public reactions to threat has resulted in several research books and monographs and in consultation roles with the National Academy of Sciences, the State Department, and defense and health agencies.

Dr. Withey has also conducted an extended series of studies on youth and the particular problems of juvenile delinquency. His current research interests are focused on developmental sequences in cognitive and attitudinal structure as seen in long- and short-range conditions of environmental stress and threat.

The Nature of Human Conflict

Part 1   Science and Conflict

1

The Nature of Social Science and Human Conflict

ELTON B. McNEIL

Quincy Wright observed that "all disciplines have tended in the modern period to become sciences, however resistant their material may be to such treatment. They usually begin as arts or histories, then become generalized into philosophies, and then struggle to become sciences" (1955, p. 19). Clearly, such has been the fate of those disciplines that presently have been loosely lashed together under the general rubric of the social sciences. Capitalizing Social Science and subdividing it to establish the Behavioral Sciences are indications that the varied fields are in a state of growth.

The sturdy growth of social science might have been less eventful had not the course of human affairs taken us to a position of possible planetary destruction. Suddenly, social science finds itself confronted by a task as immense as mankind and as vital as survival. Not only must social science see to the order of its own house, but it must also arrange its kinship with those sciences that have matured in advance of it. Human conflict has reached a global scale and, as a by-product, has laid bare the fundamental dissonance between the various intellectual endeavors. It is with this "scientific gulf" that we must first contend.

There was a time in human history when by his manner, dress, and speech an educated man could clearly be distinguished from the uneducated. Being "educated" was a way of life shared by a select few who had been exposed to an almost identical pattern of classical learning. When access to education ceased to rest on the accident of noble birth and when the expansion and diversification of knowledge in the scientific revolution destroyed the outline of the classical pattern, the stage was set for the emergence of a new cast of players. As the line blurred between educated and uneducated, new distinctions came into being—distinctions based on the specific nature of the education one received. Intellectuals—men concerned with thoughts and things of the mind—began to sort themselves out in such a way that the distance between the path of life of one discipline and the next became almost as great as it once was between the educated and the uneducated.

In its broadest outline, literary intellectuals became one species while scientific intellectuals became another. As C. P. Snow so aptly described the situation:

> Literary intellectuals at one pole—at the other scientists, and as the most representative, the physical scientists. Between the two a gulf of mutual incomprehension—sometimes (particularly among the young) hostility and dislike, but most of all lack of understanding. They have a curious distorted image of each other. Their attitudes are so different that, even on the level of emotion, they can't find much common ground (1959, p. 4).

The unleashing of the force of the atom has compelled the two cultures to face one another eye-to-eye because the urgency of the times will not let them turn away. In particular, the social and physical sciences face the greatest responsibility for merging their talents and views. From this encounter, it is hoped, they will emerge with the means to prevent the destruction of what each has sought for in its years of effort. It is regrettable that the confrontation of the two cultures could not have occurred under less desperate circumstances, but it may well be that only so grave an issue could keep the gulf from widening.

The importance of social science was most clearly underlined by Stuart Chase when he said:

> No, if war is to go it is probable that only the scientific method can hasten its going. The diplomats, the philosophers, priests, poets, and sages have not found the answer. Their hearts may have been in the right place but they have never been able to state the problem in practical terms, let alone propose a workable solution. Furthermore, while war has not been proved a cultural "universal," it is a very ancient and deeply grooved institution not to be dislodged by less than heroic means (1948, p. 273).

Yet, since its inception, social science has been viewed with an unusual degree of suspicion, anxiety, and attack by a vocal minority. Social scientists have been accused of not possessing a "true" science and have been further criticized by those who claim that even if such a science were possible it would be undesirable. It has been said that social scientists write poorly, use jargon, are too aggressive, are split into warring theoretical camps, are insecure, and imitate the other sciences. They have been labeled as frauds and described as obsessed with the trivia of everyday life. They are alternately told that their findings are useless to mankind and that they may one day convert the world into a nightmare of thought control and behavioral manipulation. A. DeGrazia (1961) has also observed that social science has been condemned for its inability to meet the social problems of the world because social scientists are noncommittal and won't take sides or a clear stand on important issues. An equally violent assault has been leveled against social scientists who have publicly proclaimed their views and taken clear stands.

In all, social scientists are seen by the frightened few as a strange breed; a breed too liberal and too radical for the average taste. This paradoxical set of accusations and contradictory group of views have in common a high degree of emotional involvement on the part of the accuser and have been the lot of social science almost since the day of its birth.

As the historian Charles A. Beard (1934) pointed out long ago, if we were ever able to develop a true science of society that could resemble astronomy, for example, we might be able to predict human affairs far into the future—to give pictures of the society of the future just as astronomers are capable of mapping the heavens centuries in advance. Groups and races of man continually grow and change, however, and refuse to remain as dependable as the heavens. Yet, the problem of the social sciences resembles that of all other sciences since accurate predictions about the physical world are also totally dependent on objects and things in nature, remaining free of influence from unexpected events. As Beard indicates, the inability of any science to predict the indefinite future is not sufficient reason for discarding all science. Comprehensive laws may be established and these laws can become effective when the proper ingredients of detail and specific limitations are added to the total mixture. In this respect, all laws have important limiting conditions. Ernest Nagel (1961) mentions that the problem that is posed is one of establishing the proper means of modifying ideal notions in terms of special conditions and that this is the great task which confronts the social sciences.

The fact that human beings are capable of modifying their habitual modes of behavior in response to the acquisition of new knowledge or as a consequence of contact with new and different methods of achieving their goals is, according to Nagel, social science's gravest difficulty. In the social sciences the means of investigation can serve to contaminate the subject under study. In this respect the situation resembles the early days in medicine when iatrogenic diseases existed—diseases that were "doctor-caused" because of unsterile techniques and ignorance of bacteriological theory.

The ease with which the forces that produce phenomena are modified provides another obstacle to the social sciences. While the stars cannot be moved by man, most of man's emotional life can. Thus, large-scale social events can be altered by informing the public of their anticipated occurrence. This is related to what has been designated as the *self-fulfilling prophecy.* Some predictions may be false at this instant (a food shortage is anticipated, for example). Yet, because people believe the prediction will come true, they respond in a manner calculated to minimize their personal discomfort and they rush to their local stores, buy in anticipation of the shortage, and produce the very situation they feared. Bank panics in 1928, for example, produced a crisis that would not otherwise have reached such intensity.

Nagel feels that the freedom of the human will constitutes another heavy burden for the social sciences. He suggests that social scientific laws must be calculated to include the possibility of human change in order to be workable. Man's will is always tempered by a number of accidents in the execution of his desires. Since man is without total mastery over his society, he cannot predict caprice, whim, or accident and he must modify his plans accordingly. In a particularly incisive example, Nagel mentions that Louis Pasteur would have been horrified at the notion that his experiments on fermentation might eventually serve as the basis for bacteriological warfare aimed at the destruction of all mankind. The discrepancy between intent and outcome in social action has managed to fill our history books.

Social science has never been able to free itself of the taint of "value judgments." A scientist might well be free of emotional involvement in the movement of the stars at the same moment that he is outraged by the course of political and social affairs. As Nagel points out, one's values may act to select the problem to be studied in the first place, they may influence the content of conclusions reached in the study, they may even hamper the clear separation of fact from belief, and they may alter the assessment of evidence. While it is well to urge social scientists to hold their beliefs in abeyance, it may not be humanly possible. The suggestion has been made that social scientists ought, at least, to make some provision to become aware of their biases and to make them explicit and manageable. As Nagel indicates, this is a counsel of perfection that does not take into account the pervasive unconscious bias that escapes even the most careful scrutiny. It is certain that judgments about "valuable" as opposed to "undesirable" forms of social action will continue to have an important impact on social scientists.

The basic question, then, remains unresolved. Can social scientists operate in the framework of society yet remain objectively removed from it? Can they become "scientific" in the classic meaning of the term? Simple observations of society or individuals in a society do not constitute science in its most rigorous sense. Science must be more than organized or classified common sense. If anything, the findings of science are highly uncommon sense because they are not achievable through everyday experience.

Nagel gives an excellent example of how complex the interrelated principles of science can become:

> Thus a few principles, such as those formulated by Newton, suffice to show that propositions concerning the moon's motion, the behavior of the tides, the paths of projectiles, and the rise of liquids in thin tubes are intimately related, and that all these propositions can be rigorously deduced from those principles conjoined with very special assumptions of fact (1961, p. 4).

Most of the common-sense rules of living have to do with things that impinge directly upon mankind—the foods he eats, temperatures, noises, and so forth—while science explores events independent of specific human concerns. Science thus examines systematically events that would not otherwise be part of the intelligence and knowledge of the average person. Most crucial is Nagel's observation that science exposes its claims to the repeated challenge of observational data and continued experiment, whereas common sense does not. Common-sense beliefs are not subjected, as a matter of regular principle, to systematic scrutiny.

Too often systems in social science tend frequently to be "single-factor" or "key-cause" theories in which some one variable such as environment, endowment, or religious belief is used to explain everything. At times, social scientists investigate problems of only moderate or unimpressive dimensions; also, it is true that in the social sciences there is nothing like the complete unanimity commonly found among workers in the natural sciences as to what is fact, what are satisfactory explanations for facts, and what are valid procedures. Social scientists continue to discuss what ought to be the central issues in the logic of social inquiry.

When the issue is raised regarding the rarity of established general laws in social science, there are several explanations. The most frequent source of difficulty is the fact that really controlled experiments on social subject matter are limited to a fairly narrow range of possibilities, because in human society there is a limit to how much you can manipulate variables or factors. Although the ability to manipulate is not the hallmark of pure science, it acts as a limiting condition on the amount of possible discovery.

A major difficulty in social science lies in the fact that most social phenomena depend not only on immediate occasions that call forth the particular behavior, but also on the culturally instituted habits and interpretations of events involved in human response to the occasion. Patterns of social behavior will vary with the society in which the behavior occurs and with the character of its institutions at a given historical period. This means that conclusions reached by the controlled study of data drawn from one society may not always be valid for a sample obtained from another society. Generalizations in the social sciences have, at best, only a severely restricted scope—a scope limited to social phenomena occurring during a relatively brief historical epoch within special institutional settings. Despite the fact that all human actions involve physical and physiological processes, whose laws of operation are invariant from one society to another, it is also true that human behavior is modified by the complex of social institutions in which it develops. As Nagel stresses, even the way members of a social group satisfy their biological needs is not determined by biological inheritance or the physical character of their geographic environment; instead, it is determined by their social institutions.

SCIENCE AND SOCIAL RESPONSIBILITY

The strides of science have increased so enormously and are proceeding at such speed that there is reason to be concerned about the path these intellectual endeavors are taking. Science has become one of those words containing so much surplus meaning and so much emotion that it has become a "thing-in-itself," mystical, venerated, unassailable. Science is pursued and practiced as though it had an existence somehow distinct from the rest of human experience. It is this magical quality of the word *science* that makes it imperative that we take a cold, hard, unemotional look at the nature of the beast that shapes so much of our destiny.

It ought to be noted that a subtle change has taken place in the public notion of the fundamental personality and character of the man labeled *scientist*. The popular stereotype of a scientist once was that of a doddering, befuddled, socially inept, absent-minded human organism who stumbled dangerously about a laboratory filled with volatile chemicals while engaged in some obscure, impractical exploration of an unessential bit of abstract trivia. Missing meals, overlooking important social events, bemused by his private thoughts, he was ridiculed by individual citizens, subject to an amused toleration by the society at large, and in need of the love of a good, self-sacrificing woman if he was to survive in a hostile environment.

From this improbable clay was formed a new image once science became an important contributor to mankind's social and personal survival. The stereotype of the typical scientist began to blur and a new image emerged in which the scientist appeared young, lean-jawed, virile, dedicated, disdainful of mere material things, alert, brilliant—in short, heroic. The Hellespont he swam was the uneasy sea of research of which —in true heroic fashion—he had no fear since even failure was noble in so great a calling. Somehow, the title *research scientist* now conjured up a mixed image of a superman and a super citizen.

Science itself is a human invention designed to solve problems. Throughout history man has used a variety of means to meet his problems, and the earliest of these probably was an appeal to the supernatural. This has continued to play a role in primitive societies, although the problems considered appropriate for modern scientific solution have been greatly circumscribed and limited. A scientist is still allowed to compartmentalize his professional work and his personal religious beliefs, but when he joins the two as a single method the conclusions are not considered the proper content of science.

Intuition, another method with a prominent place in science, still has an important function. The change that has occurred has been primarily the point in time that intuition is applied to problem-solving. Nowadays, it most often functions in the hypothesis-forming stage because there is no modern science that admits intuition as a basis for conclusion-forming. Intuition is admired and accepted if it involves insight—the sudden awareness of unique relationships and meanings.

Appeal to authority had its heyday as a method in science and from it issued what now appear to be some of the most ridiculous chapters in science. The history of science is replete with instances of stubbornness based on vested interest and a resentment of change. These instances ranged from the notion that women (being an inferior species) had fewer teeth than men to the view that the earth was flat or that the sun revolved around the earth. The birth of the age of the experiment properly relegated appeal to authority to the dusty archives of science. In much the same fashion, pure logic played an important role in the development of early science and while it still has a vital function in certain abstract disciplines, it no longer occupies the central position it once held.

Out of this diverse history came the scientific method of asking and answering questions and, as Chase (1948) said, only the scientific method *must* succeed if the right questions are asked and the proper demands are made of it. The use of curare forms a classic example. For centuries natives performed religious and mystical incantations over what they believed to be magical herbs and roots. They would then compound a brew of these herbs, dip their spears in it, and kill game. While it is not science, it works empirically. Science, with its question-asking about the form, nature, and possible related applications of curare offers something beyond simple game-killing. Science carries with it heuristic values—the promise of transporting practical knowledge to realms and reaches never dreamed of by nonscientists.

Science, according to Chase, has its laws, its rules, and its code. In this respect it is a demanding as well as satisfying mistress. It insists that things compared be of the same order, i.e., cabbages and electrons cannot be totalled to mean anything and that science has no self-evident propositions. While science may use the logic of consistency, it rests finally on experiment and observation. Science accepts no truth but the truth as one knows it alone in the night. Science believes that the scientist ought to "court many theories and wed none."

Scientific arguments are interesting too. There existed an unbelievable lag in the communication of truth before the day of experimentation. Since purely verbal controversy convinces no one, people, being human, simply argue till they weary of the topic. Sir Alexander Hamilton spent an important part of his life writing and arguing against phrenology (the study of bumps on your head as a clue to character and personality), but it endured forty years past his last paper. For fifty years after 1859, biologists and churchmen argued about Darwin's *Origin of the Species* with no clear solution. The works of Freud have been attacked for fifty years, yet they remain the core of psychiatric and psychological teachings in the major universities in America. Charles II of England, who set up the Royal Society (called the *Wise Men of Gotham*), was witness to an extended argument over the hypothesis that a live fish weighs less than the same fish when dead. This improbable issue was debated for some time before someone conducted the simple experiment which ended the discussion.

Science, then, has had a chequered career. It has faced many challenges; it has met some well and others badly. Today, it finds itself growing fantastically in public acceptance and with that acceptance has come social responsibility. Science has never before had to face this issue of responsibility because, in early times, little of science affected everyday life. The place of science in society has undergone a violent change in our lifetime and with it has come a certain degree of alienation from the culture. Theodore H. Von Lave (1963) sees a schism between scientists and humanists and he views this as one of the most ominous divisions of our times. He notes that Snow's version (1959) of the two cultures was predated by the views of George Sarton, the celebrated historian of science, as early as 1930. After a careful examination of the so-called *scientific gulf*, Von Lave concludes that "in the past half century, science has changed from a philosophic and academic pursuit into a vast social and political effort to manipulate man and nature" (1963, p. 2). In this new role science has become a potentially dangerous and destructive force—a force that may well prove fatal to the society that spawned it.

Von Lave sees little hope that the scientific gulf will ever be bridged either within the humanistic and hard science communities or between science and society. In part his despair is based on the observation that the control of science has in great part been passed on to the *administrators* of huge scientific projects. These administrators have goals that may be alien to the scientist working in his laboratory, and the transfer of power to nonscientists may prove to be a tremendously unfortunate event in the history of science.

Von Lave argues that science has become so much a social activity and integral part of the fabric of the living society that its methods and ends can easily be perverted to evil. The history of Nazi Germany and the atrocities committed in the name of science stand as mute witness to the extreme form this can assume.

Something else has happened to science. When it was a tiny, patronized, obscure activity it had little impact on the man in the street and scientists had little need to deal with social responsibility. Now we have had Hiss, Oppenheimer, the alleged atomic spies, the scientific defectors, the captured scientists of Germany, and a series of incidents which force the ethics of science to the forefront of our concern. Szilard, Teller, Pauling, and others are protagonists in an open scientific fight having little to do with the nature of science yet a great deal to do with the use of the products of science by the nonscientist public. It is in this arena that the symbolic fight is being waged and the outcome will have an impact on the nature of all science regardless of content.

As Robert Gilpin has indicated, "In substance, scientists increasingly believe that they have a responsibility for the social implications of their scientific activities and that they can no longer leave to society alone the task of assuring that scientific advance will be beneficial to mankind" (1962, p. 23). Traditionally, the view of the scientist toward his responsibility has been that expressed by Bridgman who argued that the only responsibility of the scientist was to discover the truth and to disseminate it, and that he has no responsibility concerning society's utilization of that knowledge. If, Bridgman argued, scientists are held responsible for the evils made possible by scientific discoveries, this will lead ultimately to the political control of science in the interest of protecting society. The responsibility for the utilization of science, according to Bridgman, lies solely with society.

The *amoralism* of science, or *ethical positivism,* taught by Bridgman, sought its justification in the assumption that scientific progress was the road to human perfection. In essence, positivism, as it is used here, may be viewed as an ethic which sought to separate science and politics both in the interest of human progress and the freedom of science. The freedom and amoralism of science could be supported by the thesis that science, in contrast to the disruptive force of politics, was an autonomous force working for man's welfare. This implicit ethic of positivism was clearly challenged by world events after 1935. The inhuman use to which science was put by Nazi Germany, the world's leading scientific nation, shocked many scientists.

If the scientist enters the political arena, he may indeed get slugged. The warning of Robert Hooke to his fellow natural scientists to "improve the knowledge of all natural things . . . by Experiment (not meddling with Divinity, Metaphysics, Moralls, Politicks, Grammar, Rhetoric, or Logick)" has traditionally been accepted by the American scientific community. Today, scientists are "meddling" in all manner of "Moralls and Politicks."

The political place of science is far removed from the days of World War I in which Thomas Edison advised the Navy to enlist the effort of at least one physicist in case it became necessary to "calculate something."

In addition, it is well to note here that the scientist has emotional as well as intellectual bias. James Conant observes that "The notion that a scientist is a cool, impartial, detached individual is, of course, absurd. The vehemence of conviction, the pride of authorship burn as fiercely among scientists as among any creative workers. Indeed, if they did not, there would be no advance in science" (1959, p. 114).

But he cautions that "this emotional attachment to one's own point of view is particularly insidious in science because it is so easy for the proponent of a project to clothe his convictions in technical language" (1959, p. 114) which becomes especially meaningful when applied to the scientist in government.

It must be noted that this view sets a heavy load of social responsibility for scientists. Because of this responsibility, the author insists that scientists must do some extensive soul-searching about the kind of scientific endeavor they engage in, that they maintain absolute control over the conduct of their research, that they be continuously concerned with the social use to which their discoveries or inventions are put, that they work to produce a truly international science, and that they labor in behalf of bridging the widening chasm between science and the public and between science and the humanities. Heavy as this responsibility may be, it is one that must be assumed by every scientist and not relegated only to a vocal few. The social role of science must evolve at a pace equal to that of discovery if science is to contribute meaningfully to the future of mankind.

REFERENCES

Beard, Charles A., *The Nature of the Social Sciences.* New York: Charles Scribner's Sons, 1934.

Chase, Stuart, *The Proper Study of Mankind.* New York: Harper & Row, Publishers, 1948.

Conant, James, *Modern Science and Modern Man.* New York: Doubleday & Company, Inc. (Anchor Books), 1959.

DeGrazia, A., "The Hatred of New Social Science," *The Behavioral Scientist,* V (1961), 5-12.

Gilpin, Robert, *American Scientists and Nuclear Weapon Policy.* Princeton, N.J.: Princeton University Press, 1962.

Nagel, Ernest, *The Structure of Science.* New York: Harcourt, Brace & World, Inc., 1961.

Snow, C. P., *The Two Cultures and the Scientific Revolution.* New York: Cambridge University Press, 1959.

Von Lave, Theodore H., "Modern Science and the Old Adam," *Bulletin of the Atomic Scientists,* XIX (1963), 2-5.

Wright, Quincy, *The Study of International Relations.* New York: Appleton-Century-Crofts, 1955.

The Nature of Aggression

ELTON B. McNEIL

Since modern man has the "advantage" of a cumulative wisdom of centuries of experience with the management of conflict, it would seem that with the initiation of each new member into the human race, we ought to get closer and closer to an era of peaceful interpersonal relations. That we are approaching this ideal state of affairs at a snail's pace—if we are proceeding at all—suggests that man has profited little from his awareness of the costly lessons of history. The urgency of the need for a modern-day solution to the puzzle of conflict seems now, as it has in every age, to be incredibly great. If the benefits of our historical heritage are nothing but a peculiarly human illusion, then we must search for something more palatable than the bitter and ineffective pill of disastrous human experience. To succeed where our predecessors failed, we must approach the enigma of conflict with instruments unique to the present era in order to avoid compounding the errors of the past. The importance of gaining insight into the nature of conflict, and the certainty that its causes are many in number, suggests that man's search for a solution ought to leave no possibility unexplored. It is to social science that man must look for new answers and new ways of viewing this problem. It is with man's nature that we ought to begin.

THE NATURE OF ANIMAL AGGRESSION

In a logically illogical fashion, mankind has for centuries looked to "nature" and the behavior patterns of the animal kingdom as a model of how humans ought to manage conflict. The notion that man is an animal corrupted by the devious ways of civilization has been at the base of this continuing search for "truth" in the unthinking, instinctive, rigid, blind pattern of birth, life, and death in other species. The view that "in-simplicity-there-is-truth" has accounted for a massive collection of anecdotes and animal lore purported to demonstrate a virtue or point up a moral. While fascinating in themselves, these tall animal tales produced little or nothing in the way of betterment for man's violent social condition. With the advent of a more vigorous, systematic, and less emotional approach to the study of animal behavior, modern man might benefit from the study of his "poor relations." A substantial body of research findings has appeared in recent years and it is worth taking a look at this direction in the search of a social science for the means to manage conflict.

There are several advantages to be gained from the study of animals rather than humans; there is also at least an equal number of limitations inherent in such research. In two years of work with rats, for example, it is possible to accumulate evidence which would take 150 years to acquire in a comparable study of human beings. With animals, the experimenter can exercise absolute control over mating and can construct an environment (Davis, 1958) to whatever specifications his research demands. The range of procedures which can be tried, or sometimes inflicted, on animals reaches far beyond that permissible with man.

On the other side of the ledger, we must reckon with the fact that discoveries with animals can be applied to man or another variety of animal only through reasoning by analogy. Work on one species can serve as a model only for the formation of *hypotheses* about other species. To be sure, Darwin's notions about man's evolutionary development suggest a considerable similarity between man and animal, but all analogies are imperfect and tend to cause more diseases than they cure. The freedom from evasion, defense, and duplicity in animal behavior is a singular advantage as well as a characteristic limitation on the usefulness of findings in animal experiments, for it is exactly these facets of human response which complicate man's existence. We know that the translation is less than perfect when results gained from one animal species are applied to another; the degree of error which occurs when we predict from animal to human reactions, then, must always be treated as an unknown quantity.

The task of observing aggressive behavior as it occurs in the normal course of an animal's social affairs is far from easy. Although fighting is a natural event among all the important orders of mammals, its intensity varies according to species as well as within a single species. As the psychologist D. O. Hebb (1958) has pointed out, both the reasons for anger and the nature of the hostile response differ for the various species. Among animals high on the phylogenetic scale, the causes of hostility also seem to be much more numerous. In the rat, for example, the experimenter need not deal with anger since the rat bites to protect the young, to avoid pain, or when fighting for food, but rarely for other reasons. The expression of aggression in dogs tends to be more complex and to include what looks like sulking or even attacks of jealousy. Among chimpanzees the causes of aggression appear to be even more varied and much less visible to the observer. An excellent example of specie differences is provided simply in teasing both a dog and a chimpanzee by offering and then withholding a choice morsel of food. The dog will become excited and eager to get the food while the chimpanzee may take affront at your actions, get angry, sulk, or refuse to accept it at all.

Although hostility and attack have been recorded throughout the animal kingdom, most parallels to human behavior are drawn from accounts of the group life of primates. A classic set of observations and interpretations was made by S. Zuckermann (1932) who studied a community of baboons living on Monkey Hill in the London Zoo. He noted that one of the most common causes of fighting was for the possession of objects—usually for females or food, with disputes over the possession of wives provoking by far the most serious battles. In one instance, when thirty new females were introduced into the colony in an attempt to make the ratio of sexes more even, the result was a major disaster. Within a month, one-half of the newly imported females had been killed in the continuing melee which developed over them. Such group-wide violence is only characteristic of primates and once fighting breaks out it spreads rapidly to involve others who may have no stake whatsoever in the outcome of the original dispute.

Much of the theorizing about aggression among baboons was based on these early observations by Zuckermann. In recent years, observations of baboon colonies in their native habitat have produced quite opposite conclusions (Imanishi, 1960). Under natural conditions adult males establish a strong dominance system and seldom come into conflict with one another. Zuckermann erred by reaching conclusions based on observations of a disorganized population of baboons, containing an unequal sex ratio, and living in an abnormally small and artificial area.

Extrapolation from primate behavior in such a setting to human behavior in seemingly similar situations is an interesting form of intellectual dalliance but must be approached with caution.

E. F. M. Durbin and J. Bowlby (1950) make some pointed comparisons between primate behavior and human conduct once the restraints of civilization are removed. One such fascinating example is to be found in the history of Pitcairn Island's colony of English seamen mutineers of the H.M.S. Bounty. With the forces of the English Navy in hot pursuit, nine English seamen, six native men, and eleven native women fled from Tahiti to Pitcairn Island where they lived peacefully for the first two years. Then, much as on Monkey Hill, a dispute arose over the possession of one of the females. At the end of ten years on the island, twelve of the fifteen men had been murdered and peace finally reigned when the population was reduced to a lone white man, nine native women, and twenty-five children.

A similar set of comparisons can be made between primate reactions and the basis of conflict among unsupervised groups of young children. Just as apes resent and repel the intrusion of a stranger of the same species, children too will attack another child who is perceived as being an "outsider." Children are at least as notorious for their squabbles over possessions as are the apes. Children may treat a geographical area (a corner of a sandbox) as though it were a possession and defend it accordingly. As N. Collias (1944) indicated, territorial rights are also an important and frequent source of animal aggression.

Observations of the kind, quality, and source of hostility common to animals provide us with knowledge of a hard core of basic responses from which human elaborations may be constructed. When the affairs of man are extrapolated from these findings, the most regular suggestion made is that an effective design for conflict-free human relations must at least make provision for these fundamental aspects of conflict—the intrusion of strangers and property rights.

Animals are endowed at birth with combat apparatus characteristic of their species. Battle equipment includes more than the traditional fang-and-claw of the wild; it ranges from the frog's ability to jump forcefully on the back of a fellow-frog who trespasses on his territory, to the speed with which an animal's nervous system is capable of mobilizing its resources for self-defense. This inheritance sets limits on the destructiveness of aggressive actions.

For centuries, man has capitalized on his observations of animals in their natural state; domesticating docile species (Komai and Guhl, 1960) or selectively crossbreeding other strains for aggressiveness. Work with wild rats, for example, was always complicated by the violence of their reaction to captivity and close association with humans. Such rats have been observed to die of fright when handled (Richter, 1957) or to die while fighting even when uninjured (Barnett, 1955). Thus, through planned breeding, experimenters were able to develop a compliant strain of rodent such as the now common laboratory animal, the Norway rat (Richter, 1954).

When dog-pits and gamecock fighting were in vogue, the identification of particularly aggressive breeds was of considerable practical importance. The wire-haired fox terrier has always had a reputation as a quick-tempered fighter (Fuller, 1953)—a dog that could not live peacefully with his own litter-mates. While members of most breeds of dog work out individual dominance-submission relationships with other dogs, or at times fight on a one-to-one basis, terriers have been known to band together and attack a single hapless victim. In an interesting laboratory test of the warlike qualities of these dogs, W. T. James (1951) mixed a litter of beagles and a litter of fox terriers so that half of each litter grew to maturity with litter-mates of the other breed. Before long the smallest beagle was larger than the largest fox terrier yet the beagles regularly came in second best in competition for a bone or a pan of food. Another bit of convincing evidence of terrier dominance appeared with the birth of puppies in these mixed litters—all sired by fox terriers.

A more complicated exploration of the effects of crossbreeding is reported by J. P. Scott (1954). By crossing the aggressive African basenji with the more placid cocker spaniel and then pure-breeding the offspring, he was able to make tests of aggressiveness for a series of generations containing different degrees of each strain. As a result of these experiments, Scott concluded that the percentage of aggressive individuals in each litter could be accounted for by the presence of some genetic trait.

In addition to the conclusions drawn from experiments focused on qualities of individuals and breeds, there exist a number of findings pertinent to hereditary differences in aggressiveness by sex. In studies of responses typical of each sex, aggressiveness tends to be a function of a number of elements. In some cases only one of the sexes is endowed with the apparatus needed to mount a successful offensive, e.g., only the female bee develops a stinger. In most instances, whether vertebrate or invertebrate, the average male is larger than the female and more likely to be victorious in combat. The innate gentleness often attributed to the female of the species appears to be the consequence of a delicate balance of hormones which acts to stimulate submissiveness rather than assertiveness or dominance. Of course hereditary differences in aggressiveness exist independent of sex or size and weight. At times, females can be more fierce than males, and large or lethargic animals may lose out to smaller but speedier and more vicious members of the breed. It is interesting that within a quite aggressive breed, males will be dominant over the females but in observing a more pacific breed, sex differences are not nearly as apparent (Pawlowski and Scott, 1956).

Evidence for the relationship of heredity and aggressiveness is highly suggestive but far from complete. Innate temperamental differences exist (Fredericson and Birnbaum, 1954), but, as we shall see, they represent a potential which can be drastically modified by training or altered in important respects by the accident of a whimsical environment. The facts of heredity in animals have a limited application to humans since we are not distinguished by identifiable breeds and strains. A fact of vital importance in the study of heredity is that there has yet to be an acceptable experimental demonstration of the production of aggressive humans through the sole process of mating individuals selected for their aggressiveness.

Animal responses which seem to be fully innate and present at birth may still require considerable collaboration from the environment to reach their characteristic form of expression. Even the mouse-catching of cats, as Z. Y. Kuo (1930) proved nearly thirty years ago, is a reaction the kitten usually learns from its mother. When Kuo raised kittens with a mouse or rat for a cage companion, he discovered they would not kill their cage mate and rarely killed other rodents. Kittens reared with mothers who were allowed to demonstrate rat-killing for the edification of their offspring, almost without exception became killers at maturity. We have learned, in the years that followed, that Kuo's original explanation of mouse-catching was too simple an explanation of this complicated behavior. His pioneering work gave impetus to an extensive reappraisal of many behaviors once clearly labeled *hereditary*. N. W. Heimstra and G. Newton (1961), for example, have demonstrated that the cat's killing response may be the outcome of its prior experience in competing for food.

A third, and quite different form of cat behavior, can be produced by administering an electric shock to a kitten each time a mouse appears. The effect of this treatment of the cat is the formation of a pronounced avoidance of his traditional enemy. Thus, the capacity to aggress may suffer any of a number of fates; a kitten may become the rat's playful companion, his executioner, or live in terror of him.

The malleability of aggressive urges has been demonstrated in a series of experiments devoted to inhibiting or increasing fighting through training. In five days, for example, J. P. Scott (1958) converted an inexperienced mouse into a successful fighter by "fixing" its bouts so that it always emerged the uninjured victor. According to M. W. Kahn (1951), this method of training makes mice so assaultive that, contrary to their usual habits, they may attack females and the young. Scott makes the interesting observation that methods quite similar to this are used by boxing managers who carefully match their fighters with opponents they can defeat to prevent them from undergoing a morale-killing beating. Mice who have suffered the shock of taking a beating can sometimes be retrained to become fighters, but the procedure is not uniformly success-ful. By allowing the defeated mouse to rest for a month or two and then exposing it to a mouse that has been trained to run away, B. Ginsburg and W. C. Allee (1942) were able to restore its dominant status.

If a rat learns that by fighting it can avoid an even more painful stimulus (Fredericson, Story, and Gurney, 1955), it will seek out oppor-tunities for combat with increased eagerness. Since rats can also learn to associate any of a number of cues or signals (Scott and Fredericson, 1951) with the response of attack, the range of stimuli which the experi-menter can use to provoke aggressive outbursts is almost unlimited. Just placing a rat in a cage in which it has fought in the past can be enough to evoke signs of preparation for a new contest.

The simplest method for inhibiting the expression of hostility is to reverse the procedure used to train fighters. If a rat is beaten regularly and consistently by another rat (Scott and Marston, 1953), it will de-velop an avoidance of combat that is particularly resistant to retraining. Learning to live peacefully need not involve as drastic an experience as this, however. J. P. Scott (1958) found that he could develop a "habit of not fighting" or its equivalent, a "passive inhibition" of the fighting re-sponse, by rearing inexperienced male mice with females with whom they usually do not fight. A similar passivity can be taught to puppies if they are picked up whenever they become aggressive. They are helpless with their feet off the floor so the fighting response is never allowed free reign. Scott suggests children too might acquire habits of not fighting simply by not being stimulated, or allowed, to fight. As both Scott and the average parent know full well, this is a situation much to be desired but incredibly difficult to achieve.

Another method which produces an inhibition of aggressiveness is to make some other need so urgent that it takes precedence over the urge to attack. J. P. Seward (1945, 1946), for example, learned that rats trained to fight one another on sight would fight *less* when made very hungry and then fed together in the fighting cage. It must be noted that Seward's fighting rats had not yet settled the question of which of them was to be permanently dominant over the other. When dominance-sub-mission relationships are firmly established around food, as in the goats studied by J. P. Scott (1948), then hunger *increases* the amount of aggression that appears at feeding time, but only on the part of the domi-nant goats. Goats accustomed to being submissive launched no greater number of attacks when hungry, rather they stood their ground longer while taking much more severe abuse. This, of course, might be a species difference only.

Reducing the primary stimulation to fighting is an additional means of resolving an aggressive situation (Scott, 1948). When a mouse is losing a fight but is in a cage or narrow runway from which escape is impossible, it soon remains perfectly passive or stands, with its paws extended, warding off the aggressor yet not returning the attack. Both these devices prove to be adaptive, under the circumstances, since they make the dispute a one-sided affair and eliminate any further provocation of the winning rat. "Playing possum" is a means of reducing to zero any stimulation to further a more intensive attack by the animal's antagonist and it is an effective technique since animals attack to establish dominance and not to get revenge.

Once an animal has achieved a position of dominance over other animals, it will violently resist any effort made to lower its status. J. H. Masserman (1943, 1944) and others have drawn a parallel to the human response of loss of status, noting that such a loss may result in the most extreme forms of expression of human aggression—murder or suicide. Evidently a cat, or a human, can adjust to subordinate status if he has known no other way of life, but, once having acquired a taste for being first in relationships with others, it is not abandoned gracefully. Masserman and his co-workers were able to effect a downward displacement of dominant cats by making them the victims of an experimental neurosis (i.e., forcing them to make an impossibly difficult decision with extreme punishment the penalty for failure to decide correctly). In an attempt to help the cat regain his status, the experimenter introduced a sizeable portion of alcohol into the cat's milk. The cat, suffused with alcoholic courage, became a fighting drunk and temporarily re-established his dominant position. When sober, and once again suffering from the old crippling conflicts, the cat reverted to its former status as an ineffective competitor.

The modification of social rank or dominance can be achieved for various species (Miller, Murphy, and Mursky, 1955; Smith and Hale, 1959) by a process of interanimal conditioning. If the attempt to dominate is regularly accompanied by the experience of electric shock, for example, dominance becomes a costly behavior to maintain and is abandoned. The length of time such conditioning remains effective differs in the various species.

It is apparent that the expression of aggressive urges is a plastic process capable of considerable modification through training. An animal may inherit a potential for aggressive action, but the form, intensity, and kind of expression which ultimately will characterize him is determined by the nature of his individual life experiences and what he learns from them. Each of the methods used in animal experimentation to increase or diminish aggressivity has some application to the human problem of rearing and training children. Laboratory animals provide a model of cause and effect which is most fruitfully applied to that brief period in human development when the child is sufficiently mobile to be aggressive toward others but has not yet acquired a workable system of symbolic behavior in the form of language.

An appraisal of aggression must not only encompass the conditions which provoke the animal to attack and the nature of the aggressive response itself; it ought to include an exploration of those internal physiological events which mediate between the stimulus and response. It is possible to regard the activity of the nervous system as a cause of attacking behavior, as a necessary concomitant of hostile activity, as a consequence of the expression of aggression, or, in some combination or sequence, as all of these at once. What is most important is that the internal environment of the organism provides science with yet another avenue to the modification, alteration, and control of aggressive behavior.

The network of endocrine glands, and the hormones it emits into the bloodstream, is an integral part of the functioning of the nervous system. The functioning of the endocrine system is complex and subject to a series of influences which affect it. The adrenal glands in male chickens, for example, have been found responsive to the tension resulting from being placed in pens with strangers (Siegel and Siegel, 1961). Aggressiveness per se does not seem related to endocrine weight, but social competition produces adrenal changes. In albino mice similar results have been uncovered (Vandenberg, 1960). Animals wounded in social fighting are reported to undergo adrenocortical change. This suggests that population density creates a situation that makes fighting more likely to occur and in turn produces internal changes in the animal (Southwick and Bland, 1959). Thus the population density in animal colonies can affect the endocrine functioning of the experimental animal (Thiessen and Rodgers, 1961). Since the endocrines are such active participants in the animal's general aggressive response, the history of the experimental manipulation of gland output makes up an important facet of the search for the source and determinants of aggression.

The relationship between hormone distribution and aggressive behavior can be investigated experimentally by artificially disturbing the normal hormone balance. One means of accomplishing this is to inject experimental animals with androgenic or estrogenic hormones to produce an artificial imbalance. A more drastic measure, one that is essentially subtractive in action, is to remove the ovaries of the female or to castrate the male animal. This surgical procedure eliminates part of the further production of hormones characteristic of the sex.

Typical of the experimentation that has been done in this field is the work of E. A. Beeman (1947). Since male mice usually begin to fight when they are about thirty-two days old, Beeman castrated a set of males at twenty-five days of age and then observed their reactions when given the opportunity to fight at a later date. The mice failed to display a normal aggressive response; their behavior more closely resembled the peaceful ways of the female of the species. When these placid castrates were given an injection of male hormone they began to fight immediately, but this form of response usually ceased if the dosage was discontinued. In an elaboration of this procedure, she allowed another set of males to develop fighting behavior and then castrated them after they had fought each day, for several days. If these mice were reintroduced to combat shortly after the operation, they would continue to fight vigorously despite their diminishing natural supply of the male hormone. On the other hand, if mice are castrated after learning to fight but are not allowed aggressive interaction for a few weeks following the operation, it is nearly impossible to re-establish the original aggressiveness. Findings such as these are an excellent illustration of the complexity of the interaction of an animal's life experience and his bodily chemistry. It is apparent that aggressive behavior cannot be predicted solely from knowledge of a change in the distribution of hormones.

In a series of experiments, G. Clark and H. G. Birch (1945, 1946) explored the effects of injecting hormones in a pair of castrated chimpanzees. The animals were forced to compete for food and before long they established a dominance-submission relationship based on fighting. The subordinate animal was then given injections of male hormone and in subsequent encounters he displaced his cage-mate and continued to be the dominant animal even after the injections were halted. Injections of female hormones failed to reduce his newly acquired superior status, but he again became submissive when required to compete with a strange, and more dominant, chimpanzee.

The usual effect of the male hormone is to increase aggressiveness while the female hormone acts to decrease it. That this rule applies principally to males and not to females is evident in the work of J. A. King and J. Tollman (1956) who found that one strain of mice, either intact females or those with their ovaries removed, could not be stimulated to fight even after receiving injections of the male hormone. An interesting sidelight to these results is provided by the efforts of J. W. Kislak and F. A. Beach (1955) using hamsters as experimental animals. Female hamsters, unlike most other mammals, are more aggressive than their mates, yet the removal of the ovaries of the female does not substantially alter her assaultive behavior. The effect of altering the natural distribution of hormones is to modify aggressive behavior but not to change it completely. For a complete understanding of the action of hormones we must consider the brain and the nervous system through which the hormones produce their effect.

Recent advances in technology have made it possible to implant tiny pipettes in the brain of an animal. With this technique various chemical and hormonal agents can be introduced directly into the brain and their effect studied. Such experimental control of the chemical environment of the brain will allow study of the effects on behavior of energizing and tranquilizing substances and may build a much needed bridge between brain physiology, structure, and behavior.

The paradox posed for current physiological research with hormones and aggression was presented cogently by Beach some time ago. In his extensive survey of experimental endocrinology (Beach, 1948) he concluded that no hormone is yet known which produces one and only one effect on the organism and that none of the behavioral responses thus far investigated have been found to depend on one and only one hormone. In addition, different behavior patterns may vary in their degree of dependence upon endocrine products. When genetic constitution and the animal's previous experiences is added to this, we are confronted with a tangled knot, indeed (Masserman, 1958).

As the various parts of the brain, the nervous system, and the endocrine glands interact, they function as a system of checks and balances on behavior. The raw neural excitations issuing from the more primitive parts of the brain are modified, inhibited, and regulated by those parts of the nervous system which developed later in phylogenetic history. Evolutionary progress from the lowest to the highest form of life is marked by a general increase in the relative size and complexity of the brain. With this growth comes a more intricate and delicate balance between excitation and inhibition; a balance, which, when disturbed, can release the organism's most violent aggressive actions. Although it has never been demonstrated experimentally, an intriguing speculation is that there may be hereditary differences in the stability of this equilibrium.

One important experimental procedure for studying the relation of the brain to overt behavior is to make observations of an animal's responses before and after the surgical removal of specific segments of the brain. It is roughly true that in the brain of a mammal there are genetically "newer" and "older" structures. The familiar convoluted surface of the brain, the cerebral cortex, for example, would be designated as "new," in the sense that species low on the phylogenetic scale would not possess it, while the hypothalamus and amygdala would be considered "old" and more primitive structures. When a cat has its cerebral cortex removed it responds by hissing, snarling, clawing, and arching its back, in response to a noxious stimulus, as soon as the anesthesia wears off. P. Bard (1950) points out that this rage reaction diminishes before long, but the cat remains more irritable than before. Since even the cat's cortex has newer and older portions, P. Bard and V. B. Mountcastle (1948) operated and removed only the newer parts and found this produced a peaceful, docile animal. This demonstrated that the excitatory segments were to be found in this neocortex. If part of the older cortex is destroyed by removing the amygdala, it would be expected that inhibitory control over anger would be destroyed along with it, and the result would be a bad-tempered animal with long-lasting rage reactions.

Continuing study of this problem by L. Schreiner and A. Kling (1956) revealed that when experimental animals of varying ferocity have lesions created in the amygdalois complex, they then become quite tame. This was true for animals ranging from the lynx (an animal so vicious it had to be anesthetized to remove it from its cage) to the domestic cat. It became evident that the amygdala is vital to the occurrence of a full rage reaction. When a similar set of operative procedures is applied to dogs or monkeys, a pacific response is obtained following destruction of the amygdala (Fuller, Rosvold, and Pribram, 1957). Such a dog will respond aggressively when attacked, but if left alone he will abandon this dog-eat-dog way of life. In similar fashion, the normally hostile rhesus monkey becomes tractable and placid following this operation.

The hypothalamus plays a particularly vital role in the expression of anger. When a large part of it is cut out, intense stimulation is needed to produce an aggressive response. Recent evidence (Bard and Nacht, 1958) has made suspect the simple view of the hypothalamus as the "seat" of the emotions. The hypothalamus contributes to the expression of anger primarily by magnifying and facilitating the stimulation which proceeds through it to the lower brain stem. Under normal circumstances, the cerebral cortex, in turn, exerts an inhibitory influence over the activity of the hypothalamus to filter out trivial stimuli so that they are not greeted with a full-blown reaction. This complicated sequence of inhibition-excitation-inhibition is characteristic of events in the brain and tends to make research in brain physiology a delicate affair.

Certainly no simple relationship between brain structure and aggressive behavior has been demonstrated in these investigations. Unfortunately, surgical procedures have certain drawbacks which cannot be avoided. The destruction of brain centers, for example, may produce undesirable side effects (such as loss of the ability to regulate body temperature) which can have a material effect on the animal's behavior.

Far from producing anything resembling normal function of the brain, a surgical intrusion into the animal's nervous system leaves damage which permanently distorts the normal response. Happily, an improved technique, which avoids many of the problems of drastic surgery, has now been developed. A shielded silver wire—really a tiny electrode—can be permanently inserted into specific areas of the brain. When this electrode is connected to a source of electricity, the experimenter is able to deliver an electrical impulse to a particular part of the brain, by-passing other structures and leaving the animal relatively intact physically.

When S. W. Ranson (1934) placed an electrode directly in the hypothalamus of a cat, he discovered he could generate all the signs of an intensely angry animal. In similar experiments, J. H. Masserman (1946, 1950) observed that the cat's anger lasted as long as the current is on but disappeared when it was turned off. This artificially stimulated anger was random and without focus or direction. As W. R. Hess and K. Akert (1955) found in experimentation that went a step further, if a strong and continuing shock was administered to the hypothalamus, the rage response would continue for a longer period of time and the attack would acquire greater direction and purpose. It is clear that the normal inhibitory function of the cortex can be overcome by direct stimulation of the hypothalamus.

In the experimental investigations of the influence of hormones and brain physiology on behavior, the absence of one particular discovery is of considerable importance to our understanding of aggression. Theoretically, it was possible that a close examination of the physiology of animals might reveal some instinctual drive, born of the nervous or glandular system, that would require hostile or aggressive behavior as an appropriate outlet. Had it been true that an urge to aggression was a built-in feature of mammalian life, then the task of controlling hostility would be a much more severe one. It is apparent that the necessary apparatus for aggressive response is provided at birth, but we must look to the organism's later life experiences (Levine, 1959) for a full account of the fate of hostile actions. In E. Y. Uyeno's (1960) experiments with the selective breeding and rearing of albino rats, it became evident that dominant and submissive behaviors were a complex outcome of the interrelation of both heredity and environment—each accounting for some aspects of the total variance.

D. H. Funkenstein (1955) and his fellow researchers have begun to probe exciting new areas in the physiology of fear and anger and these investigations may herald a more rewarding approach to the fundamental problems in the field. Fear and anger, although distinguishable by the person experiencing the emotion, are not easily differentiated on a purely physiological basis. The two major emotions an animal seems to exhibit are rage and fear, but man can experience anger directed toward objects outside himself, anger which he turns against himself in the form of depression or self-criticism, and anxiety or fear. Funkenstein and others are searching for reliable chemical and physiological indices of these three typical forms of response in man, and they are attempting to relate them to his environment and his early relationships with his parents. Their first experimental observations tend to substantiate the speculation that man has within him the "lion and the rabbit" and that his pattern of reaction under stress is largely determined by his early childhood experiences. Continuing experimentation (Cohen and Silverman, 1959; Schachter, 1957) is adding the necessary detail to this general premise.

The recent studies of aggression in animals provide an exciting projection of things to come. When we consider that most of these significant strides have been taken in this decade, it suggests that future discoveries may proceed at an even more rapid pace. The accumulation of new findings, the sorting out of older speculations, the invention of radically different experimental techniques, and the development of new and untried theoretical approaches all hold promise of advances in knowledge which may one day help us understand the enigma of aggression.

THE NATURE OF HUMAN AGGRESSION [*]

In man's attempt to apply the scientific method to human affairs, the study of aggression has commanded an inordinate amount of the energy of social scientists. Although recent events have expanded the scale on which human destructiveness can be expressed, and have multiplied the urgency of the need for a solution to the riddle of hostility, the primary source of anxiety about aggressive behavior is still highly personal and quite mundane. The parent whose belligerent child is rejected by playmates, the schoolteacher whose ire is provoked by negativism, the policeman whose dignity is outraged by the defiance of a delinquent, and the average citizen whose rights have been trampled on, all experience an anguish that they cannot summon up when they consider the possibility that man may one day be the instrument of his own mass extinction.

Personal frustration is woven tightly into the fabric of the life of each of us, making aggressive feelings an inevitable human experience. The paradox which aggression presents is that in all its abundance and despite the massive scrutiny it has endured since the beginning of time, it remains as enigmatic as if its presence had not yet been detected by

[*] The remainder of this chapter has been reprinted from E. B. McNeil, "Psychology and Aggression," *Journal of Conflict Resolution*, III (September 1959) 3, 195, 202-203, 209-211, 225, 227, 264-267. Reprinted by permission.

man. An apt analogy might be to liken visible aggressive acts to a tree that resists man's efforts to uproot it because he is only dimly aware of the meaning of the concept "roots." In many respects the labors of the last forty years resemble such primitive efforts in our attempt to comprehend the notion of the roots of man's emotional life—roots which twist and turn in a seemingly incomprehensible fashion and plunge to depths to which man has seldom ventured. It is not surprising, then, that an account of this toil inevitably will contain murky observation, fanciful speculation, and valid as well as irrelevant and trivial fact. It is man's inability to distinguish between the momentous and the meaningless that constrains him from discarding what looks trivial but may, in fact, be vital. [Thus, any examination of the nature of human aggression will contain as much theory as fact.]

.   .   .   .   .

The bulk of human aggressiveness can be traced directly to frustration. The civilizing of the child cannot be accomplished without frustration of his needs, for the society insists that he must learn to satisfy his needs at specific times, in specified places, by specified techniques, and in relation only to specified objects. This systematic interference with the needs of its members seems to be a necessary condition of group living, for it makes the behavior of others a dependable and predictable event and allows planning for the common good. Although most well-socialized adults encounter many frustrations in the course of their daily lives, they use established patterns of reaction to overcome them and to prevent their recurrence. The seeming ease with which adults remove, or adjust to, obstacles in their paths is a sharp contrast to the child's fumbling attempt to apply his limited skill and primitive understanding to the management of frustration. Not only do the child's needs seem to him to be overpowering, but the few alternative ways he knows of satisfying them offer little hope of an easy restoration of his emotional equilibrium. The child's methods of meeting his many frustrations tend to be quite simple and direct and until he learns a variety of ways to solve his problems he is bound to feel like the helpless victim of the caprice of his environment. It is in this setting that some of the most fundamental personality characteristics of the individual are established and his success or failure in mastering frustration has the utmost relevance for the aggressiveness with which he will manage his life.

Frustration involves interference with the gratification of a motive, need, or drive. The source of frustration may be perceived by the individual as internal or external and it may take any of a number of forms. Frustration among children, for example, frequently appears as a physical obstruction since they live in a world built to an adult scale. Frustration can be due to sheer satiation with a task from which there is no escape or it can be caused by a discrepancy between an individual's desire to solve a problem and his ability to do so. Since so many of our working and social relationships are organized in terms of employers and employees and leaders and followers, frustration can issue directly from unsatisfactory leadership which thwarts gratification of the needs of others. The interpretation of what constitutes frustration is a highly personal and individual matter and depends almost completely on the perception one has that gratification is being, or will be, withheld. To an intensely ambitious person, for example, life may be the continuous pursuit of gratification which, when achieved, is at once replaced by the demands of a new set of goals. As long as gratification is possible, it is a challenge rather than a frustration.

. . . . .

DEFENSE MECHANISMS AND AGGRESSION

No attempt to understand the vicissitudes of human aggressive behavior is adequate without concepts similar to that of the defense mechanisms and the existence of an unconscious part of the self. The efforts, for centuries, to explain the motivation of human actions on a purely conscious and rational basis always produced embarrassing paradoxes or left a host of details unaccounted for. Emphasis on the intellectual rather than on the emotional aspects of man's nature suggested that man, when faced with conflict, ought to be able to draw up a balance sheet of pros and cons and then, examining the facts, make a rational decision. When psychoanalysis shifted the emphasis of psychiatric thinking to man's emotions, it became apparent that any attempt to add up the important facts could never strike a balance because essential facts were always missing. It was from these observations that a dynamic view of human functioning was formed and the notion of defense mechanisms evolved.

The ideal way of meeting frustrations or resolving conflicts would be to approach them as problems to solve and to effect the best compromise available. In many instances in our daily lives, exactly this procedure is followed. If society set no limits on the impulses and feelings the individual could express, no more than problem-solving skills would be needed to manage one's life. In a complex fashion, the members of a culture set up an interlocking system in which acceptance and reward are issued only to those who display certain kinds of behavior and become a specific kind of person. When one fails to fit these prescriptions, he is punished by being deprived of the very things a growing child most needs. Bad little boys and girls not only lose the love and acceptance of their parents, but, once a year, Santa Claus will not bring the presents that every good child receives. Through this process of systematically rewarding certain kinds of behavior and punishing others, the adults in the society manage to force the child to conform to the specifications it has set. If the process ended here, the management of prohibited impulses would be much simpler. There would be conformity as long as the prospect of being caught and punished was immediately apparent. Since a child cannot have all his experiences in life under the watchful supervision of the parent, he must learn to heed a broad set of standards of behavior which will be applicable even in unforeseen circumstances. The standards the child must learn define the kind of person he ought to become, and the failure to achieve these standards threatens to bring rejection from the parents, in particular, and other members of society, in general. Learned in childhood, these patterns of reaction and standards of behavior get stamped into the child's psychic structure and become so much a part of him that being less than the person he ought to be will produce an intense anxiety which is painful to endure.

Having accomplished this process of internalizing maxims of good and evil and success and failure, the developing child must now sort over his wishes, desires, feelings, and impulses to determine which are acceptable to him, and can be lived with without anxiety, and which must be eliminated for psychological comfort. The simplest and most pervasive example of this process is clearly demonstrable in the feelings of love and hate the child has toward his mother. Everyone is aware that children love their mothers because mothers care for them, minister to their needs, and provide gratification. The most casual observation would reveal that when the mother spanks the child, deprives him of things he desires, or interferes with his attempt at gratification of his needs, the child, at least at that moment, hates his mother and has powerful aggressive urges directed toward her. The society insists that such hostile feelings have no place in the mother-child relationship and that the child must be free of such emotions if he is to be accepted and loved by his mother and if he is to feel worthwhile as a person. It is at this point that the child faces a conflict he must resolve and he comes to learn that a number of avenues are open to him although each will be less satisfactory than being able to accept his impulses and feelings as a normal consequence of human existence. It is at this point that the child must learn to manipulate his feelings if he is to defend himself against the onslaught of unbearable anxiety.

What are the ways the child can use to avoid being caught, by himself or others, with contraband feelings? There are four elements or dimensions of the forbidden situation that he can alter to bring about a new situation more in keeping with society's dictates and his own anxieties. Momentarily, he feels that he hates his mother and wants to kill her. There is the *source* (himself) of the feeling, the *impulse* (hate), the *object* (mother) toward which it is directed, and the *aim* (kill) of the impulse. Alteration of any one of these aspects will produce a formula which is no longer threatening to his self-esteem or to the esteem others have for him. He can, for example, change the *source* in some fashion and not tamper with the other elements; now *he* doesn't hate his mother and want to kill her. Or he can alter the *impulse* so that he *loves* his mother, not hates her. The *object* can be transformed so that he hates *school* but not his mother. Another compromise that will solve his dilemma is to admit that he hates his mother but merely wishes to *reprimand* her rather than kill her. In each instance, a slight change in his perception of the reality of hating his mother cleans up the thought and makes it presentable. In extreme circumstances the whole thought must be changed leaving no element unaltered; in a less threatening situation it is necessary only to reduce the intensity of each element of the sequence. This means that the kind, quality, and degree of distortion will always be a function of the demands made by the environment and the internal psychic resources he has available to him. In one family a child must see, hear, speak, and think no evil while in another an aggressive outburst is a natural event which must be managed but is viewed as a reasonable consequence of the frustrations of living with other people.

At first, mechanisms for managing hostile feelings are practiced in a conscious form by the child. He will, for example, retain his feelings but suppress the overt attack on the mother to insure her continued acceptance of him. Such feelings must be hidden from the self as well as from others (after all, the best-adjusted adult could not be comfortably thinking murderous thoughts about others all day), and the act of altering a prohibited situation must be invisible to the self as well as to others. Through a process we can label, but not fully understand, the effort the child once made willfully and consciously becomes an event which occurs in so subtle a fashion that no one is the wiser.

This description of the perceptual maneuvering the child must go through to escape experiencing anxiety is particularly relevant to aggressive impulses because their potential destructiveness makes it necessary that they be highly regulated and controlled. The average person in our society is made quite uncomfortable by the sight of naked hostility in himself or in others since one of the hallmarks of maturity is control over aggression. The description of the need to defend oneself makes it appear that this is a consciously willed, mechanical process—something like a bag of tricks used when appropriate to the emergency. A more apt description would be that normal persons *cope* with frustrations and forbidden impulses and only *defend* against them when no other alternative remains. When defensive tactics relieve anxiety, this very relief will reinforce the defensive behavior and tend to solidify it into a habitual and characteristic pattern of reaction when faced with conflict in the future. When this occurs, they no longer act as emergency reactions but become predictable character traits that distinguish the individual for life. Since a variety of defense mechanisms is available to the individual he usually proceeds by trial-and-error to select those that are the most effective in freeing him from guilt and anxiety. A mechanism that proves to be effective in one situation is tried in another and its use continued until it fails to accomplish its purpose. Highly flexible individuals may acquire a set of defenses which are adapted specifically to each situation; rigid or less resourceful persons may become general defenders who find one dramatic mechanism that works (such as thoroughgoing repression) and use it for a variety of situations and with all kinds of impulses.

Using hostility as the model of impulses to be dealt with, what are the ways in which it can be managed defensively? At a broad level, the choices of the individual are restricted to: *changing the situation* through the process of conscious problem-solving and working out a new relationship with the person toward whom he is hostile; *escaping from the situation* by running away or retreating into a fantasy life where the problems do not exist; *changing his perception of the hostile situation* through defense mechanisms which render it innocuous.

.   .   .   .   .

THE DEVELOPMENT OF AGGRESSION

Except in rare instances, the aggressive behavior of adults is much more sophisticated and polished than that of children. The adult not only has acquired an infinite variety of means for communicating his feelings, but he also has developed more than one kind of emotional response to frustration. These skills in managing aggression are gained during a lifetime of painful lessons at the hands of his parents, his teachers, and his peers. Only the most incorrigible of romantics would describe childhood as the golden years of carefree, happy play untroubled by the worries of the world. In retrospect it does seem that today's problems and responsibilities are more weighty and troublesome than those of youth, but this view is constructed of a combination of a hazy memory and the safe perspective of elapsed time. When we nostalgically recall a youth spent on a farm, we are likely to remember only the cool well water that slaked our thirst on a blistering summer's day. We selectively omit those memories that are painful or unpleasant in order not to disturb our idyllic image. This kind of recall has been labeled *old oaken bucket thinking*, and it is characteristic of the general conception each of us has of his own childhood. Even a casual observation of the emotional ups-and-downs of the daily life of an average child would im-immediately press home the truth that there is at least as much pain in childhood as there is pleasure. It is not that a child weeps as much as he laughs—it is rather that conflicts cut deeper than comparable joys. A tally of the number of angers, resentments, jealousies, irritations, and rebellions that accumulate in just the child's first ten years is ample evidence for the pain of maturing. During development the child does not want for the opportunity to practice managing aggression.

Theorists are in general agreement that aggression is a fundamental characteristic of existence and begins as a reflection of the action and vitality of living. Through an aggressive or active relationship with his environment and the people in it, the child becomes an active participant in the development of his own personality. If he accepts the pressures of others passively, he acquires a psychic structure not of his own fashioning. In this sense, there are positive values of aggressiveness that are more than just derivatives of by-products of the more malignant qualities of aggression. Since children grow in a setting in which there are other children, aggression seems to be an inevitable consequence of living with others. Jealousy of other children, competition with them for a place in the family, and disputes over property are inescapable.

An important aim of the study of the development of aggression is to uncover the determinants of the form aggressive response will eventually take. It is clear that the overtness of expression will depend on many factors, the most important of which will be the success the child achieves in reducing tension.

.   .   .   .   .

Since a child will learn whatever responses are rewarded by others or bring gratification of his needs, it is easy to see how he can grow in sophistication in the use of aggressive devices. When other individuals are blocking the child's way and frustrating him, he can, by accident, learn that an aggressive attack will remove them and free the path to gratification. This path, trod often enough, can become well-worn and evolve into the characteristic "style of life" of the mature individual. When the child discovers the benefits of hurting others, and as he gains experience and learns more about the motivations of others, he will become more and more skilled in using this knowledge of their motivation as a means of controlling them and getting what he wants. Early in his life he may be stubborn and negativistic toward all adult requests, yet capable only of digging in his heels in defiance. As he becomes sensitive to the emotions of others, he begins to understand that he can outwit them or outwait them and that defiance of some adult demands will not bring down their wrath on him. Thus, strangers will cow a child and cause him to be more restrained simply because he cannot predict their response. With parents, the child knows exactly what to expect and how far he can go and he acts accordingly. With strangers, he is not safe until he tests their tolerance and probes for the weak spots in their relationships with children. This, of course, is distressing to the parent who takes it as a sign of personal failure in achieving control over the child. It is not that familiarity breeds contempt; it is rather that familiarity educates the child in predicting the parents' response. As the child progresses in his education in hostility, he acquires greater finesse and soon perceives that symbolic injury and psychological pain are much more excruciating than simple physical hurts. Once this insight is gained, he stands on the threshold of graduate study in the fine art of cruelty.

.   .   .   .   .

CULTURE AND AGGRESSION

Every culture must provide a solution to the hostility among its members which threatens constantly to disrupt the smooth flow of inter-personal relations so necessary to a well-functioning society. An examination of anthropological accounts of how aggression is managed in primitive or preliterate societies reveals a number of interesting variations but probably no single pattern that contains a universally acceptable answer.

Among the Pueblo Indians, the Hopi are a society based on a notable maladjustment of its people; maladjustment in the sense of a state in which continued friction predominates in personal relations and in which the worst is regularly and anxiously anticipated. Gossip, witchcraft, fear, discord, and mutual distrust pervade the daily interactions of the tribal members. In part, the antagonistic attitudes of the adults can be traced to the sharp and consistent restriction of the overt expression of aggression by the child after an earlier period in which his aggressiveness was a successful and rewarding way of behaving. At the same time, control over the child was gained by systematically grinding extensive fears into him from his first days. Among the Hopi, physical aggression is suppressed and competition with others is held to be in particularly bad taste so that it does not offer a culturally approved outlet for the dammed-up feelings. It is pointed out that only the verbal aggression in which he excels remains to the Hopi.

The Saulteaux are an offshoot of the Ojibwa-speaking peoples living near Lake Superior. To a casual observer the Saulteaux would appear to have interpersonal relations marked by cooperation, patience, and self-control; a tribe in which there were no official records of murder, suicide, war with whites, or other Indian tribes. Although there seemed to be no manifest expression of aggression, Saulteaux patterns of social behavior created a fundamental distrust in interpersonal relations, and the outwardly placid character traits were an effective façade for deep hostility and dislike of others. The chief culturally sanctioned means for disposing of this unexpressed aggression seemed to be malicious gossip, slanderous accusations behind the victim's back, and the use of sorcery and magic as a means of retaliation. These forms of covert aggression were widely used.

The ways of regulating aggression could be multiplied with the examination of each new culture. Hostility and aggressive behavior are the most powerful obstacles to the formation of a culture which can devote its energies to constructive efforts. Institutions to deal with such feelings are a cornerstone of the ultimate pattern a society will follow. Consideration of various cultures establishes a fundamental lesson about the management of anger. Starting with the premise that an average quantity of aggression is the inheritance of each individual, it becomes clear that a dependable relationship exists between the freedom for its overt expression and the degree to which covert forms of it will make their appearance. The quantity of aggression given in the beginning seems fixed and unalterable, and if it finds no overt channel for expression, it becomes covert; the proportion of open or hidden expression tolerated in public and private life comes to characterize both the individual as well as the society in which he lives. Further, it would appear that there are few adequate substitutes for the direct expression of aggression. The variety of substitutes needed seems to be a function of the number of frustrations the society imposes and, in general, how early they are forced on the child. In some social groups the rivalry and hatred expressed openly would seem to be beyond the bounds that group life could absorb, yet the social unit survives even if at some cost to its creativity. In other cultures the suppression of all form of overt hostility, and the guilt associated with angry thoughts, is so extensive that substitute forms of outlet must carry an unreasonable burden. It may be that a self-destructive cycle exists, one that comes to an equilibrium over a period of time. A culture that permits and encourages hostility and protects itself by directing the accumulated rage against enemies outside the society may, through destructive warfare and the inevitable reduction of tribal vigor or through the circumstances of encroachment by even stronger tribes, come to follow peaceful ways by necessity rather than by choice. Through a similar process of attrition, tribes which the environment once treated kindly may find a more aggressive and warlike spirit is needed to wrest basic gratification from nature and they may gradually convert their institutions and child-rearing practices to the production and encouragement of a culturally useful aggression. Although evidence does not yet exist for this hypothesis, it seems reasonable to assume that a continual waxing and waning of cultural sanction of the proportion of overt and covert aggression is taking place in various cultures at all times. It may be reasonable, further, to assume that cultures at the extremes of both overt and covert permission of aggressive expression have within them the seeds of their own destruction. Just as the unsatisfactory results of corporal punishment drive parents to reason with their children and then dissatisfaction with this method leads to a return to spanking, it may be that at the extremes the cost of the methods of handling aggression may be so great as to force a reaction toward equilibrium and a median position. The relativism of cultural solutions to the problem of aggression are important to us because it sets a limit on human invention.

The cultural process channels aggression in directions that suit its purposes for the good of society. Once a pattern of expression is set for a society it may continue long past the time of its usefulness because it continues to be passed on to the next generation by parents who learned the lesson so well. Even within a society the relations between groups of different race, language, or religion may establish fixed patterns for the regulation of aggressive impulses. In the history of Negroes in our own society, for example, the roles they were required to take in their relations with the dominant white group allowed little variation in the expression of aggression. Before the Civil War, Negroes, as faithful slaves, were allowed to aggress only against members of their own group and were subject to an extreme penalty if open hostility toward the ruling whites were to become apparent. Since slaves depended on their masters for food, shelter, and protection, their situation was quite similar to that of the parent and child. Indeed, slaves were treated as though they were simple children in adult bodies. In this case the slave, as the child, obeyed a needed and feared master-parent toward whom aggressive feelings had to be suppressed and prevented from overt expression. Following emancipation, the Negro continued to live by the whim of the white master and was still required to suppress his hostility for fear of retaliation from his ex-masters. The overt behavior of the Negro became meek, humble, and unaggressive, concealing his true attitude from the whites and, sometimes, even from himself. In this way he assured his acceptance and continued reward for those who possessed the power to dispense the essential gratifications. Aggression became limited to fantasy life and even these feelings toward his oppressors took their toll in guilt. The masklike quality of the role of the deferential, obsequious Negro was most apparent when it was sloughed off in the company of his companions who made no demands for suppression of angry feelings and toward whom less hostility existed. Today, as the compensations are made available by direct, aggressive action sanctioned by law and social sentiment, the pattern of inhibition of the expression of hostility is undergoing a steady alteration in the direction of freedom from restraint.

The sensitivity of the developing child to the limits he must maintain over his hostility and to the approved forms for its expression help him to establish a workable pattern of behavior in relations with others. Negroes, as a minority group in this culture, must learn one pattern to fit the demands of those close to them in their own group and must interchange this pattern with another when relating to members of the majority group.

A society can give informal sanction to the most extreme forms of aggressive expression. In A. Kardiner's evaluation (1945) of early Comanche Indian culture, for example, he described a society which developed strong and uninhibited individuals devoted almost exclusively to "criminal" ends. The society established an ideal of bravery and aggressive accomplishment and allowed no escape or form of passivity for its members. Status among the Comanche was determined by prowess, daring, strength, and skill, and a warrior's position among his fellow tribesmen diminished as these powers waned with advancing age. The culture avoided its own destruction by the simple device of directing all its warlike actions against outsiders in the neighboring tribes. When the Comanche were surrounded by white men, herded into a restricted territory, and kept from further marauding, it caused the decay of the culture, for the mainstay of its vigor had been swept away.

In line with Kardiner's analysis of the structure of this Indian culture, it is a reasonable statement that for any group, wars help to externalize aggression and to reduce animosity among its members. Hostility toward an outgroup may be the prime condition for internal peace. An excellent example of this hypothesis was furnished by reports on the Teton Dakota Indians. Prior to 1850, murder of one tribesman by another was frequent and the cause could usually be traced to the frustrations issuing from an unequal distribution of the tribal wealth. For thirty years following the arrival of the white man, there was a decrease of in-group homicide while the tribe presented a united front to this enemy from without. When peace with the white man was finally achieved, in-group murder made its reappearance.

Science-fiction writers are fond of imagining the earth beset by invaders from outer space and like to toy with the idea that the world would then respond to this threat by a peaceful unification for the common good. At best such a solution would be a temporary one and it would be a detour around the problem rather than a successful conquest of it.

REFERENCES

Bard, P., "Central Nervous Mechanisms for the Expression of Anger in Animals," *Feelings and Emotions*, M. L. Reymert, ed. New York: McGraw-Hill Book Company, 1950.

Bard, P. and M. B. Nacht, "The Behavior of Chronically Decerebrate Cats," *Neurological Basis of Behavior*, G. E. W. Wolstenholme and C. M. O'Conner, eds. Boston: Little, Brown & Co., 1958.

Bard, P. and V. B. Mountcastle, "Some Forebrain Mechanisms Involved in Expression of Rage With Special Reference to Suppression of Angry Behavior," *Procedures of the Association for Research in Nervous and Mental Disease*, XXVII (1948), 362-404.

Barnett, S. A., "Competition Among Wild Rats," *Nature*, LXXV (1955), 126-127.

Beach, F. A., *Hormones and Behavior: A Survey of Interrelationships Between Endocrine Secretions and Patterns of Overt Response*. New York: Paul B. Hoeber, Inc., 1948.

Beeman, E. A., "The Effect of Male Hormone on Aggressive Behavior in Mice," *Physiological Zoology*, XX (1947), 373-405.

Clark, G. and H. G. Birch, "Hormonal Modification of Social Behavior," *Psychosomatic Medicine*, VII (1945), 321-329.

————, "Hormonal Modification of Social Behavior," *Psychosomatic Medicine*, VIII (1946), 320-331.

Cohen, S. I. and A. J. Silverman, "Psychophysiological Investigations of Vascular Response Variability," *Journal of Psychosomatic Research*, III (1959), 185-210.

Collias, N., "Aggressive Behavior Among Vertebrate Animals," *Physiological Zoology*, XVII (1944), 83-123.

Davis, D. E., "The Role of Density in the Aggressive Behavior of House Mice," *Animal Behavior*, VI (1958), 207-210.

Durbin, E. F. M. and J. Bowlby, *Personal Aggressiveness and War*. New York: Columbia University Press, 1950.

Fredericson, E. and E. A. Birnbaum, "Competitive Fighting Between Mice with Different Hereditary Backgrounds," *Journal of Genetic Psychology*, LXXXV (1954), 271-280.

Fredericson, E., A. W. Story, N. L. Gurney, and K. Butterworth, "The Relationship Between Heredity, Sex, and Aggression in Two Inbred Mouse Strains," *Journal of Genetic Psychology,* LXXXVII (1955), 121-130.

Fuller, J. L., "Cross-sectional and Longitudinal Studies of Adjustive Behavior in Dogs," *Annals of the New York Academy of Science,* LVI (1953), 214-224.

Fuller, J. L., E. Rosvold, and K. H. Pribram, "The Effect on Affective and Cognitive Behavior in the Dog of Lesions of the Pyriform-Amygdala-Hippocampal Complex," *Journal of Comparative and Physiological Psychology,* L (1957), 89-96.

Funkenstein, D. H., "The Physiology of Fear and Anger," *Scientific American,* CXCII (1955), 74-80.

Ginsburg, B. and W. C. Allee, "Some Effects of Conditioning on Social Dominance and Subordination in Inbred Strains of Mice," *Physiological Zoology,* XV (1942), 485-506.

Hebb, D. O., *A Textbook of Psychology.* Philadelphia: W. B. Saunders Co., 1958.

Heimstra, N. W. and G. Newton, "Effects of Prior Food Competition on the Rat's Killing Response to the White Mouse," *Behavior,* XVII (1961), 95-102.

Hess, W. R. and K. Akert, "Experimental Data on Role of Hypothalamus in Mechanisms of Emotional Behavior," *Archives of Neurology and Psychiatry,* LXXIII (1955), 127-129.

Imanishi, K., "Social Organization of Subhuman Primates in Their Natural Habitat," *Current Anthropology,* I (1960), 393-407.

James, W. T., "Social Organization Among Dogs of Different Temperaments, Terriers and Beagles, Reared Together," *Journal of Comparative and Physiological Psychology,* XLIV (1951), 71-77.

Kahn, M. W., "The Effect of Severe Defeat at Various Age Levels on the Aggressive Behavior of Mice," *Journal of Genetic Psychology,* LXXIX (1951), 117-130.

Kardiner, A., *The Psychological Frontiers of Society.* New York: Columbia University Press, 1945.

King, J. A. and J. Tollman, "The Effects of Testosterone Propionate on Aggression in Male and Female C57 BL/10 Mice," *British Journal of Animal Behavior,* IV (1956), 147-149.

Kislak, J. W. and F. A. Beach, "Inhibition of Aggressiveness by Ovarian Hormones," *Endocrinology,* LVI (1955), 684-692.

Komai, T. and A. M. Guhl, "Tameness and Its Relation to Aggressiveness and Productivity of the Domestic Chicken," *Poultry Science,* XXXIX (1960), 817-823.

Kuo, Z. Y., "The Genesis of the Cat's Response to the Rat," *Journal of Comparative Psychology,* XI (1930), 1-35.

Levine, S., "Emotionality and Aggressive Behavior in the Mouse as a Function of Infantile Experience," *Journal of Genetic Psychology*, XCIV (1959), 77-83.

Masserman, J. H., *Behavior and Neurosis*. Chicago: University of Chicago Press, 1943.

————, *Dynamic Psychiatry*. Philadelphia: W. B. Saunders Co., 1946.

————, "A Biodynamic Psychoanalytic Approach to the Problems of Feeling and Emotion," *Feelings and Emotions*, M. L. Reymert, ed. New York: McGraw-Hill Book Company, 1950.

————, "Experimental Psychopharmacology and Behavioral Relativity," *Association for Research in Nervous and Mental Disease, Procedures*, 1958.

Masserman, J. H. and P. W. Siever, "Dominance, Neurosis, and Aggression," *Psychosomatic Medicine*, VI (1944), 7-16.

McNeil, E. B., "Psychology and Aggression," *Journal of Conflict Resolution*, III (1959), 195-293.

Miller, R. E., J. V. Murphy, and I. A. Mirsky, "The Modification of Social Dominance in a Group of Monkeys by Inter-animal Conditioning," *Journal of Comparative Physiological Psychology*, XLVIII (1955), 392-396.

Pawlowski, A. A. and J. P. Scott, "Hereditary Differences in the Development of Dominance in Litters of Puppies," *Journal of Comparative and Physiological Psychology*, XLIX (1956), 353-358.

Ranson, S. W., "The Hypothalamus: Its Significance for Visceral Innervation and Emotional Expression," *Transactions of the College of Physicians of Philadelphia*, II (1934), 222-242.

Richter, C. P., "The Effects of Domestication and Selection Upon the Behavior of the Norway Rat," *Journal of the National Cancer Institute*, XV (1954), 727-738.

————, "On the Phenomenon of Sudden Death in Animals and Man," *Psychosomatic Medicine*, XIX (1957), 191-198.

Schachter, J., "Pain, Fear, and Anger in Hypertensives and Normatensives: A Psychophysiological Study," *Psychosomatic Medicine*, XXIX (1957), 17-29.

Schreiner, L. and A. Kling, "Rhinencephalon and Behavior," *American Journal of Physiology*, CLXXXIV (1956), 486-490.

Scott, J. P., "Incomplete Adjustment Caused by Frustration of Untrained Fighting Mice," *Journal of Comparative Psychology*, XXXIX (1946), 379-390.

————, "Dominance and the Frustration-Aggression Hypothesis," *Physiological Zoology*, XXI (1948), 31-39.

————, "The Effects of Selection and Domestication on the Behavior of the Dog," *Journal of the National Cancer Institute*, XV (1954), 739-758.

————, *Aggression*. Chicago: University of Chicago Press, 1958.

Scott, J. P. and E. Fredericson, "The Causes of Fighting in Mice and Rats," *Physiological Zoology*, XXIV (1951), 273-309.

Scott, J. P. and M. V. Marston, "Nonadaptive Behavior Resulting From a Series of Defeats in Fighting Mice," *Journal of Abnormal and Social Psychology*, XLVIII (1953), 417-428.

Seward, J. P., "Aggressive Behavior in the Rat," *Journal of Comparative Psychology*, XXXVIII (1945), 175-197, 213-238.

————, "Aggressive Behavior in the Rat," *Journal of Comparative Psychology*, XXXIX (1946), 51-76.

Siegel, P. B., "A Method for Evaluating Aggressiveness in Chickens," *Poultry Science*, XXXIX (1960), 1046-1048.

Smith, W. and E. B. Hale, "Modification of Social Rank in the Domestic Fowl," *Journal of Comparative Physiological Psychology*, LII (1959), 373-375.

Southwick, C. H. and V. P. Bland, "Effect of Population Density of Adrenal Glands and Reproductive Organs of CFW Mice," *American Journal of Physiology*, CXCVII (1959), 111-114.

Thiesson, D. D. and D. A. Rodgers, "Population Density and Endocrine Function," *Psychology Bulletin*, LVIII (1961), 441-451.

Uyeno, E. Y., "Hereditary and Environmental Aspects of Dominant Behavior in the Albino Rat," *Journal of Comparative Physiological Psychology*, LIII (1960), 138-141.

Vandenberg, J. G., "Eosinophil Response to Aggressive Behavior in CFW Albino Mice," *Animal Behavior*, VIII (1960), 13-18.

Zuckermann, S., *The Social Life of Monkeys and Apes*. London: Routledge & Kegan Paul, Ltd., 1932.

Part 2 War, Peace, and Social Science

CHAPTER

3

The Psychology of Human Conflict

ROSS STAGNER

Human conflict occurs at many levels, not the least important of which is that within the individual person. We are not, however, concerned in this volume with intrapsychic conflict except insofar as this may illuminate problems of organized conflict between groups. For the same reason we shall, in the main, ignore conflict between husband and wife, between parent and child, and similar small-scale conflicts.

The focus of this book is on large-scale, organized conflict between groups of individuals, taking in the classic instance the form of war between nations. Such conflicts are limited to human beings; it is impossible for the lower animals to achieve the kind of organization required. It is consequently appropriate to open the analysis of social conflict by examining the attributes of human beings which underlie and contribute to such phenomena. The assertion that wars begin in the minds of men points to the need for an examination of motives, emotions, perceptions, and attitudes as these make possible the violence of international conflict.

In the short run we may say that a decision-maker (or group of decision-makers) declares war because he sees no alternative course of action which will permit his nation to reach a desired goal.

Characteristically this impasse has developed because of prior choices, because other actions were seen as necessary, often because opposing groups were perceived as threatening the homeland. Most wars are described as "defensive" even by those who start them; today we speak of "pre-emptive" nuclear strikes as an attack to prevent an anticipated nuclear strike against us. If the enemy is seen as deceitful, treacherous, and belligerent, we may, remembering Pearl Harbor, find the evidence in favor of "defensive" war overwhelming. A first step in an examination of the psychology of conflict is to explore how such perceptions may arise.

PERCEPTIONS: FRIENDLY AND HOSTILE

Perceiving is the process by which an individual comes to be aware of his environment. It must be recognized, none the less, that perception is not identical to reality. Even in our observation of physical objects, errors of perceiving often creep in; for the most part these are self-correcting, because action taken with reference to such illusory percepts falls short of its goal. Further, those individuals who have grossly erroneous percepts referring to presumed physical reality (like the man who saw thousands of little red caterpillars pursuing him) are placed in mental hospitals.

Unfortunately, in the process of perceiving social reality, no such self-corrective relationship can be assumed; indeed, erroneous percepts sometimes create the "reality" they had implied, thus giving rise to the so-called *self-fulfilling prophecy*. A relevant illustration is that of the bar-room drunk who accuses others of trying to start a fight with him; by his behavior, he soon elicits the aggression he had imagined to exist in the persons around him.

We may infer how another person perceives a given external situation either from his words or from his actions. If Mr. Jones describes a labor-union organizer as "one of those stupid, violent, deceitful labor bosses," we have no difficulty in re-creating his image of the organizer. And if Mr. Smith refuses to talk to the union man except in the presence of his attorney, and trains plant guards in riot-control methods, we may arrive at a similar conclusion regardless of the words he employs.

Let me focus this discussion more sharply upon the problem of international conflict. In an interesting paper presented at a conference of psychologists, Ralph K. White (1961) has explored the "mirror image" phenomenon as it is manifest in Russian-American relations. White examined interviews with refugees and visitors to the USSR, their radio-broadcasts to the West, and other kinds of data to arrive at a statement of how they perceive the USA. Similar data were examined to get an American image of the USSR. The most striking conclusion of his study was that these two images mirror each other, as the following tabulation shows:

AMERICAN IMAGE OF USSR	SOVIET IMAGE OF USA
1. *They (the rulers) are bad.*	1. *They (the rulers) are bad.*
The men in the Kremlin are aggressive, power-seeking, brutal in suppressing Hungary, ruthless in dealing with their people.	The Wall Street bankers, politicians, and militarists want a war because they fear loss of wealth and power in a communist revolution.
They are infiltrating the Western Hemisphere to attack us.	They are surrounding us with military bases.
They engage in espionage and sabotage to wreck our country.	They send spies (in U-2 planes and otherwise) to destroy the workers' fatherland.
2. *They are imperialistic.*	2. *They are imperialistic.*
The communists want to dominate the world.	The capitalist nations dominate colonial areas, keep them in submission.
They rigidly control the satellite puppet governments.	The Latin-American regimes (except Cuba) are puppets of the USA.
3. *They exploit their own people.*	3. *They exploit their own people.*
They hold down consumer goods, keep standard of living low except for communist bureaucrats.	All capitalists live in luxury by exploiting workers, who suffer insecurity, unemployment, etc.
4. *They are against democracy.*	4. *They are against democracy.*
Democratic forms are mere pretense; people can vote only for communist candidates.	Democratic forms are mere pretense; people can vote only for capitalist candidates.
5. *They distort the truth.*	5. *They distort the truth.*
They pose as the friend of colonial peoples to enslave them.	They falsely accuse the USSR of desiring to impose ideology by force.

We can summarize White's observations on the mirror-image phenomenon by saying that *reality is not the same for observers belonging to different groups.* To the Russian, the USA is a threat, but his country is peace-loving; to the American, these relations are reversed. (It is impressive to examine racial conflicts, union-management hostilities, etc., and find the extent to which "my" group is virtuous, the opposing group untrustworthy and violent.) This principle of differential reality, in other words, seems to be of universal applicability in relation to group conflicts.

It is easy for an American to see the error in the Soviet image of our country. But we have a difficult problem: how can we induce the Russians to learn a new image of us, one closer to the facts as we see them: how is it that the Russians seem to become more convinced of the correctness of their view, rather than realizing their error?

The answer to this question is found in the principle of *selective perception*. The principle operates even in the simpler levels of perceiving objects; one learns to disregard confusing cues, e.g., when viewing through colored lenses, through inverting prisms, etc. To survive, man must learn to sift the information coming in, emphasize some items, and ignore others.

A wide variety of research experience could be cited on this point. The following are merely examples: Jerome S. Bruner and C. C. Goodman (1947) found that poor children exaggerated the size of coins, while well-to-do youngsters of the same age were more realistic about coin sizes; Henry A. Murray (1933) demonstrated the effect of fear by increasing the perceived "maliciousness" of other people.

What we must understand is that the environment is constantly bombarding us with a tremendous variety of information. It is literally impossible for the individual to take in, assimilate, and organize all of this, even on a fairly circumscribed issue such as that of the Russians. We are consequently forced into a sampling process; each of us samples from the output of news and opinion, just as in our observation of the physical world we sample from the flood of visual, auditory, cutaneous, olfactory, and other cues which emanate from external sources. The percept is thus in part a function of sampling which may be biased.

But the situation is considerably more complicated than this. Cues of different kinds do not receive equal weighting. Particularly if the person already has a "set" or attitude with respect to the presumed external object, some cues get through and others are rejected. It is easy to study this with respect to physical objects, but it is more interesting to consider social situations. Allen L. Edwards (1941) separated college students into Democrats and Republicans by an attitude scale, and then presented them with a memorized speech which contained twenty-three statements favorable to F. D. Roosevelt's New Deal program, and twenty-three statements critical of the program. When tested afterwards, the Republican students revealed that they had heard a speech denouncing the New Deal, and could give quotations in support of their views, similarly, the Democrats had heard a speech favoring the New Deal, and they too could give evidence for this interpretation.

It is hardly surprising, therefore, that procommunists (or anti-NATO observers) can find, in the miscellany of published items regarding day-to-day developments, ample cues to support their established prejudices; and the aggressive anticommunist can likewise find support for his view in the steady flow of information about world events.

Perception is, by its very nature, a subjective process. There is no answer to the question, "Who is *really* right about this?" At least psychology provides no answer. Psychological analysis may suggest that perceptual distortions are more readily identifiable in one group than in the other; but, there are no methods which tell us the true hidden nature of reality. This is a concept which lies beyond the reach of empirical research.

Estimates of intention, of trustworthiness, and of other intangible attributes are necessarily involved in international policy decisions. How we deal with the Russians over Cuba revolves, in no small degree, on how far we can trust their promises. It is thus interesting to consider the implications of a study by Mason Haire (1955) on perception of photographs. He presented a photograph of a middle-aged man to a chamber of commerce group, and asked them to "judge his personality" from his appearance. Under each photo was printed some innocuous information about his age, size of family, etc.; however, one-half of the sheets indicated that he was "treasurer of a small local corporation" while the other half designated him as "treasurer of his local union." Those who received the former sheets saw him as a solid citizen, trustworthy, responsible, thoughtful, etc. Those receiving the union designation saw him as ignorant, stupid, irresponsible, aggressive, and so on. Now it must be stressed that only the corporation or union identification differed. All other information was identical. It thus appears that a person seen as involved in a disliked organization will be perceived as having dangerous, untrustworthy characteristics.

It goes without saying that we face this problem vis-à-vis Russia. *Our* leaders are seen as belligerent, dangerous, threatening to the Soviets, untrustworthy, and so forth, simply by virtue of their role in the USA. Their leaders are so perceived over here. How can we be sure that our perceptions of Russian leaders are not as unrealistic as are theirs? The thought must give us pause.

SELECTIVE RECALL

The divergent nature of reality for differing observers becomes a more acute problem with the passage of time. Memory, too, is selective. Sigmund Freud first called attention to the repression of unpleasant memories and to false memories (fictitious stories concocted, as it were, to conceal something dangerous to inner security). Frederic C. Bartlett (1932) demonstrated the extent to which a memory image may become distorted over time, usually to fit into some familiar pattern which originally may have looked quite different; and F. Wulf (1922) showed that once a pattern forms, details that do not quite fit are likely to be eliminated. Even more relevant to our problem is the work being done on labeling as a factor affecting memory images. The study by Leonard Carmichael, H. P. Hogan, and A. A. Walter (1932) indicated that visual forms will be modified to conform to the pattern suggested by a verbal label attached to the original design. And, referring again to the Edwards study cited above, we note that his Republicans and Democrats showed greater differences in remembered content of the speech presented to them after two weeks than was found in the test immediately after the speech. Each group remembered what was favorable and rejected the unacceptable material.

The principle of selective recall, then, asserts that we will remember evidence favoring our point of view, and forget evidence which is contradictory. Thus it is easy for us to recall Russian violations of the Potsdam and Yalta agreements, whereas we conveniently forget our own deviations from those commitments. The Russians will long remember our ultimatum on Cuba, but will be quite oblivious of their coup in Czechoslovakia in 1948. Quarreling husbands and wives likewise show this selective distortion of history, but the consequences for the welfare of humanity are less catastrophic than in the case of the USA and USSR.

THE CONSTANCY OF THE IMAGE

The preceding observations lead necessarily to the conclusion that an image of a person or group, once formed, has strong resistance to modification. The term *perceptual constancy* refers to the fact that familiar objects are seen as having their "true" size, shape, and color, even though it is obvious that the image in the retina of the eye (or other sensory process) could not give rise to this kind of picture.

The principle of image constancy is of great importance in clinical psychology, where the child's picture of his parents as loving, protective, and generous, or as cold, rejecting, and depriving, persists for years, usually for his lifetime. The psychotherapist regularly deals with clients who cling to images of one or both parents in the face of extensive evidence proving (to an impartial observer) that the image is inaccurate.

This point has more than tangential relevance to the phenomena of the cold war. There is considerable evidence to the effect that the child's attitude toward his nation and national leaders transfers somehow from his image of his parents. It is no accident that we speak of "our father-land" or of the "mother country." Psychoanalytic evidence (cf. Lasswell, 1930) and questionnaire studies (Krout and Stagner, 1939; Stagner, 1944) confirm the hypothesis that children who have affectionate relations to parents tend to accept parental images of national affairs, while those who feel rejected by parents frequently react by rejecting the nation and its symbols. Thus, college students who expressed suspicion of our own national leadership showed evidence of poor relations with their fathers, as compared to a group not reacting in this manner.

While these phenomena have not been studied as carefully as they merit, it would seem that something like this goes on: if the child feels that his parents deceive him, deprive him, and so forth, he becomes selectively sensitive to such incidents. Specifically, he perceives national leaders as authority figures, resembling his parents and hence prone to show their traits. Any evidence supporting this hypothesis is eagerly seized upon and remembered, while contradictory data are ignored.

There is some evidence (West, 1947) favoring the view that those middle-class Americans and Englishmen who have become Communist Party leaders or have defected to Russia with secret documents were examples of this process. It must be conceded, however, that the data are far from complete.

MOTIVATION AND PERCEIVING

The analysis so far has stressed the notion that members of com-peting groups build up and maintain differential images of reality: images so formed that "our" group is virtuous and free from sin, hence meriting undeviating loyalty, defense, and sacrifice; "their" group is bad, aggres-sive, treacherous, and not quite human. Customary codes of ethics (within our own group) thus need not restrain us; indeed, such nasty persons really deserve to be attacked. Thus the rationale of the lynch mob, the Nazi SS men, the picket-line violence in strikes, and so on. If we can perceive the opponent as less than human, superego controls do not operate and no guilt is felt over a resort to violence.

It thus becomes obvious that we must consider ways in which moti-vation leads to the selective perceptions and memories already described. Experimental studies indicate that children who associate rewarding experiences with an outline form will see that form as brighter, clearer, and larger than a matched form not signalling reward (Solley and Som-mer, 1957). When William F. Dukes and William Bevan, Jr. (1952) showed children jars filled with candy and matched jars filled with sand, the former were seen to be larger. Numerous studies confirm this tendency to attend to (or be impressed by) cues which indicate the presence of attractive objects.

In line with this kind of laboratory research we find studies such as those of Eugene L. Horowitz and Ruth E. Horowitz (1938) on the development of patriotism in young children. Even early in the primary grades children have learned to see the flag of their own country as the "most attractive" or "nicest looking." Since few flags seem to have been designed on esthetic principles, this seems to be a clear instance of an emotional state modifying perception. Children also report that familiar houses, furniture, and so forth are "more attractive" than corresponding items from foreign cultures.

The role of the nation as a protector, and as a benefactor, becomes apparent to the child early in school, if he does not pick it up from his parents in preschool years. It would thus appear plausible that the delusion of national grandeur is supported by images which exaggerate the size and power of "our" nation as well as its virtue. National leaders may, of course, emit propaganda calculated to intensify feelings of national grandeur because these will be of benefit to the leader in one fashion or another; Daniel Katz and Stephen Withey will elaborate on this point in Chapter 4. I am concerned here only to note that these grandiose notions grow out of well-established forms of infantile thinking, and may aptly be characterized as infantile vestiges guiding adult behavior in times of national conflict. Again reverting to the analogy of face-to-face relations, we may say that "love is blind" because a young man grossly exaggerates his girl's beauty, intelligence, and charm, and this may make for a happy marriage; at any rate, it probably does no harm. On the other hand, the patriot who is blind to errors in the policies of his own nation is a threat to the lives of his countrymen, and to civilization as we know it today.

AGGRESSION AND HOSTILITY

Not all motivations take the form of attraction to and affection for objects or persons. Especially in the area of conflict, great importance is attached to the dynamics of hostility. Conflicts in their milder form, i.e., competition, may be socially beneficial. It is the destruction and violence associated with the mobilization of hostility which leads us to seek a modification of conflict patterns.

While there are two contrasting approaches to the theory of aggression, their differences in practice are minimal. The "instinct of pugnacity" described by William McDougall (1908) and the somewhat more esoteric "death instinct" postulated by Sigmund Freud (1922) at one stage in the development of his thinking represent an emphasis on heredity as the basis for aggression and violence. In contrast to this view, John Dollard and his co-workers (1939) have become identified with the view that aggression is a secondary phenomenon, a way of dealing with frustration of a positive motivation. According to this conception, man has no innate tendency toward hostility, but becomes aggressive when he is blocked from attaining some goal.

At first glance it would appear that the instinct approach is intrinsically more pessimistic than the frustration hypothesis, since it suggests that human nature carries an inevitably aggressive drive within it. But a careful reading of either Freud or McDougall indicates that these writers, too, considered some frustration to be essential to triggering hostility; and conversely, the Dollard group certainly viewed the frustration-aggression mechanism as one which was inborn, even though it was conceded that frustration may lead to other patterns than aggression. Hence the differences between the two theories may be ignored for present purposes.

There are two major aspects of aggressive-hostile behavior which must be considered in our analysis. First, there is a mobilization of extra energy when a barrier is encountered on the way to some goal. To use a simple example, a locked door is no frustration when it separates your hotel room from one occupied by someone else; but if you are in a room, hungry and prevented from leaving, you may mobilize considerable extra energy to demolish the door or to open some other exit. Aggression in this sense is obviously adaptive and useful. The second aspect, however, is that such energy mobilization, if continued and unsuccessful, tends to flow over into generalized destructive behavior. As pointed out by Norman R. F. Maier (1949), the individual may then manifest "behavior without a goal," i.e., he is simply destroying objects or attacking people because of the aggressive tension which has built up. It is this phase of the frustration-aggression cycle which represents a social danger.

Displacement

For the release of hostility in an attack upon a person or object not involved in the original frustration the term *displacement* is customarily employed. We could have used displacement to refer to the transfer of the child's affection from parent to nation; the two phenomena are quite similar. Transfer usually implies that the second stimulus resembles the original in one or more dimensions; displacement suggests that hostility may be vented on any convenient person or object without regard to this matter of resembling what is really hated. It is difficult to test the limits of this distinction, because the significant frustrations of everyday existence are human frustration, and displacements usually take the form of attacks on other, relatively helpless humans. Hence, the similarity of scapegoat and of the original frustrator may be substantial.

It will be noted that we now return to our emphasis on the process of perceiving. Persons will be seen as appropriate objects for hostility when (a) they resemble in some way the original frustrating person and (b) when they are not in a position to retaliate effectively. Consider the cases of anti-Negro violence in the old South, and of anti-Semitic violence in Nazi Germany. In both cases the dominant group denied the human attributes of the scapegoats, although they were perceptibly "human"; and the scapegoat group was relatively helpless to fight back against this ruthless aggression.

It follows that modes of perceiving which limit the category "human" to citizens of our nation, and which view citizens of Russia as less than human, will foster the displacement of aggression onto the Russians. Conversely, if they are encouraged to view us as "bad, imperialistic, warmongering capitalists" who lack human attributes, it will be easy for them to express their hostilities in the form of violence against us.

It is not my intention to suggest that the President of the United States is suffering from cold, hunger, or other frustrations, and that these lead him to feel hostility which he diverts onto the Soviet Union; nor do I imply that the leaders of the Russian government operate in any such simple-minded fashion. The displacement mechanism described here is, however, important in relation to the behavior of large populations.

It is a matter of simple fact that children must be frustrated to some extent in the process of growing up. Such experiences build aggressive tension. If these hostilities are related directly to the parents, fear of punishment, loss of love, and so forth are activated. Hence the hostility must be suppressed or repressed. In any event, it may not disappear but may crop up in disguised form as prejudice against minority groups or foreigners.

A relevant study is that by Neal E. Miller and R. Bugelski (1948), in which they obtained scores for attitudes toward minority groups before and after a "real-life" frustration of some importance to the persons involved in the survey. Prejudice was notably higher after the frustration. Since it was impossible, in either study, for the attitude-object to be the cause of the frustration, it is clear that energy or intensity of feeling can be deflected from the frustrating agent to an innocent bystander.

These observations provide contemporary confirmation for the classic advice of Machiavelli to his prince, viz., if the population is rebellious, stir up trouble with a foreign foe. The people may perceive the government as the source of their frustrations, but if they can be induced to deflect their hostilities onto a foreign enemy, the probability of a revolution is diminished.

Projection

Hostility affects perception in still another fashion. It was noted earlier that one tends to magnify desirable objects, or desirable features of approved objects. A parallel process is also found in the way we perceive objects. A hated person will be seen as having all sorts of undesirable attributes; impartial observers usually conclude that the perceiver has exaggerated the variety and extent of these traits. Citizens of neutral nations, for example, find it difficult to believe that the USA is as black as the Russians perceive it to be; likewise it it difficult to find evidence supporting the extremely negative image we hold of the USSR.

The concept of projection is relevant here because it has traditionally identified a specific case of such perceptual distortion. Projection commonly takes the form of exaggerating in other persons a disapproved characteristic which one does not wish to recognize in himself. Thus the dishonest man "sees" evidence of a great deal of cheating around him; persons with strong sex drives find that they live in a world writhing with sexual passions; and aggressive individuals feel that they live in imminent danger of attack.

The mechanism involved can be conceived again as selective sampling. Each of us engages in a variety of acts, some of which imply friendly cooperation, while others imply rivalry or dislike. The aggressive paranoid selectively screens out information which would indicate that others like him; he magnifies cues indicative of hostility.

Nationalistic persons are highly selective in their reception of international news. In totalitarian states this is guaranteed, of course, by censorship of items favorable to an "enemy" nation. But even without such press control the mechanism operates, at various levels: the "free" American newspapers do not print accounts of events as they are seen by communists, and if such accounts are available, most Americans register and remember only the material which shows communism in a bad light (cf. Edwards, 1941). For example, when the Russians reduced the size of their armed forces in 1959, this was interpreted in the USA as evidence of growing reliance upon missiles, not as proof of a wish to reduce tensions. Our demobilization after Korea was, however, cited as evidence that we did not intend to attack anyone.

The unique property of projections, as this concept is employed by psychoanalysts, is that one reduces his own guilt feelings by projecting "bad" motives onto the other party. Thus the aggressive paranoid sees another person as about to attack; he can then attack in "self-defense," releasing his painful pent-up hostility, and experiencing no guilt as an aftermath.

Whether our tendency to exaggerate undesirable attributes in nations seen as rivals to our own should be called *projection* is a matter of debate. It is possible that the chief determinant of these nasty traits seen in foreign nations is tradition, as embodied in legends, gossip, history texts, and the mass media. The dynamic energy associated with this image may derive from personal frustrations (intrafamily, for example) which are displaced onto convenient hate-objects. As will be noted in the following chapter, national leaders may exploit such hostile images to deflect aggressions which might otherwise take the form of revolution within the nation; this is what has been called the theory of *nationalism as a lightning-rod* for discharging internal disaffection without upsetting privileged persons.

THREAT AND ANXIETY

Another somewhat difficult discrimination is called for when we seek to differentiate the relevance of hostility and of anxiety for social conflict. At the extremes the distinction is easy. Aggression involves an impulse to attack and destroy; anxiety is a vaguely comprehended fear of impending disaster. But more careful examination reveals difficulties. Aggression is often triggered by fear or anxiety; the Russians fear our "encirclement" and we fear their ideology, their subversion, and their "nibbling aggression." Further, the effects of aggression and of anxiety on perceiving seem to be similar in many cases. It is possible that the major variable really is *tension*, which may appear to the observer as hostility in one context and as anxiety in another.

It is clear that percepts of physically present objects and images of those not present may be modified by anxiety. Clinicians are aware that persons suffering acute anxiety may show what is aptly called *tunnel vision*, i.e., they are so focused upon one central object that important neighboring cues may be unnoticed. Anxiety also induces *polarization*, an exaggeration of attributes which might otherwise have seemed only slightly good or bad. Joseph Kamenetzky (1955) studied judgements of persons under relaxed or anxiety-arousing conditions (threat of electric shock, of taking a blood sample, and so on). Identical stimulus materials were presented to both groups. The pattern of traits ascribed to the stimulus "persons" was similar for both sets of judges, but those under anxiety stress made more judgments at the extremes of the rating scales and fewer judgments at or near the neutral point. This reminds us of the tendency for social perceptions to become polarized in times of social stress; for example, Americans in the period 1940–1942 shifted many judgments from a normal distribution around the neutral point to bimodal or markedly skewed distributions (Stagner and Osgood, 1946).

It has been argued that these phenomena are merely extreme forms of a very common tendency which Else Frenkel-Brunswik (1949) called *intolerance of ambiguity*. This takes the form of reading meaning into ink-blots, imposing structure on unstructured situations, jumping to conclusions from inadequate evidence, and so on. Such a tendency probably has survival value. It is important for the organism, in a doubtful milieu, to conclude quickly whether this is a threatening or a safe situation. However, some people can tolerate a higher level of ambiguity than others. Those who are quite "intolerant" of ambiguous stimuli and who insist upon reading in some meaning even where cues are absent are likely to be more prejudiced, and more authoritarian. Since prejudice and authoritarian tendencies become accentuated in times of social crisis, it seems plausible to suggest that anxiety operates chiefly to intensify this need to find clear-cut distinctions in a world of ambiguities.

The foregoing comments may help to explain why the threat of nuclear devastation does not increase the probabilities of world peace as much as we would prefer to believe. Because the threat is so very great, rationality is lost; judgments move to extremes and everything is classified as black or white in a world full of intermediate grays. An anxious citizenry, no less than a desperate leadership, may elect to take a tougher and tougher stand against the enemy who is perceived as pure villainy.

We must remember that fear of injury and death has not deterred man in the past. Patriotic Americans will accept extreme sacrifices if convinced that national survival requires them. The Russians did the same in 1942. And we should remember the willingness to continue the war, shown by the British when faced with overwhelming odds in 1940.

It is at least a Western tradition, and probably a world-wide pattern, to admire the man who will fight for his principles even when he knows he will be destroyed. But this is just the problem. If both sides in the cold war continue to fight for their principles, all of us will be destroyed. As long as nationalistic perceptions guide policy, the danger persists, and the fear of catastrophe does not push it farther away.

The tendency of polarized thinking to force the world into two hostile camps is so obvious as to need little elaboration. The patriot who feels that his nation is threatened will find it difficult to tolerate nations following a policy of nonalignment. The neutral country is an uncertain quantity; and under stress, we cannot tolerate this uncertainty. "If you are not for us, you must be against us." Thus the neutral is perceived as an enemy.

The Self-fulfilling Prophecy

The phenomena of projection and polarization, separately or in combination, may give rise to what we call *the self-fulfilling prophecy.* In the case of projected hostility, one sees others as about to attack, and behaves in such a fashion as to invite attack. In the case of polarization, one may perceive the neutral as an enemy, and behave accordingly, in which case the neutral may well become an enemy.

The phenomenal attributes of national images may, of course, provide an adequate underpinning for this kind of occurrence. We, for example, perceive the Russians as untrustworthy. It will not be safe to sign a disarmament treaty with them because they would be certain to cheat. A striking example of this kind of thinking occurred in a Detroit newspaper headline during the Geneva atomic-test-ban negotiations. A banner headline read, "Soviets Set A-Test Trap." The story underneath reported that a new Soviet proposal had been received; while the details were not yet known, it was suspected that some kind of trap was involved.

If one nation assumes that another is deceitful and untrustworthy, this is likely to induce behavior confirming the assumption. If we feel that we must conceal our atomic manufacturing processes from the Russians, they will seek, by espionage or infiltration, to obtain these secrets. If the Russians hide military information, we use U-2 overflights, advanced radar and infrared sensing satellites to get information. Both sides respond by becoming more secretive and more distrustful. It is very difficult to break this kind of vicious circle once it has been established.

IDEOLOGICAL CONFLICTS

It would not be proper, in view of the attention given to the ideological aspect of the cold war, to conclude this discussion without relating it to the conflict between communism and the somewhat amorphous set of views held by the Western democracies.

It must be recognized, first of all, that ideologies with powerful emotional backing have in the past led to group unification and group violence on a level comparable with our recent wars based on nationalism. The Crusades of the Christians against the Moslems in the Middle Ages depended on the unifying and driving power of the competing religious faiths. Similarly the bloody battles of Catholics against Protestants after the Reformation drew group unity from common faith, and displaced hostility onto the opposing group. Descriptions written in those days show clearly that the out-group members were seen as agents of the Devil, inhuman, deceitful, violent; religious devotion demanded that they be destroyed, men, women, and children alike. Ultimately, recognition of a higher authority and compulsion to settle disputes without violence led to "peaceful coexistence" of these contending ideologies.

Communism has demonstrated in some degree the same capacity to fire zeal and mold group unity against perceived enemies. It has been regrettably obvious in such areas as Korea, Laos, and Viet Nam that the communist forces show high morale and dedication, in sharp opposition to groups backed by the West. It would appear that a major difficulty here has lain in our lack of any shared ideology. Belief systems can only be opposed by other beliefs, not by missiles or radar.

The extent to which the world communist parties have been dominated by the Communist Party of the Soviet Union (a domination only now weakening), and the extent to which the tools of military violence are controlled by nations, lead to grave doubt that the ideological question is the major source of world conflict. As the history of the West shows, economic and social reforms can be executed within a democratic framework. The crucial questions are those relating to perception and motivation. If privileged individuals cling desperately to traditional wealth, power, and irresponsibility, violence is almost certain. Such violence is a threat to the West only if nationalistic considerations become involved.

In any event, a psychological analysis of communism reveals the same elements so important in nationalism: a belief in the virtues of our group and in the badness of the opposition; an expectation of benefits (in the future if not at once); an opportunity to identify with something powerful; an opportunity to displace hostility onto an enemy. The patriot cries, "My country, right or wrong." The loyal communist rewrites this as "My party, right or wrong." Either slogan carries grave danger to the rest of the human race in this "age of overkill."

THEORY AND ATTITUDE CHANGE

This book makes no pretense to offering solutions for world problems. It is, however, within the general framework of our task to consider to what extent psychological theory offers any hope of dealing effectively with the conflict phenomena described in this chapter.

The discussion of attitude formation given earlier in these pages was phrased largely in terms of perceiving. This is convenient when we are dealing with phenomenal attributes, such as our image of Russia and Russian images of the United States. It is, however, possible to conceptualize attitude in terms of responses of approaching, accepting, avoiding, denouncing, and so forth. Some psychologists prefer this approach because it fits in more comfortably with the reinforcement theories which have been dominant in laboratory research on learning.

According to this view, attitudes are formed as individuals respond to certain objects (e.g., the symbolic object "Russia") and are rewarded or punished. The child might thoughtlessly say "Communists are people" and be scolded for this nonconformist behavior. Or, more likely, he merely conforms to his parents' verbalizations and receives their warm approval for so doing.

The perceptual view assumed earlier relies largely upon contiguity rather than upon reinforcement to explain learning. If information is received indicating that Russia is violent, aggressive, and expansionist, this is recorded just as one records the fact that apples are red and concrete is hard. Rewarding and punishing experiences may be involved but they are not crucial.

The difference between the two theories becomes important when we reflect on possibilities for changing attitudes. Let us consider, for a moment, the fact that the Russians have an incorrect image of our country. Our task is to devise learning experiences which will bring this image more into conformity with reality. One method is to reward them when they behave cooperatively, and to punish them when they behave obstreperously. Unfortunately, where it has been tried, the consequences were not as predicted. For example, when the Russians rattle their rockets, we brandish our Polaris missiles; this should frighten them and constitute a punishing experience, but it seems only to make them more belligerent. (When we are threatened, it does not make us more kindly disposed toward the Russians but more hostile). It is difficult to find examples of our rewarding the Russians for anything, but an examination of the 1962 Cuban crisis may be relevant. In that case the Russians withdrew their missiles and bombers from Cuba following our warlike gestures; this constituted a reward for us, and may indeed have led some Americans to conclude that we should do more of the same. Fortunately, the Kennedy administration followed this crisis with conciliatory gestures, not with renewed belligerence. Such observations suggest that at least a simple version of reward and punishment will not help us in changing international attitudes underlying conflict.

A different approach to change relies more on the perceptual model. The best statement of this formulation is given by Leon Festinger (1957) (who is not responsible for the adaptations to international situations proposed here). According to Festinger, each percept is composed of a number of "cognitive elements." If any of these elements are incompatible with the others (give rise to differing expectations), dissonance develops. The phenomenon of dissonance apparently connotes tension or discomfort; at any rate, dissonance sets up a tendency to change the percept, moving toward consonance.

Dissonance theory suggests that the way to modify an attitude toward an object is to introduce dissonance into the picture. If, for example, one person is hostile toward another, dissonance is introduced by providing evidence that the latter individual admires the former, or that he possesses attributes approved by the former. Such information tends to break up the image and induce restructuring on a more favorable level.

According to this approach, we might modify attitudes of foreigners toward the USA by introducing dissonance, i.e., by behaving in a manner contradictory to the established image. If we wished to modify the Russian image of our country, this would imply calculated policy changes which would introduce dissonance into their system. A recent volume which spells out a series of steps which might be taken by the USA to reduce tension by an application of dissonance theory is that by Charles E. Osgood (1962).

Some experimental data can be cited in support of reinforcement theory, and some in favor of dissonance theory, as devices for changing attitudes. Considerably greater varieties of research design, particularly involving populations from different nations, will be required to establish the superiority of either theory, or to define the sets of circumstances under which one approach is preferable to the other. Steps will also be needed to convince national leaders that such theories provide dependable guides to action. Nevertheless, it is apparent that progress in this area could make important contributions to the peaceful resolution of national conflicts.

REFERENCES

Bartlett, Frederic C., *Remembering*. New York: The Macmillan Company, 1932.

Bruner, Jerome S. and C. C. Goodman, "Value and Need as Organizing Factors in Perception," *Journal of Abnormal and Social Psychology*, XLII (1947), 33-43.

Carmichael, Leonard, H. P. Hogan, and A. A. Walter, "An Experimental Study of the Effect of Language on the Reproduction of Visually Perceived Forms," *Journal of Experimental Psychology*, XV (1932), 73-86.

Dollard, John *et al.*, *Frustration and Aggression*. New Haven: Yale University Press, 1939.

Dukes, William F. and William Bevan, Jr., "Accentuation and Response Variability in the Perception of Personally Relevant Objects," *Journal of Personality*, XX (1952), 457-465.

Edwards, Allen L., "Political Frames of Reference as a Factor Influencing Recognition," *Journal of Abnormal and Social Psychology*, XXXVI (1941), 35-40.

Festinger, Leon, *A Theory of Cognitive Dissonance*. New York: Harper & Row, Publishers, 1957.

Frenkel-Brunswik, Else, "Intolerance of Ambiguity as an Emotional and Perceptual Personality Variable," *Journal of Personality*, XVIII (1949), 108-143.

Freud, Sigmund, *Beyond the Pleasure Principle*. London: International Psychoanalytic Press, 1922.

Haire, Mason, "Role-perceptions in Labor-Management Relations: An Experimental Approach," *Industrial Labor Relations Review*, VIII (1955), 204-216.

Horowitz, Eugene L. and Ruth E. Horowitz, "Development of Social Attitudes in Children," *Sociometry*, I (1938), 301-338.

Hovland, Carl I., Irving L. Janis, and Harold H. Kelley, *Communication and Persuasion*. New Haven: Yale University Press, 1953.

Kamenetzky, Joseph, "Anxiety and Attitude as Variables Affecting Perception of Persons." Unpublished doctoral dissertation, University of Illinois, 1955.

Krout, M. H. and R. Stagner, "Personality Development in Radicals: A Comparative Study," *Sociometry*, II (1939), 31-46.

Laswell, Harold D., *Psychopathology and Politics*. Chicago: University of Chicago Press, 1930.

Maier, Norman R. F., *Frustration: The Study of Behavior Without a Goal*. New York: McGraw-Hill Book Company, 1949.

McDougall, William, *Introduction to Social Psychology*. London: Methuen & Co., Ltd., 1908.

Miller, Neal E. and R. Bugelski, "Minor Studies of Aggression: II, The Influence of Frustration Imposed by the In-group on Attitudes Expressed Toward Out-groups," *Journal of Psychology*, XXV (1948), 437-442.

Murray, Henry A., "Effect of Fear Upon Estimates of Maliciousness of Other Personalities," *Journal of Social Psychology*, IV (1933), 310-329.

Osgood, Charles E., *An Alternative to War or Surrender*. Urbana, Illinois: University of Illinois Press, 1962.

Solley, Charles M. and Robert Sommer, "Perceptual Autism in Children," *Journal of Genetic Psychology*, LVI (1957), 3-11.

Stagner, Ross, "Correlational Analysis of Nationalistic Opinions," *Journal of Social Psychology*, XII (1940), 197-212.

————, "Studies of Aggressive Social Attitudes: III, Role of Personal and Family Scores," *Journal of Social Psychology*, XX (1944), 129-140.

Stagner, Ross, J. F. Brown, R. H. Gundlach, and R. K. White, "Analysis of Social Scientists' Opinions on the Prevention of War," *Journal of Social Psychology*, XV (1942), 381-394.

Stagner, Ross and Charles E. Osgood, "Impact of War on a Nationalistic Frame of Reference," *Journal of Social Psychology*, XXIV (1946), 187-215.

West, Rebecca, *The Meaning of Treason*. New York: The Viking Press, Inc., 1947.

White, R. K., "Mirror Images in the East-West Conflict," American Psychological Association Convention, September 4, 1961.

Wulf, F., "Ueber die Veränderung von Vorstellungen (Gedächtnis und Gestalt)," *Psychologische Forschung*, I (1922), 333-373.

CHAPTER

4

The Social Psychology of Human Conflict

STEPHEN WITHEY

DANIEL KATZ

Wars and lesser struggles between nations are in their nature conflicts between organized structures. A social psychological analysis, therefore, must deal with those psychological factors which are relevant for an understanding of the character of the national social structure and of the actions of that structure with respect to cooperative or hostile relations with other structures.

Conflict is a more generic term than *war*—a perspective that is in back of the adage that war is just an extension of national policy in other forms. A thoroughgoing social psychology of conflict should approach the great varieties of intergroup conflict among various types of groups with some consistency and gen-

The authors wish to express their indebtedness to their colleagues Herbert Kelman and Richard Flacks for their contributions to the material on nationalism in this chapter.

erality. Understanding is probably enhanced by varying the ingredients of conflict, and the goals of conflict management are not always elimination but include restriction, control, redirection, and encouragement. However, the setting and limitation of this chapter suggests an orientation in which the focus is on the extreme conflict between nation-groups in which the ultimate power of armed conflict is approached, threatened, or utilized.

The social psychological approach to war and peace is commonly misconceived as viewing international conflict either in terms of the personalities of national leaders or in terms of a national character which suffuses the masses and the elite in similar fashion. Relevant social psychological processes are not revealed, however, by imputing to the character of the people in the system the outcome of system processes. For example, a nation declares war, hence, its people or its leaders are regarded as aggressive or warlike. This is the group fallacy in reverse, because there is the attribution of system outcomes such as belligerent or conciliatory actions to the personalities of the individual actors, as if these individuals were all acting in parallel. The facts are that system outcomes are the result of complicated interaction patterns which are a function of people operating in complementary, reciprocal, or even opposed roles. It is true that the personality make-up of key influentials may enter into the system process, but the intervention of such factors occurs only under given system conditions.

A social psychological approach, then, is not one of attempting to explain the functioning of social systems by a simple reduction of a macroscopic process to a similar microscopic process; the contribution of social psychology is the study of the complex human interrelationships which comprise the system. Conventional social science accepts social structure as the walls of the maze but is willing to have the psychologist study individual deviations within those walls. The social psychologist, however, is concerned with understanding the walls themselves as well as the individual deviations, because the walls of the social maze consist of the patterned behavior of people. There is no social structure apart from the interrelated habitual actions and attitudes of people. The patterns of reciprocity, the shared norms and values, the expectations about legitimized behavior, the interdependent actions, the acceptance and taking of roles are the appropriate subject matter of social psychology in the study of social systems (Katz, 1961).

Hence it will be our concern to explore (a) the social psychological processes which produce a social system capable of engaging in war and (b) the social psychological processes responsible for the system moving across the boundary of peace to a state of war.

THE SOCIAL PSYCHOLOGY OF NATIONAL STRUCTURES:
NATIONS THEMSELVES AS A SOURCE OF WAR

Nature of National States

National structure is one major determinant of war, since the state is the organization of the power of the society for its maintenance, protection, and expansion. Historically, states arose in group struggles in which the machinery of the state developed as the organization of sanctions and military force for purposes of conquest and exploitation on the one hand and protection and survival on the other (Oppenheimer, 1914).

Historical background is of significance, because many substructures which remain in the state were devised both to maintain internal unity and to conduct economic and political warfare against other groups. These subsystems include a military establishment, the control by the state of contacts of its nationals with other countries, the legal claim upon its citizens for military and national service, and an authority structure which is the final arbiter for resolving internal conflict.

The basic character of the national state is the subordination of all power relations within the society to the single authority structure of the state. Conflicts within the national system are thus muted, comprised, or resolved without recourse to organized violence. The failure of the state to perform this function means that it is dead or dying. Not only is the state supreme within the nation in the exercise of authority; it is also not subject to legal demands from outside powers save where it has given its consent or bows to superior external power. Moreover, it can utilize all the power of the nation to move against other countries, and once a decision has been legitimately made to take some form of international action, the decision is binding upon all of its nationals.

The fact that the state provides the final power structure for the nation means that there is machinery for handling conflicts without the use of violence save for the organized police power of the state. But it means much more than this. Since the state can intervene with its political power to settle disputes, many differences are resolved or compromised without involving the political system. As W. Levi (1964) has pointed out, many types of relationship within a nation develop outside the political structure, but in the international sphere any relationship between people of different nations can readily become a political matter involving the power of their respective nations. If the state does intervene in domestic problems, it will not necessarily be to the advantage of either side. At the international level, however, the political power invoked is not that of an international order but of the group's own nation which will be partisan to the group. Hence the most apolitical group domestically may become politically oriented internationally.

Modes of National Integration

There are four major modes for the binding of people into the national system: (a) ideological integration about a common objective, (b) normative integration based upon beliefs about the demands of specific practices, (c) functional interdependence through actually assuming roles in a system, and (d) dependence upon a focused integrative role in which an individual or small group is required or is able to assume the roles, concerns, and interests of large social units. An integration is formed around those individuals who express group ideals, who administer group activity, and who are preoccupied with group rather than with individual or narrower matters. The integration offered by focused leadership, boards of control, congresses, and parliamentary bodies is somewhat different from the functional interdependence of other parts of a system. Sometimes the integration is weak when leaders act in their schismatic role of special-interest representatives, but when they act as a body with common interests, a very real integration is accomplished. These four modes do not exist independently but serve to buttress one another in their operation. Ideological integration refers to the value systems which justify the common purpose of the structure and its perpetuation. Normative integration refers to the more specific enforceable codes about given types of behavior. Functional interdependence has to do with the reciprocal patterns of behavior based upon the assumption of mutual dependency and expectation and is related more to the task requirements than to moral demands. These different modes reinforce one another in most national systems so that the task demands of functional interdependence are backed up by specific norms requiring such behavior and often are ideological buttresses furthering the objectives of the system. Nevertheless, there can be great differences in the relative emphasis upon these ways of producing a coordinated unified system in different societies. Durkheim's brilliant analysis (1933) called attention to the contrast between the mechanical solidarity of a society in which normative integration was the dominant mode and organic solidarity in which functional interdependence was the basic pattern. In the former mode the society was held together by a collective conscience deriving from the same moral norms shared by people playing the same undifferentiated types of roles. In the latter, the heavy division of labor created an interdependence, with people assuming their reciprocal roles and accepting norms more relevant to their subsystem than the structure as a whole.

It is our thesis that the most dynamic source of international conflict resides in the first mode for binding people into a system, namely, its ideological integration. The norms which hold people to specific practices can readily transcend national boundaries and can vary within a nation according to content area. The canons of good medical practice, of good workmanship, of trust and cooperation are often international conflict. The task-demands of role interdependence is also not a dependable basis for war. It can contribute to conflict because one nation may need the raw materials or markets of another nation. On the other hand, the growth in bureaucratic structure and the development of differentiated tasks with increasing interdependence also creates pressures for international cooperation. In fact the European community has developed on this basis in spite of a long historical background of national animosity and conflict (Haas, 1958). Even the foci of leadership are constricted and pressured by national ideology. The major integrating mode which remains as a continuing source of international tension and conflict is the ideological cement or the values which justify national purpose, national goals, and national power and sovereignty. This ideology of the nation is commonly termed *nationalism*. We shall examine its system characteristics more carefully before addressing ourselves to the reasons for its acceptance by members of the nation state.

Specific Mechanisms
for Individual Involvement in National Systems

Though people may be born into a national system with its fully developed ideology, the social psychological problem remains of explaining how they come to accept enough of its core elements to tie them into the national structure.

A simple psychological explanation is the emotional conditioning to national symbols during the socialization process. For example, children recite the pledge of allegiance to the flag, sing the national anthem in unison, and are encouraged to admire national heroes and detest traitors. There is considerable validity in this interpretation, but it is too mechanical and overgeneralized to give the full story.

A second related psychological explanation would expand the conception of conditioning in the socialization process to an identification of the individual with his like-minded colleagues possessing the same culture. Books, the mass media, and school curricula identify a geographical entity, a military entity, a political entity in government, an economic entity, a social entity, and often a language, cultural, or religious entity. Only local individuals are needed to confirm membership and self-labels. The person establishes his self-identity not only as a unique personality but as an individual who belongs to an in-group sharing the same values and orientations in contrast to foreign out-groups. National identity thus is an anchoring frame for the individual's conception of himself.

In this process the individual accepts the belief in the entity of the nation as an overperson and the corresponding personification of the out-group nation as a causal agent (Allport, 1933). Thus he has a simple causal framework for assigning praise and blame to the concepts of his own nation and other nations without a discriminating analysis of the complex realities to which these concepts refer. In this sense one can say that "war begins in the minds of men."

This theory does describe a potent basis for nationalism. It does require, however, some contact and communication with members of other nations as out-groups. Otherwise the identification with a group might be with other like-minded colleagues of one's immediate social environment, e.g., other middle-class people in the South or other unionized members of the working class. Where identification with one's national group as a cultural identity is strong and is also tied to the political state, it is difficult to change. Many Englishmen living in the United States will not change their citizenship and cannot understand how any Englishman could make such a change. It would be giving up his sense of self-identity.

It should be noted, however, that a high sense of national cultural identity is not necessarily fused with statism, i.e., with beliefs about the power, purpose, and authority of the state. In the example we have given of the displaced Englishman clinging to his citizenship we have such a fusion. If we compare the English and the French, however, it becomes apparent that this integration may not be achieved in certain areas. The French have as highly developed a sense of cultural identity as the British. However, the Frenchman does not regard paying taxes to his government as part of being a good Frenchman—the Englishman does.

A more complex psychological account has become popular in recent years, namely, that national symbols and national ideology provide a compensatory feeling of security, superiority, and power for psychologically weak and conflicted people. Most psychological studies of nationalism have been concerned with this hypothesis. In fact, research evidence does show that chauvinistic nationalism is related to the authoritarian personality syndrome described by T. W. Adorno, et al. (1950) and D. Levinson (1957). Though personality conflict in individuals with repressed hostility patterns is undoubtedly an important factor predisposing toward extreme nationalistic attitudes, and though these superpatriots may play a role out of all proportion to their numbers, it is still true that we are again dealing with a single factor which exaggerates but does not account for the major process. Other types of nationalism exist, as has been shown by C. Bay and his colleagues (1950) in their study of Norwegian nationalistic attitudes. These investigators found that whereas Norwegians showing a power-oriented nationalism were characterized by the rigid, authoritarian syndrome, many others were very nationalistic in a people-oriented fashion and lacked an authoritarian personality pattern.

One of the most neglected studies in this area, by N. Morse and F. H. Allport (1952), has suggested that we may have been standing the problem on its head by seeking a simple causal relationship between personality and national ideology. Their thesis was that national involvement is the cause of ethnocentric attitudes. Their research showed that the type of ethnocentrism often assumed to be basic to nationalism could be predicted much better by knowing the degree of involvement of the individual in the national structure than by knowing his degree of personal insecurity. In other words, people may not so much be tied into the national structure through taking on its ideology as they are when they take on the ideology because their way of life ties them into the nation. The process is undoubtedly circular so that we must look at the effects of national involvement on ideological acceptance as well as on the obverse. At given periods of history for given nations, greater emphasis may have to be placed on one factor rather than on the other.

A further connection between the individual and his nationalistic beliefs is suggested by A. I. Gladstone (1962) when he describes varieties of personal relationship orientations. He specifically mentions five: (a) the undifferentiated orientation is a glossing over and submersion of differences that might be found in extreme forms of identification with people or groups; (b) the egoistic orientation involves a sharp differentiation between oneself and others and assumes an antagonistic relationship; (c) the altruistic orientation is also sharply differentiated and recognizes competing interests in favor of the other; (d) the balancing orientation represents still another approach to conflict interests, the attempt to deal justly with others so that each other receives his fair share; and (e) the integrative orientation involves a more complex awareness of both interdependence and conflict and the possibilities of mutual benefit through joint action. One would expect considerable overlap between the interpersonal orientations of an individual and the intergroup orientations adopted for his extended identifications.

The first three explanations assume a cathexis between people's emotional needs and their nationalistic beliefs. Thus individuals derive direct and consummatory satisfaction in expressing their nationalism and assuming the appropriate national roles. And in fact there are those who love their national roles as soldiers, taxpayers, or voters.

But the assumption of national roles is often an instrumental act rather than an action intrinsically rewarding. People are involved in a network of relations which are tied into the national structure. They accept the legitimacy of the system and this acceptance is a formal sign of their involvement in it. To refuse to accept the legitimate sources of authority is to reject the system. Such a rejection means a withdrawal from the way of life of the system. Hence when the symbols of authority are brought into play individuals have little recourse but to obey. There is an all-or-none quality about the matter. One is either a loyal American or he is not. The realistic alternatives to rejecting the system are prison or refuge in another country.

National involvement is thus based in good part on all the instrumental rewards which accrue to the loyal citizen in playing his part in society. When, however, these instrumental rewards are also tied to intrinsic emotional rewards, the resulting motivational force is multiplicative and of great power. The great energizing force of nationalism in the newly developing nation-states of the seventeenth and eighteenth centuries, as described by C. J. H. Hayes (1926), was a fusion of such motives. The rising middle-class groups found nationalism a highly motivating doctrine because it enabled them to ply their trades and professions more securely and profitably within wider boundaries than ever before, and at the same time met their needs for personal identity. In a similar fashion the newly emerging nations of Africa and Asia may develop a dynamic nationalism if they can master the economic problems and provide a greatly improved way of life combined with the psychic satisfactions of nationalism.

In describing the instrumental basis for national involvement we are recognizing the acceptance of the legitimacy of the demands of the nation-state as a fundamental ideological component. Without it people would not maintain their involvement in the national structure but would organize themselves into different groupings to achieve their needs. The emphasis on the rational basis for legitimate authority in any bureaucratic structure is seen in its most explicit form in the political state. In his many antisocial actions Hitler was very careful to preserve the legal forms which could be used to secure the acquiescence of the German people. Though his armed gangsters operated on the streets as the Nazi movement developed, Hitler saw to it that his ascension to power was legitimized through his being named chancellor by President von Hindenberg. When we speak of nationalism, we frequently neglect the doctrine of legitimate power residing in the established procedures of the state as one of its central aspects. In fact the ideological factor of legitimacy and the instrumental satisfactions from national involvement may in themselves account for the conduct of war by a large bureaucratic nation. The common assumption is that masses must be stirred to hate by propaganda and indoctrination for the conduct of modern totalitarian war. The facts are, however, that the war effort of the United States in

World War II was accomplished with no concerted governmental propaganda campaign of an ideological sort. Events filtered through the national ideology were often enough in themselves. The domestic propaganda efforts in the United States in World War II were limited to specific practical programs such as buying bonds, saving scarce materials, and observing the ration rules. Whatever emotional dynamics existed arose from "the conflict itself," not from a prior emotional arousal.

A large bureaucratic society as Durkheim foresaw is not based upon a collective moral conscience which is outraged by deviant behavior; it is based on the ready assumption of the roles legitimized in any given setting. The socializing process in this type of society trains the growing youngsters to be sensitive to the norms of the group and to realize that there are rules for playing the game whether it be a sport or a more serious group undertaking. Hence as adults we have developed a *role readiness,* a predisposition to accept behavioral requirements which are legitimately sanctioned. Outside of the given behavioral setting, we may react quite differently. This does not mean that people do not violate rules and laws. They do it within the context of the game, however, so that their violations escape easy and immediate detection. In spite of a certain amount of embezzlement our whole banking and financial structure is conducted with a high degree of rule compliance and a minimum of checking.

THE ASSUMPTION OF NATIONAL ROLES
AND THE GENERAL CONDITIONS FOR TAKING NATIONAL ROLES

In spite of its priority over other social structures, the role systems comprising the national state are often latent rather than active in the national population. The life of the ordinary citizen is devoted to his roles as a member of his occupation, his family, his church, his union, and so on. His national roles may make few demands in times of peace. He does vote on occasion and may even take part in the political process more actively. He pays his taxes and obeys national laws. He gives customary compliance to national rituals such as standing when the national anthem is played. His national involvement, however, does not occupy much of his psychological life space. When the nation is at war, however, the situation changes radically. More national roles are specified for him and many of his peacetime roles become national roles, e.g., his peacetime role as a worker in a plant now becomes that of a defense worker for the nation.

What, then, are the conditions which produce a shift from latent role structure to activated role performance, from minimal to maximal national awareness and action? At the one extreme are certain peaceful stages, at the other totalitarian war. There is no mystery about the fact that conflict itself, whether of open struggle or of cold war, is the most potent stimulus for evoking national roles. All the legal symbols are available for inducing acceptance of national prescriptions in war: the society is mobilized toward national effort, the emotional aspects of the struggle call for people moving into national roles, and warfare creates its own dynamics since the hostile acts of one side create hostility in the other. The problem is more of how latent national roles are maintained in peacetime with sufficient reinforcement to permit war to break out. The basic conditions for the arousal of nationalism and the assumption of national roles occur at three levels: one is the level of personal experience, a second is the level of ideational or symbolic appeal, a third is the invoking of specific authority symbols.

Personal Experience as an Arousal Condition

Individuals who do not ordinarily think of themselves as nationals, i.e., as Americans or Frenchmen or Japanese, can be brought to an immediate realization of their nationality in at least three ways. (1) They can be confronted with the divergent practices and different national character of other peoples through direct contact with representatives of other nations. It is often assumed in programs of exchange of personnel between countries and in the promotion of international travel and communication that contact in itself will produce international understanding. It is true that this is a possible outcome, but it is not a necessary outcome. In fact, the research of C. Selltiz and S. W. Cook (1962) on foreign students in the United States showed no clear relationship between the amount of contact of these students with Americans and the favorability of their attitudes toward Americans. And H. C. Kelman and L. Bailyn (1962) have demonstrated that many Scandinavian students become more nationalistic as a result of their years in the United States. The facts are that people become aware of their own nationality when confronted with the differing values of other national groups. Americans abroad will accentuate their American characteristics under the confrontation. Foreigners visiting the United States react similarly under the impact of the constant questioning of how they like it here and how conditions compare here with conditions in their home country.

The presence of foreigners working and residing in a country can also elicit the nationalism of the native population. Foreigners are often seen not in a broad frame of reference but as aspirants to a national role for which they lack an adequate sign character. The American nationalism of an older period fed upon this type of condition in which every new foreign group had to be Americanized. The reverse side of this picture is that the foreign group may become over a time more nationalistic to gain full acceptance. Many of its members will attempt to move over into the dominant culture by becoming true believers.

The arousal of national identity, however, need not lead to a chauvinistic patriotism. It can lead to a more realistic appreciation of one's own country and other countries, as H. C. Kelman and L. Bailyn have shown in their study of Scandinavian students. If, however, this arousal of national identity is associated with experiences of frustration, threat, deprivation, or unfavorable differential treatment, it can readily result in increased loyalty to one's own national symbols and hostility to the out-group. African and Asian students in the United States, for instance, may return to their own countries with an increased commitment to their own nation.

(2) Another type of contact, that of competitive trade and economic intercourse, can also result in the arousal of national identification and national roles. Businessmen, producers, exporters, and importers engaged in foreign commerce, when blocked or put at positions of disadvantage, will seek the support of their own nation. For example, the American farmers whose poultry market was destroyed by the agreements of the European common market countries turned to the American government for retaliatory actions against various types of European imports. Again the direct contact with other nationals can arouse nationalistic attitudes if the conditions are competitive rather than cooperative. R. M. Williams maintains that "Where a basis for social categorization exists, that is, in group relations, some degree of prejudice-hostility always appears when there is a combination of *visibility* and *competition*" (1947, p. 54).

(3) Another kind of personal experience which arouses national identification is the observed deviation of one's own nationals in failing to meet the requirements of a sign character for allegiance to the system. People will automatically rise when the national anthem is played or show deference to national symbols without thought or emotion. When, however, there is a conspicuous failure of a fellow national to act similarly, there is an arousal of national identification. His deviant behavior is dissonant with their expectations and a challenge to their own behavior. This is all the more true when the deviance is not merely failure to conform but an act of derogation of the symbol of custom. Thus the refusals of some college professors to take a loyalty oath or of some citizens to cooperate with the House Un-American Activities Committee can arouse feelings of national identification in the conforming majority. Even when these deviations are not matters of direct personal observa-

tion, they can have their effect through reports in the mass media or through the propaganda of certain factions of the population.

Ideological Appeals
in the Arousal of National Roles

At the ideational level the major means for arousing nationalistic attitudes and roles is the use of symbols reflecting either national ideology or legitimate authority. Four illustrative types of ideological symbols are (a) national honor, (b) national interest and security, (c) national purpose, and (d) national power and strength.

National honor
The underlying condition for rallying a people on the basis of national honor is a system in which the involvement of people is in good part one of compensatory identification (e.g., based on the authoritarian syndrome). Where many individuals find ego satisfaction in the moral superiority of their nation, an appeal to national honor can evoke their nationalism. The arousal condition here is one of a perceived attack upon or insult to national symbols. It is not the economic interests or the actual threat to human lives but the assault upon symbols which are in themselves sacred. At the level of direct experience we have noted that the deviant behavior in national observances, including acts of disrespect toward national symbols, startles people into a recognition of their own national roles. At the level we are now discussing, people have not been involved themselves as witnesses or participants in the situation. What links them to the specific situation is the polar concept of national honor. They are being told in effect that another nation has violated national integrity. The arousal condition thus is the creation of a moral idealistic frame of reference of an absolutistic sort. The creation of such an attitude is difficult in a huge, technological, and bureaucratic society where national honor has lost its personalized moral character for the role-taker.

National interest and security
In some countries national interest has replaced national honor as a polar concept. National interest is the general appeal that what protects and advances the interests of the system protects and advances the interests of the individuals in it. It is less of a polar concept than national honor because it has a more objective reference. When national interests are invoked, there is some necessity for specification and some implicit invitation of appraisal by people of the

problem. Two factors for the usessfull use of the appeal of national interests for invoking nationalism are its sponsoring leaders and its psychological closeness to the interests of groups and individuals. If the leader who attempts to arouse people about national interest speaks for a single segment of the population, he is less likely to have his message accepted than if he has some warrant for speaking for the nation as a whole. Even the President of the United States is often seen as the leader of his party; so, in emergency situations he will attempt to shift to his role as the head of the nation by enlisting the support of members of the opposed party. Thus if both President Johnson and former President Eisenhower reinforce one another in an appeal to the national interest, their combined message can arouse the American public.

A second factor in the arousal of national interest is the psychological closeness of the issue to the lives of the people. The Roosevelt administration believed that our national interests were seriously threatened by the rise of Nazi Germany, but the threat was too remote to be accepted by most Americans. Hence Roosevelt proposed aid to the non-Axis powers a step at a time until Pearl Harbor made the problem immediate and close for the American nation. Events in Cuba, because of their physical nearness, were readily seen as affecting national interest in contrast to the remote Viet Nam situation.

A third factor relative to the appeal to national interest concerns its substantive message in terms of the type of interest involved. We have used examples which relate to national security and protection against a dangerous enemy. This type of doctrine with its emphasis upon survival has the highest general potency. The need for colonies, for markets, for territory, for Lebensraum are all limited with respect to a national population and so are generally tied to, or cloaked under, other all-pervasive national interests.

National purpose

People can be mobilized toward taking national roles on the basis of some significant national purpose. National purpose is intermediate between national honor and collective economic interest with respect to ideological character. It has to do with the issue of differences in ideology as against differences in material objectives. The preservation of our democratic institutions is a national purpose and as such may bring us into ideological conflict with communistic nations. In terms of economic interests, however, there might be little basis for conflict. It is important, therefore, to distinguish between national purpose, which refers to the maintenance of our institutions as representative of national goals, and national interest, which concerns our economic well-being. The doctrine of peaceful co-existence is based upon the assumption that ideological differences between nations need not lead to overt conflict.

National roles based upon a national purpose are aroused most naturally around some specific cooperative undertaking for achieving a common goal under national auspices. In times of peace such national cooperative efforts involving the whole nation occur infrequently in a large complex heterogeneous nation-state. The smaller homogeneous country is at an advantage in embarking upon cooperative national ventures. In the United States the Roosevelt administration in the depression years attempted to rally the country around national recovery measures invoking the use of national symbols. Though certain specific measures were accepted, there was no over-all success in creating a national program for achieving common goals. In recent history the Peace Corps has received widespread support as an approved national enterprise, but it has involved only a small fraction of American citizens either directly or remotely. Totalitarian countries, however, can legislate both national objectives and their specific implementation and can attempt to carry them out through invoking national roles. Success is achieved, however, for certain emergency situations rather than as a sustained pattern. War itself is the major condition for creating a national cooperative effort in which almost all nationals contribute their energies to a specific program with a common objective.

National power and strength

To maximize national interest, to protect national honor, and to further national purpose, leaders will appeal to their people to develop the strength and power of their country. Just as international tension grows out of the push of nations to better their power position vis-à-vis, so do national roles within a country become salient when the power issue comes to the fore. One of the greatest obstacles to disarmament has been the fear by national leaders that they will be leaving their nation defenseless or they will jeopardize their positions of leadership because many of their former followers will now assume national roles. Even the minor step of suspending atmospheric nuclear testing with its many advantages to the United States resulted in some attempts to invoke the power argument by opponents of the President.

Not only does the idea of national power serve as the means for insuring honor, interest, and purpose, but it also serves as an end in its own right. The elite groups of a nation, including its officials, often see the power of the nation as an important goal rather than a means to an end. Moreover, rank-and-file citizens can more readily behave as national members if this means they can see themselves as part of the strongest, most powerful structure in the world.

PRESSURES WHICH MOVE NATIONS
TOWARD WAR

The Concept of Boundary Between War and Peace
and the Concept of Progressive Commitment

War is sometimes defined to include economic, social, and political conflict among nations without armed engagements, and peace sometimes includes armed exchanges that are hastily confined and limited. The criteria are not clear because there exists a gradient on the path toward war. There is a spiral of increasing commitment and a heightening of tensions that leaves only the last step clear—the one that puts nations into the open arena of "war."

Many of the recent efforts at reducing the likelihood of war have concentrated on slowing the pace with which nations might move toward war as well as trying to throw up roadblocks in the passage itself. Also, there have been efforts to try to blur the final step of proposing checks on misrecognition of accidental attacks and other events that would otherwise be accepted as unquestionable evidence of a state of war.

The work of R. North and O. R. Holsti (Chapter 8) points up the idea of a spiral or gradient toward war and tries to trace these paths in history. However, their work indicates that there are detours, plateaus, and points of arrested progress that do not make of this path an inevitable toboggan ride from beginning to end. What kinds of pressures push one along this path or help brake one's progress?

W. R. Ashby (1952) suggests that systems that survive have alerting mechanisms that activate attempts at adaptive behavior. These alerting mechanisms are themselves activated when conditions are such that parameters of the system approach points or zones that are critical for the system's existence. It is not necessary to posit built-in mechanisms for relieving this stress, though they may exist. All that is required is that a system have some device for starting protective behaviors when its critical parameters and characteristics are threatened. If the system is to survive, some behavior must return the critical factor from the danger zone to a more tolerable region. Such mechanisms may be trial-and-error, learned problem-solving methods, or organismically structured processes. Complicated systems can readily learn many adaptive mechanisms, but they can also learn cues for critical hazards, both of which may or may not be very efficient or accurate!

A great many critical variables approach their critical zones at a moderate pace so that there is ample time for adaptation if the changing situation is correctly assessed. Strains in population growth, the changes of technology, economic shifts, and military buildups are examples of stresses with material warning time. However, the black-or-white, right-or-wrong character of many values makes them cues for particularly hasty reactions. Where the approach to danger is gradual, one not only has extended warning time, but also a certain amount of ambiguity as to when real danger is precipitated and when emergency action is required. With values, the approach to crisis is frequently a step or cliff rather than a gradient. One is catapulted into crisis.

Values behave very much like levels of aspiration (Siegel, 1957) since the shift in evaluation from good to bad covers a very short region of some longer dimension characterizing events. For instance, an economic invasion of a market entails a buildup and gradual growth requiring counteraction over a considerable period of time. There are warnings and decisions about the criteria to be adopted before precipitating actions of one kind or another in defense of one's market interests. However, values tend to have boundary qualities like the crossing of a national border. National symbols, national honor, and values about the rightness and wrongness of policies or behaviors are sensitive reactors. Honor is untouched or abused. Sovereignty is unquestioned or threatened. A shot is fired or unfired. Thus, the involvement of values in national perspectives, as has been described, tends to provide an alarm quality to certain events rather than a prediction of a course of events that requires watching and adjustment.

Another aspect of values is that they tend to have emotional components considerably stronger than those associated with intellectual calculation and rational decision. The etiology of values as well as their either-or quality precipitates emotional decision that is inimical to rational consideration and negotiation.

The feedback on defensive and adaptive actions is not limited to information about the effectiveness of actions as they impinge on other nations and influence the international situation. There is also feedback from within the system, from within the nation, from one's supporters, from pressure groups, from special interests, and so forth, which adds clamor to the din of crisis and conflict. The coolness and objectivity required for calculation and assessment of success is very difficult to obtain under such conditions of multiple feedback and complex criteria. (See Chapter 7 [Singer].)

S. B. Withey (1962) reviews evidence in physiology, personality, and group behavior for the proposition that under threat a system will tend to adopt a course through a somewhat predictable sequence of attempted accommodations to threat, the cheaper behaviors being tried before the more expensive reactions are precipitated by the failure of initial accommodations. Commitment of a certain defense is not only an experiment in its effectiveness, but also defines the severity of the threat to which reaction is made. It is this quality that makes reversal of threat reactions difficult until one or another stage proves effective in reducing the threat. For two systems in conflict, an "effective" measure by one party may only serve as a further aggravation to the other side.

The speed of passing through a repertoire of responses to threat is accelerated if cheap defenses are ineffective or are seen as ineffective under a particular definition of the threat. Thus, a severe threat to the nation is likely to precipitate an expensive, extreme reaction by that nation at an extremely accelerated rate of response. Informational validation, authentication of expectations, exploratory negotiation of measures, or attempted arbitration is likely to be by-passed in favor of precipitous action within a very short span of time.

The cheaper defenses involve less of the nation's attention, organization, activity, and resources, but by definition expensive defenses are in themselves hazardous to the nation (if expense is defined by risk) or progressively include more of the nation's functions turned to the service of meeting the threat. Increasing involvement is itself a commitment and commits the nation to a particular, narrowing definition of what composes the threat. It is very difficult to delay these processes of narrowing commitment unless the mechanisms for slow-down are available. In domestic conflicts these slow-down mechanisms are often provided by the government and its legal structure. In international conflicts the supranational mechanisms are only embryonically developed.

It is possible, therefore, to look at a system of a single nation or the less related system of international relations, as K. E. Boulding (1962) does, in which ". . . one concept of peace would be that of a conflict system in which an approach towards the break boundary was registered somewhere in the system, whether by parties in the conflict themselves or by a third party, and in which this perception sets in force processes by which the dynamic course of the conflict might be deflected from the boundary."

It should also be mentioned that this orientation primarily deals with a mutual threat situation. This situation might be initiated by the seductions and temptations presented to one party to initiate aggression for positive rewards. The lesser importance of this factor in the present time seems to lie in the fact that the hazard of escalation in aggressive armaments is so severe that other forms of conflict and aggression are utilized to achieve such goals. The whole notion of deterrence is that no nation would court or risk the available ultimate confrontation.

The Externalization of Internal Conflict

A system such as a nation experiences internal conflict among subunits of the nation. These conflicts can cause stress for the total system and thus engage national attention. Since an organization tries to account for its problems as well as to do something about them, the option exists of locating the "cause" or the target of action within or outside of the system. There is considerable interaction and interdependence between processes within a system and external conditions that create conditions within the system. Conceptually, at least, one can often claim that certain internal problems would not exist if other external conditions could be altered. The reaction to external threat is largely an attempt to stave off internal consequences.

A government can more readily be blamed for internal conditions than for external ones. As a result it is a temptation to shift attention to external problems when internal conflicts cannot be easily managed. Sometimes this can be done with rationality, but often there is enough frustration, bitterness, anger, anxiety, fear, misunderstanding, or ignorance to make the action credible even if not very rational.

If the external conflict is not directly tied to the internal conflict, it may simply override it. Internal conflicts over production, distribution, technological change, and so forth seem to appear less significant in the face of external threat. Threats are given relative rather than absolute weights and an internal problem or conflict can be replaced or superseded.

L. Festinger's work on dissonance (1957) provides a model for the development of cognitive interpretations of this sort. The rich literature on defense mechanisms offers further examples of all sorts of distortions of thought and behavior that can gain adoption in times of emotional crisis and conflict.

The Need for Sensitivity

Because of the role of government within a national system, a sensitivity to intelligence and a sensitivity to the course of events is required in order to meet problems and conflicts before they are unmanageable. Following from the centrality of their role, allied with their executive responsibility, any efficient government is going to react strongly to minorities. It will have to react to minorities because, if a majority is aggrieved, the leaders are facing enough disaffection to cause a crisis.

As governments learn responsiveness to minorities, the obvious next step is to be sensitive to cues about what minorities are doing. This competition for information is part of the political struggle. On the international scene, where schisms are as divided as individual sovereignty interests allow. the same sensitivity creates the organization and paraphernalia of foreign-affairs sensors.

Systems that survive have good sensory equipment and pay a good deal of attention to handling information. However, the process creates a tendency toward oversensitivity. A government that considers hypothetical developments and consequences and moves from a sensitivity to the beginnings of conflict to guesses as to their portents can be very adaptive if the forecasts are right, but they can also be in error and such actions can create responses from other nations that might not have occurred if the future-influencing prophecy had not been made.

Traditionally, governments have developed certain cues and signs to which they respond with alertness, caution, alarm, or panic. Particular sensitivity exists in response to cues in the fields of economics and military intelligence. These fields are not only interlocked, they are also fields in which considerable objectivity of measurement and assessment has been achieved. There is a much lower acceptance of objectivity in assessing a political system and political intelligence. Although political trends are regarded as a sensitive area and worthy of attention, the mechanisms for data collection and analysis show relatively far less objectivity and precision.

The Dynamic for Conflict
Created by Military and Military-serving Subsystems

A portion of the national system is specialized for conflict management. In modern nations, the military is a well-organized sector of society that not only stands ready for action but is tied in with a large sector of the economy and its technology. The availability and readiness of this mechanism of conflict management with its own pressures, powers, armaments, intelligence, and so forth creates a particular dynamic for handling conflicts that are simply due to the size of this sector of society, its particular orientations, and its specific means and abilities for dealing with conflicts.

It is typical of the military, for instance, to focus their attention and preparedness planning not on the intentions of other nations but on their abilities. An equilibrium of ability is therefore unsatisfactory and a spiral of armament buildup is regarded as necessary. As an expression of the ultimate authority of the state, military actions express a particular orientation of a government that can be loose or restrictive.

When conflicts arise, any nation must interpret the situation largely on the character of other nations' behaviors. The military posture is given heavy weight in this judgment and the military has a large say in the assessment of this situation. Further, the military is the most available mechanism of government for immediate action. Thus, the emergency need for the military, the buildup of their ability, the availability of their resources, the increasing involvement of the economy in the military establishment, the close tie-in between the military and national symbols—all these factors create a particularly strong dynamic for military growth, military involvement, and military judgment.

The Dynamic
Created by Powerful Internally Threatened Groups

Any society is a process of social change. The pace may differ for different societies and for different sectors of any society. But, when a group or class in society is threatened with loss of privilege or power, it responds to threat the way any social group would. There is a struggle to maintain its advantage and its position.

Under threat a group tends to be particularly cohesive and highly tolerant of strong leadership (Mulder, 1963). This gives its actions a certain amount of temporary coordination and power that can be a stimulant to conflict. A scapegoat is usually needed for the changing turn of fortunes and, like a government, they may find one in external antagonists and external conditions.

These pressures from groups losing power create a particularly problematic input into the national system. Those who are "losing out" are doing so in a system with certain properties and characteristics that are acting to create the change and obsolescence of the threatened group. Their conflict is usually with the system itself and not with some minor subsector. Being in a position of some power their actions can be quite effective in disrupting, disturbing, and disorganizing system functioning.

The Dynamics of Policy Formulation
and Public Opinion Regarding International Actions

The bulk of international events that lead to conflict initially involve some action that is threatening to one of the parties. It may or may not have been so intended but that shadow is cast upon the stage.

The initial response seems to be one of verification and authentication. A warning is efficient in terms of what can no longer be contradicted. Inadequate warnings can be denied or exaggerated. If the "news" cannot be discounted, the following stage is one of informational search on the nature of the threat and its manageability in terms of counteraction. If the threat was unexpected, these information-gathering stages may be quite prolonged and mechanism that might prolong these stages can be somewhat efficacious in slowing down the spiral toward a hasty interpretation and hasty action. If the threat was somewhat expected, there is likely to be a triggered response which, because it overlooks information that might be more coolly assessed, may alter the interpretation of the course of events.

Once a threat is "defined" in a certain way, one begins to plan various ways of coping with the hazard. Available to consideration are counteraction, commitment of resources, counterthreats, postponing and delaying the other nation's activities, tolerating them, or perhaps simply surviving them. At the same time various less "rational" means of coping with the threat may be utilized. Inattention to the threat may reduce anxiety. Information may be distorted, selected, exaggerated, or minimized. Humor, phantasy, ridicule, anger, ranting, hate, and various emotional outbursts can occur.

What is important at these stages of reaction is the failure of certain definitions, descriptions, and assessments of the threat to fit the incoming information and the contexts of interpretation into which they are received. It appears to be psychologically easier to adopt a new interpretation or stubbornly to stick by a perspective than to backtrack to a discarded assessment of conditions. On a simple informational level, then, there is a process or spiral of increasing commitment to certain understandings of the threat situation and to what it portends.

The historical analysis of threat situations that have or have not developed into open and extended conflicts tend to indicate a rather speedy realization by involved parties of how serious a situation exists. It is sometimes difficult to see, when looking back, why one interpretation was adopted rather than another, but the process seems to occur. Many of the factors enhancing an interpretation of serious conflict have been reviewed in this chapter.

Once an interpretation of events has begun to crystallize, counteractions and defenses are developed and put into effect. These are processes that take time and organization, but they tend to commit the nation to a particular line of behavior since decisions are made that limit the number of reactions that can later be attempted or adopted. The paths of reaction further serve to define the interpretation of the situation with which they are supposed to be coping mechanisms.

Behaviors that are tried tend to focus on the supposed causes of an opponent's actions, on his capability, on the effects of his actions, or perhaps even on his existence. Along with these actions and considerations there are intrasystem responses of group cohesion and a sense of common fate that often wipe out many of the usual divisions that separate and divide society. There is a sharp increase in reactive capability. Perhaps as important as anything is an increasing acceptance of strong, aggressive, singular leadership. These are the processes of alarm reaction.

There are various studies that employ the idea of a sequence, program, or natural history of conflict of which J. Coleman (1957), R. North and O. R. Holsti (Chapter 8), or H. Guetzkow *et al.* (1963) are only examples. Somewhat similar sequential notions exist in theories about reactions to threat, fear, stress, and so on, and there probably should be some overlap or integration among these phenomena. In none of these, however, is it proposed that the course of conflict is inevitable. All propose a dynamic or process that may meet with success or failure at various points. It is these points that provide the leverage for staying, diverting, accelerating, or returning the course of events.

The social psychologist should be the first to recognize the various levels at which this process occurs. As K. N. Waltz (1959) points out and R. Aron (1957) contends, there are international relations not only in the realm of the nature and behavior of man, but also in the nation-states themselves, in the internal defects and strengths in these systems, and further in the conditions and structures that compose the international community itself. None of the three alone is a sufficient arena for an explanation for action. Perhaps one reason is that the three also describe a process of social evolution of increasingly complex social units and social interactions where conflict, its causes and effects, can occur.

FACTORS FOR STAYING
WITHIN THE BOUNDARIES OF PEACE

History has witnessed three types of armed conflicts. Early wars were limited in their involvement of the total country. With little development of the national state, wars were conducted between segments of the population: restricted groups of soldiers and mercenaries. As national structures evolved we moved toward totalitarian war in which all segments of the population became involved. For such warfare the total population had to be psychologically mobilized for assuming their appropriate national roles. By psychological mobilization we mean the personalizing of the conflict through the arousal of nationalistic ideology. The third phase is one in which modern nations, which have become large technological, bureaucratic structures, can become mobilized for conflict with a minimum of ideological and emotional preparation. Though this is terrifying in the sense that wars are more remote than ever from the people waging them, it also has far-reaching implications for peaceful solutions. The very character of large bureaucratic structures creates possibilities for nonconflictual outcomes because they mute or immobilize the aggressive impulses of people, they neutralize the warmonger, and they create pressures for organizational survival among the military.

Technological bureaucracies as national, functional systems for carrying out objectives have as their basic value systems not the polar concepts of a sacred ideology, but more empirically oriented beliefs of efficiency, productivity, and applied science. They have feedback systems based upon task accomplishment. The new bureaucratic leader is not an ideologue but a task-oriented specialist. De Gaulle is an anachronism from another age with his beliefs in the destiny of France and of de Gaulle. It is true that bureaucracies would move toward armed conflict if such conflict would make for system growth and maximization. But with mutual annihilation being the prospect in an age of nuclear weapons, the large technological bureaucracies develop pressures toward more rational problem-solving. In fact the danger of war from the large, well-developed bureaucratic states may be much less than from newly developing nations or from the more primitive Chinese system. If it were not for internal political jockeying, the Russian and American bureaucrats could have worked out an agreement on nuclear testing and disarmament long ago.

Bureaucracies can employ technology to minimize the probabilities of war as well as to maximize them. The hot line between Moscow and Washington is a case in point. The development of a disarmament agency within the United States may put their emphasis upon retaliatory capabilities rather than upon first-strike capabilities and thus reduce the mutual threat posed by their destructive armaments.

The problem, then, in the well-developed technological society is to prevent internal power struggles from using nationalism and precipitating conflict. Already forces are at work in this direction. Political leaders, though they must play their roles as protectors of the national interest, must also be the compromisers and adjudicators of internal conflict. The leader who represents the uncompromising nationalism of rightist groups has difficulty in gaining support from all segments of society.

We have pointed out earlier in this discussion that normative practices already cut across national lines. Bureaucratic society relies heavily upon such normative integration. Its explicit extension to international relations is to be found in procedural systems such as the United Nations. T. Parsons (1962) argues that there has been an historical trend toward accepting procedural obligations which made the United Nations possible and which needs to be actively encouraged even at the risk of negative decisions for certain partisan national policies. A central issue in the development of an international system in which wars will be outlawed is the question of how such integration can be achieved. R. Angell (1957) holds that it must have as its core some value consensus in the field of international morality. It may well be, however, that the value consensus will be of the most general type, namely, the acceptance of procedures and decisions of the system reached through observance of rules. In other words, it need not be agreement between the East and West on symbolic values of an ideological sort, but on traffic rules which are already so basic a part of the functioning of large-scale bureaucracies.

Though bureaucratic structure has a tendency to expand, its growth can be extended beyond national lines without overt conflict. Business organizations move across national boundaries as do other organized groups. As they do they follow international agreements and help to develop further world law. The most striking example is the development of the European community, where nations with years of bitter conflict behind them and with long histories of mutual animosity and distrust have cooperated in the interests of a more functional economic system (Haas, 1958). European economies separated by tariffs, customs, and other barriers were dysfunctional from the bureaucratic point of view. The functional, task-oriented character of bureaucratic structure prevailed to produce a more rational system. The old symbols of nationalism were not discarded but remained latent in much of the cooperative integration that took place. With time it is probable that the symbols of statism and the polar concepts will be less potent even though the cultural identity of the nations will remain.

It is also true that as networks of association transcend national boundaries, the international system will show some resemblance to a complex national system in which the crisscrossing of multiple-group membership diminishes overt conflict (Coser, 1956). The segmental involvement of individuals in many groups results in no simple line of cleavage dividing a society into warring camps: the small businessman of Protestant extraction in a small southern community will be aligned on some issues with southern workers and on other issues with northern businessmen.

One way of conceptualizing the resolution of intra-European conflict is to use M. Sherif's hypothesis (1958) of superordinate goals as the basis for conflict solution. Sherif has demonstrated that experimentally created gangs of boys in competition with one another maintained their antagonisms in spite of all efforts to establish friendly communication between them through contacts at social events. This finding has been corroborated by R. R. Blake and J. S. Mouton (1961) in their experiments on groups undergoing training in human relations. These groups were placed in competition with respect to problem-solving tasks and subsequently their representatives engaged in an intergroup conference about the problems and their solutions. The intergroup conference proved unsuccessful because the members of the various groups remained committed to their own group solutions and, in fact, could not develop an adequate understanding of the solutions reached by the other groups. In the Sherif study, however, another step was taken and a superordinate goal was created for the competing groups. For example, in one experiment the tank supplying water to the entire camp was made dysfunctional and the combined efforts of the antagonistic gangs became a necessary condition for the effective repair of the water system. Thus, when the antagonistic gangs were placed in a situation where the only solution for both groups was cooperation around objectives transcending the specific group goal, the gangs cooperated to achieve the superordinate goal. In Europe the cooperation arose not through cultural interchange nor the good offices of a third party but from the common interests of the various nations in certain new institutional arrangements. These became superordinate goals for the cooperating nations and questions of national sovereignty were side-stepped in moving toward them. The question remains as to whether the self-defeating character of nuclear war can help to create a superordinate goal of world peace among the powerful nations of the world. In the past the development of more and more destructive weapons has led pacifists to hope for such a solution, but these hopes have not been realized. Never before, however, have nations faced a common fate of annihilation. Moreover, two additional factors may help to change the picture in the future. For one thing, it is now the powerful nations which have a common interest in controlling atomic weapons. They have the most to lose, whereas the weaker powers, economically and technologically, have less to lose. Hence a superordinate goal of arms control and settlement of disputes in an international order is a real possibility for the strongest nations. Such a move on their part could exert profound influence on the less powerful nations. When Russia and the United States negotiated a treaty banning atmospheric nuclear testing, 100 other nations rushed to affix their signatures to the agreement.

Another factor making such a superordinate goal possible operates within nations. The elite groups within a powerful country in terms of prestige, wealth, and power have everything to lose and nothing to gain from a nuclear holocaust. These groups, though they may often be short-sighted, possess the information and the intelligence to develop an awareness of their position and prospects. Hence they may exert a dynamic toward their own country's push toward a peaceful settlement and counter some of the chauvinistic input from the rightist groups already losing their power.

REFERENCES

Adorno, T. W., E. Frenkel-Brunswik, D. J. Levinson, and R. N. Sanford, *The Authoritarian Personality*. New York: Harper & Row, Publishers, 1950.

Allport, F. H., *Institutional Behavior*. Chapel Hill: University of North Carolina Press, 1933.

Angell, R. C., "Discovering Paths to Peace," *The Nature of Conflict*, J. Bernard, T. H. Pear, R. Aron, and R. C. Angell, eds. Paris: UNESCO, 1957.

Aron, R., "Conflict and War from the Viewpoint of Historical Sociology," *The Nature of Conflict*, T. H. Pear, R. Aron, and R. C. Angell, eds. Paris: UNESCO, 1957.

Ashby, W. R., *Design for a Brain*. New York: John Wiley & Sons, Inc., 1952.

Bay, C., I. Gullväg, H. Ofstad, and H. Tønnessen, *Nationalism: A Study of Identification with People and Power*. Oslo: Institute of Social Research, 1950.

Blake, R. R. and J. S. Mouton, "Comprehension of Own and Outgroup Positions under Intergroup Competition," *Journal of Conflict Resolution*, V (1961), 304-310.

Boulding, K. E., "Is Peace Researchable?" *Continuous Learning* (March–April, 1962).

Coleman, J., *Community Conflict*. New York: Free Press of Glencoe, Inc., 1957.

Coser, L., *The Function of Social Conflict*. New York: Free Press of Glencoe, Inc., 1956.

Durkheim, E., *The Division of Labor*, G. Simpson, trans. New York: The Macmillan Company, 1933.

Festinger, L., *A Theory of Cognitive Dissonance*. New York: Harper & Row, Publishers, 1957.

Gladstone, A. I., "Relationship Orientation and Processes Leading Toward War," *Background*, VI (1962), 13-25.

Guetzkow, H., C. F. Alger, R. A. Brody, R. C. Noel, and R. C. Snyder, *Simulation in International Relations*. Englewood Cliffs, N.J.: Prentice-Hall, Inc., 1963.

Haas, E. B., *The Uniting of Europe*. Stanford, Calif.: Stanford University Press, 1958.

Hayes, C. J. H., *Essays on Nationalism*. New York: The Macmillan Company, 1926.

Katz, D., "Current and Needed Psychological Research in International Relations," *Journal of Social Issues*, XVII (1961), 69-78.

Kolman, H. C. and L. Bailyn, "Effects of Cross-Cultural Experience on National Images," *Journal of Conflict Resolution*, VI (1962), 319-334.

Levi, W., "Causes of Peace," *Journal of Conflict Resolution.* In press.

Levinson, D., "Authoritarian Personality and Foreign Policy," *Journal of Conflict Resolution,* I (1957), 37-47.

Morse, N. and F. H. Allport, "The Causation of Anti-Semitism," *Journal of Psychology,* XXXIV (1952), 197-233.

Mulder, M. and A. Stemerding, "Threat, Attraction to Group, and Need for Strong Leadership," *Human Relations,* XVI (1963), 317-334.

Oppenheimer, F., *The State.* Indianapolis: Bobbs-Merrill Company, Inc., 1914.

Parsons, T., "Polarization of the World and International Order," *Preventing World War III,* Q. Wright, W. M. Evan, and M. Deutsch, eds., pp. 310-331. New York: Simon & Schuster, Inc., 1962.

Selltiz, C. and S. W. Cook, "Factors Influencing Attitudes of Foreign Students Toward the Host Country," *Journal of Social Issues,* XVIII (1962), 7-23.

Sherif, M., "Superordinate Goals in the Reduction of Intergroup Conflict," *American Journal of Sociology,* LXIII (1958), 349-356.

Siegel, S., "Level of Aspiration and Decision Making," *Psychological Review,* LXIV (July 1957), 253-262.

Waltz, K. N., *Man, the State, and War.* New York: Columbia University Press, 1959.

Williams, R. M., *The Reduction of Intergroup Tensions.* Social Science Research Council Bulletin, No. 57. New York: The Council, 1947.

Withey, S. B., "Reaction to Uncertain Threat," *Man and Society in Disaster,* G. W. Baker and D. W. Chapman, eds. New York: Basic Books, Inc., 1962.

5

The Sociology of Human Conflict

ROBERT C. ANGELL

The literature of sociology is of singularly little relevance to the cold war or to the relations among national societies generally. This is in part because sociologists have paid inadequate attention to conflict, in part because when they have studied it, they have been preoccupied with class conflict, and in part because when they have looked at intersocietal conflict, they have tended to see it resulting in conquest—which is hardly a satisfactory answer to the world's problem today. Fortunately, there are signs that this neglect is coming to an end. Jessie Bernard might not now be tempted to write the article she wrote more than a dozen years ago, "Where Is the Modern Sociology of Conflict?" (1950)

The most systematic treatment of conflict by a sociologist is in a recent essay by Ralf Dahrendorf, "Elemente einer Theorie des sozialen Konflikte," in his *Gesellschaft und Freiheit* (1962). He suggests that there are six basic needs for an adequate theory of social conflict. The first is to arrive at an appropriate conception of the phenomenon and to distinguish its main types. For him the most useful definition is one in terms of opposition between two, and only two, parties, whether conscious or unconscious. He proceeds to offer a taxonomy that is here presented in tabular form because it provides a helpful framework for the discussion of the contributions of other authors. The table below is a simplified version, slightly adapted to the American context.

TABLE 1

SOCIAL UNIT	1 EQUAL AGAINST EQUAL	2 SUPERORDINATE AGAINST SUBORDINATE	3 WHOLE AGAINST PART
A Roles	Family role vs. occupational role	Occupational role vs. labor-union role	Social personality vs. family role
B Groups	Boys vs. girls (in school class)	Father vs. children	Family vs. prodigal son
C Sectors	Air Force vs. Army	Manufacturers' association vs. labor unions	Episcopalian church vs. "high church" group
D Societies	Protestants vs. Catholics	Free men vs. slaves	The state vs. criminal gang
E Suprasocietal relations	Soviet bloc vs. Western bloc	Soviet Union vs. Hungary	Common Market vs. France

(Adapted from Ralf Dahrendorf, *Gesellschaft und Freiheit*, p. 206)

For purposes of analysis Dahrendorf reduces the fifteen cells of this table to six types as follows:

1. Role conflicts (A1, A2, A3).
2. Competition (B1, C1).
3. Class conflicts (B2, C2, D2).
4. Minority conflict and "deviation" (B3, C3, D3).
5. "Proportion struggle" (D1).
6. International relations (E1, E2, E3).

Dahrendorf's second basic need for a theory of conflict is to determine what conception of society is compatible with the study of conflict. Since his discussion of this involves developments in sociology during the last twenty-five years, consideration of this problem will be postponed to a later section of this essay. His last four needs are determined by answering the following: What are the structural conditions which give rise to different forms of conflict? How does conflict evolve from these structural conditions? What are the dimensions of each kind of conflict and under what conditions does the form of conflict vary on these dimensions? How can conflict be regulated? It is interesting how closely Dahrendorf's formulation parallels a set of criteria for a theory of conflict which I had set up before reading his essay. I had thought we would expect a theory of conflict to touch upon the following questions:

1. What set of basic concepts is necessary to the study of conflict?
2. What types of conflict need to be discriminated?
3. What causal processes lead to situations of conflict?
4. What are the main processes (or developmental stages) of conflict itself?
5. What are the effects of the conflict process on the conflicting units and on the context of their conflict?
6. What sort of external factors exacerbate conflict, and what sorts tend to mollify or resolve it?
7. What are the alternative forms of termination of conflict, and how can they be reached?

We shall keep these seven points in mind as we cover the sociological literature on conflict.

The most influential theory of social conflict has certainly been that of Karl Marx. Ever since the publication of *The Communist Manifesto* in 1848, his ideas have been a force to be reckoned with. Since capitalist industrialism was spreading throughout the world and since his was a theory that promised a better life to those who felt exploited by that system, the wide acceptance of his theory is readily understandable.

Although Marx called his theory scientific and although he used historical materials to buttress it, the part that most interested him—the conflict between the proletariat and the bourgeoisie—was hypothesis rather than demonstrated theory because the industrial revolution had then not gone far enough to yield empirical data on its validity. Even today there would be wide disagreement on the degree to which Marx's theory has been validated. Perhaps someone not involved in the cold war and therefore fairly objective would declare that his great analytical abilities produced shrewd hypotheses which subsequent events have in part refuted.

In terms of our touchstones for an adequate theory of conflict Marx concerned himself with only one type—class conflict—but he did look diligently for the structural causes of that type and did construct a theory of how conflict evolves from those causes. He was little concerned with the interaction between the conflict and its context. He did not care about what effects it might have on society so long as the principal goal, the overthrow of the capitalist class, was achieved; and he was likewise uninterested in external forces that might mollify it. There was only one logical termination, and that could be reached in only one way.

To Marx, social and political conflicts spring from an economic base. Prominent in his materialistic theory are the concepts of the relations of production, the dialectic process, surplus value (stemming from his labor theory of value), class interests, class consciousness, class struggle, and the classless society. He finds the causal conditions of the conflict in the changing productive forces of the early industrial revolution, which were inconsistent with the then existing relations of production and their embodiment in principles of property. When the use of the machine made it impossible for workers to own their own tools, the private property of capitalists in plant and equipment gave them an exploitative advantage over workers. He hypothesizes that as the workers become more alienated from their work and the system in general, they become aware of their common interests, and they unite for class struggle against the ruling capitalist class, whose weapon is the state. In Marxian theory the processes of the conflict itself are bitter and unconditional. The workers can expect no quarter from the capitalists, political concessions are mere sops thrown out to confuse and weaken the workers, and the workers must press on with organization, general strikes, and preparations for violence. Finally the day of violence must come, and out of it will emerge the dictatorship of the proletariat. The workers will then root out the last vestiges of capitalism, preside over the withering away of the state, and usher in the classless society.

Because Marx was both an analyst and a reformer his doctrine contains a curious mixture of inevitability and voluntarism. To him the proletarian revolution is inevitable, but at the same time he wished to incite the workers to exert themselves—to hasten the day. The polemical aspect of his work has of course made many writers question whether he deserves to be called a social scientist at all. Can anyone who is so ardent a champion of a cause possibly explore the complexities of social organization objectively? We are so used these days to hearing Marxian thought condemned without examination that it may be worthwhile to note the high praise bestowed upon his work by the first professor of sociology at the University of Chicago, Albion W. Small: "I confidently predict that in the ultimate judgment of history Marx will have a place in social science analogous with that of Galileo in physical science" (1912, p. 810). In order to evaluate so extravagant a statement, let us turn to another work by Dahrendorf, *Class and Class Conflict in Industrial Society* (1959). Approximately half of this book is given over to an evaluation of the Marxian theory.

Dahrendorf believes that the greatest contribution of Marx to sociology was his realization that internal conflict derives from the existent social structure and that it produces changes in the structure. Thus, as against cumulative theories of progress, he saw the vital role of conflict in social change. As motive forces in the conflict, Dahrendorf also approves the Marxian concept of class interests. He does, however, quarrel with Marxian theory at a number of points.

First, he finds that Marx was wrong in his assumption that all structural change is brought about by class conflict. He points out that external conflict may well produce change in social patterns and that in addition there are internal conflicts between religious and ethnic groups that do so.

A second point of difference is that Dahrendorf denies that all class conflicts must eventuate in revolution before they achieve structural change. He believes that the history of Western nations thoroughly refutes this. An allied criticism is that though it is true that classes have conflicting interests, Marx was wrong in holding that they are always in acute and violent conflict. Dahrendorf believes that conflict may remain latent during national emergencies or through negotiated "armistices" between workers and employers.

Of great interest for sociological theory is Dahrendorf's contention that instead of relations to the means of production being the crucial fact in class formation, it is relations of authority. Difference in structured power—such as in modern industrial, governmental, religious, and educational bureaucracies—are, he thinks, the determinants of interest.

Finally, Dahrendorf is critical of the identification which Marx makes between the economy and the society. The notion that those who win the means of production therefore automatically control the destinies of the government and all other social institutions seems to him undemonstrated. He asks how Marx would explain the labor governments in England.

What is the picture of Marx that emerges from Dahrendorf's critique? It is that of a great pioneer in sociology who got a firm grasp on an original idea—that internal conflict is a method of transition from one pattern of social structure to another. He gave this idea undue centrality in a general theory of change and embellished it unconvincingly in several directions. When, however, these mistakes are stripped away, there remains a solid contribution.

Ten years after the *Communist Manifesto* Darwin and Wallace published their joint article on biological evolution. It gave rise to a completely different line of thought that was also concerned with social conflict, but this time with external conflict. This doctrine, now called *Social Darwinism*, was to gain great popular acceptance in the latter part of the nineteenth century. It is concerned with cell E1 of Dahrendorf's table.

The fundamental idea of Social Darwinism, that societies and groups are engaged in a struggle for existence in which the fit survive, had been anticipated long before, especially among political writers dealing with the origins of the state. A great precursor was Ibn Khaldun of Tunis, the Mohammedan historian (1332–1406). He developed the theory that sedentary agriculturalists occupying villages and towns succumb to luxury and vice and are thus easily conquered by pastoral nomads who have been hardened by the rigorous life in the desert. The conquerors, however, soon adopt the ways of the conquered with the result that the cycle repeats itself approximately every 120 years.

Jean Bodin (1530–1596), the French political philosopher, had similar ideas. He thought that the state originated in the conflict of societies and that its particular nature was the subordination of the conquered by the conqueror. Hence, the unstratified character of pre-existing societies is replaced by a stratified system once the state is born. David Hume (1723–1816) accepted the conflict theory of the origin of the state, but believed that the principle of forceful subordination is gradually replaced by the development of consensus.

The first book attempting to apply Darwinian ideas to society was Walter Bagehot's justly famous *Physics and Politics* (1872). He did not emphasize the biological element in social selection, but rather used the struggle for existence among societies as one stage in a three-stage process by which civilization has developed. First, each society had to harden its "cake of custom" so as to become a true competitor in the struggle. Second, there ensued a conflict between societies in which strong states were created by conquest. Such states, however, were in danger of stagnation once they had stabilized their position. Hence a third stage is necessary for continuing progress, the so-called *age of discussion*. This breaks down the "cake of custom" by the development of tolerance for innovations.

The most extreme of all Social Darwinists and therefore the scholar who most heavily relied on external conflict in social explanation is Ludwik Gumplowicz (1838–1909), a Pole living in Austria. His most famous work, *Der Rassenkampf* (1883), bases social evolution on biology in the sense that he posits different genetic stocks which have an absolute animosity toward one another. As they expand and come in contact, they engage in violent conflict, and thus begins the incessant process of war and conquest. The state is always born of conquest, and hence is always heterogeneous internally. Thus what was originally external conflict is carried on internally as the ethnic groups retain their animosities. Here Social Darwinism, on the assumption that different stocks find themselves in different relations to the means of production, connects with the Marxian theory.

Gustav Ratzenhofer (1842–1904) was a fellow citizen of Austria with Gumplowicz and a fellow Social Darwinist, but in the first instance he focused on the person, not the group. Like Marx he developed a theory of interests, but rather than class interests, he emphasized the individual interests of self-preservation and propagation (1898). The person's hostility to other persons is, however, overlaid by the strength of the kin tie and thus he discovers that others have similar interests that can form the basis of organized groups. At this point his theory is much like that of Gumplowicz, endorsing as it does the conquest theory of the state and explaining the development of internal conflict. However, much like Bagehot, he believes the conquest state evolves into the culture state through compromise among competing interest groups. There is the same danger in this that Ibn Khaldun recognized long before—that the culture state may become weak and fall before a less evolved opponent.

Lester F. Ward (1841–1913), the pioneer American sociologist, despite his emphasis on the psychic factors in civilization, followed Gumplowicz and Ratzenhofer completely in their behalf that the state and systems of law arose from conflict. He does see a more beneficent process taking over, however, after the state is well established. The heterogeneous elements are cemented into a *people*, and thereupon there develops a sentiment of patriotism and the formation of a *nation* (1903, p. 205).

There is no need to pursue the conflict theory of the origin of the state through its definitive expression in Franz Oppenheimer's *Der Staat* (1908). It is by now obvious that the Social Darwinists were simply trying to prove that there had been a process analogous to biological selection in the struggle for existence among societies. For the most part they saw the units of struggle to be societies, and the process, wars of conquest. When Bagehot comes to his "age of discussion," and when Ratzenhofer, Ward, and Oppenheimer come to their "cultural states," where law has superseded exploitation, they concentrate on the internal evolution of the society-state. They do not make clear what happens in the realm of external conflict.

As perhaps might be expected, it is only a critic of Social Darwinism, Jacques Novicow (1849–1912), who states a theory about external conflict. This French scholar of Polish origin devoted his life largely to the refutation of the cruder doctrines of the Social Darwinists. While admitting that man had passed through physiological, economic, and political struggles, he believed that conflict was destined to be carried on in the future on an intellectual plane. Such conflicts will be both internal to societies and between the members of different societies. Since the best people and the best ideas will win out, justice will grow and, with it, peace among men (1893). It is interesting to note that in 1901 he wrote a prophetic book entitled *La Federation de l'Europe*.

If we look back at our criteria for an adequate sociological theory of conflict, we see that the Social Darwinists fall far short. They have simple sets of concepts like Gumplowicz' absolute hatred, conflict, and conquest, or Ratzenhofer's individual interests, the conjunction of individual interests in collectivities for survival, conflict, and conquest. This is because they have not faced fully the types of conflict possible, even external conflict. Novicow made a real contribution here. Most of the attention of the Social Darwinists is devoted to the third and fourth points in our list: the causal processes leading to conflict and the main processes of conflict itself. Only Bagehot has much to say about the effects of the conflict on the nature and structure of the societies involved with the process of conflict. And almost nothing is said about the external factors which may influence the course of the conflict. The termination of conflict is seen in the simplistic terms of the conquest of the less fit by the more fit.

The first sociologist to consider conflict as a separate subject, without reference to any larger subject, like the historical dialectic or evolutionary survival, was Georg Simmel (1858–1918). He believed that the progress of sociology depended upon a searching exploration of particular aspects of society, such as secrecy, monetary exchange, and the role of the stranger. His imaginative and subtle mind found pleasure and stimulation in these explorations. The result was a series of essays full of penetrating insights and delicate nuances of thought.

Because he was treating conflict as a separate subject, Simmel ranges all over Dahrendorf's table. He was interested in both internal and external conflict, in both causes and results, and in both personal and group involvement (1955). These interests weave in and out of the essay in a manner that sometimes masks from the reader the full significance of his thoughts. Lewis A. Coser has performed a notable service, therefore, in giving us a learned, critical restatement of Simmel's essay in his *The Functions of Social Conflict* (1956). He sorts out sixteen propositions, puts them in an analytic framework, and comments extensively on each.

If one can summarize so diffuse a piece of work, the central idea in Simmel's essay is that conflict is constructive. It is his belief not only that it gives rise to social change, as Marx would have it, but also that in many ways it is immediately integrative. This of course is obvious in the case of external conflict producing internal integration—to the spelling out of which three of Coser's propositions are devoted. But it is not at all obvious (and perhaps it is questionable) that internal conflict gives rise to internal integration or that external conflict unifies the antagonists.

Three of Coser's propositions in particular deal with the effect of internal conflict on integration. The most general one is represented by Simmel's words:

> Conflict is designed to resolve divergent dualisms; it is a way of achieving some kind of unity. . . . This is roughly parallel to the fact that it is the most violent symptom of a disease which represents the effort of the organism to free itself of disturbances and damages caused by them. . . . Conflict itself resolves the tension between contrasts (1955, p. 15).

Coser very well comments that these ideas of Simmel are valid only if one assumes that at the basis of the relations between parties there is strong consensus, so that the conflicts he speaks of concern less fundamental questions that do not bring that consensus into question. In that sense Simmel is here stating, at most, a half-truth. But, as Coser points out, there is perhaps implicit here another truth that Simmel did not clearly see: that open societies, which permit internal conflict on many fronts, by that very fact make it less likely that any one conflict will endanger the basic consensus. The numerous conflicts will crisscross each other in a confusing way that prevents their cumulation to form a basic line of cleavage (1956, p. 80).

Another of Simmel's ideas made into a proposition by Coser is that the more stable the relation between the parties, the more they will be willing to express hostilities through conflict. Thus it is not sound to judge the instability of a relation by the amount of conflict expressed within it. Quite the contrary, much conflict can occur even in a stable relation. People are willing to become embroiled in conflict if they have no doubt of their ultimate cohesion. In reality, then, we have a threshold phenomenon. Below a certain integrative threshold, conflict betokens the possible breakup of the unity and is therefore negatively indicative of its stability. Above the threshold the amount of conflict is positively related to the stability of the relationship. This is a most significant insight which has no application to contemporary cold war conditions, since the relationship between the two sides is so fragile; but, it is an insight that may become applicable to the common market, which may show its strength by the amount of internal conflict that develops.

The third of Coser's propositions derived from Simmel's thoughts on internal conflict is much more dubious. After indicating that internal conflict is a cause of integration, Simmel says:

> Thus, the Hindu social system rests not only on the hierarchy, but also on the mutual repulsion, of the castes. Hostilities not only prevent boundaries within the group from gradually disappearing . . . often they provide classes and individuals with reciprocal positions which they would not find if the causes of hostility were not accompanied by the feeling and the expression of hostility (1955, pp. 17-18).

What this proposition amounts to is saying that the expression of hostility in conflict clarifies the positions of the contending parties and thus defines the situation more clearly. Once clearly defined, orderly processes of control and accommodation tend to set in. The lingering doubt about the validity of this proposition arises from two other possibilities: (a) that latent hostility will be gradually allayed from the very indefiniteness of an unstructured situation and (b) that the more structured situation, if it arises, will not necessarily give rise to the controlling mechanisms, but rather tear the society apart.

To put the matter in contemporary terms, do we really believe that clear positions on either side of the cold war are more conducive to peace than more elusive ones?

Three of Coser's propositions deal with external conflict. These are the most relevant of Simmel's ideas to the present world situation. The first one states that if there is any limit at all to violence, conflict binds the antagonists. Simmel says: "One unites in order to fight, and one fights under the mutually recognized control of norms and rules" (1955, p. 35). Coser believes this to be true provided the conflict initiates other forms of interaction between the antagonists and especially if these other forms of interaction stimulate new rules, norms, and institutions (1956, p. 128).

Even if true, the contribution of this proposition to human welfare is not great under modern conditions, since the risk of conflict between nations going over into nuclear war is so great as to dwarf the chance benefits from the formation of new normative controls. We had better aim at control directly rather than hoping that it will spring out of conflict before millions are dead.

Another proposition suggests that in external conflict each side wants the other to be unified, because it is then easier to deal with and its commitments can be trusted. This is no doubt true if each party is sure the other will survive the contest. But if one side thinks it can break down the resistance of its opponent and thus win a clear victory, it will surely prefer the opponent not be well unified. Coser makes this point.

The third proposition in this field is one involving the balance of power. Simmel says, "The most effective prerequisite for preventing struggle, the exact knowledge of the comparative strength of the two parties, is very often attainable only by the actual fighting out of the conflict" (1904, p. 501). This principle too gives us scant consolation in the present world situation. If accommodation between the parties is only possible when relative strengths are known, and if these can be known only through conflict, World War III is a necessary prelude to accommodation—a dismal prospect.

Five of the other seven propositions drawn out by Coser are less relevant to our interest here. Four of them concern personal conflict in intimate or small-group relations. Though these may be suggestive for conflict among large aggregates, the parallels are not close enough to be very profitable. Another makes the obvious point that conflicts create associations and coalitions. Whether it is classes or other units within a society, or whether it is societies that are in conflict, the desire for allies is inevitable and understandable.

The other two propositions have to do with variables that affect the intensity of conflict. The first states that the closer the relationship of parties, the more intense the conflict if it breaks out. The more central in the lives of its members a collectivity is, the more bitter will be the conflict after schism. The American Civil War is a case in point. This is a proposition that has little relevance to the international situation today, but it is one that might lead to caution in approaching a unified world society. If such a society were merely to represent a semblance of unity, the chances of breakup and succeeding world annihilation would be great.

The final proposition states that conflict is intense if it is ideological. Personal goals and ambitions are more easily compromised than impersonal causes. Coser suggests that an exception to this rule occurs when self-interest is given moral sanction, as in the Protestant Ethic. He concludes that the real principle at stake is not that ideological conflict is intense, but rather that conflict entered upon with a good conscience is so. This is a proposition that emphasizes the perilous nature of the cold war, since both sides are so sure of the justice of their respective causes.

One of Simmel's ideas which Coser does not propositionalize, but which has relevance to the contemporary international situation, is that slight dissonance will give rise to more intense conflict when the parties expect a high degree of consonance than when they do not (1955, p. 44). In other words, the United States, not expecting the Soviet Union to act on our principles, can accept unpalatable behavior on her part much more easily than we can take such behavior from a country of similar ideology. The question arises whether this idea does not contradict the last proposition above. The reconciliation of the two seems to be as follows: Strangeness makes us slow to anger because our expectations are not high, but once conflict has started, it will be more bitter the more it is a conflict of conscience.

A special section of Simmel's essay is given over to competition, which he defines as that form of conflict where the parties are vying for a prize that is not under control of either, where efforts are therefore parallel rather than offensive and defensive. Here he points out the great civilizing effect of competition. It socializes because its competitors have to adapt to third parties or to public wants and tastes and standards generally if they wish to carry off the prize. This notion is of course already of great relevance in international affairs, since there is enough of world public opinion already to make the United States and the Soviet

Union compete for the favor of unaligned nations. We are, however, as Simmel points out, a long way from the development of agreed rules of competition such as have developed within national societies.

These few paragraphs on Simmel give a very inadequate conception of the richness of his essay, but perhaps enough has been conveyed to make it apparent why sociologists in the last fifty years have returned so frequently to it. He goes further than his predecessors in refining concepts, in discriminating different types of conflict, in discussing causal processes that lead to conflict (although we have not set forth these ideas here), in analyzing the actual processes of conflict, and in subtly treating the side factors and the side effects that come into play during the conflict. Although he really says little about the last point in our paradigm, the termination of conflict—possibly because he finds it so constructive that he may not wish to terminate it—he does not wholly neglect the matter. "The sociology of conflict thus requires, at least as an appendix, an analysis of the forms in which a fight terminates. These forms constitute interactions not to be observed under any other circumstances" (1955, p. 110).

Long before the Coser analysis of Simmel was published, Simmel's ideas had had a strong influence on American sociology through the impress of his work on two scholars in the great department at the University of Chicago. Robert D. Park attended Simmel's lectures at the University of Berlin as a graduate student at the turn of the century and subsequently wove many of his ideas on conflict and competition into the justly famous *Introduction to the Science of Sociology* written by himself and Ernest W. Burgess (1921). Albion W. Small, Park's older colleague and chairman of the Chicago department, was also interested in Simmel and translated his work extensively for the *American Journal of Sociology,* including an earlier essay on conflict (1904).

More than two hundred pages of the Park and Burgess work are given over to the processes of competition, conflict, and accommodation, and in the chapters treating them there are seven long excerpts from Simmel. According to the authors, competition can exist without any recognition of it on the part of the parties. In nature, trees compete for sunlight; in the human economy, a wheat farmer in Saskatchewan is competing with one in North Dakota to sell his crop on the international market at the best possible price, though neither has ever heard of the other. The lines of effort are parallel since they are directed at the same goal, but there is no conflict. Competition becomes conflict when the competitors identify each other and try to impair each other's efforts toward the common goal. Since means of communication make possible contact between distant parties, there is always the likelihood that competition will become conflict.

Park and Burgess point out that competition is continuous and impersonal, whereas conflict is intermittent and personal. There is obviously an area of overlap—where competitors, in trying to reach the prize, become embroiled with each other. It is to keep conflict to a minimum and to retain the social value of competition that standards are set in morality and law to achieve fairness in the struggle. Wherever there is an attentive public watching the behavior of the competitors, there is a force limiting the unscrupulousness and the violence of the conflict. The authors believe that rivalry is best conceived as the struggle for public approval, status, or prestige. To the degree that the conflicting parties feel that appeal lies in the judgment of the public, they are rivals.

Conflict goes over into accommodation when a *modus vivendi* is worked out. One frequent form of accommodation is superordination and subordination. Another is mutual adjustment through compromise. Since the equilibrium almost always involves a power differential, conflict remains latent even when there is surface accommodation. If the power position of the parties shifts before the accommodation has become thoroughly embedded in the cultural tradition, the conflict may be renewed.

The Park and Burgess volume does not so much make new contributions to the sociology of conflict as it familiarizes American students with the analyses of earlier writers, especially Simmel, and systematizes the treatment of the subject. There is a section on war, instincts, and ideals, but as the title suggests, the selections presented here are psychological in orientation, not sociological. Hence there is no specific contribution to the sociology of international conflict.

Since the work of the great pioneer American sociologists between 1880 and 1920, two outstanding influences have been felt in American sociology, neither of them conducive to a theoretical concern with conflict. The first was the trend toward empiricism manifested in the great sociology department at the University of Chicago in the Twenties and Thirties. Reacting somewhat to armchair theorizing, Park, Thomas, Burgess, and Ogburn sent their graduate students out into the community to investigate the ongoing processes of life. This example was widely copied in other universities, with the result that studies were made on every conceivable front. Conflict processes were often part of the data of such studies—conflict between workers and management, race conflict, religious conflict—but rarely were the studies focused on these processes in such a way as to give them broad conceptualization. The general theory of the subject was not advanced because each student was looking at too small a segment of reality.

The second influence has been the rise of structural-functional theory in sociology under the lead of Talcott Parsons immediately following World War II. The best known expression of this point of view is Parsons' *The Social System* (1951). The essence of the theory is that a community or society forms a system of action, each part of which has one or more functions to perform, all the parts being integrated into the ongoing system by virtue of some value consensus. This way of looking at a society tends to make conflict appear as deviant or abnormal, since the central concern is the successful integration of the various parts into a smooth-running whole. The tremendous vogue which this approach has enjoyed has therefore tended to distract American sociologists from attention to conflict processes.

Dahrendorf has been one of the major critics of this approach. In his essay on the theory of social conflict he argues that there are only two solutions to the Hobbesian problem of order: that of coercion or compulsion, which Hobbes himself took, and that of consensus, which Rousseau took and which Parsons is taking. These two solutions rest on quite different assumptions regarding the nature of society: the latter rests on the assumptions that society is inherently stable, its parts in equilibrium, each part performing functions for the system, all integrated through common values; the former rests on the assumptions that every society succumbs to change, is made up of a contradictory and explosive set of elements, each of which contributes to change, the society being integrated through coercion. Dahrendorf does not argue that the coercive answer has the sole claim to truth, but he does argue that without this perspective there can be no theory of conflict (1962, pp. 207-212). This is what he meant when he said that the second basic need for a theory of social conflict was a conception of society compatible with it.

To Dahrendorf the value of social conflict is that it produces change. In another essay in the same volume, "Die Functionen sozialer Konflikte" (1962, pp. 112-131), he takes Coser to task for seeing the functions of social conflict entirely in terms of its contribution to the ongoing system. He agrees that it is true that sometimes conflict contributes to functional effectiveness, but he asks—to him—the devastating question: "Is the only sociologically relevant consequence of a strike or even of a revolution that it constitutes a tie between the hostile parties?" He would answer with a resounding "No." The chief contribution of conflict is to keep the system from ossification.

We have discussed Dahrendorf's general theory of conflict, his critique of Marx, and his criticisms of the structural-functional school. Before turning back to American sociologists, we should perhaps present his own ideas on class conflict as set forth in the latter half of his *Class and Class Conflict in Industrial Society* (1959).

Dahrendorf defines an interest as a structurally generated orientation held by the incumbents of a defined position. There is no psychological assumption here—the interests of classes are objective. As indicated earlier, he believes that the positions in industrial society that are important are defined on a continuum of authority. Broadly there are those who have authority, and their interest is domination; and there are those who have little or none, and their interest is to change the situation. Class conflict is therefore best understood as conflict over the legitimacy of existent authority relations.

Because the interest of a class may be latent as well as manifest, he adopts the concept of quasi-group (perhaps better, potential group) whose members have an interest in common that is not manifested. Such quasi-groups are recruiting fields for real interest groups which are the agencies of class conflict. He points out that a single quasi-group may give birth to more than one interest group, as where the proletariat becomes the recruiting ground for communist, socialist, and Christian labor unions. Some quasi-groups never give rise to interest groups—for instance, the peasantry in many European countries.

The organization of interest groups is affected, he thinks, by three sorts of conditions: (a) there must be sufficient communication to realize that the community of interest in a class and that members of the class must have the same objective interest (i.e., they must not have arrived there by chance or for irrelevant reasons); (b) there must be freedom of speech and association, so the interest group can form; and (c) the interest group must have sufficient material means, able leadership, and a clear ideology to attain success.

It is Dahrendorf's belief that class conflicts are never resolved; they are only regulated. Regulation is most effective when both sides recognize the reality of the conflict (that they must deal with the opposition), when both sides are organized in interest groups, and when agreed rules of the game have been developed. Since rules of the game can last only so long as they put the parties on a relatively equal footing, and since new conditions may change their effect, rules for changing the rules are very important. This is the value of a constitution (1959, p. 227).

Nothing could point up more clearly the difference between internal and external conflict. Classes are interdependent parts of a larger whole, and if they do not themselves realize the worth to them of rules of the game, they can in the last analysis be coerced by the state to structure their conflict. If they do not adopt an agreed way of changing the rules of the struggle, the encompassing society can do it for them. This is exactly what is lacking in the external conflict of nation with nation—an encompassing society to see to it that conflict is stabilized through rules of the game.

Dahrendorf has worked out a most complete modern theory of class conflict. Although we have not outlined his theory in its entirety, he does in fact cover almost every point in the paradigm of an adequate theory of conflict with which we commenced. Perhaps he gives too little attention to the effects of the conflict on the parties during the process. But the thirty-nine propositions which he enumerates at one point are a major contribution (1959, pp. 237-240).

The subject of internal community conflict seems to have received its first careful consideration, at least in the United States, in the volume *Community Conflict* published by The Inquiry (1929). The editors have gathered together studies of actual cases in American towns and drawn generalizations from them. The generalizations, however, have an action rather than a theoretical emphasis. The chapter, "Integrating Community Interests," stresses the importance of finding the common interest among the divisive interests and bringing it to dominance in the community. The philosophy behind this work seems to be that of Mary P. Follett, so ably expressed in her *The New State* (1918) and *Creative Experience* (1924). This approach to conflict resolution seeks to recognize all valid interests in the final accommodation. If successful, this accommodation is not merely a dead compromise, but involves a new factor, a social invention as it were, that is the result of the interpenetration of the several conflicting interests. Although the idea of a new level of organization is not required, it is compatible with this approach. In any event, the conflicting interests must be transcended by a new integration. This is a line of thought that has obvious application to international problems.

Almost thirty years later, James S. Coleman published a monograph also called *Community Conflict* (1957). He too looked at specific conflicts as reported by journalists and social scientists. His generalizations aim to be scientific. Perhaps his most interesting findings revolve around the dynamics of controversy. He sketches the following natural history of community conflict: Once a controversy has started, there is a tendency for the agenda of conflict to widen and for its bitterness to increase. Particular organizations develop to fight the battle, and more extreme leadership emerges. The traditional organizations in the community are either forced to take sides or are immobilized by internal splits on the issues. Among the factors that may help in the solution are the interlocking of memberships in organizations so that there are bridges across the battlelines, and an increased sense of community identification, however aroused, which conduces to the finding of Miss Follett's common interest.

A well-known American sociologist, Robin M. Williams (1947), wrote a valuable monograph just after World War II surveying the social science research literature on tensions and conflict between groups in the United States. This work will not be treated here because the research examined was largely sociopsychological. The monograph is therefore being dealt with in Chapter 4.

A recent work that is not oriented directly to conflict, but which nevertheless has interesting comments to make about it, is *Political Man* by Seymour M. Lipset (1960). It is his basic assumption that democracy is a system whose policies are the product of conflict. The system requires both enough consensus to give it legitimacy and enough effectiveness to make it work. But conflict must never be stifled. He believes that the usual classification of political parties as left, center, and right needs to be supplemented by a cross-classification in terms of moderate and extremist attitudes. Those who take extremist attitudes, no matter where they lie on the left-right continuum, are antidemocratic in their methods. The moderates use parliamentary methods. It is his view that wherever the social structure naturally isolates an occupational group, as in the case of miners, lumbermen, and sailors, there is a tendency to extremism in political conflict. And extremist parties, once established, try to control the context of their members' lives so as to ward off influences that might shake their morale.

The relevance of this insight to international relations is obviously that totalitarian societies will tend to limit the communication and contact that they will permit to their citizens and, contrarily, that the greater the communication and contact that can be arranged from the outside, the less extremist they will be in their policies.

The Nature of Conflict, a volume published by UNESCO, contains three essays by sociologists (International Sociological Association, 1957). The first is a broad survey of recent work in the sociology of conflict by Jessie Bernard. This is a most valuable source, since Bernard has thrown her net very wide and has brought together for our scrutiny some two hundred studies by a wide variety of scholars. She distinguishes the sociological conceptualization of conflict from two other conceptualizations. One of these, the semanticist, she quickly dismisses as invalid because the evidence is overwhelming that conflicts are not simply the result of misunderstandings; the other, the sociopsychological conceptualization, she discusses at some length. As research on international tensions this is treated elsewhere in the present volume.

Bernard's main interest is in conflict seen from the standpoint of social systems. Her basic theory is that conflict arises when there are mutually exclusive goals espoused by the parties, in the sense that if the goal of one is fulfilled it will be at the cost of the other. In internal conflict the goals are sought by different segments of the total system, and the cost will be suffered by the less successful segment. In external conflict, one whole system will benefit at the expense of the other if it wins. She divides her discussion of systematic studies into (*a*) a consideration of how systems fall apart or are built up when there is cost involved in the process (that is, when there is conflict) and (*b*) a consideration of how costs can be minimized through proper strategies by the parties. Under the first head she considers a wide range of studies, including mathematical treatments of conflict by such scholars as Richardson, Rashevsky, Rapoport, Zipf, Deutsch, and Firey; experimental studies by Sherif and Hare; studies in the integration of systems, like Crane Brinton's *From Many One* and the present writer's *The Moral Integration of American Cities;* and less theoretical works dealing with conflicts in many parts of the world and such special fields as racial, religious, political, and industrial relations. The twenty-five pages of her essay devoted to these matters is a rich bibliographical source for sociological students of conflict.

The section of Bernard's essay that deals with strategies is unique in the sociological literature. It considers the evaluations by scholars of strategies in a number of fields: race relations, anti-Semitism, the problems of organized religion, industrial relations, social and political movements, international relations, and the use of violence. Both cases where sociological research has been used as a basis for strategy and cases where the success or failure of strategies have been determined by sociological research are discussed. A short explanation of the theory of games and its relevance for a sociology of conflict concludes this section.

Finally Bernard reviews the literature on techniques for ameliorating conflict in small, face-to-face groups. She sees both the sociological and the social psychological approaches as contributing to the development of these techniques.

A second essay in *The Nature of Conflict*, "Conflict and War from the Viewpoint of Historical Sociology," is by Raymond Aron. The author's purpose seems to be to call into question the sociopsychological approach to the study of conflict implicit in the UNESCO Tensions Project and to show the greater suitability of historical studies of particular conflicts where diplomacy's failure has produced war. He believes that the likelihood of war in any particular set of circumstances can only be gauged when the answers to six questions are known. The first of these is: What is the area of diplomatic relations? Here Aron is referring to the set of national societies that might become involved in a threatened conflict. Second: What is the disposition of power within the area? This is the main question the "realists" among political scientists ask. Third: What is the method of warfare which is more or less clearly in the minds of statesmen when they estimate the importance of positions or relations? Nuclear weapons have obviously made a great difference in the sense that no one may be the victor in future war.

Aron's last three questions are closely related to one another: To what extent do the contending states recognize one another, so that the issue at stake is the frontiers and not the very existence of the states themselves? What bearing does domestic policy have on the decisions of statesmen? How do statesmen understand peace, war, and interstate relations? These three questions get further away from the traditional questions of foreign policy and more into the area of culture, social psychology, and sociology. Aron sees the statesmen as influenced by the forces that surround them. In any particular historical instance those forces have to be estimated and their impact evaluated. If the enemy is seen as ruthless and likely to wage a war of extermination, if there are internal troubles for which an external war might prove healing, and if the ideology of the leaders is Marxist, rather than Gandhian or Jeffersonian—these things will make a difference.

Aron's approach is particularistic. He distrusts broad theories that social scientists might try to apply to all international conflicts. Analysis has to be undertaken, he thinks, in the context of the individual case. But when this is done, and rigorous analysis is applied to the six questions he asks, fruitful results may be obtained. Since his is an approach that centers on the forces playing upon national decision-makers, we may call his the approach of the political sociologist.

The last essay in *The Nature of Conflict* is entitled "Discovering the Paths to Peace," and it is by the present author. Like other papers of mine since 1951 (1951, 1955, 1962) this one deals more with the processes of resolution of conflict than with conflict itself. The general position taken is that the causes of conflict between national societies are very deep-seated and not likely to be removed. If the world is to avoid nuclear war, there must therefore develop "a more exclusive set of relations that will bring the contending elements into a single social system." National interests must ultimately be transcended by some sense of world interest. The main question is therefore how to work toward that transcendence. It is accepted that the new system will develop not by the abolition of nationalism, but by its transformation. Nations must be brought to the point where they can agree on a few principles of international morality on which a rule of law can be built.

How can we bring national societies to agreement on the necessary minimum set of principles? The essay in question suggests that there are two essentials and that social science research can be of service in the attainment of each. First, a firmer set of cooperative relations across national boundaries is required in order to build trust and to start the convergence of moral standards which alone can support a world rule of law. (In a later paper [Angell, 1962] this is phrased as a convergence of conceptions of the good world.) In the attainment of the prerequisite web of cooperative relations social science studies of three kinds are seen as potentially helpful: (a) studies of analogous situations in the past such as Crane Brinton's *From Many One;* (b) studies of the existing tentative developments toward a more inclusive system to determine which of these are in fact bringing a greater compatibility in the normative standards of the nations; and (c) studies of experimental programs aimed at achieving the result desired. The second type of study is seen as most promising because of the numerous opportunities for such research on exchange of students, on the effects of work, study, or military service abroad, on the activities of international nongovernmental organizations, and on the programs of the United Nations and its specialized agencies.

The second essential for initiating the process of transforming nationalism is seen as the cultivation of a group of leaders in all the principal nations who are devoted to the building of a world order. The contributions of social science to the building of responsible world leadership could be many. How knowledgeable are present leaders in various countries about international affairs? What are their attitudes toward the development of a world social system? What are the factors in the careers of leaders that have inclined them toward or away from an internationalist position? What kind of selective processes have leaders come through in their rise to the top, and have these selective processes favored or handicapped those with an interest in the development of a world social system? Who are the gatekeepers in these selective processes, and how can they be influenced?

Though it is true that my own interest in studying possible approaches to a world social system is not one of pure curiosity, I would hope that investigators could proceed with absolute objectivity. It would be calamitous if someone's pet scheme were given wide support only to find that important side-effects of it had not been looked into when it was scientifically evaluated.

The most recent paper by a sociologist relevant to our subject is "Polarization of the World and International Order," by Talcott Parsons, included in the volume *Preventing World War III* (Wright, Evan, and Deutsch, 1962). Parsons starts from the premise that the polarization represented in the cold war implies that there is a world constituency to which the opposing parties are appealing and which therefore attests to the existence of a world community. He believes that the values of economic productivity and of national autonomy are common throughout that community (including both developed and underdeveloped societies). He suggests that the path to peace is to institutionalize these values by a threefold process: (a) to develop procedural norms in the U.N. and otherwise to implement them; (b) to facilitate in every way possible the breaking up of monolithic national interests into differentiated interests so that some of them can be shared across borders (e.g., interests in science, art, recreation); (c) to dissociate the elements of the world value consensus from the opposing ideologies and to foster objective social science research to give an agreed basis for the application of the value consensus.

The suggestions for institutionalization are unexceptionable, and the second one is a peculiarly sociological idea. The crucial question is whether there is in fact the *common value* consensus that Parsons assumes. The European nations before World War I had the same sharing of a way of life, but they were devoted to no inclusive system (like the common market), so that their diverse interests brought them into conflict. It would seem that they had like values rather than common values. Do the nations today value economic productivity or autonomy for anyone but themselves? And if they do not, is polarization any help toward a world order? Is not perhaps Parsons guilty of the myopia with which Dahrendorf charges him?

This brief résumé of the work of sociologists on conflict reveals the truth of what was said at the outset: Very little has been accomplished that is pertinent to the greatest problem of our day—the threat of nuclear war. Few sociologists since the Social Darwinists have been concerned with the interaction of national societies. If the sociological contribution is one that needs to be made before the world can find lasting peace, then the present generation of sociologists faces a tremendous challenge.

It would be presumptuous to prescribe how that challenge should be met, but it may not be amiss to set down a thought or two on the subject. At least others may be thus provoked into developing their own ideas.

Obviously, if sociologists are to make a contribution, they must begin to envisage intersocietal relations as part of their discipline. To date few of them have. It would not matter much whether they were interested mainly in conflict or mainly in cooperation. The study of one would almost inevitably lead to the study of the other. It is hopeful that the man whose work led to the preoccupation with processes within a single social system, Talcott Parsons, has now turned some of his attention to intersocietal relations. Perhaps others will follow.

It is my own belief that one of the most urgent items on the agenda of the sociology of conflict is to develop a typology that is particularly relevant to intersocietal relations. The situations that fall under international relations (E1, E2, and E3 in Dahrendorf's table on page 92) can be elaborated. The cell E1—where equal confronts equal—is the one most crucial to the study of the cold war. In the same essay Dahrendorf suggests that two dimensions of conflict are particularly important: the degree of intensity and the degree of violence (1962, pp. 220-224). For intersocietal conflict I have thought that the degree of violence and the degree to which agreed principles or rules were applicable were key dimensions. If only polar positions on these two dimensions were to be recognized, a fourfold table would result as shown in Table 2.

TABLE 2

	VIOLENT	NONVIOLENT
NO RULES	Combat without rules	Unprincipled peaceful conflict
RULES	Combat with rules	Principled peaceful conflict

The conflict between the Soviet Union and the United States today would seem to be unprincipled peaceful conflict. The costs of nuclear war are greater than either party wants to risk, but their differences are so great that they cannot agree on any rules. The danger is that the relationship will move to the left into combat; the hope is that it will move down into principled peaceful conflict. There is some chance that if the United States and the Soviet Union are drawn into a war that has started between other parties, they will at least tacitly agree on the exclusion of nuclear weapons, thus illustrating the condition of the cell "combat with rules." The chart remains one of conflict even if the parties do manage to reach the lower right cell. They still see each other as obstacles to their own goals, but they have accepted a set of rules under which the conflict can take place. This is essentially the kind of relation we find in intercollegiate athletics, but it is rarely found in intersocietal matters.

Some such typology as this should make it possible for sociologists to get further with the study of conflict than they have so far managed to do. The forms and processes of each type could be analyzed separately. The transitions from one to another could be charted and the causal factors examined. This would bring the sociology of conflict close to modern-systems theory and would possibly open up new vistas for research.

Although the most we could hope for in the next generation would be to bring the world to a state of principled conflict among nations, there may be theoretical advantages in widening the agenda of sociological interest to include processes of competition and cooperation. On first thought the inclusion of competition might seem futile. If there are to be less than 150 nations in the world, the number is too few for competition among nations as wholes. It is difficult to imagine reaching a condition in which no society feels that any other society is its opponent— which is the definition of competition. But just because competition does not seem a promising concept for reactions among societies as wholes, we cannot conclude it is no help at all. If monolithic national interests do break down into pluralistic interests, as Parsons hopes they may, there could be world competition among subnational interest groups like business enterprises, research institutes, universities, and churches. The nature, limits, and rules necessary for such competition could be explored.

Cooperation as a concept complements conflict in a different way from competition. Although conflict and competition have in common the fact of struggle, they differ in the main objective of struggle—for conflict, it is defeat of the opponent; for competition, it is to appropriate a scarce resource. Conflict and cooperation have in common the orientation of the parties to each other, but they do not share the process of struggle. Thus two industrial nations are likely to conflict, whereas an agricultural and an industrial nation are likely to cooperate. It is the incompatibility of interests that is crucial.

It is obvious that principled conflict might prepare countries for competition in some fields and for cooperation in others. The Soviet Union and the United States, for instance, might in time find their universities in lively but friendly competition for students from the underdeveloped parts of the world. At the same time Soviet undergraduates might be coming to the United States to learn English, and our undergraduates might be going to the Soviet Union to learn Russian.

The suggestion that the agenda of the sociology of conflict be widened to include competition and cooperation is tantamount to saying that we need a sociology of involvement. How do separate social systems become involved with each other? What are the types of involvement and what are the consequences of each? It is the belief of the sociologist that increasing involvement requires increasing social structure. Hence a central concern of such a sociology would be to learn under what conditions a structure develops between social units and what the processes of its growth are. Such questions could be studied at all levels. Perhaps the best example to date is the work of Muzafer Sherif, a social psychologist, experimenting with two groups of boys in a summer camp (1958). There are a great many examples in the international field of the development of structure, both intergovernmental and nongovernmental, on which data could be secured. So far no one has systematically gathered such data and tried to subject it to theoretical analysis.

Although a truly integrated world society may never come into being, a sociology of involvement would be of great assistance in the struggle to achieve it. How separate social systems, growing together by the force of circumstance, achieve a more inclusive structure is a puzzle whose solution we have hardly begun to study, let alone solve.

REFERENCES

Angell, Robert C., "Sociology and the World Crisis," *American Sociological Review*, XVI (1951), 749-757.

————, "Governments and People as Foci of Peace-oriented Research," *Journal of Social Issues*, XI (1955), 36-41.

————, "Discovering the Paths to Peace," International Sociological Association, *The Nature of Conflict*, Vol. XI. Paris: UNESCO, 1957.

————, "Defense of What?" *Journal of Conflict Resolution*, VI (1962), 116-124.

Aron, Raymond, "Conflict and War From the Viewpoint of Historical Sociology," International Sociological Association, *The Nature of Conflict*. Paris: UNESCO, 1957.

Bagehot, Walter, *Physics and Politics*. London: H. S. King and Co., 1872.

Bernard, Jessie, "Where Is the Modern Sociology of Conflict?" *American Journal of Sociology*, LVI (1950), 11-16.

————, "The Sociological Study of Conflict," International Sociological Association, *The Nature of Conflict*. Paris: UNESCO, 1957.

Coleman, James, *Community Conflict*. New York: Free Press of Glencoe, Inc., 1957.

Coser, Lewis, *The Function of Social Conflict*. New York: Free Press of Glencoe, Inc., 1956.

Dahrendorf, Ralf, *Class and Class Conflict in Industrial Society*. Stanford, Calif.: Stanford University Press, 1959.

————, *Gesellschaft und Freiheit*. München: R. Piper & Co., Verlag, 1962.

Follett, Mary P., *The New State, Group Organization, and the Solution of Popular Government*. New York: David McKay Co., Inc., 1918.

————, *Creative Experience*. New York: David McKay Co., Inc., 1924.

Gumplowicz, Ludwik, *Der Rassenkampf*. Innsbruck: Wagner'sche Universität Buchhandlung, 1883.

Inquiry, The, *Community Conflict*. New York: The Inquiry, 1929.

Lipset, Seymour M., *Political Man*. Garden City, N.Y.: Doubleday & Company, Inc., 1960.

Novicow, Jacques, *Les Luttes entre sociétés humaines et leurs phases successives*. Paris: Alcan, 1893.

Oppenheimer, Franz, *The State*, J. M. Gitterman, trans. Indianapolis: Bobbs-Merrill Company, Inc., 1914.

Park, Robert D. and Ernest W. Burgess, *Introduction to the Science of Sociology*. Chicago: University of Chicago Press, 1921.

Parsons, Talcott, *The Social System*. New York: Free Press of Glencoe, Inc., 1951.

Ratzenhofer, Gustav, *Die Soziologische Erkenntnis*. Leipzig: F. A. Brockhaus, 1898.

Sherif, Muzafer, "Superordinate Goals in the Reduction of Intergroup Conflict," *American Journal of Sociology*, LXIII (1958), 349-356.

Simmel, Georg, "The Sociology of Conflict," *American Journal of Sociology*, IX (1904), 490-525, 672-689, 798-811.

————, *Conflict*, Kurt Wolff, trans. New York: Free Press of Glencoe, Inc., 1955.

Small, Albion W., "Socialism in the Light of Sociology," *American Journal of Sociology*, XVII (1912), 810.

Ward, Lester F., *Pure Sociology*. London: The Macmillan Company, 1903.

Williams, Robin M., Jr., *The Reduction of Intergroup Tensions: A Survey of Research on Problems of Ethnic, Racial, and Religious Group Relations*, Social Science Council Bulletin 57. New York: The Council, 1947.

Wright, Quincy, William M. Evans, and Morton Deutsch, *Preventing World War III*. New York: Simon and Schuster, Inc., 1962.

CHAPTER

6

The Anthropology of Human Conflict

MARGARET MEAD

RHODA METRAUX

The contribution of anthropology to problems of conflict resolution on the world scene lies essentially in anthropologists' familiarity with and use of the concept of culture (Mead and Metraux, 1962). On the international scene, conflicts do not occur between isolated individuals, for whom adequate solutions may be found by the formulations of individual psychology; nor do they occur between groups made up of individuals who are similar to one another, to whose interactions as groups certain laws of group behavior may be applied. International relations and, within nation-states, the relations among groups with historically different identifications (e.g., in the United Kingdom, the relations of the Scottish, the Welsh, and the English peoples; in France, the relations of Provencals, Bretons, and French) occur in contexts in which ethnic, regional, caste or class, racial, and national identifications are salient in the minds of the participants. The same individuals, in other contexts, may exhibit behavior to which some other set of explanatory principles may be applied—the principles of genetics, situational or role analysis, or economic determination; but, in contexts in which group loyalties are involved, the cultural components of behavior are maximized (Bateson, 1942).

Human beings are involved in international and intranational group conflicts not only as human beings, as men and women, as individuals
having specific childhood experiences, as fathers, as mayors, as stock-
brokers or physicists, but also as Britons, Americans, Puerto Ricans,
Pathans, Copts, Muslims, and so forth. Where conflicts occur between
groups in terms of these and other cultural identifications, any discussion
of group interaction which fails to take culture into account will inevitably lack cogency.

In general, the situations in which Group A–Group B formulations—
of the kind made by L. F. Richardson (1960a, 1960b)—are useful are
those occurring within a culture area, within which certain premises
about diplomatic exchange, the rules of war, war technology, and so on
are shared by members of different groups (Taylor, 1963). In situations
of this kind (as, for example, in the relations of the European Allies and
the central powers among and with one another in World War I), intergroup responses may be superficially and misleadingly similar, and quite
plausible formulations may result from analyses that are pursued without reference to culture (Tuchman, 1962). In contrast, in situations in
which conflict occurs between national groups with clearly different
ideologies, the need for cultural analysis is more readily discernible
(Benedict, 1946).

For example, examination of the handling of submarine crews during World War II showed that all the European participants hit on a
common solution to the dangers of intragroup conflict within the confined
space of the submarine—continuous access to food. The types of food
differed by nationality, but the solution was the same. However, a more
complex situation developed after the fall of France in the relations
between the occupying Germans and the French civilians, as, initially,
civilian prisoners of the Wehrmacht were treated within the context of
internationally understood rules of wartime trial and imprisonment (a
fact substantiated in postwar trials of German officers in French courts),
while the civilian prisoners of specifically Nazi agencies were subjected
to entirely different modes of treatment. And in the war in the Pacific,
it was the Japanese definition of bomber range—enough gasoline to reach
the target—which upset early American calculations, since these American calculations of range included, by definition, an allowance of fuel
to *return* to base.

The common solution to the problem of handling men confined in
submarines may be attributed to certain common attitudes towards men
in confinement developed in Western Europe in the course of a long
history of military and naval exchanges of ideas. Differences in the treatment of French civilians by professional Wehrmacht officers and Nazi
elite officers are to be understood in the light of the Nazi version of

German culture. And, of course, culturally different conceptions of human life were expressed in Japanese and American calculations of bomber range.

During World War II a group of American anthropologists, to which the authors belonged, devoted considerable time to the development and application of methods of analyzing culture, stated in the form of national character; these were relevant, on the one hand, to problems of international cooperation both within a nation and between nations and, on the other hand, to problems of warfare. Most of the dimensions used in this work had already been developed in studies of primitive societies and in studies of enculturation. One problem area in which these methods were used with considerable success was that concerned with estimates of relative strength and weakness (e.g., the definition of situations in which it is culturally permissible to put forth full strength and the delineation of culturally determined conceptions of behavior which could be expected to lead to the overestimation or the underestimation of the enemy's strength). As these wartime studies were pursued in an atmosphere of emergency, the same dimensions were not used for every study. Several different applications of technique can be seen, for example, in Geoffrey Gorer's early analysis of Japanese culture (1943), which drew heavily on our knowledge of character formation, Gregory Bateson's analysis of the American and the British handling of relationships of dominance and submission (1942), which also was based on a parent-child model but focused more sharply on interaction, and Ruth Benedict's analysis of conflicting loyalties in Japanese culture (1946). Yet, although differently structured, these analyses were directed successfully to particular points of conflict between allies and to estimates of mutual strength and evaluations of intention between enemies.

When social scientists attempt to make analyses involving the behavior of a national group or several national groups without the intervening variable of culture, their results are likely to be ambiguous or confused—or both. A case in point is the recent study of disaster behavior edited by George W. Baker and Dwight W. Chapman (1962), in which the behavior of groups belonging to several different nationalities is summarized without any allowance for culture, and the results reported are almost wholly indeterminate. It is possible to analyze and structure Dutch responses to disaster—or English responses or American responses, as Martha Wolfenstein did in her analysis of American disaster material (1957)—and to come out with a coherent pattern of action. But without the intermediate step of cultural analysis it is not possible to compare culturally different styles of response, to predict responses to new sets of circumstances, or to expand the area of understanding. One of the most significant failures during World War II—the evaluation of civilian responses to different types of bombing (whether by enemy planes over England or Germany or by Allied planes in France in the later stages of the war)—must be attributed to a definition of civilian morale which was basically individual in its derivation and to the absence of cultural determinations of effect (U. S. Strategic Bombing Survey, 1947). The inclusion of culture is crucial to an understanding of all such events as the Japanese kamikaze operations, the German failure to invade England after Dunkirk, or, alternatively, the English rally after Dunkirk, the defense of Stalingrad, the sacking of Cyprus by Australian troops, English fury at the American treatment of the role of antiaircraft in the German buzz-bomb campaign, shifting American attitudes toward Yugoslavia, American responses to Finnish debt repayments, the French insistence on being publicly and ceremonially included in secret agreements, Khrushchev's lack of concern with face-saving over the Cuba episode, or the behavior of Americans mourning the death of a president aged forty-six as if he were a youth in his twenties.

Application of the knowledge of culture to international and intranational situations brought with it a developing ethic both among those who worked in war-making agencies and those who were concerned primarily with intranational morale-building (Mead, Chapple, and Brown, 1949). Experience with both short- and long-run effects made it clear that it was necessary to set very definite limits to the exercise of this kind of understanding and, particularly, that there is a great difference between working with cultural strengths and with cultural weaknesses. Knowledge of the strengths of a culture, it was recognized, can be useful in calculating the chances of victory and also in estimating the probable initiatives and responses of an enemy. Such knowledge is equally useful in developing a cooperative relationship with an ally and in invoking the highest degree of participation of one's fellow citizens in a national activity. But it was also recognized that the effects of work on cultural weaknesses, whether as a wartime measure or as part of psychological warfare, are likely to boomerang. Those anthropologists who worked inside security, especially those who were concerned with "black" operations (which might, for example, involve an attempt to weaken a people by the secret dissemination of frightening statements disguised as solicitous warnings from their own government), became convinced that the application of anthropological methods to activities of this kind is ultimately destructive, however effective the results may appear to be in the short run.

An understanding of the Russian preoccupation with the full use of strength, their insistence on testing the limits, and their willingness to abide by them provides a framework within which Soviet behavior becomes more intelligible and therefore more predictable. The characteristic Russian response to opposing strength greater than their own is strategic withdrawal accompanied by the sense that this will enable them later to return to the conflict in greater strength because of the maximum effort made previously. But if this strategic withdrawal is interpreted by Americans as a sign of weakness and defeat, two undesirable results obtain. Americans begin to act in ways which are appropriate (in American culture) for us with those whom we believe can be bluffed by a show of strength—as in the Dulles type of brinksmanship; and Russians, in response, must keep their stance of intransigency (Gorer, 1962). In contrast, when Russian negotiators recognize that the opposition respects their strength, their pride in this recognition is a facilitating factor. Spelling out these conditions for the interpretation of a set of United States-Soviet Union negotiations means taking into account the culturally crucial question for Russians: "Did I put forth my full strength?" and the culturally crucial question for Americans: "Did I win or lose?" Where English values must also be included, a third culturally crucial question must be taken into account: "Was this the best possible compromise?" (Mead, 1948)

The kind of pressure exerted by the United States on the Soviet Union in the 1950's and the interpretation to Americans of both our own and Soviet behavior in this situation was a poor preparation for an American understanding of the sequence of events in the Cuban crisis. One result was that we erroneously worried about Russian "face-saving"—a misapplication to the Russians of our misunderstood ideas of Chinese (or even "Oriental") standards of behavior.[1]

Estimates of cultural strengths, even those which are formulated in an atmosphere of enmity, are applicable in a very wide range of circumstances and can survive shifts in international relationships, as, for example, when a nation which has been defined by Americans (or in its own terms) as a neutral becomes, instead, an ally—or vice versa. But the usefulness of such an estimate can be fully realized only if the phrasing of a nation's cultural characteristics is one that is acceptable to its own members. It is enlightening, in this connection, to contrast the widespread acceptance in Japan of Ruth Benedict's *The Chrysanthemum and the Sword* (1946) and in Mexico of Oscar Lewis' successive studies of poverty, *Five Families* (1959) and *The Children of Sanchez* (1961) with the general German reaction to various phrasings of German culture in terms of "authoritarianism" (Adorno *et al.*, 1950). While this phrasing demonstrated a German vulnerability (as well as a strength of a sort),

---

[1] In fact, analysis of *American* statements about the "face-saving" behavior of other peoples suggests that these are primarily reflections of a cluster of American attitudes rather than insights into the behavior of the people whose activities are so defined.

it split off certain components of a more complex structure (Dicks, 1950; Levy, 1948; Schaffner, 1948) and resulted in a distorted delineation of German national character.[2] A further distortion (one which reflected a perversion of both psychiatric and cultural methods of analysis) occurred when Richard M. Brickner's idea that the behavior of German nationals and the responsive behavior evoked in others had the characteristics of the behavior of a paranoid and his family (1943) was extended in attempts to demonstrate that certain individual Germans—in contrast to other Germans—had an "authoritarian" character structure.

It is the essence of the cultural approach that *all* members of a given culture share the same cultural character. The expression of cultural character may take various forms, as individuals within a society differ in temperament, capacity, and experience, but all these forms will display regularities in relationship to one another and to the culture as a whole (Mead, 1942b). Within a nation one may identify groups whose version of the national character may appear to be an antithetical one, but, in fact, each version will contain the others as possible modes of behavior. The existence of such different versions may be acknowledged within the formal framework of the culture. The French Bohemian, living in an accepted setting, may deny family responsibility; French law, however, provides the means for him to legitimize his children. And when Polish Jews migrated to Israel to set up a national, agrarian-based state, one of their models of behavior in their new setting was their conception of Polish bravery. What in Poland had been a counterimage and a way of maintaining a separate identity became available as an accepted form of behavior after they had migrated to Israel.

The generalization can be made that the larger the group about which it is desirable to make a prediction based on national character, the more accurate the prediction will be, and also that a prediction will always be a statement in terms of limits or alternatives, subject to the historical situation at the time at which an action takes place (Mead, 1950b). The smaller the number of persons involved, the smaller and less representative the group, the less useful will be a knowledge of the culture, as such, and the more necessary it will be to introduce an understanding of situational and individual experimental factors. But where national leadership is concerned, however idiosyncratic the behavior of a specific leader may be, it must be interpreted in the light of the cooperation, the enthusiasm, and obedience evoked on a national scale. The most particularistic interpretation of the character of a Hitler or a

---

[2] The use of this definition by Americans in an estimate of German weakness has had demonstrable effects on the ability of Americans to make differential judgments about superordinate-subordinate relationships, confusing rather than clarifying certain of our own cultural attitudes toward, for example, dependency.

Churchill must include the culture of the people to whom they addressed their programs and by whom their programs were carried out.

The formulations made by political scientists, economists, sociologists, and psychologists can be linked together with the findings of anthropologists into a coherent working program. To accomplish this it will be necessary to establish ways of including culture in formulations of conflict, resolutions of escalating states of hostility, and stabilization of relationships. That is, any statement about A and B, defined as nation-states, as subgroups within a nation, or as individuals who are treated as paradigms of conflict, must include culture as part of the total statement: Group A (culture: Italy) vis-à-vis Group B (Yugoslavia): minority members (Germans) of the textile workers union in the American town of X in conflict with the majority members (Italians): head of international agency A (a Pole) in conflict with the head of international agency B (a Lebanese).

When formulations of this kind are made as a matter of routine, it will be evident that larger cultural structures must also be included, that is, that the cultures of nation-states are only one kind (though in our thinking an almost overwhelmingly important kind) of cultural structure that exists in the contemporary world. The communist bloc, the Western bloc, the Afro-Asian bloc—cultural structures which are ideological rather than national—must also be included, and other, older identifying allegiances—Christianity or Islam, for example—may also be entirely relevant. Writing statements in this way will clarify the orders of information which it is necessary to obtain for the full specification of a particular situation. In considering a Pole vis-à-vis a Lebanese, for example, it is important to recognize not only the contemporary position of the Pole, as a member of a nation within the Eastern bloc, but also the historic position of Poland (as seen by Poles), as a Roman Catholic outpost in Eastern Europe; from this description of one of the members of a pair, joined in conflict, it becomes clear that the description of the Lebanese will be incomplete without the inclusion of his membership in the Muslim, Eastern Christian, or Jewish community in Lebanon.

In fact, full specification of the relevant aspects of cultural character demands the participation of a wide range of disciplines: the disciplines traditionally concerned with social, economic, and political behavior, those concerned with the products of creative behavior, those especially concerned with philosophy and with religion, linguistics, psychology, and psychiatry—which is needed especially to provide models for the interpretation of culturally stylized defenses (Wolfenstein and Leites, 1950). A well-trained anthropologist with a working knowledge of psychological and sociological theory may be expected to produce an organized account of a small primitive preliterate society. This would, however, not be possible for a complex modern culture. The anthropologist working alone (or even a group made up only of anthropologists) could not handle the mass of available material critically or establish all the necessary lines of communication with those trained in other disciplines—especially political science, history, and law—who play active roles in the conduct of public affairs.

The method by which the formulation of relevant cultural statements is arrived at is intrinsic to the uses which can be made of such formulations in the process of national and international conflict resolution. However accurate formulations may be, if they are to be operationally useful, they must be so phrased that the statements are intelligible to the members of the culture (or cultures) who are to take the advice provided by the researchers; they must be acceptable in the cultures of those about whom statements are made; and, not least important, they must be intelligible to the members of at least one other culture who are not directly involved in the conflict.[3]

After World War II we conducted, in extensive researches financed by the Office of Naval Research, RAND, and (under a subcontract) the Massachusetts Institute of Technology, a series of carefully recorded experiments in the construction of hypotheses about the national character of different modern nations (Gorer and Rickman, 1950; Leites and Bernaut, 1954; Mead, 1950b, 1951b, 1952; Mead and Metraux, 1953; Mead and Wolfenstein, 1955; Metraux and Hoyt, 1953; Metraux and Mead, 1954; Zborowski and Herzog, 1952). It was our experience that subsequent acceptance of the formulations by members of the nation studied was a function of the presence within the research group of members of that nation who participated as full members of the research and discussion team.[4] No amount of interviewing of nationals or painstaking

---

[3] Certain exceptions must also be pointed out. In a situation in which the ruling power in a country includes in its ideology an explicit repudiation of some aspect of the social science of a national or an ideological group with which it sees itself in conflict, then all statements made within that particular frame of reference will, of course, be repudiated. In addition, it must be borne in mind that members of governments in exile, refugees, and first-generation immigrants all are likely to be in a state of conflicted loyalty and, as a result, may have a seriously diminished capacity to make use of statements about the country from which they are, voluntarily, purposefully, or involuntarily, absent. So also, the convinced and committed immigrant may have difficulty in absorbing and making use of statements about the new culture to which he is still in the process of adapting himself. Such diminutions of cultural perspective may be compared to the shrinking of the field of awareness under conditions of danger (Bahnson, 1962).

[4] The single exception, in the research done in the late 1940's, was France. In this case, it appeared not to be possible to devise a group context within which French participants worked easily over a longer period of time. It was not then (as it is not now) possible to assess fully the difficulties that were encountered. Part of the difficulty undoubtedly lay in the composition of the group into which attempts were

analysis of historical documents or cultural products, such as literature, paintings, or films, was an adequate substitution for such participation. On the basis of less formal experience, it may also be said that it is essential to include nationals of both sexes and, ideally, members of three generations in order to represent the culture in its biological completeness.

This is, of course, a way of restating the fact that our model for culture is a generation continuum in which cultural transmission and reinforcement are not a one-way process from parent to child and from elder to younger, but are instead expressions of a network of responses, in which all members of a society, persons of both sexes and all ages, are continually making prefigurative, configurative, and postfigurative contributions to the maintenance of the cultural system from the viewpoints of their particular sex, age, generational, and ordinal position (Mead, 1961). Attempts to reconstitute and so define a cultural system at a distance usually suffer from the absence of a full set of personnel. This makes it all the more important to undertake research on each national group as any one of them becomes, perhaps only temporarily, accessible to a cooperative exploration of its relevant cultural strengths.

The analysis of national cultures is essentially applied research. It lacks the rigidly confined conditions within which research is ideally undertaken—the conditions of the laboratory for the experimentalist and of the small isolated homogeneous culture for the anthropologist. Research of this kind will, therefore, only be undertaken in a climate of opinion in which decision makers are willing to make use of the results. Such a climate of opinion existed during World War II, when the large number of social scientists who had been recruited for work inside the government assured the reception and use of cultural analyses, whether these were produced within a government agency, such as Naval Intel-

---

made, too late, to introduce French collaboration. But part of the difficulty may also be attributed to the deep conflicts which rent France at that time and which affected the ability of French men and women, living abroad, to do research on their own culture together with the nationals of other countries. In this one case, we finally adopted the expedient of working through all our tentative formulations with individual, high-level French informants. However, it is worth remarking that disagreement with certain of our formulations (e.g., the idea that it was possible to define a "national" culture, which included regional versions of that culture, for France) was influential in initiating research on French culture by French investigators—which, at a later time, led to substantial agreement on basic points about French culture.

It must also be pointed out that participation by members of the nation studied in a research group means that the style and the pace of the research must be geared to their style of participation. This means, in turn, that the organization of the research as a whole must be sufficiently flexible to permit variations in approach, speed, type of discussion, and so on, as each particular research group adapts itself to the styles of all the participants—and learns to use this adaptation as an additional research tool.

ligence, the Office of Strategic Services, the Office of War Information, the Office of Civilian Defense, etc., or were prepared outside of government and were presented to one of these agencies. This receptive atmosphere continued to prevail within government for about five years after the war; as a result it was possible to make follow-up studies in which wartime methods were refined and tested (Gorer and Rickman, 1950; Leites and Bernaut, 1954; Mead, 1950b, 1951b, 1952; Mead and Metraux, 1953; Mead and Wolfenstein, 1955; Metraux and Hoyt, 1953; Metraux and Mead, 1954; Zborowski and Herzog, 1952).

After 1950, however, areas of receptivity within government began to shrink visibly. During the Korean War almost no attempt was made to apply in new ways the types of insight which had proved useful in World War II. In the decade of the 1950's, the cold war atmosphere of secrecy and reciprocal espionage, the general distrust of social science, and the desire of anthropologists to return to their own research work meant that almost no use was made of the research that had been done and that virtually no new research of this kind was undertaken.

It is also important to realize that research on national cultures, as well as on subgroups within a national society or on the shared ideology of supranational blocs, must be contemporary. Definitions of historical continuities in a culture are extremely useful to research workers, but policy-makers must receive their information in a phrasing which takes into account national pronouncements of recent date and which refers to contemporary events. Furthermore, with the tremendous changes that are occurring the world over, in almost every nation, the dimensions of an analysis which were adequate for application at one period may become quite inadequate in another.

In the Soviet Union, today, we are dealing with individuals and groups which include in their membership both old Bolsheviks and a young generation who have experienced only the postrevolutionary (and among the youngest only the post-World War II) state. For England, the formulations of Anglo-American conflict and cooperation in foreign relations—the original models for which were the "public school" Englishman and the American businessman (Mead, 1948)—need to be revised in the light of contemporary changes in participation in policy-making. So, also, the formulation of England as a nation which always acts from strength needs to be rephrased in terms of moral strength instead of the traditional phrasing based on the British Empire's scope and the paraphernalia of military and economic power. Geoffrey Gorer's postwar survey-study of English character (1955) demonstrated the importance of working within a narrow time span in situations in which regional variation is relevant. So also, in the United States, research on immediate responses to the launching of the first Soviet satellite indicated the importance of work within a narrow time span whenever it is important to assess the components that enter into and may affect the long-term reactions to a new situation. In this case, research carried out within one locality seemed to suggest that an event of local concern outweighed interest in *Sputnik* as a preoccupation; but, simultaneous research carried out across the country indicated that such an upsurge of interest in a local preoccupation was, in itself, one of the forms of response to a larger event whose implications were at that time unclear.

Research which has already been carried out and the applications of such research in meeting specific needs make possible a statement of the steps necessary for the inclusion of the cultural variable in studies of conflict resolution and for policy recommendations. Ideally, we would carry out explorations of the same relevant dimensions on a large number of significant cultures—the United States, the Soviet Union, the United Kingdom, Germany, France, the United Arab Republic, India, China, and so on. The research would be done by interdisciplinary and international teams, each containing research workers of at least three nationalities, including nationals of the country studied (Mead, 1953b). As part of this exploration, firsthand field work would also be done by research workers who would continue to be members of the team. After the initial work was completed, the team would remain in existence in order to work on new problems for which contemporary materials would be gathered as they were needed.[5]

The importance of these three basic conditions—initial exploration, the maintenance of a trained group of observer-analysts, and continuing scrutiny of changing circumstances—has been underlined also in those situations in which anthropologists have acted (or may be called upon to act) as advisers in technical change. It is never enough to make a baseline synchronic study of the culture and then to base all planning on this analysis. In all applied situations one is dealing with a historical process, whose course of development is shaped in part by other historical processes and also by fortuitous events outside the single system; without a continuing awareness of how a cultural system is affected by such cross-currents, it is possible to make predictions only in terms of

---

[5] We have one case in which this formula (with the exception of the field work, which was impossible at that period) has been applied. In 1950 the senior author was asked to help a research group at the Massachusetts Institute of Technology assemble an interdisciplinary team of Russian specialists to take part in a communications study. In the interests of research economy, we reassembled the team which had worked in Studies on Soviet Culture (many of whom had previously worked in the Russian section of Columbia University Research in Contemporary Cultures) and, in addition, enlisted new interviewers to provide materials to be analyzed by the expert group, who were accustomed to working together (Mead, 1952).

very wide alternatives. But once a particular situation or complex of events is known, the already systematized knowledge of the culture can be brought to bear on an immediate problem—ideally by a team whose members were responsible for at least part of the basic systematization (Mead, 1944).

This approach is based on the assumption that there are many variables in systematic cultural behavior which we do not have any means of quantifying and that the most effective procedure, therefore, is to work with groups of human beings who, quite literally, embody the culture. Such a procedure yields more usable results than procedures which yield skeleton statements about a culture which must then be fleshed out with the reality.[6]

But at the same time, we should be adding to the dimensions which can be identified in and are relevant to all cultures, and we should be creating a pool of available systematic statements which would enable us to stimulate conflict situations in a laboratory context so designed that the cultural variables would be contained within the stimulation. For it must now be recognized that there are some situations which are so dangerous that the only way their occurrence and their outcome can be anticipated and prevented is through their analysis in laboratory simulations.

For the sake of illustration, the following list is a preliminary indication of the cultural dimensions on which it would be essential to obtain information in any culture:

1. The relative proportions (and the location) of symmetrical, complementary, and reciprocal types of behavior (Bateson, 1936, 1942; Mead, 1949, 1953a, 1963).
2. The definition of attitudes toward relative strength and weakness, and the definition of solutions of the order of "compromise," "surrender," "settling for," and so on.
3. The phrasing of part-whole relations, boundaries, inside and outside, centers, types of recognized segmentation.
4. The definition of relationships to groups of identification—as one among peers, parent, child, total embodiment, and so on.
5. Ascribed and achieved statuses of decision-making groups and of those involved in carrying out decisions.
6. The definition of types of time perspective.

---

[6] If it is desirable to turn a dried food, bearing no resemblance to the actual food of any nationality, into "food" which will be acceptable to Greeks or Norwegians or Netherlanders, one could follow the procedure of analyzing the principles of cookery and taste in the particular culture and, from this analysis, develop suitable recipes. But the more rapid and certainly the more satisfactory procedure would be to ask Greek or Norwegian or Dutch women to use their knowledge and skills in cookery to turn this potential nutrient into a culturally recognized "food."

In cultural analysis, each specific culture which is analyzed in terms of dimensions of known importance reveals the usefulness of hitherto unidentified dimensions which, superficially, may be less salient but which are nevertheless relevant in the analysis of other cultures. For this reason, if for no other, it is economical of research time to have a series of analytical teams working simultaneously on different cultures and in active communication with one another on their research problems and their research findings.

COMMON DENOMINATORS AND CROSS-CULTURAL AND CROSS-IDEOLOGICAL COMMUNICATION

Anthropology can also make an important contribution to the problem of handling cross-cultural communication. The cultural dimensions outlined above provide a framework within which meaningful communications can occur. For example, in a situation in which Englishmen, Americans, and Russians are involved as participants, it is useful to know that the English regard compromise as a positive outcome, that Americans regard compromise negatively, and that Russians define behavior which, in English and American eyes, would be regarded as compromise, as a necessary and quite admirable strategic retreat after having put forth all available strength.

But even when a framework for communication has been established, there remains the further problem of a common language through which it is possible to arrive at a resolution. In recent European history, so-called *diplomatic French* served this purpose. One necessary research problem is a detailed study—while we still have living informants of different national backgrounds who are versed in the usages of diplomatic French—of the ways in which this language of international communication differed from ordinary French, and what the limitations were on idiom and excursions into fantasy couched in one's mother tongue. Exploratory work on this problem, in general, makes possible a few preliminary generalizations (Capes, 1960; Glenn, 1960; Chapple, 1951).

Natural languages, which have been modified by users of both sexes, all ages, different temperaments, and different levels of intelligence and degrees of education, are more suitable—because of their redundancy—for cross-boundary communication than are artificial languages—which lack redundancy. For communication in which it is intended that the several participating communicators should feel on an equal basis, the language used should not be the mother tongue of any one of the participants, as idiomatic fluency gives the group whose language is spoken a felt advantage. If simultaneous communication is to be successful, serious attention must be given to the sequential structure of the sentence and to other elements of the discourse style. Seating together members of one linguistic group, the timing of whose responses is slower than that of another group—so that bloc laughter or bloc vocal resentment occurs— may have disastrous results. The choice of interpreters (especially sequential interpreters, who have greater license) is a matter of vital and continuing significance. In Soviet-American discussions, fluent and facile simultaneous interpreters often assume that they know what will be said next and rattle off speeches ahead of a speaker, giving an air of insincerity and a sense of a stereotyped performance to the whole discussion (Cousins, 1962a, 1962b, 1962c).

The *Relay II* communications satellite and its proposed successors present the world with a situation in which appropriate forms of cross-national and cross-ideological communication, in visual forms equally communicative and loaded with comparable affective weight, may reduce conflict and sources of conflict by promoting a perceptual consensus or, alternatively, may enormously exacerbate conflict. To understand what some of the effects of this new kind of communication may be and to make the most of positive effects, it will be necessary to undertake research on appropriate forms and on the identification, standardization, and popularization of appropriate glyphs (Teltsch, 1964) (formal signs having the same meaning but a different verbal content in different languages; international road signs are one example). It will be necessary, for example, to establish cartoon forms which can stand for a human being of any race or creed or nation. Like all anthropological research on the problem of conflict resolution, research of this kind will require exploration, experimentation with selected members of different cultural groups, and careful attention to first attempts to put recommendations into practice. Considerable work has already been done on cross-national and cross-ideological communication in the fields of language, interpretation, and conference techniques. In contrast, little research has as yet been done on the use of glyphs or cartoons, the choice and modification of a secondary, politically nonsensitive language, and the principles of cross-ideological communication. Anthropologists should, therefore, be working closely with those organizations, new and old, which are majorly concerned with problems of cross-national visual presentation and especially in those situations in which cross-ideological communication is one focus of interest (Brown and Federov, 1962; Cousins, 1962a, 1962b, 1962c).

At one level it is necessary to scrutinize carefully current comments and repartee. When, for example, D. W. Brogan, writing on "The Presidency" in *Encounter* (1964), states that the White House is a "court," this statement, on the one hand, is certain to exacerbate American opposition to federal power and, on the other hand, is certain to decrease American understanding of Britain, however well it may serve unilaterally to increase British understanding of the American institution of the presidency. At this level it is worth analyzing the kind of communication involved in standardized exchanges, for example (in the early 1940's) the American comment, "What about India?" to which the British reply was, "What about your slums?" Or the satirized American-Soviet study in which the comment, "Your subways don't run very often," evoked the question, "How about the Negro problem?"

At another level in the field of cross-national and cross-ideological communications sensitive art historians and students of comparative literature can work together with anthropologists to provide better forms of communication than now exist. One outcome of such cooperation could be new strategies in which statements that are acceptable to several communicators and are meaningful and acceptable to listeners-in would be developed.

NEW MODELS FOR A PLANETARY SOCIETY [7]

A third way in which anthropology can contribute to conflict resolution is in the design of organizations which will facilitate social order. One of the reasons for investigating and recording the various ways in which human beings, as groups, behave in different cultures has been to widen our imagination about the possibilities for organization that are open to mankind. Nowhere is this more important than in the analysis of groups of varying degrees of simplicity and complexity organized for the purposes of war-making and peace-keeping. Anthropological studies document the fact that warfare is a human invention made possible by the symbolic assignment of the role of predator or prey to other conspecifics (Masserman, 1963). In addition, studies of primitive societies provide us with evidence of the kinds of experimentation in social order which became progressively less likely as towns and city-states, each drawing on each other for inspiration, began to develop within a single area of trade and contact stretching from the Middle East into Europe (Frankfurt, 1956; Muller, 1958). The very fact that it is possible to erect

---

[7] Based on plans made in 1963 by a subcommittee of the Committee for the Study of Mankind for a joint conference with anthropologists.

a vast scheme, such as that contained in Karl Wittfogel's study of societies organized around the provision of water (Wittfogel, 1957), or to speak of a "feudal system" in Japan (Allen, 1962) or a "bureaucracy" in China (Wittfogel, 1957) is a testament not to limited possibilities but rather to the extent to which each developing urban civilization drew on the experience of the past, thus narrowing the margin of experimentation. One of the urgent reasons for anthropological research has been, therefore, the necessity of keeping open our sense of the possibility of quite different solutions to human problems through careful explorations of societies which, through isolation and limited resources, have taken or have kept to quite different cultural paths. Without research of this kind there is always the danger that our thinking may be progressively trapped by our preoccupation with the very limited and special solutions which the human civilizations to which we have historic access happened on and found useful more than five thousand years ago.

In recent years there has been a growing interest in the interconnectedness of civilizations, even when they are separated by political boundaries, and there has been a tendency to discount the brief moments of harmonious configurational integration and to emphasize, instead, ubiquitous trade (Conklin, 1953, 1955), languages which have extended far beyond political boundaries, and ideologies which have swept across cultural lines (Deutsch, 1953).

The patrilocal band and the tribal unit exposed to trade in goods and the exchange of women, with all borders open to change, has been a favored model of man's early evolutionary development (Huxley, 1956; Sahlins and Service, 1960; Simpson, 1960)—a model which emphasizes formal similarities and tends to bind the imagination into a kind of determinism based primarily on technical advances in the use of energy.

Given this frame of reference, island cultures represent a kind of anomaly. So, for example, those who have attempted to explain pygmy populations as a gradual, progressive, and reversible adaptation to forest life and poor nutrition regard the Andaman Islands as a special case (Brace, 19–). And it has even been suggested that the models of cultural balance and harmony constructed by A. R. Radcliffe-Brown (1922) and by Bronislaw Malinowski (1922)—as well as analyses, such as those by Eliot D. Chapple and Carleton S. Coon (1942), deriving from this work and emphasizing dynamic equilibrium—owe their form to the accident that both Radcliffe-Brown and Malinowski did their definitive ethnographic research on whole cultures on islands. It is interesting also that Julian Huxley selected an island, Bali, to pose the question of conscious human involvement in the evolutionary process (Huxley, 1958).

Between the first attempt made by members of the Society for Applied Anthropology to develop a professional ethic in 1949 (Mead, Chapple, and Brown, 1949) and their second discussion of this problem in 1960, the launching of space satellites ushered in the space age. In this same period there was an increasing dissatisfaction with the treatment of human societies as closed systems. The idea of dynamic equilibrium was felt to be both confining and false. However, while these changes in theoretical emphasis were taking place, it was becoming clear that this planet is rapidly going through the process of becoming—functionally if not yet structurally—a single interconnected community in which events occurring at any point in the intercommunicating network may affect any other part of the whole. It was becoming clear, in fact, that this planet has become an island society. The possibilities of space exploration, space colonization, and discovering intelligent life in outer space have had immediate repercussions on human thought and on social planning and may, within our lifetime, have very significant technological repercussions (for example, National Aeronautics and Space Administration, 1963). However, the chances of finding or of coming into active contact with intelligent life beyond this planet—an event which would provide a major challenge to an earth system of community—seem minimal during the next decades or centuries (depending on the calculations which are made [Simpson, 1961; von Hoerner, 1962]). So, for all present practical purposes, this earth is becoming an island. Looking to the past, societies in continuous and also intermittent land contact with members of other cultures and other societies provide the most significant models for man's earlier development. But looking ahead, very useful models for our future development are to be found in island societies, particularly those island groups which drew on cultural forms worked out where there was much more contact and interaction between groups and later, after they established themselves on isolated islands, developed special versions of these forms. In the present circumstances of a developing world civilization, studies of the island cultures of single isolated islands are becoming a new source for the creation of social systems appropriate to the state of man on earth.

But there is also another way in which knowledge of the varieties of human social organization may be useful to planning for types of world order in which lethal conflict will be minimized. Primitive societies provide us with small-scale living models of a great variety of arrangements by which man's protective and conserving potentialities have been mobilized or, on the contrary, by which his destructive and divisive potentialities have been maximized (Berndt, 1962; Gardner [film]). Studies of primitive societies thus can be used to clarify our thinking about a wide variety of related questions: the danger that incentive may be minimized within certain types of social organization; the conditions within which high motivation can be maintained (McClelland, 1961); the relationship between socioeconomic and political organization and cooperation and competition (Mead, 1937); and the relationship between means and ends (Mead, 1942a, 1950a)—a crucial problem in the choice between totalitarian, democratic, and other as yet undeveloped forms of political order.

As we devise new social forms we shall necessarily depend both on anthropology, with its records of contrasting social solutions, and on history, with its detailed documentation of success and failure within our own historical tradition (Mead, 1951a). But we shall not be wholly dependent on past experience. Simulation, by providing us with analyses of compatibilities and incompatibilities between potentially freely combining elements of social structure—based on actual, carefully specified cultural regularities—can also become a source of new organizational forms. But to be fully productive of such new forms, and not merely exercises in ingenuity, simulation must completely take into account the information which can be provided by history, anthropology, comparative sociology, and political science on the possibilities of and the limitations on man's abilities. When the state of our own research permits us to undertake simulation of this order of complexity, we should be able both to develop new forms and to examine the inherent possibilities of actually existing new forms, such as the type of acephalous organization, from which rebellion and older types of fission are less possible, which has been described in connection with the modern mineral industries in Africa (Wolfe, 1964).

In conclusion: In the 1940's and early 1950's a tremendous amount of research time, devotion, effort, and money went into the development of an applied anthropological specialization—the use of anthropology in conflict situations. Lack of any disposition on the part of those conducting international relations or dealing with intranational conflicts to make use of such findings and such research resulted in a decade of disuse, loss of momentum, dispersion of personnel, and loss of experts. The proper use of anthropologists in this complex and desperately important field is as team members. The understanding by members of other disciplines of what anthropology can contribute and the understanding by anthropologists of other disciplines both are essential to productive research. In the early 1940's, as the Nazi tyranny was sweeping over Europe, the phrase "it is later than you think" had the effect of mobilizing every kind of necessary activity. Today, looking at the spade work which still must be done—and the cooperation which must be achieved—if we are to create an applied behavioral and social science that is capable of dealing with large-scale human affairs, we may well say: "It is earlier than you think!"

REFERENCES

Adorno, T. W., *et al.*, *The Authoritarian Personality.* New York: Harper & Row, Publishers, 1950.

Allen, George C., *A Short Economic History of Modern Japan, 1867–1937,* 2nd ed. London: George Allen & Unwin, 1962.

Bahnson, Claus Bahne, "Emotional Reactions to Internally and Externally Derived Threats of Annihilation," *Symposium on Human Reactions to the Threat of Impending Disaster,* Part III, 129th Annual Meeting of the AAAS. Philadelphia, Pa., December 28, 1962.

Baker, George W. and Dwight W. Chapman, eds., *Man and Society in Disaster.* New York: Basic Books, Inc., 1962.

Bateson, Gregory, "Morale and National Character," *Civilian Morale,* Goodwin Watson, ed., pp. 71-91. Boston: Houghton Mifflin Company, 1942.

————, *Naven.* New York: Cambridge University Press, 1936; 2nd ed., Stanford, Calif.: Stanford University Press, 1958.

Benedict, Ruth, *The Chrysanthemum and the Sword.* Boston: Houghton-Mifflin Company, 1946.

Berndt, Ronald, *Excess and Restraint: Social Control Among a New Guinea Mountain People.* Chicago: University of Chicago Press, 1962.

Brace, C. Loring, "A Nonracial Approach Toward the Understanding of Human Diversity," *Critical Examination of the Concept of Race,* Ashley Montague, ed. New York: Free Press of Glencoe, Inc., in press.

Brickner, Richard M., *Is Germany Incurable?* Philadelphia: J. B. Lippincott Co., 1943.

Brogan, D. W., "The Presidency," *Encounter,* XXII (1964), 3-7.

Brown, Harrison and E. K. Federov, "Too Many People in the World," *Saturday Review,* XLV (February 17, 1962), 16-20, 86.

Capes, Mary, ed., *Communication or Conflict: Conferences—Their Nature, Dynamics, and Planning.* London: Tavistock Publications, Ltd., 1960.

Chapple, Eliot D., "Technical Assistance Program Film Planning Reports." Society for Applied Anthropology, International Motion Pictures Division, U.S. Department of State, Contract SCC-la-1723, 1951. A series of unpublished reports. Committee on Food Habits, National Research Council, "Manual for the Study of Food Habits," *National Research Council Bulletin,* No. 111. Washington, D.C., 1945.

Chapple, Eliot D. and Carleton S. Coon, *Principles of Anthropology.* New York: Holt, Rinehart & Winston, Inc., 1942.

Conklin, Harold C., "Buhid Pottery," *Journal of Asiatic Studies,* III (1953), 1-12. Published by the University of Manila.

————, "Hanuo'o Color Categories," *Southwestern Journal of Anthropology,* XI (1955), 339-344.

Cousins, Norman, "Experiment at Andover," *Saturday Review,* XLV (November 10, 1962a), 24-25.

————, "Talking to the Russians," Part 2, *Saturday Review,* XLV (December 1, 1962b), 24.

————, "Talking to the Russians," Part 3, *Saturday Review,* XLV (Decem-15, 1962c), 14.

Deutsch, Karl W., *Nationalism and Social Communication.* New York: John Wiley & Sons, Inc., 1953.

Dicks, Henry V., "Personality Traits and National Socialist Ideology," *Human Relations,* III (1950), 111-154.

Frankfurt, Henri, *The Birth of Civilization in the Near East.* Garden City, N.Y.: Doubleday & Company, Inc. (Anchor Book A89), 1956.

Gardner, Robert, *Dead Birds.* A film about the Dani of western New Guinea.

Glenn, E. S., "Washington Conference on Interpretation," *Communication or Conflict: Conferences—Their Nature, Dynamics, and Planning,* May Capes, ed., pp. 206-212. London: Tavistock Publications, Ltd., 1960.

Gorer, Geoffrey, "Themes in Japanese Culture," *Transactions of The New York Academy of Sciences,* V, Ser. 2 (1943), 26-51.

————, *Exploring English Character.* London: Cresset Press, Ltd., 1955.

————, "Introduction—1961," *The People of Great Russia,* 2nd ed., Geoffrey Gorer and John Rickman, eds., pp. xxix-xli. New York: W. W. Norton & Company, Inc., 1962.

Gorer, Geoffrey and John Rickman, *The People of Great Russia.* New York: Chanticleer Press, Inc., 1950.

Huxley, Julian S., "Evolution, Cultural and Biological," *Current Anthropology,* William L. Thomas, Jr., ed., pp. 3-25. Chicago: University of Chicago Press, 1956.

————, "Cultural Process and Evolution," *Behavior and Evolution,* Ann Roe and George G. Simpson, eds., pp. 437-454. New Haven: Yale University Press, 1958.

Leites, Nathan and Elsa Bernaut, *Ritual of Liquidation.* New York: Free Press of Glencoe, Inc., 1954.

Levy, David M., "Anti-Nazis: Criteria of Differentiation," *Psychiatry,* XI (1948), 125-167.

Lewis, Oscar, *Five Families.* New York: Basic Books, Inc., 1959.

————, *The Children of Sanchez.* New York: Random House, 1961.

McClelland, David C., *The Achieving Society.* Princeton, N.J.: D. Van Nostrand Co., Inc., 1961.

Malinowski, Bronislaw, *Argonauts of the Western Pacific.* London: Routledge & Kegan Paul, Ltd., 1922.

Masserman, Jules, ed., *Science and Psychoanalysis.* New York: Grune & Stratton, Inc., 1963.

Mead, Margaret, ed., *Cooperation and Competition Among Primitive Peoples.* New York: McGraw-Hill Book Company, 1937. Rev. ed., Boston: Beacon Press, Inc. (BP123), 1961.

————, "The Comparative Study of Culture and the Purposive Cultivation of Democratic Values," *Science, Philosophy and Religion,* Lyman Bryson and Louis Finkelstein, eds., pp. 56-69. New York: Conference on Comparative Study of Cultures and the Purposive Cultivation of Democratic Values, Second Symposium, 1942a.

————, "Educative Effects of Social Environment as Disclosed by Studies of Primitive Societies," *Environment and Education: A Symposium,* Supplementary Educational Monographs, No. 54, pp. 48-61. Chicago: University of Chicago Press, 1942b.

————, "Contemporary Anthropology: Summary of a Communication by Dr. Margaret Mead: 5 October, 1943," *Man,* XLIV (1944), 48-49.

————, "A Case History in Cross-national Communication," *The Communication of Ideas,* Lyman Bryson, ed., pp. 209-229. New York: Harper & Row, Publishers, 1948.

————, *Male and Female.* New York: William Morrow & Company, Inc., 1949.

————, "The Comparative Study of Cultures and the Purposive Cultivation of Democratic Values, 1941–1949," *Perspectives on a Troubled Decade: Science, Philosophy, and Religion, 1939–1949,* Lyman Bryson, Louis Finkelstein, and R. A. MacIver, eds., pp. 87-108. New York: Harper & Row, Publishers, 1950a.

————, *Soviet Attitudes Toward Authority.* New York: McGraw-Hill Book Company, 1950b. Reissued, New York: William Morrow & Co., Inc., 1955.

————, "Anthropologist and Historian: Their Common Problems," *American Quarterly,* III (1951a), 3-33.

————, "Research in Contemporary Cultures," *Groups, Leadership and Men,* Harold Guetzkow, ed., pp. 106-117. Pittsburgh: Carnegie Press, 1951b.

————, ed., *Studies in Soviet Communication,* 2 vols. Cambridge, Mass.: Center for International Studies, Massachusetts Institute of Technology, 1952.

————, "End Linkage: An Analytical Approach," *The Study of Culture at a Distance,* Margaret Mead and Rhoda Metraux, eds., pp. 365-393. Chicago: University of Chicago Press, 1953a.

————, "The Organization of Group Research," *The Study of Culture at a Distance,* Margaret Mead and Rhoda Metraux, eds., pp. 85-101. Chicago: University of Chicago Press, 1953b.

————, "Cultural Determinants of Sexual Behavior," *Sex and Internal Secretions*, 3rd ed., William C. Young, ed., pp. 1433-1479. Baltimore: The Williams & Wilkins Co., 1961.

————, "The Factor of Culture," *The Selection of Personnel for International Service*, Mottram Torre, ed., pp. 3-22. Geneva and New York: World Federation for Mental Health, 1963.

Mead, Margaret, Eliot D. Chapple, and G. Gordon Brown, "Report of the Committee on Ethics," *Human Organization*, VIII (1949), 20-21.

Mead, Margaret and Rhoda Metraux, eds., *The Study of Culture at a Distance.* Chicago: University of Chicago Press, 1953.

————, "The Participation of Anthropologists in Research Relevant to Peace." Manuscript prepared for the Center for Research in Conflict Resolution and the American Anthropological Association, January 1962.

Mead, Margaret and Martha Wolfenstein, eds., *Childhood in Contemporary Cultures.* Chicago: University of Chicago Press, 1955.

Metraux, Rhoda and Nelly S. Hoyt, "German National Character: A Study of German Self-images," *Studies in Contemporary Cultures–B.* New York: American Museum of Natural History, 1953.

Metraux, Rhoda and Margaret Mead, eds., *Themes in French Culture.* Stanford, Calif.: Stanford University Press, 1954.

Muller, Herbert J., *The Loom of History.* New York: Harper & Row, Publishers, 1958.

National Aeronautics and Space Administration, "Symposium: Space Biology," "Part I: Biosatellites"; "Part II: Bioregenerative Systems." Joint Program of the American Physiological Society and NASA, cosponsored by the Ecological Society of America, presented at the 130th Annual Meeting of the AAAS, Cleveland, Ohio, December 29, 1963.

Radcliffe-Brown, A. R., *The Andaman Islanders.* New York: The Macmillan Company, 1922.

Richardson, L. F., *Arms and Insecurity*, Nicolas Rashevsky and Ernest Trucco, eds. Pittsburgh: Boxwood Press; Chicago: Quadrangle Books, 1960a.

————, *Statistics of Deadly Quarrels*, Quincy Wright and C. C. Linaw, eds. Pittsburgh: Boxwood Press; Chicago: Quadrangle Books, 1960b.

Sahlins, Marshall D. and Elman R. Service, eds., *Evolution and Culture.* Ann Arbor: University of Michigan Press, 1960.

Schaffner, Bertram, *Father Land.* New York: Columbia University Press, 1948.

Simpson, George G., "The History of Life," *Evolution after Darwin, I: The Evolution of Life*, Sol Tax, ed., pp. 117-180. Chicago: University of Chicago Press, 1960.

————, *Life of the Past: An Introduction to Paleontology.* New Haven: Yale University Press, 1961.

Taylor, Edmond, *The Fall of the Dynasties.* Garden City, N.Y.: Doubleday & Company, Inc., 1963.

Teltsch, Kathleen, "UN to Use Glyphs to Promote Unity," *The New York Times,* March 29, 1964.

Tuchman, Barbara W., *The Guns of August.* New York: The Macmillan Company, 1962.

U.S. Strategic Bombing Survey (Morale Division), *The Effects of Strategic Bombing on German Morale.* Washington, D.C., 1947.

von Hoerner, Sebastian, "The General Limits of Space Travel," *Science,* July 6, 1962, pp. 18-23.

Wittfogel, Karl A., *Oriental Despotism.* New Haven: Yale University Press, 1957.

Wolfe, Alvin W., "The African Mineral Industry," *Social Problems,* XI (1964), 153-164.

Wolfenstein, Martha, *Disaster.* New York: Free Press of Glencoe, Inc., 1957.

Wolfenstein, Martha and Nathan Leites, *The Movies: A Psychological Study.* New York: Free Press of Glencoe, Inc., 1950.

Zborowski, Mark and Elizabeth G. Herzog, *Life Is With People: The Jewish Little-town of Eastern Europe.* New York: International Universities Press, 1952.

**The
Political
Science
of
Human
Conflict**

J. DAVID SINGER

From the time that Thucydides dwelt upon the Peloponnesian Wars to the present, the study of international relations has passed through an interesting and disparate number of phases. The subject has been alternately the domain of theologians, philosophers, soldiers, courtiers, statesmen, historians, and lawyers. The latter two professions tended to dominate during the late nineteenth and early twentieth centuries until, during the interwar period, political scientists increasingly pre-empted the field (Ware, 1938). But even as our near monopoly was being consolidated, the devastation of the Second World War and the spectre of a third helped to bring a new array of scholars into the area of inquiry. These were the behavioral scientists, primarily from the disciplines of psychiatry, psychology, and sociology, seasoned with a smattering of anthropologists and economists. These newcomers, in turn, had barely begun to stake out a claim when they were joined by an indefinable breed of strategists, systems analysts, and operations researchers.

As the "legitimate" and "traditional" proprietors of international relations, we in political science have watched this influx of newcomers with a mixture of awe, inadequacy, and dismay. Should we fight them, ignore them, or join them

(Singer, 1961)? It seems to me that we can—and must—do all three, and the purpose of this paper is to illustrate such a "mixed strategy" via the presentation of one possible model of international conflict, viewed primarily from the political scientist's perspective. I propose to begin with a delineation of the major social systems involved in international conflict, then discuss the relationships and processes which seem to characterize such conflict, and then close with some observations on the role of the various disciplines concerned.

THE STRUCTURAL SETTING
OF INTERNATIONAL CONFLICT

International relations are perhaps most fully understood in terms of the interactions within and among four different levels or classes of social system. The most comprehensive of these is the *international* system, a weakly organized social system whose territorial and cultural base is nearly global. The major components of this system are *national* states, or societies with a well-defined territorial base and relatively discernible and differentiable cultural characteristics, organized into that particular form of political system we call a *sovereign state*. The national state (or nation, which we will label it, since almost all nations in the world today are organized into states) is, in turn, composed of a multiplicity of *subnational* groups or social organizations, each characterized by a distinctive subculture, but not necessarily associated with a fixed territorial base. These subnational organizations might be political parties, religious sects and hierarchies, labor groups, professional associations, or adherents of a particular ideological doctrine. The important thing about these subnational groups is that, unlike the national states, individuals can and do "belong" and owe some measure of allegiance to several at once.

It is this overlapping membership which makes possible, and leads to, our fourth class of social organization—*extranational* associations. That is, people who belong to the Christian Democratic, Social Democratic, or Communist parties, the Roman Catholic or Protestant Episcopal Church, the Congress of Industrial Organizations, the American Political Science Association, the Japan Society of Mechanical Engineering, or the Humanist or Esperanto movement in their own national societies also find branches of these or similar organizations in many other nations (White, 1951). These extranational associations of subnational groups, though growing in numbers and influence, still exercise only a minor impact on the diplomatic behavior of nations, primarily through their role as indicators of gradually changing norms regarding nationalism and cosmopolitanism. Though they may ultimately shape the political organization of the international system, at present their role is considerably subordinate to that of the nations. On the other hand, the subnational groups, acting upon the separate national states in which they are located, often exert an appreciable impact, though not always in the cosmopolitan direction.

THE BASIC MODES OF CONFLICT MANAGEMENT

In a cluster of social systems such as this, it is not only inevitable that international conflict will be recurrent and widespread, but that a variety of modes for the resolution and management of such conflict will be germane. Normally, the social scientist thinks of three such modes. The first is moral consensus, in which case a more or less universal understanding of, and commitment to, justice and equity permits conflicts to be settled by appeal to such norms. The second basis is physical coercion, in which case the recognized and legitimate agencies of enforcement impose settlements and solutions according to their own operational code, which may or may not reflect that of their constituents. Finally, there is the utilitarian basis for conflict management. In that case, participants are generally thought to be able to measure expected utilities and disutilities against their own and their opponents' value-preference hierarchies, and then select the most rational of the solutions available. Conflict solutions thus eventuate out of a bargaining process, and the assumption is that with a multiplicity of such bargaining processes always underway in the social system, the resultant outcomes will be advantageous to the system in both the short and long run and to the individual parties to conflict in the middle and long run. Subject to the vicissitudes of some short-run inequities for the parties, the general welfare is expected to prosper, thanks to the invisible, unseen hand of the collective separate interests.[1]

In every social system, some blend of these three elements is at work, producing conflict-management results that range from relative harmony to near chaos. Within the national societies, given the complexity of differing subgroup interests and values, successful pluralism requires somewhat more in the way of coercive capabilities than within the subgroups themselves. The capabilities, of course, need seldom be applied in the physical sense; awareness of their legitimacy and their effectiveness suffices to impose severe inhibitions on conflict participants, especially in those cases when one of the participants is an agent of the

---

[1] Note the parallel between this notion and the classical economic model. The most thorough espousal of its applicability to the international system was made by the historian and diplomat George F. Kennan (1951; 1954).

national government. On the other hand, national subgroups, since they tend to be formed around common interests or highly compatible ideologies and in which membership is often voluntary,[2] rely much less upon the coercive element.

The question that concerns us here, of course, is the way in which the interactions between and among the four social-system types generate, and permit the effective resolution of, international conflict. An exploration of that question might best begin with a closer look at the reciprocal influences that occur between the nations themselves and the international system.[3]

TWO MODELS OF NATIONAL BEHAVIOR
IN THE INTERNATIONAL SYSTEM

Though we may already be, without fully recognizing it, entering into a transitional stage in the development of the international system, in which the relative influence between national and extranational organizations may be radically redistributed, that stage has barely begun. To put it another way, the monopoly of power in the system has been, and remains, largely in the hands of the national states, acting through their governments.

What is it that these national governments do in that system?[4] Several models might be offered, each compelling in its own terms, but I shall restrict myself to two which, though incompatible at first glance, may well be complementary to one another. The first might be called the "passive-isolationist" model, and it postulates the nations as essentially inward oriented, with their governments preoccupied by the welter of domestic problems peculiar to that nation's physical, societal, and attitudinal conditions. Their political elites are seen as trying to solve the eternal dilemma posed by the desire to: (a) remain in power and (b) render social justice as it is understood in their particular milieu. Alloca-

---

[2] The importance of the voluntary-involuntary distinction seems to have been overlooked by social scientists in their studies of social and political organizations; we normally just postulate membership, overlooking the extent to which genetic and territorial probabilities determine the lifelong associations of all men.

[3] Elsewhere, I have argued at some length for the need to maintain a clear delineation between these two of the four named systems (Singer, 1961a).

[4] Some readers may boggle at any effort to generalize, however abstractly, about all or most nations. While recognizing the structural and behavioral diversity and the nonsimultaneous developmental stages which all are passing through at any particular time, I would urge that political science's preoccupation with the unique has been a major inhibition to the development of systematic theory. Any science requires empirical generalization, and this can hardly proceed from an N of 1 (Deutsch and Singer, in press).

tion of attention or resources to foreign affairs is kept to that minimum permitted by their immediate international environment, or necessitated by their domestic inadequacies. This is the passive-isolationist concept of the national state, actively engaging in international politics only as a loss-avoiding stratagem.

Close to the opposite end of the continuum is the "active-interventionist" model, postulating national elites vigorously (and even exuberantly), engaging one another in a wide and diverse range of competitive and collaborative relations on behalf of their respective national societies. Adherents of this model see alliances, conventions, trade, and war not as occasionally imposed upon reluctant leaders but as the normal and inevitable preoccupation of those who rise to political power in national states.

There would seem to be two ways in which one's theoretical orientation to international relations might handle these two diverse models of national motivation. One is to argue that the world is, in fact, divided into two kinds of nations; some tend toward the passive, loss-avoiding pole while others lean in the more vigorous, gain-maximizing direction. From such a dichotomous model, in turn, two alternative extensions are possible. In one, we assume that those nations manifesting vigorous interventionism are likely to survive and thrive, while the passive ones are, in the Spencerian sense, doomed to eventual decay and demise. The other strand of reasoning, and the one which most concerns us here, argues that it is exactly this dichotomy which produces international conflict: if all the nations would only concentrate their energies on domestic needs and follow a live-and-let-live policy, international conflict would disappear and peace would be the inevitable consequence.

Returning to the problem of relating the active and passive models again, another line of reasoning would suggest that most nations are most accurately viewed, not as one type or the other, but as a combination of the two. This is essentially an ambivalence model of national motivation, and it looks for an explanation of the dominance of one or the other of the two tendencies, not in the distinguishing domestic characteristics of the diverse and separate nations, but in the nature of the international environment at the time under examination.

More specifically, we postulate that our nations will be more inwardly or outwardly oriented, depending on the mixture of incentives and restraints present in the system, which is, after all, their external environment. If the political organization of the system permitted or encouraged domestic preoccupation and relative isolationism, we might see markedly different national behavior patterns. But it does not. To the contrary, it demands—of all but a handful of geographical and historical aberrations—a constant vigilance, lest their vital interests be jeopardized.

Though it may not be a Hobbesian world of each warring against all, it is certainly a world in which no nation takes the uprightness and virtue of its neighbors for granted, at least over an extended period of time.

Since I have more or less rejected the nations' internal characteristics as a possible explanation of this state of affairs, I must, of course, justify it in terms of the system's characteristics. Thus, let me argue at the outset that the system—primarily because of the inadequacy and incompleteness of its political institutions—exhibits as its dominant characteristic the phenomenon of scarcity. Though this scarcity extends to resources, locations, markets, and so forth, it applies most directly to national security. That is, even if the tangible commodities which nations value were plentiful, there would still not be sufficient security to go around.

This is because one nation's security must inevitably be—in an environment of relative anarchy—another nation's insecurity. In such a poorly organized system, the relative degrees of justice and power which go into the distribution of valued objects and arrangements are heavily skewed in the direction of the latter. The human race has admittedly made some impressive advances in the development of norms of justice, equity, and morality,[5] but these are still far from sufficient to generate a world-wide sense of national security. Furthermore, some serious normative regressions have occurred in the present century, most notable of which is the general acceptance of genocide as a means of protecting the interests of one's own nation.[6]

Returning to our three possible bases of conflict management, we must conclude that moral consensus is, for the relevant future, a fairly unreliable one. As to the second, nearly all of the means of coercion are at the disposal of those who most need to be coerced (i.e., the national states) while those international institutions and organizations responsible for and preoccupied with the general—as distinguished from the parochial—welfare, remain almost incapable of coercing the would-be aggressor.

Thus the nations are left to rely primarily upon the intelligent calcu-

---

[5] Two practices which are now widely held in disrepute, but which formerly met with general approval, are slavery and racial subordination and exploitation. Even poverty, which was formerly thought of as the inevitable lot of the morally inferior, is now almost universally condemned as unjust.

[6] Though those of us who are not advocates of unilateral disarmament do not think of ourselves as defenders of genocide, and hope that the act need never be committed, we are nevertheless quite prepared to resort to it in an alarming range of contingencies. Some would accept the use of strategic nuclear weapons (a mass-destruction technique par excellence) only if an enemy used them first, but others accept—and often advocate—their use as a bargaining ploy, as a credibility demonstrator, or as a response to the use of conventional weapons. My own ambivalence has already been recorded (Singer, 1962).

lation of their own and others' utilitarian interests if they are to minimize recurrent threats to their security and remain free from war as the most frequent consequence of such threats. In the following section, I shall attempt to identify the factors which tend to inhibit, if not preclude, the effective operation of that "invisible hand."

POLITICAL PAY-OFFS AND CONFLICT MANAGEMENT [7]

For the invisible hand of the separate "national interests" to provide an even moderately effective process of conflict management in the international system, the pay-off structure of that system (i.e., the environment within which the nations act and interact) must produce at least as much in the way of incentive as of disincentive for such behavior, that is, the rewards for irrationality must not exceed, and should be significantly fewer, than those for rational behavior.[8] In addition, the system's payoff structure must be one in which there is some basis for each nation's decision makers to assume that their opposite numbers will adhere to the dictates of rationality. Furthermore, the *domestic* environment must also reflect such a payoff matrix for the decision makers.

To put it bluntly, the recent and present international system makes these requirements extremely difficult to meet, and when we combine the pay-offs of national domestic politics with those of the larger system, the picture is bleak indeed. Why should this be so? As I suggested earlier, the absence of sufficiently powerful normative and coercive forces at the international level compels nations to rely heavily (some might say exclusively) upon their own power as a means of protecting their interests in the inevitable conflicts to which they are parties. And that power, in turn, is an amalgam of many factors, of which military capability is only one, albeit still a crucial one.

Military power must be based upon, and supplemented by, a mobilized national population. If the national society is to provide the men, the money, and the material willingly—or even passively—with

---

[7] Needless to say, international conflict is not thought of here as a phenomenon to be condemned or eliminated. It is assumed that conflict must occur in an environment of such complexity, especially one characterized by scarcities. Our concern is with the management of international conflict to the extent that war might be virtually eliminated as a mode of conflict resolution.

[8] If pressed, I might define rational behavior as that which: (*a*) is able to identify all available alternatives; (*b*) enumerates all possible outcomes arising out of each available alternative; (*c*) assigns subjective probabilities to all possible outcomes; (*d*) assigns subjective utilities and disutilities to each such outcome; (*e*) combines probabilities and utilities according to consistent rules; (*f*) selects the optimum alternative; and (*g*) allocates the necessary resources to execute the action selected.

which to make any threat of military force credible, the population must be persuaded that a genuine threat is posed by the adversary of the moment.[9] Furthermore, the citizenry must be persuaded to accept such ancillary costs of preparedness as a serious erosion of civil liberties, and in the mid-twentieth century, the additional burden of genetically harmful radioactivity.

Since none of these are traditionally thought of as inherent in the human condition (though even this set of norms may be changing), the national political elites find it necessary to paint an increasingly treacherous, if not omnipotent, picture of the opposing nation(s) in the conflict. The consequence need not necessarily be Lasswell's "garrison state," but it inevitably becomes some approximation thereof. That is, as the symbols of legitimacy are constantly associated with, and invested in, the preparedness program and its parallel activities, organized or individual resistance to the train of events becomes ever more costly and difficult. In the language of cybernetics, we get what is termed a *positive feedback* process, replete with all the attributes of any self-aggravating (as distinguished from a negative feedback, self-correcting) dynamic. Almost every articulation, act, or allocation of resources made in response to the state of affairs serves to advance it further.

The tragedy is, of course, that at about the time the political elites discover what they have set in motion, it is extremely costly to seek to slow or reverse it. They discover that their domestic pay-off structure is full of rewards for continuing to feed the hostility and the jingoism, and loaded with penalties if they hesitate to do so. Normally, the would-be peacemaker loses out (at the polls, in the smoke-filled rooms, or whatever the path to political power) to the sabre-rattler and the demagogue. As a consequence, the holder or seeker of domestic power finds himself seriously inhibited from "doing business" with the enemy. Bargaining is seen as appeasement, *quid pro quo* concessions represent capitulation, and serious negotiation may well be denounced as treason.

The irony, of course, is that a similar pattern is reproduced within the society of the other conflicting nation. The two national systems not only produce this positive feedback process *within* themselves, but by their consequent external behavior produce exactly what is required to strengthen and accelerate it within the other.[10] The distribution of power among the subnational groups is ultimately such that those who favor the "hard line" acquire a strangle hold over the domestic political process.

---

[9] In order to keep the discussion manageable, we postulate a simple bi-lateral conflict, but a more accurate model would have to account for the role of allies and neutrals in almost any international conflict.

[10] A mathematical description of this interaction prior to World War I is in Lewis F. Richardson (1960).

Not only are the probabilities of a "co-existence" faction achieving national office extremely low, but those already in office find it increasingly necessary to placate and reinforce the more aggressive groups in order to retain legitimacy. The result is, of course, a tacit and indirect alliance between the "hard-line" groups in each of the nations, with the titular power-holders trapped in a pay-off matrix (admittedly of their own making in some measure) in which punishment for cooperative diplomatic gestures comes from both their own national subgroups and their opposite numbers in the other nation.

If this general model—though perhaps slightly overdrawn for emphasis—is an accurate one, it would seem that escape in the short run [11] can only be found (if at all) via a modified strategy on the part of certain crucial subgroups in each of the nations involved. In the longer run, major transformations in the political organization of the international system would seem both necessary and desirable. But between the present and the time when such organization might possibly approximate that found at the national level, less radical restructuring will have to suffice.[12]

INITIATING A PROCESS REVERSAL

Returning to the cross-national alliance and the positive feedback process which it sustains, the question becomes one of identifying alternative modes by which that relationship and process might be reversed. More specifically, what are the sorts of initial measures that might conceivably constitute a break in the normal feedback cycle and set in motion a self-enforcing process in the opposite direction?

One such possibility, which has attracted the interest of many political scientists is known as the *functional approach,* and though its ultimate concern is with radical modification of international organization, its initial phases are quite germane to our consideration of process reversal.[13] The assumption here is that, as industrial technology and communications improve, as economic and social interdependence increase, and as human aspirations for the good life become increasingly strident, national elites will gradually discover the inadequacy of national solutions to these new problems. As a consequence, they will be increasingly

---

[11] Identifying the relevant future is an important and challenging task, but social science has made little operational progress on that score. But see Wilbert Moore (1963).

[12] For several comparisons suggesting the relevance of national models to the international system, see Alger (1963), Parsons (1962), and Russett (1963).

[13] Perhaps the best known and most fully developed articulation is found in David Mitrany (1944).

willing to support the creation, and strengthening, of intergovernmental international organizations handling specific functional problems in the economic and social realm.[14]

Once established and consolidated, national governments will find it increasingly rational to turn over more and more national functions to these agencies, and before too long a well-established pattern of international cooperation will have developed. Then (but only then) it is suggested that national elites will, having discovered the virtues of cooperation in these essentially nonpolitical fields, be willing to turn to international organization for cooperation in the more sensitive political and security realms.

The model is appealing, but it tends to overlook the incentives for irrationality which normally operate upon national elites. Thus, even though the functional approach, once initiated, might possibly lead in the direction of political transformation of the international system, there is serious doubt as to the probability of the process being perpetuated, via "spill-over," [15] for example, once the sensitive threshold of political and security concerns is approached.

To put it another way, it may strengthen the bonds between and among those subnational groups whose professional interest is in sanitation engineering, wood technology, social welfare, or space communications—and this is all to the good—but these are seldom the subnational groups which have much influence on the diplomatic behavior of their national governments.

Another strategy, more current and consequently better known, is the *unilateral initiatives approach;* though widely advocated and under constant consideration in the United States government at least, it is given its most systematic formulation by Charles Osgood (1959, 1962), a social psychologist. Briefly summarized, it calls for policy-makers to select a repertory of diplomatic and military measures which would, at the outset, not seriously jeopardize their nation's security if not reciprocated, but which convey to the adversary an inclination to slow down and then reverse the internation positive feedback process. Though less attention is given to the domestic politics aspect, the assumption is that sufficiently concerned and powerful subgroups already exist (again, in the United

---

[14] The specialized agencies of the U.N. system (and those few which existed prior to the formulation of the U.N., such as Universal Postal Union, International Telecommunications Union, and International Labor Organization) are precisely what is meant by these functional organizations.

[15] This concept is borrowed from a study by Ernst Haas (1958), which is perhaps the most important one of its kind to date on the development of supranational organization. Haas did discover some evidence of the spill-over phenomenon, but his study deals with nations whose interests are far more compatible than incompatible.

States, if not elsewhere) and if mobilized into political activity could so modify the policy-makers' pay-off matrix as to make such moves relatively attractive.

From the international point of view, the major weakness of this strategy probably stems from the incompatibility between the two requirements of any initiative. Unless the move were a relatively dramatic one, seriously weakening the nation militarily, the adversary's response is likely to be exactly as in the past: suspicious or disdainful. For any single initiative or sequence of initiatives to engender reciprocity, it would have to come pretty close to "exposing the jugular," and the domestic resistance could be expected to be extraordinarily powerful.

The difficulty with either the functional or the unilateral initiatives approach seems to be in their failure to deal in a systematic way with the domestic as well as with the diplomatic processes, and more important, the interaction between the two. As a matter of fact, I cannot think of a single comprehensive effort to work out a model which embraces these two processes, along with the social structure within and among which they occur. Many of us, in a variety of disciplines, are working on parts of the problem, but a compelling synthesis—even if purely deductive and nonempirical—remains to be produced. In the section which follows, let me attempt to spell out some of the more fundamental requirements of this highly necessary—but improbable—irreversible process, and then go on to explore the kinds of research necessary to generating a theory within which that process must be understood.

SOME REQUIREMENTS OF IRREVERSIBILITY

It would seem that, for any process which aims to reverse the normal conflict processes, and itself become essentially irreversible, it must meet four conditions. First, it must be either initially acceptable to the policy-making subgroups (i.e., those who act on behalf of the national state) or of such a nature as to change the pay-off structure in the direction of diminishing their resistance to it. This distinction is, of course, pretty much a matter of time scale; some measures are initially acceptable because they appear to offer, for example, a sufficient mix of rewards at the national and international levels to compensate for the predictable losses or penalties from both of those environments. Others (and this is our concern here) seem to presage such changes in one or both of those environments that *future* gains and rewards are seen as compensatory for the losses which dominate the *immediate* pay-off mix.

Second, in order that the policy-makers' pay-off matrix can be modified, one of two domestic phenomena must occur. Either those subgroups which reinforce the hard-line tendencies must be weakened vis-à-vis the "moderates," or the former must experience a shift in attitudes such as to move them away from the implacable hostility end of the foreign-policy continuum.

This requires, in turn, the fulfilling of a third set of conditions, that is, the hard-line subgroups must be persuaded that continued resistance to a co-existence strategy will be costly to them in the middle as well as the long run. And that conclusion is unlikely to be reached unless one or both of their two major sources of support and power seem to be turning away from them and thus depriving them of the legitimacy which is the major pillar of that power. One of those sources is generalized public opinion (responding either to the nation's political leadership or to those other reference figures who dominate most of the subgroups) and the other is the political elite itself.

For the latter condition to obtain, of course, we come full circle, and must then look, *inter alia,* at the international environment again. The adversary nation must be expected (despite all of the experiential evidence to the contrary) to respond to co-existence moves in a manner such as to reward the policy-makers diplomatically in order to minimize their losses (and hopefully, maximize their gains) domestically. The fourth condition, therefore, is diplomatic reciprocity, and this requires, in turn, that essentially the same processes be set in motion within the adversary nation, at approximately the same pace.

In suggesting these minimal requirements, I am, of course, raising by implication a host of applied social science questions. Just to indicate the flavor of these, let me make a few of them explicit, first in the context of an initiative coming directly from the top national policy-makers and then with certain key subgroups viewed as the possible instigators.

What are the probabilities of any major-power head of state engaging in such a concerted effort? Are there any prior cases? Are there any compelling analogues from other social settings? To what extent would the probability be a function of his personality (Lasswell, 1930, chaps. 4, 6, 7, and 8), socioeconomic status (Matthews, 1954), mode of power acquisition, party structure, national character, geographical location, control of media, and so forth? If the effort were made, what variables would predict to its degree of success, both in the domestic setting and in terms of engendering reciprocity?

To take another, and intuitively more attractive, scenario; suppose that some of the major subgroups in one society decided that the conflict process might best be modified or reversed by attempting to create a tacit cross-national alliance between subgroups which are highly concerned and perhaps moderately influential. What sort of research base exists from which we can make adequate predictions regarding the likely sequence of events? For example, will the probabilities of process reversal be increased if the subgroups on each side act simultaneously, or is a time lag necessary? What sort of action ought to be contemplated: public statements? private pressure? threats? promises? ignoring whom and targeting on whom? Which groups are most likely to receive most attention where it counts?

CONCLUSION

The model of international conflict outlined in this paper is not only a pessimistic one, but one which requires far greater elaboration before any compelling theoretical basis for escape from it can be formulated. As the above questions indicate, the relevant relationships are unlikely to be understood, or the correlations among them measured, by any single-minded social scientist. The traditional international relations specialist from political science would tend to have neither the concepts nor the methods for dealing with the factors which generate specific attitudinal change, nor would the psychologist, for example, be particularly sophisticated in his examination of the precise institutional restraints within which our various national subgroups must operate.

Given these lacunae in our normal professional preparation, which approach to peace research looks most promising? On the one hand, any coherent model of international relations must rest upon psychological, sociological, and anthropological variables and measures, but on the other hand, the most crucial ones seem to be political.[16] One strategy would suggest the creation of interdisciplinary teams, recruited according to the specific needs of a given project, bearing in mind the likelihood that a traditional single-disciplined scholar would be little more successful in *designing* an interdisciplinary study than in carrying it out. Group-designed studies are quite likely, however, to be diffuse and incoherent, representing an awkward cluster of compromises.

The other extreme, and the one toward which I would lean, calls for some sort of "new breed" of social scientist. He must, of course, understand the principles of international relations (as well as they are known) and have a working familiarity with the data, concepts, and bibliography of politics. But this does not necessarily imply a Ph.D. in political science; already, a good number of people with other training have acquired and demonstrated an impressive grasp of the subject. Representatives of any of the disciplines or approaches suggested in this volume can make im-

---

[16] If I seem to be slighting history it is not because historical analogues are not appropriate, but because I assume that every social scientist is something of an historian in his own discipline.

portant individual contributions to our understanding of international conflict. But there is a "hooker": the tendency to concentrate upon the structures and processes most familiar and to assign more of the variance to them than the data (when we have it) would seem to allow. Many psychologists (from clinical to social), for example, seem determined to describe, explain, and predict the behavior of any of the complex social organizations mentioned here as if they were nothing but the individual writ large. Among the crucial factors overlooked in this sort of analogizing is the fact that the large social system has a far more restricted repertory than the "normal" individual, that response time tends to be considerably greater, and that utility preferences are subject to far less frequent and rapid shifts.

Less extreme, but nearly as misleading, is the tendency of many psychologists to see public opinion as the major independent variable in the foreign policy of a large, industrialized democracy such as the United States. Though no compelling empirically based theory exists to challenge the hypothesis, most students of the subject would argue that the role of public opinion in any major power is quite modest, probably differing only in degree from democratic to authoritarian societies, and largely molded by the very people who then claim to be responding to it.[17]

In conclusion, then, one must be affirmative, and at the same time cautious, regarding the influx of nonpolitical scientists into the international relations field. We who have dominated it for the past several decades have failed rather badly in developing a rigorous social science discipline. We have, with only a handful of exceptions, remained ignorant of, or have turned our backs on, the impressive advances which sociology, psychology, and economics have made since the turn of the century. Moreover, we have all too often failed the simple test of objectivity, and on many occasions our writing, our teaching, our lecturing (and especially our governmental consulting) have been virtually indistinguishable from that of either the passionate patriot or the man who is too interested in telling his audience what he believes they want to hear.[18]

There is, in sum, no more important or exciting field of research in the world today, and as we political scientists are joined by colleagues from other disciplines, the rate of theoretical progress cannot help but

---

[17] This latter factor is, of course, one of the reasons for pessimism regarding any reversal of the self-aggravating processes described earlier. One of the interesting paradoxes is that, while political elites seem to be aware of the degree to which they can and do encourage public bellicosity, they become very bearish at any suggestion that they might likewise be able to modify mass opinion in more pacifistic directions.

[18] It is not that patriotism among scholars is to be deprecated, but that there is little point in our doing what others do as well, while leaving undone the crucial job of building a body of knowledge.

accelerate. And if we turn out to be lucky, as well as diligent, creative, and skillful, we may even discover enough about international conflict to permit policy-makers to find a rational exit from an interaction process which now looks very much as if it is, in fact, not reversible.

REFERENCES

Alger, Chadwick F., "Comparison of Intranational and International Politics," *American Political Science Review*, LVII (June 1963), 406-419.

Deutsch, Karl W. and J. David Singer, "The Organizing Efficiency of Theories." In press.

Haas, Ernst, *The Uniting of Europe: Political, Social, and Economic Forces, 1950–1957*. Stanford, Calif.: Stanford University Press, 1958.

Kennan, George F., *American Diplomacy, 1900–1950*. New York: Mentor Books, 1951.

———, *Realities of American Foreign Policy*. Princeton, N.J.: Princeton University Press, 1954.

Lasswell, Harold, *Psychopathology and Politics*. Chicago: University of Chicago Press, 1930.

Matthews, Donald, *The Social and Political Background of Political Decision Makers*. New York: Random House, 1954.

Mitrany, David, *A Working Peace System*. London: Royal Institute of International Affairs, 1944.

Moore, Wilbert E., *Man, Time, and Society*. New York: John Wiley & Sons, Inc., 1963.

Osgood, Charles, "Suggestions for Winning the Real War Against Communism," *Journal of Conflict Resolution*, III (December 1959), 295-325.

———, *An Alternative to War or Surrender*. Urbana: University of Illinois Press, 1962.

Parsons, Talcott, "Polarization and the Problem of International Order," *Preventing World War III*, Quincy Wright *et al.*, eds. New York: Simon & Schuster, Inc., 1962.

Richardson, Lewis F., *Arms and Insecurity*. Pittsburgh: The Boxwood Press, 1960.

Russett, Bruce M., "Toward a Model of Competitive International Politics," *Journal of Politics*, XXV (May 1963), 226-247.

Singer, J. David, "The Level of Analysis Problem in International Relations," *World Politics*, XIV (October 1961a), 77-92.

———, "The Relevance of the Behavioral Sciences to the Study of International Relations," *Behavioral Science*, VI (October 1961b), 324-335.

———, *Deterrence, Arms Control, and Dissarmament: Toward A Syn-*

thesis in National Security Policy. Columbus: Ohio State University Press, 1962.

Ware, Edith, *The Study of International Relations in the United States: Survey for 1937.* New York: Columbia University Press, 1938.

White, Lyman C., *International Nongovernmental Organizations.* New Brunswick, N.J.: Rutgers University Press, 1951.

The History of Human Conflict

OLE R. HOLSTI

ROBERT C. NORTH

Modern social science methods coupled with the use of computers may transform history into something approaching a laboratory of international behavior. With machines and appropriate techniques, the scholar can now reduce documentary materials from various national archives into replicable, countable units and analyze quantities of data which would have required a battalion of research assistants by traditional standards. With these methods, moreover, it is now feasible to order new concepts, test new kinds of hypotheses, and derive new types of findings from the usual documents of history. Aided by machines capable of handling vast quantities of data and large numbers of variables, scholars may eventually find ways of linking individual behavior and small-group behavior with the behavior of states and coalitions of states—all within a single body of theory.

What can these new historical approaches offer to the social scientist who is interested primarily in contemporary phenomena, or to the policy-maker whose focus is on the present and on the future? What relevance, for example, does an historical crisis have for crises of today—crises in a nuclear age? Clearly the circumstances are different, the nations and leaders are different, and the weapons are different. Why dig into the half-forgotten past? What can we learn that will be useful in meeting problems of the future?

Social science approaches to historical situations are based upon the fundamental assumption that there are patterns, repetitions, and close analogies throughout the history of human affairs. The circumstances and paraphernalia will differ between the Peloponnesian War and the War of the Roses or between World War I and World War II, but the patterns of human fears and anxieties and perceptions of threat and injury may not be dissimilar. A fundamental part of the problem lies in identifying the levels of abstraction where likenesses can be found between problems or events that are widely separated in time and also in space.

For example, if the leaders of State A (correctly or incorrectly) perceive that State B is posing a threat, there is a strong possibility that they will initiate hostile "defensive" activity. If the leaders of State B then (correctly) perceive this hostile behavior on the part of A, it is likely that B, too, will behave with ("defensive") hostility. This threatening behavior of State B will soon endow A's perceptions of threat with further "reality," whereupon A's leaders will further increase hostile "defensive" activities. From that point forward the perceptual exchanges between the two parties—whether they live in ancient Greece or mid-twentieth-century Europe or Asia or the Americas—are likely to become more and more emotional, or "affective," and less and less "reasoned" in their content. With time the exchange of hostile perceptions and threats may give rise to exchanges of lethal strikes—whether with swords, spears, crossbows, cannon balls, or nuclear missiles.

There are important advantages in using historical situations for this kind of research.

With the whole sweep of human history to choose from, the scholar can select situations where the archives are open and the documents are relatively numerous, complete, and illuminating. Clearly, in view of security restrictions, it is impossible to obtain materials of this quality in a more contemporary situation. We are almost compelled to turn toward history, then, in our major attempts at developing a theory of international behavior.

Beyond this, historical situations offer the advantages of an algebra book with the answers in the back. A scholar thus enjoys the possibility of working at a problem—even making a prediction—and comparing his "answer" with the way things really turned out. In this way he can compare in minutest detail what statesmen have said with what they have actually done—and determine what perceptions have shaped their decisions.

It is also feasible, by adapting the same data, to play simulations against archival records, thus combining history with laboratory (or near laboratory) technique. For example, a Northwestern University research team recently used mathematically controlled simulations to play groups of live decision-makers against the events which led to the outbreak of war in 1914. By using a psychological test, the investigators divided their subjects into separate groups—one group that more or less matched the personalities who made major decisions in the 1914 crisis, and one group that did not match. Each group was divided into decision-making teams to correspond with leadership roles in major European capitals nearly five decades earlier, and then placed in semilaboratory situations analogous to 1914. As simulated events unfolded, the subjects received historical messages which had been "masked" so that items revealing the particular crisis would be suitably camouflaged. After the two separate groups had worked their way through the crisis simulation, their own records were subjected to the same processes of content analysis that had been used on documents from the outbreak of World War I. In this particular case study, a significant similarity emerged between the real actors of 1914 and the psychologically matched simulation teams. The nonmatched teams found other ways of handling their conflicts: they negotiated, called a conference, and avoided war (Hermann and Hermann, 1962).

Many more case studies must be completed before conclusions can be drawn, but such experiments open a whole new range of possible ways for linking history with the present and for closing at least a part of the gap between the abstractions of simulations and game theory on the one hand, and behavior in the real world on the other hand.

There is a further important consideration. In fact, history of one sort or another provides the sole key we have into the future: "The only way to judge what will happen in the future is by what has happened in the past" (Horst, 1963, p. 12).

Wisdom about the present and future is derived wholly from what we have experienced—or learned about—in the past. It is by comparing new problems with old experiences, by looking for similarities and differences, that we move into the future. "Other things being equal, the more frequently things have happened in the past, the more sure you can be they will happen in the future" (Horst, 1963, p. 12). As human beings without occult prevision we have no other way of assessing, judging, and deciding.

Essentially, then, it is by projecting past experience into the future that human beings make decisions, and statesmen, in this respect, are not exceptions. Thus, foreign-policy decisions, like other human decisions, imply not only an abstraction from history, but also the making of a "prediction," the assessment of probable outcomes. These two operations may be undertaken almost unconsciously, but they are nonetheless real and inescapable. The Marshall Plan was based upon a prediction, derived from some combination of experience, that systematic aid to European nations would bring about certain consequences. Viewed in retrospect, this prediction seems to have been generally sound. The basic prediction inherent in Khrushchev's decision to establish long-range missiles in Cuba was much less accurate.

There is nothing magic in this kind of prediction. Even the weatherman is correct only a part of the time, and international politics, being human, is considerably more perverse than the weather. Prediction depends always upon knowledge, and knowledge is necessarily an offspring of the past. This principle is basic, not only to science, but to all knowledge, and herein lies the crucial importance of history, in one form or another, to all the social sciences.

The weeks just prior to the outbreak of war in 1914 offer a particularly useful laboratory for studying the behavior of states, the processes of international conflict, and the escalation of limited war into major war. Embedded in archival data lies something close to a prototype of crisis against which a contemporary crisis—or future crisis—can be measured profitably.

II

The Archduke Francis Ferdinand, heir apparent to the throne of Austria-Hungary, was assassinated June 28, 1914, in Sarajevo by a young Serbian nationalist. Within a week Imperial Germany had promised "blank-check" support of the Vienna government in an action which was perceived as likely to eventuate in a "localized war" against Serbia. On July 23 the Austro-Hungarians presented Serbia with an ultimatum, and five days later Vienna declared war against its neighbor.

On July 29, the day following the declaration of war, Imperial Russia—acting to support a small, fellow-Slav nation and to "deter" Austria-Hungary—ordered, and then cancelled, a general mobilization. Efforts were made to shape a mobilization clearly directed against Austria-Hungary, but technical difficulties intervened, and on July 30 St. Petersburg reversed its decision in favor of general mobilization—in spite of German warnings and misgivings.

The Berlin government then proclaimed a "state of threatening danger of war" on July 31 and dispatched to St. Petersburg a twelve-hour ultimatum which demanded a cessation of Russian preparations on the German frontier. On the following day Germany ordered mobilization, and at 7:00 P.M. declared war on Russia, who had not replied to Berlin's ultimatum.

Foreseeing a two-front war, prosecuted from the east by Russia and from the west by France, the Berlin government tried to gain an initial advantage by invading Luxemburg and demanding permission of Belgium to cross Belgian territory. On August 3 Germany declared war against France, and the following day Great Britain declared war against Germany. Within three weeks what began as a local Balkan dispute had exploded into a major European war, and in the years that followed a large part of the world became involved. When the fighting finally stopped in the latter part of 1918, the Austro-Hungarian Empire was in dissolution and Imperial Germany was on the edge of collapse.

Essentially, then, the summer of 1914 provided two wars: a war between Austria-Hungary and Serbia, which most European statesmen of the time hoped to keep localized, and a major "world war," which escalated from the smaller conflict in spite of widespread intentions.

Like many historical situations, the crisis culminating in World War I has been studied for a multitude of purposes. Early studies were largely characterized by single-minded searches for a culprit or culprits upon whom to lay full blame for the war. Among the most important of these were the analyses made by Lenin and Hitler, each of whom was using history in order to support the necessity for activist political movements. Whatever the shortcomings of their analyses in terms of scientific objectivity, their practical effect cannot be denied; our present world has been shaped in large part by the movements led by Lenin and Hitler.

As archives containing the documentary evidence were opened and the passions aroused by the war subsided, historians searching for scapegoats were largely superseded by the work of historians who were more concerned with determining "what really happened" rather than "who was to blame." Here the work of Sydney B. Fay (1928) and Luigi Albertini (1953) stands out.

Finally, the events of 1914 have been investigated with purposes of determining the patterns of behavior of decision-makers in crisis (Abel, 1941; Russett, 1962). The remainder of the present chapter illustrates this use of history. Specifically, how can the 1914 crisis be used to test the hypothesis that the knowledge of inferior capabilities may fail to deter if perceptions of injury are great enough?

It was postulated in a pilot study of June-August 1914 by content analysis that *a state will not go to war* (ie., commit aggression or allow itself to be drawn into an avoidable war) *if it perceives its power* (or the power of its coalition) *as "significantly" less than that of the enemy at the time that such a decision must be made* (Zinnes, North, and Koch, 1961, p. 470).

The assumption underlying this hypothesis is that states commit aggression—or allow themselves to be drawn into a war that could be avoided—only when they have assessed the outcome as minimally favorable. On the other hand, a confrontation of superior force, if accurately perceived, will serve to deter the weaker state. An empirical testing of this hypothesis with data from the summer of 1914 required the formulation of the following special case:

> If a state's perception of injury (or frustration, dissatisfaction, hostility, tension, or threat) to itself is sufficiently great, this perception will render perceptions of insufficient capability much less important a factor in a decision to go to war. Under such circumstances a state may go to war even though it perceives its power as relatively weak (Zinnes, North, and Koch, 1961, p. 470).

Historical evidence revealed that Germany perceived itself as seriously unprepared for war in 1914 and essentially incapable of prosecuting a major armed conflict against other leading powers without risking national disaster. Why, then, did the Kaiser and his colleagues allow Germany to be drawn into World War I? Under what circumstances, or by what processes, did Germany's perception of injury (or frustration, dissatisfaction, hostility, tension, or threat) to itself become "sufficiently" great to offset perceptions of insufficient capability?

III

The data used in analyzing the 1914 crisis included all verbatim documents of unquestioned authenticity authored by key decision-makers in Austria-Hungary, Germany, Great Britain, France, and Russia. Key decision-makers—of which three to six men were selected for each state —are those who, by virtue of their positions, were able to commit the resources of the state in the pursuit of foreign-policy goals. The documents yielded over five thousand *perceptions.*

It will be recalled that the leaders of State A and State B in the basic-conflict model acted on the basis of *what they perceived* and not necessarily on the basis of what was "actually" happening. Thus, it was possible that the leaders of State A might perceive themselves threatened by State B whereas, in fact, B harbored an entirely different intent.

To encompass possibilities of this kind it is convenient to use the *perception* as a basic unit for counting and for scaling by intensity along a variety of dimensions. This unit is abstracted from primary documents of state in terms of the following elements: *the perceiving party or actor; the perceived party or actor; the action or attitude element; and the target party or actor.*

Content analysts can be trained to recognize these basic capsule units with a reasonably high degree of consistency, and scalers can be trained to rate them along scales according to intensity. Electronic computers can also be programmed to recognize, retrieve, count, and even scale these perceptions, provided certain basic subscript identifiers have been added to the documentary text (Stone *et al.*, 1962, Holsti, 1963).

Depending upon its content, the text of each perception is placed in categories such as hostility, friendship, frustration, satisfaction, and so on. After masking, the perceptions within each category are rated for intensity of expression by a series of judges on a scale of 1 to 9, using the Q-Sort method (Block, 1961).

In order to satisfy the special case of the deterrence hypothesis, three requirements must be met. First, the failure of superior forces to deter must be shown. The culmination of the crisis in a general European war satisfies this condition. Second, knowledge of inferior forces must be ascribed to one of the parties. The pilot study of the 1914 crisis showed that top German decision-makers were fully cognizant of Germany's inability successfully to wage a general European war in 1914 (Zinnes, North, and Koch, 1961). Finally, it must be shown that the same leaders perceived themselves to be the victims of injury during the course of the crisis which led to the outbreak of war.

A systematic scaling of the 1914 data reveals that for each of the major participants—and therefore for the system as a whole—perceptions of hostility rose markedly from the time of the assassination of Francis Ferdinand up to the outbreak of hostilities.[1] (See Figure 1.)

The finding that perceptions of hostility showed a marked rise is hardly surprising in itself. Figure 1 does suggest, however, that the actual unfolding of events is accurately reflected in the "profile" of crisis as revealed through the analysis of the verbal behavior of decision-makers.

In order to test our hypothesis it is necessary to distinguish between two aspects of hostility: that which the decision-makers of State A express toward State B (State A as the *agent* of hostility), and that of which the leaders of State A perceive themselves to be the recipient (State A as the *target* of hostility). Perceptions of friendship may similarly be divided into the decision-maker's perceptions of his nation as the *agent* of friendship and the *target* of friendship.

The term *perception of injury* may now be operationalized in terms of two components:

1. Perceptions of a hostile environment in which decision-makers regard their own nation to be primarily the target rather than the agent of hostility. On the basis of this definition an "index of persecution" may be expressed as:

$$\frac{Units \ of \ hostility \ as \ target}{Units \ of \ hostility \ as \ agent}$$

---

[1] The time periods in Figures 1 and 2 were determined by the amount of data rather than by calendar time in order to insure an adequate number of perceptions for each period.

INTENSITY

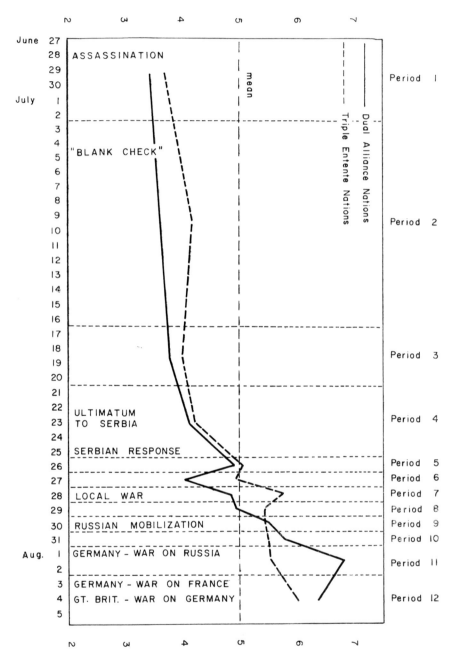

FIGURE 1   PERCEIVED HOSTILITY

A unit of hostility is defined here as the product of the *frequency* and the *mean intensity* of perceived hostility.

2. Perceptions of an unsupportive environment in which decision-makers view the policies of their nation to be friendly toward other nations, but in which at the same time they regard that friendship to be unreciprocated. An "index of rejection" or unrequited affection, similar to the index of persecution, may be expressed as:

$$\frac{Units\ of\ friendship\ as\ agent}{Units\ of\ friendship\ as\ target}$$

The unit of friendship, like that of hostility, is the product of the frequency and the mean intensity of perceptions of friendship.

The results of the coding and scaling of the 1914 documents reveal that the decision-makers of each major power in the crisis felt their own nation to be the undeserved victim of a hostile environment. (See Table 1.)

Three of the five major participants in the events of 1914 (Austria-Hungary, Germany, and France) felt themselves to be primarily the target rather than the agent of hostility. For the system as a whole the nations involved perceived more than twice as much hostility—as measured by both frequency and intensity—directed toward themselves as they directed toward other nations.

The results for perceptions of friendship are even more conclusive. Decision-makers for each of the five major powers regarded themselves as predominantly the agents of friendship, a friendship which was not reciprocated.

The results for both perceptions of hostility and friendship are combined in Table 2. The "index of injury," combining both the index of persecution and the index of rejection, is calculated by the formula: [2]

$$\frac{Units\ of\ hostility\ as\ target\ +\ units\ of\ friendship\ as\ agent}{Units\ of\ hostility\ as\ agent\ +\ units\ of\ friendship\ as\ target}$$

Were these perceptions of injury accurate? In a sense the question is beside the point, for if the Kaiser believed that England, Russia, and France were preparing a "war of extermination against Germany," [3] *and*

---

[2] The "index of injury" might also be used as an "index of paranoia." For a somewhat different technique of identifying paranoic actors in the system through content analysis, see Boulding (1959).

[3] In one of his marginal notes, the Kaiser wrote, "England, Russia, and France have agreed among themselves—after laying the foundations of the *casus foederis* for us through Austria—to take the Austro-Serbian conflict for an excuse for waging a war of extermination against us" (Underlining the Kaiser's) (Montgelas and Schucking, 1924, p. 350).

TABLE 1

PERCEIVER	AGENT OF HOSTILITY			TARGET OF HOSTILITY			INDEX OF PERSE-CUTION
	No. of Percep-tions	Mean Inten-sity	Units of Hos-tility	No. of Percep-tions	Mean Inten-sity	Units of Hos-tility	
Austria-Hungary	81	4.17	338.69	190	4.40	835.34	2.47
Germany	66	5.63	371.32	125	6.41	799.63	2.25
Great Britain	22	4.28	94.35	9	6.23	55.99	0.60
France	6	7.00	41.99	39	6.65	258.31	6.30
Russia	13	5.20	67.67	8	5.04	40.33	0.59
Totals	188	4.86	914.02	371	5.36	1989.60	2.18

PERCEIVER	AGENT OF FRIENDSHIP			TARGET OF FRIENDSHIP			INDEX OF REJEC-TION
	No. of Percep-tions	Mean Inten-sity	Units of Friend-ship	No. of Percep-tions	Mean Inten-sity	Units of Friend-ship	
Austria-Hungary	55	5.29	291.50	32	5.40	173.50	1.69
Germany	87	5.52	480.50	19	5.03	99.00	5.04
Great Britain	49	5.20	255.00	11	5.00	55.00	4.63
France	44	4.75	209.00	23	5.69	131.50	1.59
Russia	24	4.76	114.50	3	6.17	18.50	6.20
Totals	259	5.21	1350.50	88	5.40	474.00	2.84

if he acted upon that assumption, then this circumstance endowed his perception with a "reality" quite apart from what the real intentions of the Triple Entente powers may have been. Yet it may be instructive to ask how the other participants in these events—both allies and prospective enemies—viewed each other's situations. Austria-Hungary, for example, perceived itself to be the victim of undeserved injury at the hands of Serbia and Russia. Did Germany share Austria-Hungary's view in this regard? Did the nations of the Triple Entente? In all cases nations viewed *themselves* as the victims of injury, but regarded their *political enemies*

TABLE 2

	1	2	3	4	col. 2 + col. 3 / col. 1 + col. 4
PERCEIVER	AGENT OF HOSTILITY	TARGET OF HOSTILITY	AGENT OF FRIENDSHIP	TARGET OF FRIENDSHIP	INDEX OF INJURY
Austria-Hungary	338.69	835.34	291.50	173.50	2.21
Germany	371.32	799.63	480.50	95.50	2.73
Great Britain	94.35	55.99	255.00	55.00	2.07
France	41.99	258.31	209.00	131.50	2.70
Russia	67.67	40.33	114.50	18.50	1.80
Totals	914.02	1989.60	1350.50	474.00	2.40

as primarily the targets of friendship and agents of hostility. More significantly, in no case did even a nation's allies share to the full degree that nation's sense of injury. (See Table 3.)

A comparison of self-perceptions (Table 2) with the judgments of other nations (Table 3) reveals that, without exception, the decision-makers of State A failed to see State B as the victim of injury to the degree felt by the decision-makers of State B. One can only speculate on how the course of events might have been changed had leaders in the various capitals of Europe been able to judge more accurately the "bind" in which their counterparts in other nations felt themselves to be caught.

Finally, we may ask whether this sense of injury felt by each of the major powers increased during the course of the crisis. In other words, is there evidence that this sense of injury was cumulative and that, as the crisis wore on, decision-makers in Berlin, Vienna, St. Petersburg, London, and Paris felt themselves increasingly pushed into a corner by hostile neighbors? Firsthand accounts strongly suggest that, after the initial shock of the assassination, crisis-hardened diplomats did not on the whole regard the events in the Balkans as being serious. Few appeared to expect anything more destructive than a localized war of the type that had broken out so frequently in that region. Oddly enough, the nearly senile Emperor Francis Joseph of Austria-Hungary was one of the few who gave some indication of foreseeing the probable course of events. After the Kaiser had granted Austria-Hungary the "blank check," he remarked, "now we can no longer turn back. It will be a terrible war." The reaction of Sir Arthur Nicolson, British Undersecretary of State for Foreign Affairs, was more typical: "I have my doubts as to whether Austria will take any

TABLE 3

		1	2	3	4	col. 2 + col. 3
						col. 1 + col. 4
				AGENT OF	TARGET OF	
		AGENT OF	TARGET OF	FRIEND-	FRIEND-	INDEX OF
PERCEIVER	PERCEIVED	HOSTILITY	HOSTILITY	SHIP	SHIP	INJURY
Germany	Austria-Hungary	320.27	409.98	76.00	243.00	0.86
Triple Entente*	Austria-Hungary	700.33	232.34	12.50	117.00	0.30
Austria-Hungary	Germany	22.66	9.37	97.50	57.50	1.33
Triple Entente	Germany	548.89	165.01	127.50	111.50	0.49
France and Russia	Great Britain	17.33	3.33	58.00	135.00	0.40
Dual Alliance **	Great Britain	75.66	19.00	79.00	25.00	0.98
Great Britain and Russia	France	3.33	46.34	60.50	57.00	1.77
Dual Alliance	France	538.29	117.01	40.50	50.00	0.27
Great Britain and France	Russia	109.64	89.67	187.00	195.50	0.91
Dual Alliance	Russia	583.97	244.63	90.00	158.00	0.45

* France, Russia, Great Britain.
** Austria-Hungary, Germany.

action of serious character and I expect the storm will blow over." [4]

In the latter days of the crisis, however, the pressures became almost unbearable. The usually confident and swaggering Kaiser appears to have undergone an almost complete personality change during the critical night of July 29-30. His marginal notes from that time on reveal a man who felt himself desperately pushed into a corner and no longer the

---

[4] The Russian Minister of War wrote that as late as July 27, Tsar Nicholas showed no awareness of anything "that might affect in any way the peaceful life of Russia" (Taylor, 1963, pp. 209, 222).

master of his destiny—or of the destiny of his nation.[5] The eyewitness reports of close confidants support this view. Bulow later wrote, "Wilhelm II did not want war. He feared it. His bellicose marginal notes prove nothing. . . ." Admiral Tirpitz graphically illustrated the impact of the crisis on Wilhelm. "I have never seen a more tragic, more ravaged face than that of our Emperor during those days" (Taylor, 1963, pp. 219, 228).

The content analysis of documents for the period—probing below the level of literal, dictionary meanings of official texts—reveals much the same picture. Figure 2, in which the "index of injury" for all five major powers is plotted against the actual course of events, reveals two major peaks which correspond to the two phases of the crisis—the local war in the Balkans between Austria and Serbia, and the general war involving all five major powers.

More significant, perhaps, is the finding that each nation (through the nervous systems of its key decision-makers) most strongly felt itself to be the victim of injury precisely at that time when its leaders were making policy decisions of the most crucial nature. Table 4, in which the "index of perceived injury" is calculated for each of the nations involved for that period in which its most crucial decisions were made, reveals the intensity of this sense of injury, even when compared from the vantage point of the crisis as a whole.

TABLE 4

PERCEIVER	DATES OF "CRUCIAL PERIOD"	INDEX OF INJURY "CRUCIAL PERIOD"	INDEX OF INJURY JUNE 27–AUGUST 4
Austria-Hungary	July 17–July 25	4.08	2.21
Germany	July 30–Aug. 5	2.70	2.73
Great Britain	Aug. 3–Aug. 5	2.43	2.07
France	Aug. 1–Aug. 2	9.53	2.70
Russia	July 30–Aug. 2	1.70	1.80
Totals		2.97	2.40

[5] Only a few days earlier the still confident Kaiser, when informed of the contents of Austria's ultimatum to Serbia, remarked, "A spirited note, what?" (Taylor, 1963, p. 214) Compare this reaction with his later marginal notes, especially in documents 368 and 401 of the Kautsky collection (Montgelas and Schucking, 1924, pp. 322, 349-350).

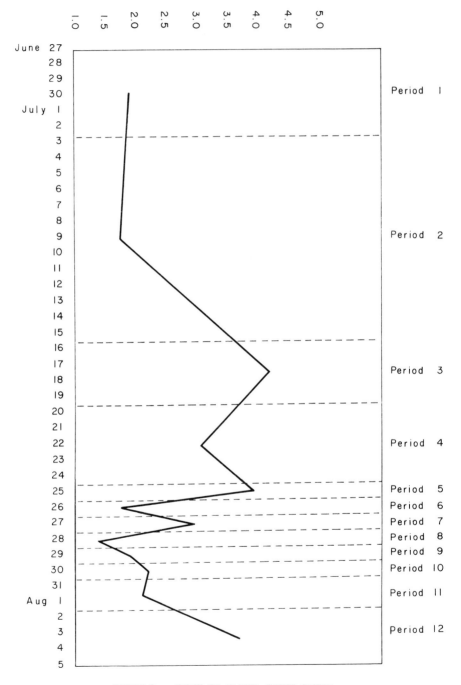

FIGURE 2   INDEX OF INJURY—ENTIRE SYSTEM

IV

Theodore Abel, in his analysis of decisions to go to war—including the case of 1914—concluded, ". . . in no case is the decision precipitated by emotional tensions, sentimentality, crowd behavior, or other irrational motivations" (1941, p. 855). The evidence presented here strongly supports the contrary hypothesis: *Perceptions of inferior capability, if perceptions of anxiety, fear, threat, or injury are great enough, will fail to deter a nation from going to war.*[6]

The Kaiser's desperate reaction to the events which were engulfing him—perhaps best characterized by his assertion that "if we are to bleed to death, England shall at least lose India" (Montgelas and Schucking, 1924, p. 350)—is the reaction of a decision-maker under such severe stress that any action is preferable to the burden of the sustained tension. The sharp drop in the mean intensity of perceived hostility by German leaders after the decision to gamble on war (Figure 1) suggests how that crucial action, the long-range consequences of which were disastrous, provided an immediate relief from the tension—however brief the respite.

The Kaiser's reaction in the face of an adversary's greater capabilities—a reaction strikingly similar to instances in the Peloponnesian Wars, the wars between Spain and England during the sixteenth century, and the Japanese decision to strike Pearl Harbor—are not unrelated to the dilemmas of our own age of missiles and nuclear warheads. These findings underscore the need for re-examining that "common sense" and almost irresistible "conventional wisdom" which argues that deterrence is merely a matter of piling up more and better weapons than the opponent can amass.

Do the events of the summer of 1914 conform to the basic-conflict model described earlier? Does the model provide insights which help in understanding the escalation of a local incident into a general war? The answer would appear to be yes, with some qualifications.

World War I was not originally a conflict between two monolithic and mutually antagonistic blocs. Initially State A and State B did not correspond to the Triple Alliance (termed Dual Alliance in this study inasmuch as Italy did not enter the war—to join the Entente powers—until 1915) and the Triple Entente. Rather, the initial spiralling of tensions, of perceived threats and counterthreats, occurred within a series of lower-level relationships. Serbia and Austria-Hungary had been linked in such

---

[6] The present study appears to support Bruce M. Russett's assumption that "the outbreak of war, at least on a scale involving several major powers, was an accident rather than the result of a deliberate aggressor's plot" (1962, p. 4). This does not preclude the possibility of "accident proneness."

a situation well before the assassination of Francis Ferdinand. That act of violence was only one of a series of events which led to the outbreak of local war between them. Russia and Germany, which had made binding commitments to Serbia and Austria-Hungary respectively, were similarly linked. For a variety of reasons Russia was unable to make clear to Germany its intention to aid Serbia without attacking Germany. The Kaiser's reaction not only brought Russia into conflict on a larger scale by triggering off the "unalterable" Schlieffen Plan,[7] but Wilhelm also extended the war to Western Europe. Thus France and Great Britain, hardly more than bystanders in the early phases of the crisis, and neither of which had made clear its position, were drawn in.[8]

Thus, like a series of separate eddies, the various nations were at first linked in a number of local situations as described by the conflict model. But as eddies, when they come in contact, form a whirlpool, so the major powers of Europe were drawn into a general conflict which none had desired and few had even foreseen, at least consciously.

In conclusion, it should be pointed out, the present example only illustrates rather than exhausts what is capable of being tested in historical situations such as the 1914 crisis. If international relations is to attain some of the predictive powers which characterize a mature science, it will be the result of systematic analyses of history (as well as of ongoing events and of laboratory simulations) which enable investigators to develop both the general theory and the analytical tools with which to cope with the future.

REFERENCES

Abel, Theodore, "The Element of Decision in the Pattern of War," *American Sociological Review*, VI (1941), 853-859.

Albertini, Luigi, *The Origins of the War of 1914*. New York: Oxford University Press, 1953.

---

[7] To the Kaiser's last-minute hopes of a single-front war ("Now we can go to war against Russia only. We simply march the whole of our Army to the East"), Moltke replied, "Your Majesty, it cannot be done. The deployment of millions cannot be improvised. If your majesty insists on leading the whole army to the East it will not be an army ready for battle but a disorganized mob of armed men with no arrangements for supply. Those arrangements took a whole year of intricate labor to complete and once settled, it cannot be altered" (Tuchman, 1962, pp. 78-79).

[8] "After eight years as Foreign Secretary in a period of chronic 'Bosnias,' as Bulow called them, [Sir Edward] Grey had perfected a manner of speaking designed to convey as little meaning as possible; his avoidance of the point-blank, said a colleague, almost amounted to a method. Over the telephone, Lichnowsky, himself dazed by the coming tragedy, would have no difficulty misunderstanding him" (Tuchman, 1962, pp. 77-78).

Block, Jack, *The Q-Sort Method in Personality Assessment and Psychiatric Research*. Springfield, Ill.: Charles C Thomas, Publisher, 1961.

Boulding, Kenneth E., "National Images and International Systems," *Journal of Conflict Resolution*, III (1959), 120-131.

Fay, Sidney B., *The Origins of the World War*. New York: The Macmillan Company, 1928.

Hermann, Charles, and Margaret Hermann, "On the Possible Use of Historical Data for Validation Study of Inter-Nation Simulation." Prepared under Contract N123 (60530) 2875 A for U.S. Naval Ordnance Test Station, Northwestern University, 1962.

Holsti, Ole R., "Working Papers on Computer Content Analysis." Stanford, 1963. Mimeographed.

Horst, Paul, *Matrix Algebra for Social Scientists*. New York: Holt, Rinehart & Winston, Inc., 1963.

Montgelas, Max and Walther Schucking, eds. *Outbreak of the World War: German Documents Collected by Karl Kautsky*. New York: Oxford University Press, 1924.

Russett, Bruce M., "Cause, Surprise, and No Escape," *Journal of Politics*, XXIV (1962), 3-32.

Stone, Philip J., Robert F. Bales, J. Zwi Nemenwirth, and Daniel M. Ogilvie, "The General Inquirer: A Computer System for Content Analysis and Retrieval Based on the Sentence as a Unit of Information," *Behavioral Science*, VII (1962), 484-497.

Taylor, Edmund, *The Fall of the Dynasties*. Garden City, N.Y.: Doubleday & Company, Inc., 1963.

Tuchman, Barbara, *The Guns of August*. New York: The Macmillan Company, 1962.

Zinnes, Dina A., Robert C. North, and Howard E. Koch, Jr., "Capability, Threat, and the Outbreak of War," *International Politics and Foreign Policy*, James N. Rosenau, ed. New York: Free Press of Glencoe, Inc., 1961.

CHAPTER

9

The Economics of Human Conflict

KENNETH E. BOULDING

Sociologist Jessie Bernard distinguishes between two kinds of conflict, conflicts which are *about* something on the one hand which she calls *issue conflicts* and conflicts which are in some sense illusory, which are not really about anything, but which are simply developed out of dynamic reactions or misunderstandings. Most people would probably regard economic conflicts as falling into the first category. When we think of conflicts which are about something, we think of situations in which if A gets more, B gets less. Conflicts about land, about money, about the ownership of commodities, about the terms of exchange, and the like seem to most people to be about something. The fundamental characteristic of an issue conflict is that there should be scarcity of some desired resource or good, in the sense that what I have sometimes facetiously called the *Duchess's Law*—after its classic statement in Alice in Wonderland, "the more there is of yours, the less there is of mine"—dominates the situation. Scarcity, however, is the peculiar province of the economist and hence we would not be surprised to find concepts of conflict at the very center of economics. Only where there is scarcity in the economists' sense can there be issue conflicts, for the only thing that conflicts can rationally be about is the distribution between two or more parties of some good which is both scarce and valued.

There are, however, two kinds of issue conflicts, those which arise out of the use of threats and those which arise out of exchange. With the first kind, economists have not been much concerned. When an armed robber accosts you with "your money or your life," though this may look superficially like an exchange it is fundamentally a very different system. It is certainly an issue conflict. If you give him your money there is a redistribution of economic goods, for he has more and you have less. This is, however, at best a zero-sum game (his gain equals your loss), and insofar as the actual robbery diverts both the parties from productive activities or produces disutilities it is a negative-sum game in which there is a redistribution of a diminished total. This problem, however, we can leave to the political scientists and concentrate on the kind of conflicts which arise out of uncoerced exchange. Here we find a curious paradox. Exchange is a positive-sum game in the sense that it will not take place unless both parties feel themselves to be better off. On the other hand there is clearly a conflict about the distribution of the larger utility product which results. The product in this case has to be measured in some kind of utilities and the difficulty involved in making interpersonal comparisons of utility prevents us from expressing it as a cardinal number. It is clear, however, that while there is a community of interest between the two parties in the *fact* of exchange in the sense that both parties would be worse off if the exchange does not take place, there is conflict of interest in the *terms* of the exchange, that is, in the price or the exchange ratio at which the exchange takes place. Let us suppose, for instance, that A is selling wheat and B is buying it for money. There is some price of wheat below which A will not sell because he prefers the wheat he has to the money which he might get for it. Similarly there is some price of wheat above which B will not buy because he prefers the money which he has to the wheat which he might get for it. At any price between these two prices the exchange is profitable to both parties. The distribution of the gains from the trade, however, depends on whether the price is high or low within this range. If the price is at the lower limit, A gains practically nothing and B has all the gains from the trade. If the price is at the upper limit B gains practically nothing and A has all the gains from the trade. As the price moves from the lower to the upper limit, therefore, A's share of the total gains from the trade increases and B's diminishes. Many of the peculiarities of the exchange relationship and the bargaining situation arise because of this ambivalence.

In a typical bargaining situation, we suppose that we can move from a state of the world X, before the bargain, to a number of states of the world, after the bargain Y_1, Y_2, and so forth, so that within the range of bargaining terms and the movement from X to any of the Y's means that both parties are better off. The bargaining process, however, involves deciding which one of the Y's to move to and this decision may be very difficult—so difficult in fact that it may not be arrived at and both parties stay at X where they are both worse off than in any of the Y's. Wars, strikes, and divorces frequently, although not always, represent situations of this kind, where the parties fail to accomplish a positive-sum game or even worse get themselves into negative-sum games because of the inability to decide on the terms of a bargain which would be profitable to both parties.

The various relationships involved in economic conflict can be illustrated by a simple diagram (Figure 1). In this we suppose two parties, A and B, and we measure A's welfare horizontally and B's welfare vertically. The measure of welfare we leave up to question; it may be meas-

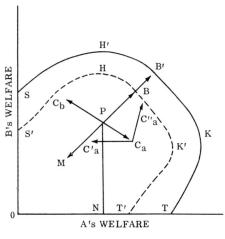

FIGURE 1

ured in dollars or in more subtle units of utility. To any given state of the world there corresponds a point in this field; at the point P, for instance, A's welfare is ON, B's welfare NP. A change in the state of the world is likely to change the position of P in the welfare field. Such a change is called a *move*. Not all changes in the state of the world will change the position in the welfare field, for there may be a number of different states of the world each corresponding to the point P. A change in the welfare-field position, however, always signifies a change in the state of the world. Four cases may be noted. A move in the generally northeasterly direction, such as from P to B, is what I have called a *benign* move, in which both parties increase their welfare. The opposite is a move in the southwesterly direction, such as PM in which both parties become worse off, and is a *malign* move. Moves in a southeasterly or northwesterly direction are "conflict" moves in which one party is getting better off and the other is getting worse off. Thus a move from P to C_b is a conflict move with B getting better off and A getting worse off. A move from P to C_a is a conflict move with A getting better off and B getting worse off.

Benign moves can originate in a number of ways. They may originate by an agreement among the parties. This is necessary if the change from state of the world X (yielding P in the field of Figure 1) to state of the world Y (yielding B in Figure 1) can only be accomplished by prearranged and concerted action. When one man sells a house to another, for instance, there must be agreement on the price between the two parties before the transaction can be completed. If two men are going to cut down a tree with a crosscut saw there must be at least a tacit agreement between them on a mutual course of action and the way each is going to react to the action of the other. In a disarmament treaty each nation agrees with the other what course of action it shall pursue in order to achieve a mutually agreed end. Agreement, however, is not the only avenue to a benign move. This is fortunate because agreement is often very difficult, and if men had to agree before anything could be done, not very much would be done. A special case of a benign move is a *trading move* in which uncoerced exchange takes place between two parties. This is benign because, as we have seen, it will not take place unless both parties feel that they benefit at the time of the decision. There are problems which arise out of erroneous or fraudulent exchanges where one or both of the parties decide at some future date that the exchange was not worthwhile and should not have taken place. These will be discussed later. A trading move can be initiated without formal agreement by one party who sets up what might be called a *trading opportunity*. In exchange, for instance, one party may publish his intent and willingness to exchange at a stated price. The bulk of exchanges in our society are in fact accomplished by this means. We do not bargain about most prices. The storekeeper sets a price on the good which is as it were a declaration that he is willing to sell the good at this price, and the customer is free to take it or leave it. If the customer takes it and an exchange is consummated, exchangeables, usually money and goods, are redistributed among the parties in such a way as to make all parties feel better off, at least at the moment of the exchange. In the language of strategic science, when the storekeeper sets a price upon the good he takes a unilateral initiative and he leaves it up to the potential customer to respond, or not to respond, as he wishes. In simple bilateral exchange there may be a whole series of initiatives of this kind, and a succession of unilaterally initiated trading moves are performed by the parties in turn. Thus, suppose we return to our two parties, A, who has wheat, and B, who has money. Let us suppose that A announces a price at which he is willing to sell in unlimited quantities, and at this price B is willing to buy so much and no more. That is, B buys a quantity such that any increase in purchases would not be worthwhile to him in the sense that the increase in his holdings of wheat would not be worth to him the decrease in his holdings of money. At this point if the price remains constant, exchange will stop. A may still wish to continue exchange (sell), for he may still feel that the increase in his money stock at this point is worth the wheat that he would give up. If B is unwilling, however, A is powerless to increase his sales. This time, however, A may take a further initiative in altering the terms at which he is offering to sell. If he lowers his price, B may take more, and so the process may go on. A succession of trading moves, however, tends to exhaust the possibility of further trading moves and eventually lands the parties on what the economists have called the *contract curve* or what I have more generally called the *conflict set*. From such a point we can move either to another state of the world in which both or all parties are worse off, that is, in terms of Figure 1, a malign move; or we can move to a state of the world in which one party is better off and the other party is worse off; or more generally in which some parties are better off and some parties are worse off; that is, a conflict move. Where a number of related parties are on the conflict set, exchange is no longer capable of organizing or resolving the conflict. In terms of the economic abstraction the solution of the problem is indeterminate, and if a determinate solution is to be found it must be in other systems of analysis such as the analysis of threat systems, or perhaps rhetorical systems by which people persuade each other, bargain, and reach agreement. The important point here is that once we are on the conflict set the repertoire of unilateral initiatives has been exhausted and there is no possibility of moving from where we are to another state of the world except through agreement on the one hand, or threats on the other.

Figure 1 again is useful to illustrate the principles involved. In such a field the conflict set expresses itself as a conflict boundary such as HK beyond which the system cannot go, that is, points representing welfare combinations beyond the boundary are unobtainable in any state of the world which is open to the parties concerned. Benign moves if carried far enough will land the parties in the state of the world which corresponds to a point on the conflict boundary such as B's. From this point only conflict moves such as toward H or K or malign moves towards P are possible. Ordinarily we think of the conflict boundary as possessing a roughly northwesterly or southeasterly direction as between H and K, in which case only conflict moves are possible. It is not impossible, however, for this boundary to be nonlinear and indeed to bend back so that it takes the form such as SHKT. This will be the case where there is a certain amount of empathy between A and B. From H to S, as A's welfare diminishes B's welfare does too, reflecting the fact that B cannot be happy if A is miserable. Similarly between K and T, B's misery makes A more miserable too. From any point between S and H or T and K, it is possible to make benign moves, in spite of the fact that we are on the conflict boundary, simply because each party rejoices in the other's welfare. We know therefore that as long as we confine ourselves to benign processes, these must end up somewhere between H and K; where they end depends on the particular dynamic system itself as we note in the previous paragraph. If A and B are extremely altruistic, the points H and K may move together and coincide. At this point there is only one position of equilibrium of the system at the point of maximum welfare for both parties. As drawn in Figure 1, however, B's maximum welfare is at H and A's at K and on the line HK there is genuine conflict between them, even though they exhibit a certain amount of altruism.

An important principle which is often overlooked is that the parties that have reached a conflict set relevant to a state of the world defined by only a few variables can frequently break the impasse and open up opportunities for further trading and further benign moves by widening the agenda, that is, by introducing new variables into the relationship. We notice this phenomenon, for instance, in collective bargaining in industrial relations where there is a strong tendency to proliferate clauses in the contract, partly at least because this opens up further opportunities for bargaining. An impasse in bargaining about wages and hours may be broken if various other fringe benefits, job security, procedural relationships, and so forth are thrown into the bargaining process. This is a special case of a general proposition, that within the ultimate outermost boundary of the welfare field at SHKT, there may be sub-boundaries such as S'H'K'T' which correspond to a particular state or process of the dynamic relationship between the parties. Thus, S'H'K'T' might be the boundary including all the points in the welfare field which could be reached by unilateral initiative without agreement. The development of skills in agreement, or of a dynamic process which can lead to agreement, will then widen the boundary to SHKT and further benign moves will be possible.

We need to know something about agreement, therefore, and the processes which might lead to it if we are to exploit all possibilities for benign moves. A very simple theory of agreement is outlined in Figure 2. Let us suppose that to fix our ideas we are considering a labor-management bargain about a wage; in Figure 2a wage increases as we move

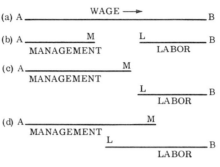

FIGURE 2

from A to B. In Figure 2b labor will agree to any wage above L, management will agree to any wage below M, but M, however, is less than L and
no agreement is possible. Under these circumstances a bargain cannot
be struck; other forces then come into play aimed at changing the positions of M and L. They may be rhetorical forces, and labor may appeal
to cost-of-living indices, to what is happening to other industries; or,
labor may bring out facts and figures to show that management can
easily afford a wage increase. Management likewise will employ rhetoric
to persuade labor to move the point L closer to A. If rhetoric and argument fail there may be a recourse to threats. Labor may threaten to
strike in order to bring M closer to B, management may threaten to lock
out and to bring L closer to A. If the threats do not produce the behavior
they expected, they may have to be carried out. Here, however, both
labor and management may get into a negative-sum game, imposing losses
on each other in order to bring M closer to B or L closer to A. As soon as
the distance between M and L diminishes to zero, a bargain can be struck
as in Figure 2c. The exact position of M and L at this time depends, of
course, on the dynamics of the situation and on the extent to which the
rhetoric or threats have moved M or L. Many of the difficulties in conflict situations arise out of the fact that in the actual division of the spoils
of the bargaining process, victory tends to go to the recalcitrant. On the
other hand, recalcitrance may prevent the accomplishment of the bargain
altogether and may turn the positive-sum game into a negative-sum game.
Recalcitrance, therefore, increases the chance both of gain and of loss.
Which side will be recalcitrant and how much, therefore, depends a great
deal on the relative estimates of gain and of loss. The more fearful of
loss we are, the less recalcitrant we are likely to be and the less our bargaining gain. We are here rapidly getting into game-theoretical considerations which are somewhat outside the boundaries of formal economics,
even though they may be considered a legitimate offspring.

The situation of Figure 2d exhibits some interesting peculiarities. In this case the lines A-M and L-B overlap so that there is a range L-M within which agreement can be obtained. There is nothing in the situation as hereto described, however, which will tell us where the agreement will be obtained, and a great deal depends upon the realism of the perception of the parties. If, for instance, labor realistically appraises the position of management and offers to settle at L', the bargain may be struck at labor's end of the range of mutual benefit. Similarly if management offers to settle at M', labor may accept and in the distribution of the gains of the bargain the bulk goes to management. This illustrates the great importance of social perception in the bargaining process, but this again carries us far beyond the formal boundaries of economics.

We now come to a proposition which is essential in economic theory and which yet has an appearance of paradox: the more perfect competition becomes, the less economic conflict there is. The economist defines perfect competition as a situation in which there are so many buyers and so many sellers, each of whom is free to contract with any other and each of whom has full information about the offers which all the others are making, that no action by any one of them can effect a noticeable difference in the total market situation. Under these circumstances, all transactions at about the same time will take place at about the same price. Any seller who is offering to sell at a price above the others will not find any buyers; any buyer who is offering to buy at a price below the others will not find any sellers. The limits of the bargaining situation under these circumstances are, therefore, very narrowly circumscribed. In terms of Figure 2 two parties which are in a relationship such as Figure 2b are simply not in the market, that is, there is no relationship between them. They are not in effective contact and, therefore, there is no conflict between them. There are always parties in the market who are in the position of Figure 2c and who are, therefore, consummating exchanges. If at the price which is prevailing in the market there is a surplus of offers to sell a series of unilateral initiatives on the part of the sellers, the price will be reduced by a series of very small stages and this in itself will diminish the offers to sell and increase the offers to buy until these once more come to equality. The market itself, therefore, provides as it were the rhetoric and the threats which enable bargains to be consummated simply because any person who is not satisfied with his existing potential partner in exchange can always find another. In the light of the economists' abstraction therefore, economic conflict only arises as a result of either monopoly or monopolistic organization of some kind which limits the number of potential partners with whom to exchange, or, as we shall see later, it arises through immobility of resources.

This proposition may seem surprising to many people who think of economic conflict as something extremely important and pervasive, whereas the economist sees it developed as a result almost of a quirk or defect in the economic system. This is perhaps because the organizing power of the market is so quiet and persistent that it is largely imperceptible. We notice the occasions when the market breaks down, but we do not notice the occasions when it operates successfully. Hence, we tend to attribute to the institution itself phenomena which are essentially associated with its breakdown. This has led to a great deal of the intellectual "flight from the market" which has been so characteristic of socialist and liberal thought in the last 100 years. What people do not generally realize here is the extraordinary pervasive power of unilateral initiatives in economic life, as long as there is reasonable freedom to make them. Because of this it is quite difficult to achieve genuinely long-run conflict moves in the economic system, that is, it is difficult to move the economic system from position X_1 to position X_2 in which one group of people is permanently worse off and another group permanently better off. An economist would argue indeed that this is virtually impossible to do in uncoerced exchange and that it is possible only if we employ either the coercive power of the organized threat systems, or a monopoly of the means of rhetoric and persuasion.

Some illustrations may serve to demonstrate the point. The most convincing case of economic conflict is that of enslavement, where one group of people conquer another and make them their slaves. This is obviously a conflict move in terms of Figure 1; if A are the slavers and B the enslaved, this is a movement from say P to C_a. This is, however, a threat system, not an exchange system. It is a system also with a low developmental horizon. There is no incentive to increase productivity, and, by and large, societies which have been based on slavery have stagnated. The slave has every incentive to work as little as possible and produce as little as he can get away with. The ruling class often becomes corrupt and degenerate and the society moves in directions from C_a to C'_a, where the master as well as the slave gets worse off and the general result is a malign move for all parties.

Karl Marx argued that a similar process of class conflict is likewise a characteristic of the free-market societies which succeeded slave- or serf-based feudal societies. The argument is that even if the worker possesses a property in his own mind and body, so that he sells services to an employer in a labor market and receives in return a money wage, he is still in a position of helpless inferiority in the bargaining process and his real wage therefore will be driven down to a subsistence level not much above that of a slave. The crucial phenomenon here is also a process arising out of a threat system, namely, what Marx calls *primary accumulation*. This is the initial seizure of the nonhuman capital of the society, in the first instance—of course, mainly land—by a small ruling class. This is indeed descriptive of many feudal societies where the ownership of land is based essentially on the coercive power. In the capitalist societies which follow feudalism Marx predicted a sharp class differentiation between the capitalists who owned the nonhuman capital of society and the workers who possess nothing but their own bodies and minds. Under these circumstances the capitalists would be able to force down wages; this is a real conflict process with the workers continually getting worse off and the capitalists getting better off. In the Marxian dynamic this process continues until finally the working class revolts, the newly found coercive power of the proletarian dictators is used to overcome the old coercive power of the ruling class, and again a conflict move results in which the workers benefit and the capitalists lose. Marx seldom contemplates benign moves; in his scheme society seems to oscillate between C_a and C_b. First one class and then another gains the ascendancy.

The Marxist dynamic is, however, a very special case; so special indeed that it is hard to find examples in history in which it really operated. Once slave labor has been abolished and a genuinely free labor market is established, the sheer "positive-sum" aspect of exchange easily transmutes conflict into a benign move. Marx postulated that the working class would remain at subsistence level, and therefore all the increase in the product which resulted from the accumulation of capital and the development of technological progress would accrue to the capitalists. What has happened in fact is that the proportion of the total product going to labor has either remained fairly stable or has even tended to rise, so that in the advanced countries the working classes shared more than proportionally in the increase of total income which has resulted from economic development. This is particularly true of the skilled urban working class. In many countries it has been less true of the rural and peasant class, which has remained relatively stagnant while the rest of the society has advanced, thus creating severe social tensions such as in Cuba. Thus, the Marxist dynamic applies fairly well to conditions of slavery or serfdom, but as soon as anything like a free labor market develops, it is upset simply by the enormous and cumulative positive-sum process which a free market will set up. If a man has a property in his own mind and body, even if he has no property in nonhuman capital, any increase in the value of his mind and body will accrue to him. There is therefore a strong incentive to increase that value by becoming more highly skilled or by going into other occupations which are more rewarding. There are therefore pay-offs for increasing the total product of the society, and the more the total product increases the more benign moves become possible in which everybody is better off. Thus the gradual development of free labor in the Middle Ages seems to have been responsible at least in part for the long, slow improvement of economic life, and once serfdom had been abolished and free labor spread to agriculture, especially free labor in the shape of the farmer with a little capital, economic development accelerated enormously.

The failure of the Marxist predictions regarding the proportion of the total product going to labor underlines the importance for any theory of economic conflict of a satisfactory theory of distribution, especially a theory which will account for the proportional shares of the product going to the various classes, regions, or industrial sectors of the economic system. This is an area, unfortunately, where there is little agreement among economists and where a satisfactory theory still seems a long way off. The most widespread agreement can probably be obtained on the factors which determine the distribution of the total product among different industrial sectors of the economy. It is well recognized that in the course of economic development the proportion of the total product contributed by the various industrial sectors changes radically. Technological development, in agriculture for instance, which increases the productivity of labor in agriculture is likely to result in a fall in the proportion of the labor force engaged in agriculture simply because of the low-income elasticity of demand for agricultural products. Thus, in a society in which the farmer can produce only enough food for himself and one other family, there will be 50 per cent of people in agriculture and 50 per cent in other things. If one farmer can produce food for ten families there will be 10 per cent in agriculture and 90 per cent in other things.

In the course of technological improvement, therefore, the proportion of the population in agriculture has continually declined. In the United States, for instance, it has declined from about 90 per cent at the time of the Revolution to about 10 per cent today, and it is likely to decline even further. Similarly, in the course of technological development many old trades become obsolete and sometimes disappear altogether, like that of the coach-builder or the hand-loom weaver, while new industries, like electronics, arise and grow rapidly. In this process there is, of course, a conflict between the rising industries and the declining industries. Incomes in the rising industries are usually above the average for the society, and incomes in the declining industries are usually below. Agriculture is a particularly good case in point, as incomes in agriculture have averaged well below incomes in the society at large for a very long time. This, however, is almost certainly necessary to the process of adjustment. Unless incomes in the declining industries are below normal the industries will not decline, because people will not move out of them. Unless incomes in the expanding industries are above normal, people will not move into them.

There is a real dilemma here between the claims of social justice, which laments these disparities of income and the claims of economic adjustment, which sees them as strictly necessary. From the point of view of economic conflict, the situation is highly mixed. A technological improvement will create an economic conflict between those who participate in it and who practice it on the one hand and those who continue to practice the obsolescing or declining industry on the other. The rise of machine looms unquestionably worsened the lot of the hand-loom weavers. We can see, therefore, technological progress as in some respects a conflict move which increases the welfare of the people who take advantage of the new technology and diminishes the welfare of those whose activity is in competition with it. If the people are fairly mobile as between occupations, however, the initial conflict easily turns into a benign move. This, again, may be illustrated in the field of Figure 1. In this case let us suppose B represents our hand-loom weavers and A represents the rest of society. The invention of the machine loom is unquestionably a conflict move in this field, again let us say from PC_a. The hand-loom weavers are worse off, but everyone else is better off as a result of the greater plenty of cloth. If, however, the hand-loom weavers are mobile, they will soon get into other occupations which pay better. As they do so, the welfare of the rest of society likewise improves as the one-time hand-loom weavers will now be producing other things for which the society has a greater demand. There is a move, therefore, from C_a to C''_a. The net result of the whole operation is a benign move from P to C''_a.

The possible catch here, of course, is that the labor force in the declining industries may not be mobile. The hand-loom weavers of England themselves took two generations to die, and their agony is one of the grim stories of the industrial revolution. The coal miners of the southern Appalachians linger on in unemployment and poverty, while their more fortunate brethren in the mechanized mines earn high wages. In the absence of mobility, therefore, technological developments can cause very sharp economic conflicts. These conflicts, however, are best resolved not by preventing the technological improvements, but by increasing the mobility which will enable them to bear their full fruit. The case of agriculture again is of peculiar interest. We have had a long period of technological improvement in agriculture, coupled with inadequate mobility out of the occupation. As a result, agricultural incomes have been depressed for a long period of time. The remedy here again, however, is not to prevent the technological improvement nor to subsidize agriculturalists indefinitely through the public treasury, but rather to increase their mobility out of agriculture into more productive occupations. This has been going on at a great rate in the United States, but just not fast enough. Here oddly enough the conflict originates mainly from within agriculture itself. The technological developments in agriculture have mainly come from within the industry, assisted in some measure by the public sector of the economy supporting land-grant colleges and agricultural research and extension. These technological developments have unquestionably benefited most of those even within agriculture who seized upon them first. For those who have lagged technologically, however, and for those who have been squeezed out of agriculture, a very real economic conflict exists.

The distribution of income and, therefore, the conflict among regions follows principles which are not unlike those which govern the conflict among industrial and occupational groups. A region which is strongly attached to a declining industry will itself suffer from the low income which the declining industry produces. A region which is backward technologically will likewise often suffer in competition with those which are more advanced. Regions where the economy is tied to a natural-resource base, such as mining, likewise suffer as the lands become exhausted.

In a world of relatively stationary population the solution of interregional conflicts will be much the same as the solution of interoccupational or industrial conflicts, that is, the encouragement of a free mobility of people among regions. A poor region will then have an outflow of population and it will get poorer. This may look like a conflict among regions, but it is not necessarily a conflict among people. The people who migrate get better off as a result of the migration. The people who are left behind in the declining region also become better off as the population of the region becomes better adapted to its resource base. Paradoxically, the people who previously lived in the underpopulated region will not necessarily be any worse off either, as the newcomers should increase the product of the region by at least as much as their own income. There may, of course, be occupational conflict within the region, but this again, as we have seen, can be resolved by mobility.

This idyllic picture, unfortunately, is somewhat clouded by the existence of differential rates of population growth. A region which is poor because it has allowed the growth of population to proceed unchecked by anything but misery will not necessarily solve its own problems by emigration and may simply export its poverty to others. In a truly Malthusian situation where the population is indeed limited by the means of subsistence and the rising mortality which these limited means create, emigration is no solution to the problem at all. Every adult who emigrates releases enough food so that probably two children survive who might otherwise have died, and in a single generation the population is as great, if not greater, than before. Suppose we had a world, for instance, in which only one region refused to limit its population while the rest of the world limited its population. Then if there was unlimited mobility between all regions, the feckless and fecund region could in the course of time reduce all the rest of the world to its own level of misery and poverty. There are conflicts here of a very subtle nature not only among regions but also between the generations. A generation which uses its fortunate economic position for unlimited procreation is in effect enjoying itself at the expense of its descendants.

When we examine the nature of economic conflict carefully, it may well appear that conflict between the generations is the most "real" of all conflicts, in spite of the fact that it is one of the least visible and the least organized. Rapid economic development for instance frequently involves the ruthless sacrifice of an existing generation, especially of youth, for the sake of posterity. This seems to have been true in the early days of the industrial revolution in England, and it is certainly true of the Soviet Union. Economic development requires a large proportion of the economic product in what might be called the *growth resource*, that is, education, science and technology, and capital-goods industries. This means that less is available for the needs of the present.

The fact that the course of economic development usually seems to entail fluctuations and that development rarely proceeds smoothly means again that a severe conflict can exist between the generations, that is, between different cohorts of the population. Studies have indicated, for instance, that the unfortunate generation which entered the labor market in the early thirties never really recovered from the experience of the Great Depression. Similarly, some generations get caught in wars and some do not, and the date of birth is often one of the most important predictive factors in determining economic welfare. As severe as these conflicts may be in real terms, however, they seldom result in organized strife, although juvenile delinquency at the one extreme and Townsendism at the other are symptoms of intergenerational strife. The main problem here is that youth, for instance, ages too fast to organize itself as youth, and by the time an exploited generation of youth has realized the fact, it is middle-aged or old and is itself doing the exploiting. Similarly, it is hard to sustain a political movement among the old simply because of the rate of attrition through death.

The recipe which we have given for the resolution of interregional, or interoccupational, conflicts, namely, mobility, is less applicable here simply because there is mobility only in one direction. The young get old, the old never get young. It is perhaps fortunate, therefore, that the very elements of the situation which make the conflict less resolvable also make it harder to organize. Ideally, the institutions of the capital market should assist in resolving this conflict just as the existence of the labor market helps to resolve the conflicts of occupational groups. At any one time those in middle life are supporting both the young and the old, that is, those in middle life who constitute the labor force produce more than they themselves consume, and the excess, in part, goes to support both the young and the old who consume more than they produce. When we are young, as it were, we run up a debt to society; in middle life we pay this off, and indeed reverse it so that by retirement society is in debt to us and in the older years society pays this debt off. In an ideally functioning market economy the rate of interest would, as it were, adjudicate this conflict between the young, the middle-aged, and the old, for the higher the rate of interest, the more, in effect, the young must pay and the more the old will receive. The capital market, however, is so imperfect and has so many other functions to perform that people by and large are completely unaware of this aspect of the rate of interest. The market has, therefore, performed this function rather poorly and we have consequently had to devise nonmarket machinery both for supporting the education of youth and for supporting the retirement of the aged. The conflict passes over from the economic to the political arena as the competing claims of aid to education and youth services on the one hand or to old age and dependency on the other are fought out in the competition for the budgets of states and federal governments.

The last field of economic conflict is the class struggle in the Marxist sense of the word, that is, the conflict between those who own property and those who do not. Oddly enough, in this field it is surprisingly difficult to state firm propositions. If we take the distribution of national income between labor income and nonlabor income as the crucial variable in this conflict, it is surprisingly hard to identify any particular acts or norms of action which move this proportion clearly one way or another. It is even harder to identify those decisions which change the absolute amounts falling to labor or to nonlabor income. It is fairly clear, for instance, that deflation, such as we had from 1929 to 1932, increases the proportion of national income going to labor, which rose from 59 per cent in 1929 to 72 per cent in 1932. It increases also the proportion going to interest and diminishes enormously the proportion going to profits. However, in those years the national product itself fell so drastically that the total amount going to labor fell in spite of the increase in the proportion. Furthermore, within the labor force itself a sharp differential developed between those who still held jobs and those who were unemployed. Those who held jobs were probably better off in 1932 than they had been in 1929, whereas those who were unemployed were much worse off. Furthermore, the rise of the labor movement and the extension of collective bargaining to large sectors of American industry seems to have had remarkably little effect on the over-all distribution as between labor income and nonlabor income. Between 1932 and 1942 the membership in American labor unions increased from under four million to about fifteen million, and an even larger number of workers enjoyed some spill-over from the presumed benefits of collective bargaining. Yet in these years also, because of the recovery of profits, the proportion of national income going to labor actually declined from 72 per cent to 63 per cent, though the absolute amount of labor income increased because of the increase in the national income itself. What does seem to be clear is that the general movements of inflation and deflation are much more powerful in changing the distribution of the national income as between the labor income and nonlabor income than any change in the organization of the labor market itself. The rise in real wages in the last few decades which has been so spectacular in the United States, has clearly not been due to any direct influence of labor unions on wages, although their indirect influence may have been substantial. It is the rise in the total product itself, however, especially the product per man, rather than in the proportion going to labor which has been the major factor in the long-run increase in real wages.

Even the influence of taxation on the distribution of income as between labor and nonlabor is extraordinarily difficult to assess. The corporation tax, for instance, would seem at first sight to fall mainly on nonlabor income. There is a good deal of evidence, however, that much of it is, in fact, shifted in the form of increased prices of products, most of which are bought by the working class. Property taxes are in many cases passed on in the form of increased rents and again paid by the working class, whereas the social security tax on wages can easily result in the diminution of profits. All one can say about the situation is that it is extraordinarily confused and that the distribution between labor and nonlabor income is dependent on so many decisions of so many different people that no clear conflict emerges, because it is very hard to specify particular decisions which will, in fact, move the distribution of income away from one class or towards the other. In the light of this fact, the defect of the Marxist scheme as an interpretation of history becomes clear indeed, and it is not surprising that Marx's predictions were, for the most part, falsified. Economic life is so complicated, in fact, that very frequently decisions which are taken with one objective and with the object indeed of making a conflict move in favor of a decision-maker turn out ironically enough to produce effects quite opposite from what was intended.

Many of these ironies of economic conflict could be cited. In the United States, for instance, measures which have been intended through the years to benefit the farmer, perhaps at the expense of the rest of us, in fact have prevented agriculture from making the adjustment which it should have made but has also, as a by-product, set off a remarkable process of technological development which has benefited the nonagricultural population much more than it has benefited agriculture. One of my favorite examples of these ironies was something that happened in Great Britain in 1934 when the British government, seeking to assist a slovenly and inefficient English pig industry, imposed a quota on imports of Danish bacon, no doubt with a view of injuring the Danes and bene-fiting the British pig producer. This is a perfect example of a decision intended to produce a conflict move. What, in fact, happened was that, because in the eyes of the British housewife Danish bacon was so superior, the price of Danish bacon rose substantially and the British ended up paying the Danes more money for less bacon than they had before. The British consumer was injured, the Danish producer was benefited, and the British pig producer remained pretty much where he was before.

Another example of these ironies of conflict are the many attempts which have been made to regulate the production of agricultural com-modities by means of quotas. Attempts to reduce the output of cotton in the United States by means of acreage quotas actually resulted in so much more fertilizer being put on the diminished number of acres that the total output of cotton rose! Marketing quotas, such as we have in tobacco, are successful in limiting the output of a product. The subsequent rise in price, however, is almost invariably capitalized and the quota becomes a valuable commodity which represents, as it were, a free gift to the people who happen to be producing the commodity at the time the quota was imposed. In the American tobacco regions, for instance, a farm with a quota now sells for many times the price of a farm without one. In Britain the right to produce hops has become a salable commodity representing, as it were, a free gift to those people who happened to be producing hops in 1934 when the marketing scheme went into operation.

Even the tariff, which is regarded as a typical example of economic conflict, seldom has the effects which are expected. The imposition of a tariff is usually regarded as a conflict move intended to benefit the home producers of the commodity in question and to injure the foreign pro-ducers. The more sophisticated might recognize that it also injures the home consumers and benefits the foreign consumers, but as consumers form an incoherent mass of little or no political significance, their voice is not usually heard and their interests are not taken into account. If, however, there is free mobility into the affected industries, the results of the tariff on the distribution of income will very soon be diffused. In the country imposing the tariff, the protected industry may be unusually profitable at first, but its high profits will soon attract other resources into it and its profits will come down to normal again. In the foreign countries producers will leave the industry and its profits will rise. The long-run effects of a tariff are impossible to predict because of the extreme com-plexity of the dynamic results. It has often been the case, however, that a protected industry has stagnated, whereas sometimes an industry which finds itself in a suddenly more adverse position responds to this challenge and reorganizes itself and, as a result, is often in a stronger position than before. In the cynical mood one sometimes feels that the worst possible thing one can do for anybody is to help them.

It is clear that the prime characteristic of economic conflicts is that they are hopelessly muddled, and it is surprisingly hard to make a really intelligent conflict move in the economic area simply because of the complexity of the system and the enormous importance of side effects and dynamic effects. Even where economic conflict is clear, however, it has one obvious method of resolution, which is by economic development. If the total product is constant, then if I get more, somebody else must get less. If the total product is increasing, I can get more without anybody else getting less; indeed, everybody can get more together. This is why economic development is such an extraordinary mollifier of economic conflict. It is only where economic development is heavily concentrated in one sector of an economy to the exclusion of the other sectors that it produces a sense of economic conflict and eventual alienation from the society of those who fail to benefit.

This is a real dilemma for the poor countries. In many ways the easiest path of economic development is to have it start in some sector of the economy and to have the developed sector expand to one field after another until the whole economy is developed. We visualize economic development as something like the growth of the chicken in the egg. As the chicken, that is the more highly organized and developed part of society, grows, the yoke, that is the poor undifferentiated technologically backward folk society, declines. Unfortunately, a process of this kind inevitably produces tensions within the society and a sense of conflict. It is quite possible for the declining sector actually to be getting worse off as a result of the development. If the individual finds it easy to move from the declining sector into the advancing developed sector, this may not cause any great sense of personal frustration and alienation. If, however, the tightly drawn lines of the traditional society prevent this movement, the envy and frustration of those who are held back in the declining sector will gather steam and may even generate a revolution. It may be better, therefore, to develop more slowly and more uniformly, or perhaps tax the "chicken," not severely enough to stop its growth and yet enough to keep the "yolk" integrated into the total society.

We thus see that the management of economic conflict has many things in common with the management of conflict in general, even though in the immensely complex network of the economy it is not always easy to see where the lines of economic conflict are drawn. Even in cases where conflict is clear, however, the problem still remains as to how to make a succession of conflict moves have benign rather than malign

over-all consequences. The problem is illustrated in Figure 3 which repeats the field of Figure 1. From position P_0 suppose A makes a conflict
move to P_1 increasing his welfare at the expense of B's, B may reply with

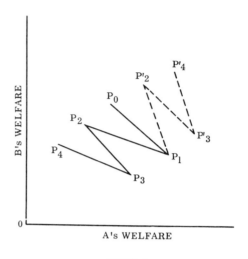

FIGURE 3

a further conflict move, say to P_2. A may reply in turn to P_3, B to P_4, and
so on. It is clear that the net result of this succession of moves is a malign
process leading both parties to positions of lower welfare. A quite small
change in the parameters of the system, however, can reverse the process.
Instead of going from P_1 to P_2 and so on, we might go to P'_2 to P'_3 to P'_4,
and so on in a process which has an over-all benign trend in which both
parties are getting better off as a result of the succession of moves.

The difference between benign and malign processes is often a mere
quantitative difference. This is one of the most vivid illustrations of the
one principle of Marxism to which I am willing to subscribe whole-
heartedly, namely, that a sufficient difference in quantity can produce a
difference in quality. One principle of the general theory of conflict which
has important applications to economic conflict arises clearly in this very
diagram. The condition for a benign series is a little hard to formulate in
words. If we think of a conflict move on the part of A as P_0P_1, followed
by a countermove on the part of B as $P_1P'_2$, and the whole process as a
succession of moves and countermoves, then the countermove must leave
the injured party in a better position than he was before he made the first
move. If we call the slope of the line P_0P_1 the *coefficient of conflict*, that
is, the loss to one party per unit gain of the other, then the condition for a
benign process is that the coefficient of conflict in the countermove must

be less than that in the move. The more empathy and goodwill present among the parties, the more likely is this condition to be fulfilled. Hostility and malevolence increase the probability of malign processes. Hatred injures the hater as well as the hated. Love blesses the lover as well as the loved. This is hard economics as well as good ethics. One may venture the hypothesis that there is some critical level of general hostility in a relationship above which the conflict processes will be malign and below which they will be benign. It will be a most exciting and critical enterprise to try to identify this level of hostility and apply it to particular cases. We see this, for instance, in the high economic cost of racial prejudice, and we see it also in the high economic cost of international tension. Hostility is probably the costliest emotion man harbors. If psychologists can contribute to its relief, the economic gains will be enormous.

Part 3 The Mutant Disciplines

The chapter entitled "The Future of Human Conflict" contains the suggestion that our academic and intellectual disciplines have evolved with characteristics that may be ill suited to the task that now confronts them. The specialization in subject matter taken to be the proper concern of a single discipline most often is achieved by the deliberate exclusion of certain realms of thought and areas of application. A trade-off is usually arranged historically in which a clear view of the microcosm is substituted for the often more blurred perception of the macrocosm. The satirical definition of an expert as one who knows more and more about less and less is an adequate description of academic history over the last half-century. It is apparent that the bulk of the forces in scholarship press in on the scholar to compress his grasp of things intellectual and the favorite villain of the piece has been a combination of limited time and expanding knowledge.

Beyond the constraints exercised by an almost explosive expansion of information and experience in every discipline, and beyond the enormous increase in the number of human beings engaged in the pursuit of science, lies the problem of the intellectual organization of society. Once great value and clear meaning get attached to intellectual efforts of a particular variety, the society tends to organize the means to assure its expansion and continuation. This organized social activity is the kiss of death since by its very nature (rules, regulations, administrative conveniences) it must surgically remove the annoying and complex deviations that always mark true invention and discovery. The mass production of art and the mass production of invention along disciplinary lines are chillingly equivalent. The organization of intellectual effort by discipline within the social sciences has produced a series of tiny fragments that defy reassembly into a meaningful whole form. The task of devising a unified science of man will be an Herculean one.

That social science cannot "pull itself together" to meet the challenge of the nuclear age is distressing, but disciplinary narrowness has had an even more important facet. Teaching, training, and orientation to the close quarters of a single discipline has acted to prevent the appearance of new approaches to global problems, since one must break the bonds of past experience even to think in other than familiar patterns. If one attempts to depart from the traditional ingredients of thought, he must do so alone and without the comfort of sympathetic colleagues immersed intellectually in similar problems. The deviant thinker must often invent new tools, methods, and techniques to meet his unique needs and much of his time is devoted simply to equipping himself to tackle the task he faces. Disciplinary limitations and departmentalization probably exact their greatest toll in making certain kinds and classes of approach to problem-solving simply "unthinkable."

It is not surprising, then, that so few relatively unique attacks on war and peace have been born in this age of widespread science of all kinds. What looks like a fertile ground has been unaccountably barren. Some "thinking out of the usual categories" has taken place and the outcome has been the formation of fields of inquiry and methods of viewing international relations that do not comfortably fit any of the established academic subdivisions. It is to these we now turn our gaze to see if some of these unaccustomed combinations hold a kind of promise absent from those approaches which have been longer and more formally organized. Some familiar and recognizable parts will make up these new assemblages, but their application in a new context produces a qualitative as well as a quantitative break with the past.

10

Game Theory and Human Conflict

ANATOL RAPOPORT

Although from a certain point of view, game theory appears as a basis *par excellence* of a theory of conflict, the road that leads from the beginnings laid down by game theory to a full-fledged science of conflict is beset with pitfalls of misunderstandings. One of these misunderstandings is easy to dispose of: game theory is not, as is sometimes assumed, a branch of behavioral science; no proposition of game theory relates to how people (or animals or organizations) behave in conflict situations. However, this disclaimer is frequently taken to imply that game theory purports to be a *normative* theory of rational conflict, that is, that its propositions relate to how rational participants in conflicts ought to behave. This characterization of game theory is only partly accurate. The limits of its validity will be delineated in our discussion, which, we hope, will bring out both the positive contributions of game theory to a theory of conflict and the unfortunate by-products which have emerged from assuming too wide a range for the normative aspects of the theory.

It is true that certain aspects of game theory deal with rational decisions, and all of it deals with conflicts of interest. Where the two areas intersect, one might speak of a rational theory of conflict. However, as we shall see, a theory of rational decision cannot be extended to all conflict situations. In some situations, game theory ceases to be normative: it cannot prescribe decisions to "rational players." We have already implied that neither is game theory descriptive: it does not state principles according to which participants in conflict situations actually behave. If game theory is neither prescriptive nor descriptive, what is it? It is essentially a structural theory. It uncovers the *logical structure* of a great variety of conflict situations and describes this structure in mathematical terms. Sometimes the logical structure of a conflict situation admits rational decisions; sometimes it does not. The discovery of logical structures of conflict situations therefore allows a classification of conflicts. This classification abstracts entirely from the *content* of conflicts. This is what any mathematical theory does, namely, abstracts the structures of events or situations entirely from their content.

The widespread notion that game theory is essentially a rational theory of conflict derives from the observation that one part of game theory, namely, the theory of the two-person zero-sum game, is a natural extension of a theory of rational decisions to situations where two or more decision-makers with conflicting interests are involved. In the context of the two-person zero-sum game, game theory can indeed be a normative (prescriptive) theory in a sense analogous to that in which the theory of rational gambling is normative. The principal notions of the latter theory, which is a much older and simpler theory, serve as a good introduction to the notions of game theory. Let us therefore take a brief look at the classical theory of gambling.

CHOICE AMONG RISKY OUTCOMES AND UTILITY

Consider the following drastically simplified form of poker. The (single) player is dealt a hand of five cards. He gets a pay-off from the House depending on the strength of his hand, the largest pay-off for the royal flush and so forth, down to three of a kind, two pair, one pair, and bust. The question faced by the rational player is how much he should be willing to pay for each hand before it is dealt. The following answer seems reasonable. Multiply the pay-off for each type of hand by the probability with which it can occur and add the products. This is the expected gain of the gamble. The rational gambler ought to be willing to pay any amount less than the expected gain. Similarly the House ought to charge an amount in excess of this quantity. In fact this is what all gambling houses do, so that the expected gain of any gamble is always in favor of the House. The House is therefore always the rational gambler, while the customer is not. Why the latter continue to gamble and to keep the Houses in business is a psychological question, beyond the scope of rational gambling theory and of this discussion. We shall, however, examine the justification for designating the acceptance of bets with positive expected gains as "rational."

One such justification is eminently acceptable on intuitive grounds. If bets can be repeated a large number of times, the expected gains become almost certainly actual long-run gains. The expected gain principle then says in effect that gains are preferable to losses, a rational preference by any usual standards.

Now the transformation of expected gains into actual long-run gains is guaranteed ("almost certainly") by the so-called *Law of Large Numbers* of the probability theory, which states roughly that in a great number of trials the frequency of an event will be proportional to its probability. What the Law of Large Numbers does not say is how large a large number of trials should be for this law to operate. Failure to take this qualification into account can lead to bizarre conclusions concerning the rationality of accepting bets with positive expected gains. This was dramatically demonstrated by James Bernoulli in the so-called *St. Petersburg Paradox*. In the St. Petersburg Game, the House pays the gambler 1 cent if a head turns up on the first toss of a coin; 1 cent + 2 cents if the first two tosses are heads, 1 cent + 2 cents + 4 cents . . . 2^{k-1} cents if heads come up on k consecutive tosses. A play of the game is defined as a sequence of tosses up to the first tails. How much is the gambler justified in paying for each play of the game?

According to the principle of expected gain, the gambler should be willing to pay any amount smaller than the expected gain. It turns out, however, that the expected gain to the gambler in the St. Petersburg Game is *infinite*. That is, in the long run, the occasional windfalls brought on by long stretches of consecutive heads will give the gambler a positive gain no matter how much he agrees to pay for each play of the game. One is faced, therefore, with the uneasy conclusion that the gambler ought to be willing to pay any amount per play, even, say, a billion dollars, if the pay-offs are as indicated above.

Now in practice, paying a nickel a play will bring in profitable returns fairly soon. Paying a dime will do so after some hours of tossing. But paying 10 dollars a play will not wipe out the losses in a lifetime of tossing. So the catch is the length of the "long run." We are thus forced to re-evaluate the "rationality" of the expected-gain principle. At the very least, the principle ought to be qualified by introducing a cost of waiting for the long run, not to speak of the very real possibility that the gambler will lose his capital long before a windfall comes. Since the capitals of individuals vary and so does their patience, the hope of establishing a *universal* objective-rationality principle for gambling dims.

In an attempt to save the expected-gain principle, Bernoulli introduced the notion of utility. This notion is also indispensable in game theory, and so we must examine it in some detail. Bernoulli argued that pay-offs of gambles should be expressed not in money but in what money is "worth" to the gambler. Thus 10 dollars may not be worth ten times as much as 1 dollar but only, say, three times as much. The diminishing return idea applied to the "worth" of money seems reasonable in view of the fact that rich people spend money more freely than poor people and will not do the things poor people will do to get a given amount of money. Specifically Bernoulli proposed a logarithmic utility function for money, assuming that the worth of an amount of money is proportional to its logarithm instead of to the actual amount. When the utility of money returns replaces the returns themselves in the calculation of expected gains, the rational gambling policy becomes more conservative, because the utilities of the big gains (those associated with the big risks) become smaller. In particular, the expected (utility) gain of the St. Petersburg Game game becomes finite, its magnitude depending on the parameters of the utility function assigned. Thus the maximum amount to be paid per play can be prescribed.

When the concept of utility is introduced into normative gambling theory, the prescriptions of the theory become dependent on the utility function of the particular gambler. Thus the normative theory loses its purely rational character. Here we distinguish between the rational and the empirical aspects of a theory. The former consists of the compelling, logically determined elements; the latter consists of elements that are arbitrary in the sense that empirically determined facts must be simply taken as they are. To be sure, these arbitrary elements can be by-passed, if one assumes the utility function of a gambler as given, so that gambling theory is confined to the calculation of maximum expected-utility gains, leading to the prescription of the optimal course of action. It is noteworthy, however, that in the *magnum opus* of game theory (von Neumann and Morgenstern, 1953) considerable attention was devoted to the method of determining the utility function of a player. If this method is followed in the context of gambling theory, the latter loses its prescriptive character entirely. The "prescriptions" become obvious tautologies. This curious result will be an important element in our later discussion. Let us examine the underlying argument.

Suppose we wish to rank order an individual's preferences among a set of alternatives (objects, events, outcomes of decisions, or what not). As an example, let us take three desserts offered on a menu: cake, pie, and custard. A simple method of determining preferences is to ask a man which of the three he would like, and, if that one is not available, which would be his second choice. Suppose the man indicates pie as first choice, cake as second, and custard as third. We have now determined the rank order. But if we wish to assign numerical values to how much each is "worth" to him, we have an embarrassment of riches. *Any* three numbers will do provided the number assigned to pie is the largest and the one assigned to custard is the smallest. An indication of the preference order tells us only that cake is between the other three; it does not tell us whether cake is nearer to pie or to custard and by how much. One could of course ask the man how much he would be willing to *pay* for each of the three desserts. But the amounts he names would establish only the exchange value of the desserts in money units. We do not know how much the *money amounts* are "worth" to the man, so we have only displaced the problem, not solved it.

To circumvent this difficulty, von Neumann and Morgenstern have proposed the following procedure. Suppose the man is offered a choice of two tickets. One of the tickets entitles him to cake, while the other is essentially a lottery ticket with which he can win one of two prizes, pie or custard. Which will the man choose, the cake ticket or the pie-custard lottery ticket? We feel that the answer depends on two things: (*a*) the chance of getting pie as against custard if the lottery ticket is chosen and (*b*) where on the preference interval between pie and custard cake is located. With regard to *a*, the bigger the chance of getting pie, the more likely is the man going to choose the lottery ticket. With regard to *b*, the closer the cake is to custard on the preference interval, the more likely is the man to choose the lottery ticket.

The method of determining utilities proposed by von Neumann and Morgenstern amounts essentially to examining risk-taking behavior in situations such as the one just described. We ask the man whether he prefers cake to a 50-50 chance between pie and custard. If he prefers cake, we increase the chance for pie; if he prefers the gamble, we decrease the chance for pie. Thus repeating our offers, we establish the odds of the lottery ticket which make the man indifferent between the ticket and cake. We then assign the sizes of intervals on his preference scale inversely proportional to these odds. The bigger the odds for pie must be to make him just accept the lottery ticket, the closer we put cake to pie. When this is done, we have established the man's utilities for the three desserts on an *interval scale*. (The rank order establishes the preferences on a weaker *ordinal scale*.) The numbers so assigned are not unique; but they are far less arbitrary than the numbers which reflect only the rank order of the utilities. The zero point and the unit of the interval scale can still be chosen arbitrarily, but the relative magnitudes of the intervals between the utility values are determined: they remain the same no matter how the zero and the unit are chosen.

Game theory, like gambling theory, requires for its utility scale an interval scale. The position of the zero point and the size of the unit on this scale are arbitrary. Therefore the problem of assigning utilities, in terms of which the results of the theory will be derived, is in principle solved by the method just described.

Now let us see what has happened to the normative aspect of gambling theory, if the above method is used for determining utilities. We have seen that Bernoullian gambling theory prescribes the maximization of expected utility gain. If utilities of outcomes are given, preferences between options involving different risks associated with different pay-offs are prescribed. For example, if numerical utilities of pie, cake, and custard are given, Bernoullian gambling theory will prescribe the choice between cake with certainty or the pie-custard lottery ticket, depending on which expected-utility gain is greater. (The "expected-utility gain" of cake with certainty is simply the utility of cake.) But now we have assumed that the respective utilities of pie, cake, and custard have been determined by the von Neumann-Morgenstern method, that is, by an investigation of the man's preferences among various gambles as compared to cake. The determination of these preferences amounted to a *definition* of utility in such a way that the option with the greater expected utility was always the option chosen. Thus the prescription of the choice with the maximum expected utility becomes in this context a *tautology.* One is told simply to choose the option which one prefers most! Only if the utilities are determined in some other way does Bernoullian gambling theory actually instruct the gambler how to choose. The status of prescriptive gambling theory, then, is the following. In order to prescribe choices among risky options, utilities on an interval scale are needed. If these utilities are defined in the sense of von Neumann and Morgenstern, the prescriptions of Bernoullian theory reduce to tautologies and tell us nothing. If prescriptive content is to remain, the utilities must be determined independently of preferences among risky options. This conclusion is related to similar limitations of game theory. Let us therefore keep it in mind.

We now turn to the problems of game theory proper.

THE ZERO-SUM GAME WITH DETERMINED OUTCOME

The choice between cake with certainty and the lottery ticket can be schematized as shown in Game 1.

The situation is represented by a so-called *game matrix.* One of the players A is the man who makes his choice between cake and the lottery ticket. The other player B is Chance. The man chooses either the first row or the second row of the matrix. The choice of the first row A_1 gives

	B_1	B_2
A_1	Cake 3	Cake 3
A_2	Pie 5	Custard 2

GAME 1

him cake. If he chooses the second row A_2, he gets pie or custard, depending on what column Chance chooses. Let us generalize the situation somewhat by having the man choose between two lottery tickets. Suppose one of the tickets gives him cake or fruit, and the other pie or custard as before. Let us also change the man's preferences, so that they are as shown in Game 2.[1]

	B_1	B_2
A_1	Fruit 10	Cake 1
A_2	Pie 5	Custard 2

GAME 2

The essential difference between a gamble and a two-person game can now be illustrated in this example. If the choice is between two lottery tickets (a game against Chance), this choice will be determined (according to Bernoullian gambling theory) by the probabilities associated with Chance's choices. If Chance chooses between columns 1 and 2 with equal probability, then clearly the lottery represented by A_1 with its expected gain of $5\frac{1}{2}$ is preferable to that represented by A_2 with its expected gain of $3\frac{1}{2}$. It would take 5-to-1 odds in favor of B_2 to equalize the preference between the two rows.

The essential feature of a game against Chance is that Chance gets no pay-offs and hence is indifferent to the outcome of the choices. To be sure, this indifference does not mean that Chance always chooses her alternatives with equal probabilities. She may favor some alternatives over others, but this preference is quite independent of the pay-offs that accrue to the gambler. In a two-person game, on the other hand, the chooser of the column is also a player, who also gets pay-offs. This player

---

[1] The preferences are changed so as to lead more naturally into the zero-sum game, examined below.

will not choose his column randomly. He will be guided by "rational" considerations, i.e., he will make his choice with a view of maximizing his pay-off within the constraints of the game.

Let us now enter the other player's pay-offs into the game matrix. In general we can enter any pay-offs we wish. However, a very important case is where the pay-offs of the second player are equal to those of the first with the signs reversed; what one player wins, the other loses. Such games are called *zero-sum games* (because the sum of the pay-offs in each matrix entry is always zero). Zero-sum games represent, then, the purest form of conflict of interests, namely, one where the interests of two parties are diametrically opposed.

	B_1	B_2
A_1	10, –10	1, –1
A_2	5, –5	2, –2

GAME 3

Game 3 is the same as Game 2 but now with the pay-offs of both players shown. (The first number of each pair is the pay-off to A.) Let us see now how a rational player, choosing a row, will be guided in his choices. Facing a "rational" opponent, he cannot now assume that the latter will choose his column in some random fashion with some pre-assigned probability. Instead a rational player will expect the other (rational) player to be guided by his own interests. It is now clear that it is in the interest of B to choose B_2, because his losses in that column are both respectively smaller than the corresponding losses in B_1. On the basis of this knowledge it is clearly in the interest of B to choose B_2. A cannot hope to get the attractive outcome 10 in row 1, column 1, because B cannot be expected to choose B_1.

We have examined the simplest type of game studied in game theory, namely, a two-person zero-sum game with a perfectly determined outcome. What is the range of application for this model? We have already said that a zero-sum game represents a conflict between two parties whose interests are diametrically opposed. In real conflicts, on the other hand, partial coincidence of interests frequently occurs, especially in situations where more than two parties are involved, as evidenced by coalitions among some of the parties. In a two-person zero-sum game coincidence of interests and hence coalitions are excluded. This restriction on the range of conflicts represented by the zero-sum game is of crucial importance, as we shall see. But there are also other limitations.

Another characteristic of the two-person zero-sum game model of conflict is the assumption that the players are rational. In this context, rationality can be naturally and unambiguously defined, and this is the principal basis for a claim that game theory is a logically perfect model of rational conflict. The range of application of game-theoretical models, however, is no larger than the range of situations in which rationality can be clearly defined.

Finally the zero-sum game model of conflict, like all the game models studied in game theory, is applicable only if the situation represented in the model is indeed a "game," to be presently defined.

A game is defined in game theory as a situation in which there are (a) two or more "players," each of whom has (b) a set of choices of "strategies," (c) knowledge of all possible outcomes of all possible combinations of strategy choices, and (d) a preference ordering on an interval scale among the outcomes. The last two parts of this definition define the rationality of the players.

In our simple example of a zero-sum game (Game 3), each of the two players has a choice of two strategies. There are four outcomes, represented by the four pairs of pay-offs. These pay-offs are known to the players. The entries have already been translated into utility units. Consequently, they reflect the preferences of the players on an interval scale.

It is a simple matter to extend this conceptualization of a game to a situation where each player has a choice of an arbitrary number of strategies. The matrix then becomes one of N rows and M columns. If M and N are very large, it may be unrealistic to suppose that the players have full knowledge of the pay-off matrix. But *conceptually* the model remains the same.

Now game theory justifies its name by the following remarkable result. Whenever a situation exists in which a finite number of choices are presented to the players in some sequence of stages and whenever a termination rule exists for the process, the whole process can be represented as one in which each player has only a *single* choice of strategy, whereby both players make their choices *simultaneously* (i.e., independently of each other).

To illustrate, take the simple game of tic-tac-toe. In this game, the first player has nine choices where to put a cross. Thereupon the second player has eight choices where to put his circle. Then the first player has seven choices where to put a cross and so on. The game is terminated when either three crosses or three circles appear in a straight line or else when all the nine boxes of the grid have been filled.

In poker, the rules are more complicated but no less definite. Upon seeing his hand, a player has a set of choices (namely twenty-seven) of which (if any) cards to exchange, or else to fold.[2] Thereupon, the dealer has only one "choice" (i.e., actually no choice)—to deal him the number of cards he has thrown off. Then the player has a choice of various amounts permitted to bet or else to fold. The dealer has a choice of folding, seeing, or raising, and so on. The play of the game ends when either of the two players has folded or has asked to see. The pay-offs are determined by the amounts contributed to the pot.

The sets of choices open to the players at each stage of a game are called moves. The moves and the conditions of termination (plus certain bylaws governing details of behavior) are called the *rules of the game.*

The possibility of "collapsing" all the possible moves open to a player upon a single "strategy" is proved as a principal theoretical result of game theory. A choice of strategy is a statement by a player (to himself) of what he would do in any of the situations which could ever arise in the course of the game. The number of such situations is finite; consequently, the number of strategies available to each player is also finite. The number of strategies is vastly larger than the number of possible situations. For example in tic-tac-toe, the number of possible situations in which the first player has a choice (disregarding the symmetries of the grid) is 3,139. But the number of strategies is over 65 trillion. It is possible to learn to play perfect tic-tac-toe in a few minutes, but it is out of the question to list all of its strategies.

However, the fact that it is impractical to actually list all the strategies of even a very simple child's game does not detract from the importance of the notion of strategy. This notion enables the game theoretician to *conceptualize* a two-person game as a single pair of choices by the players, consequently to represent such a game by a matrix and so to develop a theory based on certain properties of the matrix. It is a certain mathematical property of the game matrix of tic-tac-toe (derived by mathematical considerations) which establishes rigorously the well-known result that the outcome of every game of tic-tac-toe (played perfectly by both players) must end in a draw. Game theory has established a much larger result, namely that the pay-off outcome of *every* game of perfect information (to be presently defined) played by two rational players is determined. Games of perfect information are those in which all the choices made by the players are known to both players. Chess, checkers, and go, as well as tic-tac-toe, are games of perfect information. It follows that the outcome of every game of chess between rational players is theoretically determined. Whichever is the outcome of one such perfectly played game (win for White, draw, or win for Black) the

---

[2] We are assuming three-card draw.

same outcome will be the result of every perfect game. If the best strategy choices of both players were known (as they are essentially known in tic-tac-toe, although they are not easy to state), it would be as pointless to play chess as tic-tac-toe.

If game theory were confined to games of perfect information, its object would be clear and destructive: to find the best strategy choice (or choices) for each player and thus to render every game pointless. Such situations actually occur even in games as complex as chess, when, for example, it becomes clear that one of the players can force a win or that neither can. In such situations, experienced players stop the game. Similar situations used to occur in war in times when wars were fought by "gentlemen" and were largely devoid of emotional content, that is, when wars were thought of as matches of strategic skill, as in eighteenth-century Europe. Armies finding themselves in disadvantageous positions surrendered gracefully; negotiations were often preferred to battles of attrition, and so on.

The scope of game theory is both smaller and larger than the problem of "solving" theoretically determined games. It is smaller in the sense that specific solutions of specific games are seldom undertaken, except as exercises or as illustrations of the method. (Most of the interesting games are too complex to be solved.) The scope is larger in the sense that the investigations cover a far wider class of games than those of perfect information. In so defining its scope, game theory reveals its distinctly mathematical character. The mathematician, having indicated a method of solution for a class of problems, is usually not interested in solving specific problems of the class. This task can be relegated to mathematical technicians or, in our day of mathematical technology, to computing machines. Frequently, the mathematician is satisfied with having proved that solutions to a class of problems exist, even though straightforward methods of solving them have not been found. Much of game theory has been developed in that spirit. The result that a unique pay-off outcome is determined in every game of perfect information is what mathematicians call an existence theorem. Such theorems are important for indicating whether further work in the search of solutions is at all feasible and also what sort of solutions one can expect to find.

CLASSIFICATION OF GAMES AND CONFLICTS

Having established an existence theorem for games of perfect information, game theory seeks to establish corresponding results for different kinds of games. It turns out that the character of these results differs widely in different kinds of games, and this leads to a theoretically fruitful classification of games. The importance of game theory for a theory of conflict may well be suggesting an analogous classification of conflicts—a classification which may bring out features of conflict situations not hitherto considered, some of which may turn out to be more profound than those immediately apparent.

By way of analogy, compare the child's classification of animals with the biologist's. To a child, a mouse is more like a frog than like a whale, but to a biologist it is the other way around. The child judges by superficial aspects, like size; the biologist sees the more essential biologically significant relations. Similarly, a layman may classify games according to whether they are played indoors or outdoors, for money or for fun, whether chance or skill are predominantly involved, whether the games are simple or complex. These are apparent features. They may or may not be essential for understanding just what is involved in the contests represented by the games. Most adults will agree that whether chess is played with wooden pieces or plastic ones, whether the squares are colored white and black or blue and yellow does not matter for the character of the game. Upon some reflection, most will agree that even the presence of a board and pieces is not necessary to describe the essential features of chess. It is the *rules* which make the game. The pieces, and the board, are only devices for keeping track of what has happened in the course of the game. That they are not necessary is apparent from the fact that a record of the game, such as one finds in a chess journal, is entirely sufficient for its reconstruction. Game theory carries out such "distillations" of games even further, until even the specific rules are ignored. What is left is the underlying logical structure of a class of games. Of these logical structures, as we shall see, there are several, and they provide the bases for game-theoretical classifications.

Now conflicts too have been classified, largely by social scientists, e.g., according to the nature of the participants (individuals, corporations, interest groups, ethnic groups, national states, and so on), according to the issues involved (economic, ideological, political), according to intensity and extent, and so forth. There is no question that all these matters are essential if we are interested in the content or the genesis of conflict. But many of these matters are not relevant to the *logic* of conflict. Whether a game of poker is played for pennies or for human lives is not relevant to the strategic considerations of poker. The fact that one might play more conservatively if larger stakes are involved simply reflects different utilities of the outcomes. But utilities, we have seen, are given *before* game-theoretical analysis begins. Strategic analysis is performed on the basis of these given utilities of outcomes, regardless of the content of the outcomes.

Similarly, the genesis of the conflict is a matter of indifference to the game theoretician. Whether the "game" is played because the players are forced to play it by authority (as in war) or because they are driven to play it by inner compulsions (as in the playing out of hostility), or whether the players have amicably agreed to play the game (as in parlor games), is of no consequence to the game theoretician. Finally whether the rules are results of agreement or merely formalized statements about what is physically possible in a given situation (e.g., which roads are open to an advancing army) is not relevant to strategic analysis. What is of consequence to the game theoretician is only the strategic structure of the situation represented by the rules of the game, after the rules and, be it especially noted, the utilities of the outcomes have already been specified.

Having pointed out what we believe to be the essential difference between the behavioral scientist's and the game theoretician's approach to the theory of conflict, we return to the theoretical development which the game-theoretical approach has made possible.

We have seen that the most definitive game-theoretical result concerns the outcome of a game of perfect information. All such games have "saddle points" in their matrices, i.e., entries which are at the same time the minima of their rows (among the pay-offs to the row-chooser) and the maxima of their columns. (In Game 3 the entry 2,—2 is saddle point.) If there are several such saddle points, it is shown that the corresponding pay-offs in a zero-sum game must all be equal. The pay-off at the saddle point, then, is the determined pay-off of every such game. The strategies prescribed to each player are the strategies which intersect at a saddle point.

It should be noted that in order to determine the saddle-point strategies, it is not necessary to know the utilities on an interval scale but only on an ordinal scale; each player needs only to give the rank order in which he prefers all the possible outcomes. This requirement can certainly be met in many cases and simplifies tremendously the prescriptive task of game theory. Thus while the number of ways a game of chess can be played is superastronomical, only three classes of outcomes need to be rank ordered, namely, win, draw, and lose, and it is certainly reasonable to assume that each player prefers them in that order. Where pay-offs are in money, it is reasonable to assume that whatever the utility of money may be for a player, larger amounts are always preferred to smaller amounts. Since only the rank order of outcomes is important in solving a zero-sum game with a saddle point, the problem of assigning utilities to outcomes is not a difficult one.

Once we leave the realm of games with saddle points, a simple rank ordering of the outcomes is not enough. Utilities of outcomes must now be established on an interval scale, as we will now show.

THE MIXED-STRATEGY GAME

Consider Game 4, which has no saddle point.

	B_1	B_2
A_1	-3, 3	10, -10
A_2	8, -8	2, -2

GAME 4

What are the best strategy choices for each player? A little reflection shows that whichever strategy is chosen by A, there is an argument against it (provided B is rational). Suppose A chooses A_2 on the grounds that 2 is the greatest amount which he can *certainly* win in this game. If this is a rational choice, B will also assume that A will so choose, and on the basis of this assumption, he will choose B_2 (preferring a loss of 2 to a loss of 10). But if B chooses B_2, clearly A_1 is A's best choice. Now suppose A chooses A_1 on the grounds that it offers the possibility of winning the greatest amount (10). But B, acting on this supposition, will then choose B_1. But if he does, clearly A_2, not A_1, is A's best choice.

We see that the clear choice of a "best" strategy cannot be defended in games without saddle points. To get around this difficulty, the game theoretician has introduced the concept of *mixed strategy*. A mixed strategy is characterized by a distribution of probabilities apportioned among the player's available strategies. In the example just cited, there being two available strategies, a mixture of them would be a pair of complementary probabilities, e.g., .75, .25, indicating that the first strategy is to be chosen with probability ¾ and the second with probability ¼. To play such a mixed strategy, the player would let some random device choose one of the available strategies for him. For example, in a toss of two coins, the probability that both come up heads is ¼. The player would play the second strategy whenever two heads occur; otherwise the first.

The importance of the mixed strategy concept is that it enables the game theoretician to extend the prescriptive role of game theory to zero-sum games without saddle points. We have seen that it is impossible to prescribe the "best" single strategy in such cases. But it is possible in a certain sense to prescribe a "best" mixed strategy to each player.[3] The prescribed mixed strategy is best because it guarantees the maximum *expected*-utility gain under the constraints of the game. This choice can be claimed to be "rational" in one of two ways. If the utilities are additive, i.e., each player simply accumulates the pay-offs (positive or negative) that accrue to him, the expected utility will be in the long run very nearly equal to his actual accumulated pay-off per play of the game. The optimum mixed strategy guarantees to each player that this amount will be maximized under the constraints of the game. Another interpretation of the rationale of expected-utility pay-off is that it reflects the rank order of preferences of the players among all possible "lotteries" in which the pay-off entries are prizes. In other words, if the rows and columns of the game matrix with probabilities assigned to each were to represent the mixed strategies open to the players, and the entries the rank-ordered utility values of the gambles which would result from each pair of mixed-strategy choices, the prescribed mixed strategies would meet at a saddle point.

Admittedly, the rationale of mixed strategy is not nearly so straight-forward and intuitively acceptable as the rationale of saddle-point strategies. Also the rationale depends on the possibility of determining utilities on an interval scale. Not only must such utility functions of both players "exist" in some objective sense, but they must be known to both players. Unless these conditions are fulfilled, the prescriptive role of game theory cannot be realized in this context. We shall have more to say about this below.

THE MIXED-MOTIVE GAMES

The two-person zero-sum game, we have noted, represents conflict in its purest form, in which the interests of the players are diametrically opposed. Although this situation is typical in parlor games, it is not typical in real-life conflicts. In real-life conflicts, the interests of conflicting parties often partially diverge and partially coincide, although vested interests often lead those who analyze such conflicts to emphasize the one or the other aspect. For instance, Marxist analysis of capitalist economics makes it appears that the interests of the entrepreneurs and of the workers are diametrically opposed. And so they are, if one considers the value of the product as a constant to be apportioned between the two parties. If, on the other hand, the value of the product (or the productivity) is not a constant, while the ratio of the apportionment is, then clearly the inter-

---

[3] The best mixed strategy for A in Game 4 is 6/19,13/19 and for B, 8/19,11/19.

ests of the two parties coincide. They can both act so as to increase the value of the product or the productivity, and so the absolute magnitude of both shares. This is precisely the aspect of capitalist economics emphasized by those who wish to direct attention away from the "class struggle."

Again in the current struggle between the communist and the Western blocs, their respective interests appear diametrically opposed to those who see the pay-offs of the outcomes in terms of power or prestige. On the other hand, the interests appear to be nearly coincident to those who see the main issues in terms of the welfare of the populations (especially in view of the threat of nuclear war, associated with the intense struggle for power).

In actuality, most real conflicts are governed by mixed motives. There are outcomes which both parties would prefer to other outcomes. Sometimes, however, these outcomes are difficult or impossible to realize because the conflicting interests of the parties interfere. A very simple and dramatic illustration of such a situation is shown in Game 5.

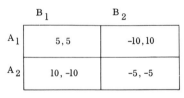

GAME 5

Clearly, it is to the joint advantage of both players to have the outcome 5, 5, since their joint pay-off is greatest there. Nevertheless it is in the interest of each of them *individually* to choose A_2 (or B_2), no matter what the other does. In fact, the outcome −5,−5 is a saddle point in the pay-off matrices of both players. Neither can depart from this saddle point without worsening his pay-off. Both could improve their pay-off by departing from it *together*, namely, from −5,−5 to 5,5. But for this to happen an agreement is necessary. If an agreement is impossible (e.g., if no communication opportunity exists or no enforcement machinery is effective) game theory cannot prescribe a choice of strategy which would be intuitively acceptable on all counts. If A_2 is prescribed to A (on the grounds that it is the best answer to whatever B chooses), then B_2 must also be prescribed to B for the same reason. But the resulting outcome −5,−5 is certainly not the best that the players can do. On the other hand, if A_1 is prescribed to A, then A must be assured that B will choose

B_1, and even then, A must somehow resist the temptation to doublecross B by choosing A_2, i.e., to take advantage of B's goodwill.

There are two ways out of this dilemma. One is to introduce into the analysis of conflict concepts which are not derived from calculations of individual self-interest. Thus the outcome 5,5 can be recommended to the two players, even in the absence of a specific enforceable agreement, by appealing to collective interest and to mutual trust. The idea of collective interest still fits into the conceptual framework of a rational theory of conflict, but the idea of mutual trust hardly does. Therefore this reformulation of the problem carries us outside the realm of game theory.

The other way out is to assume that coalitions among players are always possible. Clearly the concept of coalition is of prime interest in any theory of conflict, since mergings of policy decisions to enhance collective interests are common by-products of multilateral conflicts.

We note in passing that whenever a conflict is represented by a nonzero-sum game, such as Game 5, it can be conceptualized as a zero-sum game by the addition of a third (fictitious) player, who pays out what the others have won collectively and takes in what they have lost. We shall call such a player the *House*. The agreement on the outcome 5,5 in Game 5 is then seen as a coalition of A and B against the House. Such a coalition provides an intuitively acceptable solution, since it gives the players their biggest joint pay-off. However, not all such games can be solved as neatly by the simple expedient of allowing coalitions. Consider Game 6.

	B_1	B_2
A_1	1, 10	-2, -5
A_2	-10, -3	10, 1

GAME 6

In this game the outcomes A_1,B_1 and A_2,B_2 are clearly more advantageous to both players than either of the other two outcomes. However it is by no means a matter of indifference to each player which of the two preferred outcomes obtains. Clearly A prefers A_2,B_2, while B prefers A_1,B_1.

Suppose at first that no communication is possible. How should each choose? B might argue as follows: "Of the two undesirable outcomes, A_2,B_1 is worse than A_1,B_2, since our collective loss is greater in the former. Therefore it is more advantageous to both of us to avoid A_2,B_1 than A_1,B_2, and A should see this as well as I do. He should therefore abstain from A_2 with its greater risk for both of us (and incidentally for him personally). He should play A_1, in which case I can safely play B_1."

Now if A thinks the way B would like him to think, the two players will end up at A_1,B_1 just as B hopes. However A might reason as follows: "B should see that $-10,-3$ is worst for both of us collectively and he should therefore avoid B_1. He should choose B_2, in which case I can safely play A_2."

If B thinks the way A would like him to think, the players will end up at A_2,B_2 as A hopes. But if each expects the *other* to avoid the collectively worst outcome, the result will be precisely what they both wish to avoid, namely, A_2,B_1.[4]

On the other hand, suppose they both think as B thinks they should and so end up at A_1,B_1. Will A be satisfied with this? Will he not raise the question why B should get ten times as much as he. If the game is repeated several times, will not A rebel and choose A_2 occasionally in an attempt to force B to B_2? This question can be answered only experimentally and so is beyond the scope of formal game theory. (We must keep in mind that no result of game theory is either derived from or justified by experimental evidence.)

Suppose now that communication is permitted between the two. Now bargaining becomes possible. A wants B to agree on A_2,B_2; B wants A to agree on A_1,B_1. What are the means of persuasion open to each player? We see that each has a threat with which to back his case. If B persists in his intention to play B_1, A can threaten him with A_2, where B loses 3. But how effective is this threat in view of the fact that A will suffer a loss of 10 if the threat is to be carried out? On the other hand, if A intends to play A_2, B can threaten with B_1, where A stands to lose 10. How credible is B's threat if he himself risks to lose 3 in carrying it out?

Theories of bargaining which have developed in connection with problems arising in nonzero-sum games are centered upon attempts to find solutions of such games which would somehow reflect the relative "bargaining powers" of the players. One such solution might be the following. Note that a nonzero-sum game can be made into a zero-sum game if we enter the algebraic differences between the pay-offs into the game matrix. Our game now becomes that shown in Game 7.

The entries in A_1,B_1 are now $-9 = 1 - 10$ and $9 = 10 - 1$, i.e., the algebraic differences of A's and B's original pay-offs and similarly for

---

[4] Note also that the undesirable outcome A_1,B_2 results if each thinks as the *other* expects him to think. This result can also be interpreted as a case of uncoordinated altruism (each trying to give the bigger pay-off to the other), as illustrated by O. Henry's famous story, *The Gift of the Magi*.

	B_1	B_2
A_1	-9, 9	3, -3
A_2	-7, 7	9, -9

GAME 7

the other entries. Now this game is a zero-sum game with a saddle point, namely, at A_2, B_1. Therefore the outcome of this game is determined. This zero-sum game can be interpreted as conflict of interest between the two players with respect to the respective relative advantage of each over the other. The solution of this game, $-7,7$, states that B can win from A a relative advantage of 7 units for himself. Once this point is settled, the players can jointly maximize their pay-offs in accordance with the relative advantage prescribed by the zero-sum game and within the constraints of the game. Figure 1 shows how this is done.

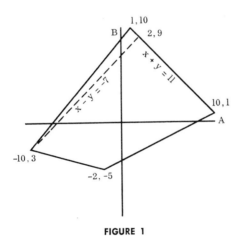

FIGURE 1

The horizontal and the vertical axes represent pay-offs to A and to B respectively. The coordinates of the four corners of the quadrilateral are the four pay-off pairs of the game. All the points inside the quadrilateral are pay-off pairs which are realizable if A and B choose mixed strategies jointly (which they are able to do because communication is allowed). The line joining 1,10 and 10,1 represents the so-called *negotiation set*. The sum of the pay-offs associated with any point on that line is 11. Any such point is realizable if A and B agree to choose A_1, B_1

jointly a certain fraction of times in repeated plays and A_2,B_2 the remaining fraction of times (or else, if the game is played once, one of these strategy pairs would be chosen by a random device with corresponding probability settings.) The dotted line represents the result of the zero-sum game played to determine the relative advantage. It is the line on which all the pay-off pairs with the determined relative advantage are situated. The intersection of this line with the negotiation set is the maximum amount the players can get within the condition of the relative advantage and within the constraints of the game. The solution of this game gives 2 units to A and 9 to B. It can be realized if A_1,B_1 is chosen eight out of nine times. We note that A gets the short end of the bargain. This reflects the fact that B's threat is more effective than A's.

Now this "solution" has a serious drawback. Recall that the pay-offs are in "utiles" and so are to a certain extent arbitrary. Only the interval ratios between the numbers are fixed on the utility scale. The absolute magnitudes of either player's pay-offs could well be a different set of numbers without the interval ratios being disturbed. The resulting pay-offs would represent the player's utilities just as well.

Let us see what happens if we multiply all of B's pay-offs by 2. By the nature of utility, these are still the same "pay-offs" and so the operation should not affect the solution. But it does. Our matrix is now that in Game 8.

	B_1	B_2
A_1	1, 20	-2, -10
A_2	-10, -6	10, 2

GAME 8

The relative advantage game becomes Game 9.

	B_1	B_2
A_1	-19, 19	8, -8
A_2	-4, 4	8, -8

GAME 9

The saddle point is still at A_2,B_1, but B's relative advantage is now only 4 units.

The resulting diagram is shown in Figure 2. The solution 6,10 can be obtained by choosing A_1,B_1 four times out of nine.

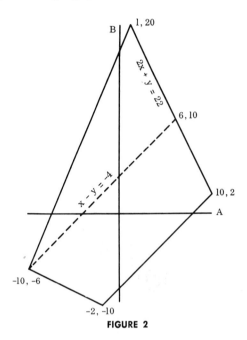

FIGURE 2

Does this solution represent the relative bargaining powers of the players more or less accurately than the preceding one?

The whole matter hinges on the nature of the pay-offs. If the pay-offs are in transferable units whose total measure is conserved (like money) and whose utilities are assumed to be equal for both players, then Game 6 and Game 8 are different games, and it is not surprising that they have different solutions. In fact, in that case the players would do better in Game 8 to agree to play A_1,B_1 *all* the time, since the absolute joint pay-off is greatest there. (If the pay-offs are in money, they can settle their differences by side payments.) If B has a relative advantage of 4 units over A, then the solution could be $12\frac{1}{2},8\frac{1}{2}$ instead of 6,10, and both players would do better. If, however, the pay-offs are not transferable (e.g., like health), they must be measured in utility units. In that case, if a bargaining principle (like that of relative advantage) is to provide a solution, we must demand that this solution remain the same regardless of the units (and the zero points) of the utility scales.

One way of solving this problem is to agree on some standard scale, to which the utilities of both players should be converted before the solution is calculated. For instance one can agree to assign the value 0 to the respective lowest utility pay-offs of the players, the value 1 to the highest values, and then subdivide the intervals proportionately to the other values. If we do this, both Game 6 and Game 8, and also any other game resulting from simply changing the units and/or the zero point of the utility scale of either player, will reduce to Game 10.

	B_1	B_2
A_1	11/20, 1	8/20, 0
A_2	0, 2/15	1, 6/15

GAME 10

Here the relative advantage line becomes $x - y = \frac{2}{15}$. The negotiations set line is represented by $80x + 60y = 96$. The solution is given by the intersection of the two lines, namely $x = \frac{24}{35}$; $y = \frac{86}{105}$. The solution is realized if A_1, B_1 is chosen forty-four out of sixty-three times. If this proportion is applied to Game 6, A would get a pay-off of about 3.7 and so would be better off than if the utility scales had not been standardized. On the other hand if the same proportion were applied to Game 8, A would also have obtained 3.7, this time instead of 6, and he would have been worse off than in the nonstandardized game.

In what way does the standardization of utility units and the procedure outlined above contribute to a justification of the resulting theory of bargaining and hence to a theory of conflict and perhaps to conflict resolution?

This question is posed here, because we feel it is strongly suggested at this point. We are not yet ready to answer it. First we must follow the development of game theory to its next and, so far, highest stage, namely, the theory of the N-person game.

We have seen that when game theory is extended to nonzero-sum games, the prescriptive aspect of the theory is seriously impaired if communication between the players is not allowed because of the frequent incongruity between individual and collective interest. If communication and bargaining are allowed, "solutions" of nonzero-sum games can be designed, based on certain bargaining principles or norms. There is no unique set of these norms as evidenced by the fact that several kinds of solutions to bargaining games have been proposed (Raiffa, 1953; Luce and Raiffa, 1957; Nash, 1953; Braithwaite, 1955). Still, underlying all the proposed solutions are attempts to take into account the bargaining "strengths" of the players. Thus there emerges a notion of power which can be operationally defined and possibly quantified.

So far we have only considered the case where two players in a non-zero-sum game join forces to maximize their joint return. Power comes into play in determining the way the joint return will be split. The coalition of the two players in a two-person game is against the House. The House participates in the pay-offs but has no bargaining power. Suppose now there are more than two players, so that some can join in a coalition against others. The bargaining problem now becomes much more complex, because there are now many ways in which the coalitions can be formed.

In the theory of N-person games, it is usually assumed that whenever a subset of the N players, say k of them, form a coalition, the remaining N − k players will form a countercoalition. (Actually it is always in their collective interest to do so.) The result is a two-person game of one coalition against the other. By adding another (fictitious) player who gets the collective losses and pays out the collective gains, any N-person game can be viewed as an N + 1 person zero-sum game, which, after a coalition and a countercoalition have been formed, becomes a two-person zero-sum game.

Now the theory of the two-person zero-sum game is complete in the sense that the pay-offs to the two parties (at least the expected pay-offs) are determined. These pay-offs are the collective pay-offs to the members of the coalition and of the countercoalition. Therefore the only problem remaining in the theory of the N-person game is that of deciding which coalitions are to form and, once they are formed, how the collective pay-offs are to be apportioned among the coalition members. It turns out that this is a formidable problem.

Note that the phrase "which coalitions are to form" is ambiguous. We recall that game theory does not discover rules or laws which actually govern behavior, hence is not in a position to predict behavior. Can then game theory *prescribe* the formation of coalitions as it prescribes the strategy choices in zero-sum games? Let us see on what basis such prescriptions could possibly be made.

An N-person game, we have seen, can be viewed as a two-person zero-sum game between two coalitions. Depending on how the N players split, a certain *collective* pay-off will accrue to one of the coalitions and its negative to the other. Some of the 2N subsets of the N players will be able to get the maximum collective pay-off that any coalition can get. Let us call such a coalition a winning coalition and its complement a losing coalition. Shall then one of these winning coalitions be prescribed? The answer cannot be a clear affirmative for the following reasons: (*a*) there may be several winning coalitions; (*b*) a winning coalition may lose its attractions for some of its members. Presumably players are induced to join the coalition by a promise of a certain share in the take. However, the losing coalition may be in a position to lure certain members away from the winning coalition by promises of greater individual shares, since it can become a winning coalition if others join it.

To take the simplest example, suppose three individuals, A, B, and C are after a prize which can be captured by any two of them. If A and B form a coalition to capture the prize, they are a winning coalition, while C by himself is the losing coalition. Suppose A and B agree to split the prize evenly. Even though C has nothing to offer of his own, he is in a position to offer B a greater share of the prize if B deserts A and joins with C. But if this happens, A will be in a position to offer C (the recipient of the smaller share from B) a larger share if he deserts B. No matter which winning coalition is formed and no matter how the prospective prize is shared among its members, the third, the losing party, is in a position to break up the coalition by bribing one of its members. Obviously no prescription of a coalition and its associated allocation of spoils can be definitive in such a situation.

In spite of these difficulties, N-person game theory has come up with certain types of "solutions" of N-person games. However, for reasons just stated, these "solutions" can by no means be considered as definitive prescriptions of coalition-forming strategies. Rather the "solutions" are classes of outcomes which have certain mathematical properties. These properties may or may not have a bearing on certain notions of stability of coalitions, or on a rationale for forming the coalitions in question, or on equity, or any other notions which we may believe to be relevant to conflict situations. It is difficult to say whether the game-theoretical solutions of N-person games are relevant to such matters, because most of the associated notions have emerged from game theory itself, that is, from its mathematical structure rather than from any observed or postulated characteristics of conflicts.

PITFALLS OF STRATEGIC THINKING

The foregoing discussion was meant to serve as a background to our evaluation of game-theoretical contributions to the theory of conflict. The issues we have brought out are all familiar to the game theoreticians, but many of these issues are still, it seems, outside the nonspecialist's conception of game theory. The nonspecialist, coming in contact with the elementary aspects of game theory, is still easily seduced into thinking that game theory is a straightforward extension of rational-decision schemes to conflict situations. Such a conception is based on a tacit assumption that in any situation involving a range of decision choices, there exists an objectively "best" decision and hence a rational procedure for determining it. For instance if each of the possible decisions leads to a definite single outcome, one needs only to find out which decision leads to which outcome in order to choose the decision which leads to the most preferred outcome. In this context the decision-maker solves his problem by simply obtaining sufficient information about his environment.

Next consider the situation where each decision can lead to a number of different outcomes, each with a known probability. If one is able to assign utility pay-offs to the outcomes, rational decisions can be made in the context of a rational gambling theory with its central concept of calculated risk, that is, a decision based on a comparison of expected gains. In this context, too, a prescriptive theory can be rationalized.

The decision problem is further complicated if a rational opponent enters the picture. At this point, decision theory becomes game theory proper. Game theory can prescribe best strategies (pure or mixed), provided the utilities are given, both the decision-maker's and his opponent's. Here, indeed, game theory appears as an important extension of a rational-decision scheme to situations involving not only risk but also conflict.

Now in our society two classes of decision-makers wield great power in the sense of directing the organized efforts of great masses of people. These are business and military leaders. The business leader's "rational decisions" are frequently in the context of calculated risk or of a conflict of interests (e.g., labor-management relations, economic competition, and so on). Moreover, in many contexts, the business leader is accustomed to thinking in terms of naturally quantified utility units—profits, volumes, share of market captured, efficiency indices, and so on. He therefore readily interprets game theory as a theory of rational decisions applicable to situations involving the uncertainties of economic life and to competition.

To the "scientifically oriented" military leader, game theory also tends to appear in this light. He too has become primarily a "rational decision-maker" (rather than, say, a charismatic leader, as he frequently was in earlier days). One might guess, therefore, that "enlightened" business and military leaders would tend to view game theory as a science created to help them solve their problems, namely, how to make rational decisions under risk and in conflict situations, decisions which will help them make more money or enhance the power and prestige of organizations or nations which they serve.

From our analysis of game-theoretical problems it appears that the prescriptions of game theory are clearest in purely competitive situations, in which the utilities of all outcomes have been determined on interval

scales. Therefore if a game theoretician wishes to *apply* his theory of conflict in business or military contexts, he will experience a pressure to cast
conflict situations in just such terms: he will assume utilities as given and
will emphasize the purely competitive aspects of the conflict.

Now it is not possible to substantiate the conjecture that game
theoreticians actually distort real situations in order to make them amenable to game-theoretical treatment. Nor is it possible to assess the influence of game theoreticians in the formulation of business or military
policies. The number of game theoreticians working as business advisors
is probably negligible, if not nil. Some game theoreticians, to be sure,
work on strategy research in such organizations as the Rand Corporation
and the Systems Development Corporation, but certainly their number
must be quite small, since there are not many genuine game theoreticians
to begin with, and many of these work in mathematics and economics
departments of universities rather than in the paramilitary think factories.
On the other hand, many individuals who apply "rational methods" to
the working out of strategic-policy recommendations disclaim with perfect
right the designation of *game theoretician*. We cannot therefore hope to
demonstrate lines of influence from the mathematical theory of games
to the current conceptions of conflict among decision makers, let alone
to the current nature of national policies. We rather suspect that both the
lively interest manifested toward "game theory" (or rather certain conceptions of it) in circles far removed from the mathematical community
and the energetic development of game theory itself are symptomatic of
our times and of the prevailing notions about conflict and, more generally, about the nature of collective human existence. Competition and
conflict of interest, as well as science as a source of power, are at the
center of attention in our society. The glamor of game theory stems from
the notion that it is a science devoted to the investigation of means which
enable the participants in conflicts to conduct conflicts effectively. From
our analysis it should be clear that this is a distorted view. A thorough
knowledge of game theory will not make anyone a better chess or poker
player or a more brilliant military strategist, although such knowledge
can impart a profound understanding about the basic nature (i.e., the
underlying logical structure) of a great variety of conflicts.

However, the pressures to view game theory as a contribution to
competitive know-how persist. It seems to us that this view contributes
to the already prevailing misconceptions about the nature of real-life
conflicts. For example, an idea that a common denominator of value
exists derives from the role of money in a market economy. Money makes
every commodity exchangeable with every other. The great convenience
of money as a means of exchange makes for pressures to view it also as a
common denominator of value and so to view all values as commodities.

One can buy for money not only hay, buttons, and pork, but also a man's services. If one can buy his services, one can perhaps buy his loyalty and even his integrity. The corrupting role of money as a universal standard of value has been noted since the days of the prophets. But a rational analysis of conflict, we have seen, *presupposes* a determination of utilities and this, in turn, implies *some* common standard of value. Money serves admirably in this capacity and suggests other "objective" standards. For example, it has become commonplace in discussing alternative defense policies to measure outcomes of nuclear exchanges in "megadeaths" and to apply this measure to assess the relative "degrees of deterrence" possessed by each side in the cold war. The pernicious influence of this mode of thought is not so much in its implied callousness as in the absurdly simplistic conceptions of conflict and of the psychology of threat. The vastly complex global conflict with profound ideological and possibly psychopathological roots is cast by the strategists into a football-game model with an implied objective of achieving a higher (megadeath) score than the opponent.

In short, the pressure is toward conceptualizing conflict in terms amenable to rational analysis. Rational analysis is predicated on the knowledge of one's own *and* of the opponent's utilities of outcomes. We have already shown what it takes to obtain an interval scale of utilities —a list of preferences among options involving risky outcomes. How is one to construct a list of one's own preferences in situations involving national-policy decisions? "Oneself" in the context of national policy is a fiction. Does it refer to some poll-determined average? To the person of the head of state? If so, on what grounds are his preferences to be equated to the hierarchy of national interests? Suppose, however, for the sake of argument, some hierarchy of preferences among risky outcomes is chosen to represent "one's own" utility scale. *Then the notion of so-called calculated risk becomes meaningless.* If the notion means anything, it means a maximization of expected gain. But we have seen that if utilities are determined by the risk-preference method, maximization of expected gain becomes nothing more than a restatement of these preferences and so has nothing to do with "rational decision." To be sure, in the context of a game involving mixed strategy, the calculation of the latter still remains as a "rational act." However this too is meaningless unless the utility scale of the *opponent* is known. No such knowledge can be realistically expected to be available. Consequently, to preserve the appearance of rational analysis in the formulation of strategy-problems standards of utility tend to be chosen essentially arbitrarily. A degradation of human values and a brutal oversimplification of conflict issues are the by-products of these persistent attempts to formulate conflicts as problems which yield to available tools of analysis.

Since the most definitive results of game theory (hence of rational analysis of conflicts) appear in the context of the two-person zero-sum game, there are pressures to *see* conflicts in this context. In the present global conflict, it is frequently tacitly assumed that what hurts "their" side *ipso facto* benefits ours and vice versa. Again this oversimplification cannot be laid directly at the door of game theory, since two-valued thinking of this sort is moldy with age. Nevertheless the "we-they" thinking is reinforced by casting conflicts into game-theoretical terms. Zero-sum games have straightforward solutions; consequently the associated models are the most tractable and so the most attractive.

The assumption in the zero-sum model is that whatever the "enemy" can *possibly* do to gain an advantage (therefore to harm our side) he *will* do. Possibilities become certainties (as with the paranoiac). The main problems associated with any agreements with the "enemy" become overwhelmingly problems of detecting and punishing violations and sometimes even problems of how to get away with violations. I have witnessed a presentation by a game theoretician at a conference on arms control, in which the problem of inspection (associated with a hypothetical arms control or disarmament agreement) was cast into a two-person zero-sum game, with inspectors and evaders as the players. The solution of the game was a pair of prescribed mixed strategies, one for the inspectors, one for the evaders, which would maximize the chance of detection for the former and minimize it for the latter.

Now there is no denying the value of such investigations in providing some estimates of what it would take to be reasonably sure of effective inspection and what it would take to evade an agreement with reasonable impunity. The results do, in principle, furnish us with relevant information, as long as the problems continue to be viewed in the same zero-sum context. But it seems to us also that the pursuit of these investigations tends to keep attention fixed on this particular context and to discourage alternative approaches to the analysis of conflict and of the issues involved.

Whether or not they are zero-sum, two-person games permit a more definitive treatment than N-person games. Further pressure for simplification operates here. Although the problem of the N-country arms race is sometimes mentioned in strategic circles, attention is still riveted on the bilateral arms race and how to win it. The simplicistic view of game theory fosters the illusion that if one is smart enough one can "win" any strategic contest. A fuller understanding of the N-person game should dispel these illusions. But the utilitarian interest in game theory is not conducive to fuller understanding.

Finally, the preoccupation with rational analysis of conflicts in the spirit of game theory (whether specific game-theoretical techniques are

involved or not), by directing attention exclusively toward strategic issues, directs it away from fundamental ones. In a game there are only
strategic issues. The justification of a move in chess is exclusively in terms
of the strategic advantage it confers. Its utility is measured by its contribution to the prospect of winning. One does not ask why one wants to
win the game itself. Similarly, a purely strategic analysis of conflict de-
tracts from the issues of the conflict. In our time a question like why one
should want to "win" a nuclear war (or "to prevail" in one, as some nuclear strategists would have it) is simply not raised. Similarly, the genesis
of a conflict, its psychological overtones, in short, its meaning, are totally
beyond the scope of strategic analysis, such as is epitomized by the game-
theoretical approach.

THE POTENTIAL POSITIVE CONTRIBUTIONS OF GAME THEORY

It should be clear that our critique is not directed at game theory
itself, which as a branch of mathematics has absolutely nothing to do with
conflict or any other sector of human affairs. Our critique is directed at
the facile formalizations of real conflicts which have been encouraged
by the appearance of game theory and, in its wake, of the idea that a
rational theory of conflict is about to confer strategic superiority on those
who master it. On the other hand we do not contend that the value of
game theory is confined to its contributions to mathematics. We do believe that game theory can contribute significantly to the theory of conflict. But it will do so by suggesting revealing insights into the nature of
conflicts, not through utilitarian applications of techniques. Paradoxically
the very limitations of game theory are the sources of its greatest theoretical contributions. This is quite in accordance with many other analogous
situations in science where the recognition of limitations induced new
important developments. For example certain phenomena are understandable in the light of mechanics alone, e.g., in terms of the conserva-
tion of mechanical energy. So the motion of the clock can be explained
by the compressed spring within it. But if a seventeenth-century physicist
tried to explain the action of a steam engine in this way, his search for
the compressed spring would prove futile. At this point, he could persist
doggedly in his search for a compressed spring, or else he could abandon
the search and invent thermodynamics.

We have seen how, in progressing from gambles to the two-person
zero-sum games with saddle points, to games without saddle points, to
nonzero-sum games, to N-person games, the game theoretician is forced

to introduce additional, more sophisticated concepts, without which even an analysis let alone solutions of these games is impossible. In this way the game theoretician has enriched the conceptual repertoire of the theory of conflict, and moreover, he has done so not by an *ad hoc* introduction of concepts to explain isolated phenomena (as frequently occurs in isolated speculations of social scientists), but rather in the course of a tightly reasoned *sequential* expansion of the logic of conflict. This process began long before game theory; it began in the introduction of the expected-gain concept into gambling theory by Pascal and Fermat in the seventeenth century. This expected-gain idea allowed the extension of the notion of rational decision to risk situations. When the expected gain alone was shown to be inadequate by Bernoulli, another concept was introduced, that of utility.

Both the expected-gain concept and that of utility are essential in game theory. The function of the former, however, is not such that it enables the decision-maker to *cope* with uncertain outcomes (as in gambling theory), but rather that it enables a player to *impose* uncertainty on his strategy choices in order to confound the opponent (as in the use of mixed strategies). The existence of this principle was, of course, intuitively known to military commanders and poker players for a long time, but it was in game theory that the mixed-strategy concept was given its exact formulation and so endowed with theoretical power.

Next, we see how in the nonzero-sum game without communication, strategic considerations can become self-defeating, as in Game 5. The analysis is provided in the context of game theory but in our search of satisfactory solutions, we are forced to give consideration to concepts like "trust," "trustworthiness," and "suspicion," which stem from psychology or even from ethics. In this context game theory ceases to be prescriptive in the usual sense of rational decision. But the analysis suggests an extension of the theory to the experimental domain. How *do* people behave in situations where self-interests conflict with collective interests and where a decision to pursue the collective interest depends on trusting the other to do the same? Experimental evidence on these matters would certainly be a contribution to a theory of conflict in its usual sense as a branch of behavioral science.

The introduction of the coalition concept introduces still another class of ideas into the analysis of mixed-motive conflicts. Solutions of bargaining problems associated with coalition formations depend on a definition of bargaining power and suggest definitions of *equity*, since these solutions represent, in a way, equitable divisions of joint gains.

In this connection it is noteworthy that the first problem suggested by Chevalier de Méré to Pascal, which gave the impetus to the development of mathematical gambling theory, involved a question of equity.

The problem was how the stakes in a game of chance ought to be divided if the game is interrupted before either player has reached a winning score. It was in this context that the notion of expected gains ("moral expectation") was born, later to be applied also to gambling strategies.

There is no natural definition of equity. All such definitions are based in the last analysis on social norms. An achievement of bargaining theory (an extension of the theory of the nonzero-sum game) has been in laying bare the assumptions which underlie this or that definition of equity. Some definitions may eschew comparisons of utility scales of the contending parties on the grounds that the units and zero points of such scales are necessarily arbitrary. But other definitions may wish to take such comparisons into account. A compromise which implies a small loss to one of the parties and at the same time a big gain to the other seems more attractive than one in which one party gains little at a large expense to the other. But this idea cannot be utilized in bargaining theory unless the utilities of the bargaining parties are compared. In making the axiomatic bases of bargaining schemes explicit, game theory at least clarifies the ethical issues involved.

Finally the theory of the N-person game with its labyrinthine analyses and inconclusive "solutions" should impress the participants in multilateral conflicts with the immense complexities of the situations in which they find themselves.

The greatest lesson to be derived from "higher" game theory, that is, the theory of games beyond that of the two-person zero-sum game, is that purely strategic considerations are not sufficient for a basis of "rational decision," indeed that the very concept of rational decision becomes diffuse in most real-life conflict situations. This lesson should serve to direct the attention of would-be rational decision-makers to other than strategic problems of conflict—to psychology, to problems of communication, and to ethical questions, all of which are sadly neglected in our technique-worshipping and competition-dominated age. If this lesson is learned, the potential contributions of game theory to an understanding of conflict will be more fully realized.

REFERENCES

Braithwaite, R. B., *Theory of Games as a Tool for the Moral Philosopher*. New York: Cambridge University Press, 1955.

Luce, R. D. and H. Raiffa, *Games and Decisions*. New York: John Wiley & Sons, Inc., 1957.

Nash, J. F., "Two-Person Cooperative Games," *Econometrica,* XXI (1953), 128-140.

Raiffa, H., "Arbitration Schemes for Generalized Two-person Games," H. W. Kuhn and A. W. Tucker, *Contributions to the Theory of Games:* II, *Annals of Mathematical Studies,* XXVIII (1953).

von Neumann, J. and O. Morgenstern, *Theory of Games and Economic Behavior.* Princeton, N.J.: Princeton University Press, 1955.

CHAPTER

11

World Law and Human Conflict

RICHARD A. FALK

"The observance of law and the establishment of a stable international legal order are a necessary preliminary to universal peace . . ." (Korovin, 1962, p. 7). This is the conclusion reached by Y. Korovin, a leading Soviet international law expert, in an article appearing recently in *International Affairs* (Moscow). President Kennedy's *Law Day, USA— 1963* proclamation similarly suggests that: "In a time when all men are properly concerned lest nations, forgetting law, reason and moral existence, turn to mutual destruction, we have all the more need to work for a day when law may govern nations as it does men within nations" (Kennedy, 1963, p. 817). This convergent reliance by rivals upon law as the means to attain the common goal of enduring peace is a significant, if somewhat curious, item of consensus in this era of imminent danger and global antagonism. Perhaps law as a neutral common denominator, more than morality or alliance systems, can after all provide the norms and procedures by which to safeguard the existing order and transform it into something both more durable and beneficial.

Of course, it is not realistic to rely upon law as an *independent* instrument of order and change. For law provides only the method and ritual by which deeply held values and policies can be preserved and promoted. Law is an integral aspect of a functioning social system. It is not an autonomous force that can ignore the expectations that remain dominant in a relevant community. Thus so long as the effective elites of major states are conflict-oriented and deferential to the habits of sovereignty, the prospects for the qualitative growth of world law are not good.

An assessment of the role of world law in the future of mankind is a problematic subject. In one sense, a unified legal order represents the common dream of men of goodwill otherwise separated by morality, culture, and ideology. In quite another sense, world law is a delusive expectation, leading us to ignore the extent to which we are trapped by the social and moral variables of a political heritage of ardent nationalism that opposes the assumption of the most minimal risks (acceptance of the compulsory jurisdiction of the International Court of Justice or ratification of the Genocide Convention) to bring a stronger world legal order into being. This dual reality poses a formidable challenge: the discovery of intellectual tools adequate for the depiction of the constructivist mission of law in world affairs that is yet able to avoid the deceptions of a facile and false optimism. We need a vision of the goal to guide our actions toward the kind of future that we seek, but we also require an accurate account of the obstacles that impede its attainment.

There is a second delicate balance to be maintained. Law can serve either to promote conflict or cooperation. Law can serve to provide a self-justifying explanation for a conflict position, and hence provide a respectable explanation for aggressive and destabilizing behavior; the Soviet Union, the United States, and Cuba could each plausibly describe its relation to the 1962 emplacement of Soviet missiles in Cuba by reference to the right of self-defense as sanctified by law. But law can also provide a series of techniques to overcome conflict. The Antarctica Treaty creates a cooperative regime that makes a legal allocation of rights and duties to the participating states. Therefore, it is necessary to examine the status of law and conflict in a series of specific settings. To describe the role of law requires the observation of its variable impact upon human behavior as well as its differential use as an instrument of change and order. Law is available in conjunction with the relevant index of capability to implement whatever policies achieve dominance for decision-makers, including the increase of national power, prestige, and wealth at the expense of others or the gradual conversion of a system based on conflicting sovereign states into a global peace and welfare system. There is, of course, a spectrum of law possibilities, not just a choice between the sectors of pure conflict or pure cooperation; in fact, the mix of various proportions in various settings is the most significant sector. These comments about the role of law are applicable to its operation in any social system, not just to the way law functions in world affairs.

Law, and especially international law, has a special concern with the control of violent conflict. Every legal order does seek to minimize recourse to unauthorized violence by those subject to its norms and to monopolize for itself the effective right to use violence when necessary. This general proposition points to the special problems of developing legal control over international conflict, namely, the continuing dominance of national decision-making in the realm of international conflict combined with a virtual monopoly by nations of the instruments of violence. This raises a question for world affairs: What can law contribute to the regulation of human conflict in a social system that is as decentralized as is the present international system? The response to this question is the central, if deferred, undertaking of this essay. It will become clear that legal technique promotes stability even in situations of crisis and violence by moderating, or at least by providing actors with a way to moderate, if they so wish it, conflict before it generates devastation. International order, as a primitive social system that contains dangerous and powerful rivalries, imposes upon law a primary task—to prohibit effectively violence and threats of violence. Nonviolent means must be developed to resolve conflict. The promotion of human rights and economic welfare are also increasingly germane to the avoidance of violent conflict and must become susceptible to legal control if law is to succeed in keeping the peace.

Law provides a disciplined interpretation of social phenomena that is capable of taking significant account of the totality of social reality, including political, moral, and historical variables. But law, unlike the other social sciences, is a functioning part of social reality to be understood, as well as a specialized way to understand it. Thus the relevance of law to conflict is an empirical *and* a methodological inquiry, and so far as the claim to consider a warless world is accepted, then it is also a speculative inquiry.

THE QUEST FOR LEGAL CONTROL
OVER INTERNATIONAL VIOLENCE

Legal order has enjoyed reasonable success in its efforts to manage conflict arising out of the relations between social units other than states. The legal control of international conflict is hampered by the weakness of centralized sources of authority and by the concentration of the instruments of violence on the national level. Therefore, unauthorized violence as a means to resolve crucial conflicts has been rather frequent and of spectacular magnitude in the history of international affairs. The absence of an international legislature has often allowed unauthorized coercion to play a constructive role bringing about desirable social changes in the history of international relations. Just as the opportunity for, and threat of, revolution are available to challenge domestic oppression, so the possibility of international war has created the opportunity for the more exuberant and progressive nations to expand their beneficial influence in international society; at least this rationalization has been widely accepted and can be supported with considerable evidence.

The special crisis of the contemporary world arises because the costs and dangers of unauthorized national violence, always high and occasionally intolerable, have become unacceptable because the major use of thermonuclear and missile weaponry would be so permanently destructive. Thus the traditional willingness to allow violence to serve as a means to resolve international conflict, a tolerance that has long been tormenting to many of those familiar with the brutality and suffering occasioned by warfare, is now challenged by the dismal prospect of an eventual catastrophe of global proportions. This objective situation, accented by radical changes in the status and outlook of the less industrialized states, prompts a search for new ways to gain control over national capabilities to use violence for conflict resolution. There is a much smaller margin of tolerance for violence in international affairs than in domestic society. We read of unsolved homicides in daily newspapers without losing confidence in the viability of the domestic legal order. Not so with an international delinquency. For the instances of international violation are often perceived as so decisive as to undermine the credibility of the regulative authority claimed on behalf of international law. And especially with nuclear warfare as a serious possibility, a legal system that cannot give virtually perfect assurance that it can prevent unauthorized violence will be perceived, and quite prudently so, as almost worthless, providing inadequate protection against potential dangers. Thus the devastating consequence of inadequately controlled international conflict imposes a requirement upon international order that no domestic society has been yet able to satisfy. It is well to appreciate that it is the special nature of international conflict more than the deficiencies of international law that account for the failure of a peace system to emerge. Our conception of peace on the international level is much purer than it is for domestic affairs, for there is less capacity to withstand the impact of a single diligent violator if it happens to be a major state.

Skepticism about the reality of international law also emanates from the divisive tendency of nations and national jurists to use law as a rationalization for national policy no matter how evident the illegality of conduct might appear to an impartial observer. The availability of legal explanations for contradictory courses of action underlies the adversary nature of law and is a well-understood attribute of domestic legal process. Thus the United States may claim that principles of self-defense or collective security legitimize its insistence in October 1962 that the Soviet Union remove missiles from Cuba, whereas the USSR and Cuba can invoke their interpretation of self-defense (against an American invasion) or assert that bilateral military arrangements are matters within the domestic jurisdiction of the transacting states to support their allegation that the United States claim of removal underlying the quarantine was illegal. It is not the availability of these opposed legal arguments, each rather plausible, that helps to disclose a deficiency of international legal order, for this is the characteristic mode of adversary contention in any legal system (Cardozo, 1921; McDougal, 1962). Rather, it is the absence of any acceptable means for *authoritative* resolution. There is no regularly available and respected neutral decision-maker that will provide the community with a principled and reasoned determination of which side is "correct" about its claim of what it is that the law permits. This situation is aggravated by the patriotic habits of jurists who, in the rhetoric of scientific objectivity, provide their governments with legal apologia. Scholars, detached from an exclusive identification with national welfare, might contribute a rather authoritative interpretation of legal requirements if they were not drawn into the political process as experts in the instrumental manipulation of legal doctrine. One's nation becomes a client that expects a brief; international law, especially when it is invoked in crisis situations, functions more as a self-righteous rhetoric to describe national policy than as a constraining set of limits. This feature of the juristic approach to world affairs has been quite properly condemned as "legalism." It is true that even if nationalism continues to dominate the juristic imagination, international law facilitates routine or noncrises transactions; as part of the bureaucratic apparatus of the modern state, international law is mechanically applied and scrupulously adhered to so long as legality is not perceived to impair the defense of vital national interests. Therefore, acceptance of this point does not imply a rejection of international law *in toto*, although it does confine its operations to rather trivial subject matter, especially if a concern is with what can be done to prevent nuclear war.

SOME CONTRIBUTIONS OF LAW
TO THE CONTROL OF WORLD CONFLICT

The reality of conflict is pervasive and multifaceted. However, in world affairs, the urgency of concern about the prevention of war encourages a concentration upon the relevance of conflict to the control of political violence in interstate relations. This orientation conditions thought about law. It leads law to be conceived frequently, albeit simplistically, as the one alternative to force in the resolution of international disputes; this dichotomy is much too sharp as it overlooks the dependence of law upon force and neglects to appreciate the moderating effects that law can have even when violence has been introduced into social relations by threat or use. Nevertheless, this essay accepts the premise that the regulation of violence is the proper focus for a study of the relevance of law to international conflict, an acceptance predicated upon the paramount importance of maintaining nuclear peace.

There has been a tendency on the part of those who view law and force as mutually exclusive alternatives to devote their attention to the description of existing procedures and institutions—as well as the invention of new ones for the pacific settlement of disputes (e.g., Larsen, 1961). Pacific settlement provides a significant series of opportunities for international actors locked in conflict to resolve their difference in a nondestructive manner. As such, these procedures and institutions are important, especially as anticipations of a more ordered world; but, a present emphasis distracts one from an appreciation of the role that law can presently play in world affairs. For although the renunciation of force must be accompanied eventually by reliable substitutes, there is not yet in sight a significant disposition on the part of nations to entrust the settlement of vital disputes to legal tribunal and procedures. And, in fact, much misunderstanding is caused by "rule-of-law" movements that act as if the truly urgent obstacle to the growth of world law is the Connally amendment. Diplomacy, rather than law—although the divorce is not a separation (law affects the course of diplomatic negotiation)—is the realm for fruitful pacific settlement (Corbett, 1959).

A major criticism of the approach taken by specialists in international relations to the contribution law makes to the control of international conflict arises from their tendency to overstress formal apparatus: the World Court and treaty-making procedure (e.g., Hartmann, 1962, pp. 111-130; Stoessinger, 1961, pp. 240-256). If this apparatus is extolled as even potentially adequate to guard the peace, it encourages a naively optimistic outlook. If law is categorically dismissed because the apparatus is unable to regulate reliably the more fundamental aspirations of states for power, wealth, and security, then an equally naive cynicism emerges which is quite misleading (most notably Morgenthau, 1962, pp. 282-307). For legal process and order have contributed, and continue to contribute significantly, to the avoidance of destructive conflict and to the reduction of its destructiveness, but *not* by providing the kind of institutional structure or law-making procedure that has led us to rely so heavily upon the judiciary and legislature in our domestic life. As has been argued already, the character of law in world affairs is shaped by the decentralized distribution of power, producing a horizontal law system that, by its very nature, emphasizes substitutes for central or vertical institutions.

It is the aim of this section to outline some of these contributions that law presently makes to the control of conflict. The first task is to discuss how the classical concerns of international law must be updated to take recent developments into account. This discussion will, secondly, be supplemented by a description of law as a process for the communication of national claims to act; this is a characteristic of classical international law, but it has not been appreciated to be so until recently (McDougal *et al.*, 1960, pp. 987-1019). Third, it is necessary to deal with the special importance of nuclear weaponry for the operation of law in world affairs. Fourth, it is useful to consider the role of the United Nations—a significant centralizing tendency in the existing world-order system. Fifth, a short description will be given of certain unfamiliar functions fulfilled by international law in the contemporary world. And sixth, some comments will be made about those developing areas of world law that pertain to the control of international conflict in the decades to come.

On the Continuing Relevance of Classical International Law

There are several relevant categories to be distinguished: recourse to violence, rules of conduct, permissible instruments, belligerent objectives, and responsibility (national and individual).

Recourse to violence

It should be recalled that until after World War I a state was regarded as entitled to have recourse to force and war whenever it saw fit. Now, of course, law attempts to regulate *recourse* to force in international relations, restricting its legitimate role to situations of individual and collective self-defense or to security operations that have been authorized by the United Nations. The prohibition of force produced a search for precise limiting standards, explaining the frequent attempts to persuade nations to agree upon an authoritative definition of aggression (Report of the Secretary General, 1952; Stone, 1958). The complex reasons that explain the failure to reach an agreement about a definition of aggression cautions against a reliance upon the present capacities of law to exercise control over national decisions to make use of force in world affairs.

This failure of implementation should make one skeptical about appraising the significance of the Charter claims. Nevertheless, the willingness of nations to subscribe, even in principle, to the renunciation of their rights to use (except in self-defense) force is a significant step, an expression of willingness to move in one direction rather than another, and a disclosure of consensus on the most important aspect of political order in world affairs. And there is more to this consensus than a mere gesture of goodwill. However, a prohibition of force is not even a guide to behavior if its scope is not uniformly understood by the nation. Each state remains free to adopt a broad definition of self-defense that is capable of rendering the Charter renunciation of force almost meaningless. Even if an acceptable definition could be agreed upon by major states, it would not inspire confidence, unless it is accompanied by procedures to enable reliable and effective implementation. For if law is to control behavior, then it is necessary to provide an assured way to translate its standards into action, and thereby construct a sturdy bridge between the realms of authoritative utterance and behavior. Nevertheless, the record of United Nations control over national dispositions to violence is encouraging. It is especially impressive, if one takes into account the absence of centralized power in the United Nations, that is, of a regular police force and a reliable basis for fiscal support, that the organization has been so successful in frustrating the significant attempts (Korea, Suez) to commit outright aggression that have taken place since it came into existence. The passionate persistence of several claims by colonial powers to perpetuate their control has challenged the efforts of the United Nations to implement a peaceful but expeditious decolonialization process.

Rules of conduct

A second area of legal activity involves the establishment of rules and procedures for the conduct of war, the traditional "laws of war." Such matters as treatment of prisoners, care for the sick and wounded, and the rights and duties of belligerent occupation are governed by fairly clear and widely accepted rules, many of which are contained in international agreements and are included in national field manuals for the guidance of personnel (see generally, Greenspan, 1959). The further application of these rules developed, primarily, to govern international wars to the conduct of civil or internal wars is an important area of potential growth for law. Humanitarian considerations, as well as the moderating psychological impact upon even belligerents, of adherence to a common regime are contributions that are usually overlooked by those who conceive of war as the contradiction of order. Law can contribute by moderating the effects of violent conflict, including the provision of efficient termination procedures, as well as by acting to prevent the occurrence of international violence altogether.

Instruments of violence

There is also evidence of concern on the part of lawyers with the legal status of particular instruments of violence, especially with the status of nuclear weapons (O'Brien, 1960; Singh, 1959; Schwarzenberger, 1958). This kind of concern goes back at least as far as 1868, when the Declaration of St. Petersburg required the parties "to renounce, in case of war . . . the employment . . . of any projectile of less weight than four hundred grammes, which is explosive, or is charged with fulminating or inflammable substances" (Scott, 1908, pp. 381-382). There is disagreement about whether it is legitimate to use nuclear weapons in the pursuit of traditional military objectives; as well, there is some disagreement about a demographic military strategy that proposes cities as targets. Legal controversy has also involved the right to use the high seas and atmosphere to test nuclear weapons, despite uncertainties about the effect of fallout and the receipt of objections by nonnuclear states (cf. McDougal et al., 1960, pp. 763-843). The historic debate about the legal status of poison gas as a military weapon indicates that international law has long sought to regulate those instruments of violence responsible for indiscriminate suffering and permanent destruction.

Belligerent objectives

The subject of belligerent objectives has also always been on the borderland of law. If it is permissible to use force, it remains necessary to specify whether limits condition the objectives that can be sought. Under existing conceptions, this involves, primarily, a definition of the scope of self-defense; other national uses of force are agreed by most to be illegal. But is the state that properly claims self-defense entitled to compel its attacker to surrender? Or is there a norm of proportionate response that limits the defender's objectives to a restoration of the status quo ante? (Tucker, 1960, pp. 97-162; Falk, 1963, pp. 16-20). What limits apply when a regional organization undertakes collective security measures or applies sanctions for wrongful behavior? Or when the Security Council, General Assembly, or Secretary General employ force? These questions are just beginning to be seriously raised. There is no consistent response provided by law at this stage; the formulation of the issues, however, suggests a new source for limits upon the competence of all international actors, not just states, when force has been used in the course of conflict. This further suggests that an attempt to control force by even a perfectly defined and implemented definition of aggression and a coordinate concept of self-defense is insufficient. We need, as well, to know more precisely about the relations between a nation acting in self-defense and an international organization acting within the scope of its authority. This is an area badly in need of normative clarification.

Responsibility: national and individual

The victorious side after World Wars I and II attempted to emphasize the responsibility of the losers for the war. A peace treaty, no matter how much a product of duress, represents a valid legal instrument; therefore, "victor's justice" is "law," in the international system. There was a considerable shift in the attitude of the victors toward the vanquished after the two great wars, a shift dramatized by a comparison of the Versailles Treaty with the Nuremberg Judgment.

The prevailing idea after World War I was to make Germany suffer as a nation for the destruction and suffering caused by the war. Reparations were claimed and restrictions were imposed upon Germany's freedom to re-establish its military prowess. There was some attempt to prosecute the Kaiser as a war criminal, but it was thwarted by his unavailability for prosecution. The casual relationship that many people believe connects the austerity of Versailles to Hitler prompted a virtual abandonment, especially by the West, of any attempts to punish Germany as a nation after World War II. Instead, the responsibility for the war was attributed to the evil apparatus of government as administered by its leaders. This produced the Nuremberg and Tokyo judgments, and in Germany, a multitude of lesser military and civilian trials imposing responsibility upon individuals who carried out the inhumane or aggressive designs of the Axis governments. Despite the deficiencies of these trials from the perspective of domestic due process, there is a growing willingness to make individuals responsible for carrying out government policies that are in flagrant disregard of world-community values. It is significant that no member of the Security Council questioned Israel's authority to prosecute Eichmann, even though the allegedly criminal acts committed by Eichmann were committed abroad in accord with territorial law prior to the existence of Israel, the prosecuting state, and, of course, before the statutes defining the offenses upon which the prosecution rested were enacted. National courts in the existing system act as agents of the world community, deriving the mandate and authority from the presence of a supranational consensus rather than from a mere assertion of national authority (Falk, 1961).

The effectiveness of symbolic retribution against national officials is certainly undemonstrated as a deterrent. Nevertheless, from the standpoint of the possibilities for world law, these developments are encouraging. For there is disclosed a willingness to accord significance to world-community perspectives in the appraisal of human conduct. The growth of a transnational consciousness is essential preparation for further transfers of power and authority to supranational institutions, especially if it is our intention to prevent violent resolutions of internation conflict.

Law as a Claiming Process

There is a frequent tendency to understand law statically as a system or corpus of rules. A major divide between the positivist and sociological approaches concerns whether or not processive elements of legal order are included within the jurist's province (McDougal, 1953; 1960a). It is strongly urged here that one of the major contributions of law in conflict situations is to provide a regular and highly articulated procedure for the assertion and refutation of national claims. The claiming procedure enables precise communication to take place in a horizontal authority structure. The failure to assert such claims and to justify them with reasons gives action an arbitrary appearance that undermines the reliance of international law upon a regime of self-imposed restraints. Myres McDougal emphasizes this point by identifying legality with reasonableness in context (McDougal et al., 1960, pp. 871-889). Thus a United States claim to develop a communication system based on copper needles in the atmosphere (Project West Ford) acquires some legal status if the United States gives its reasons for doing this and attempts to meet Soviet and British objections, but not otherwise. The entire pattern of behavior surrounding the assertion and withdrawal of claims appears to be critical for the maintenance of present stability and the encouragement of future changes. In no other setting can one perceive quite so clearly the reality or delusiveness of national intentions to give up or insist upon short-term advantages in exchange for the improvement or sacrifice of the intermediate and long-term prospects for world order. The acceptance of this obligation to demonstrate the reasonableness of controverted national claims is a development of legal accountability that extends beyond the classical notion that a sovereign state is entitled to do whatever it is not forbidden from doing (Case of the S. S. *Lotus*, 1927).

In crisis confrontations the communication of claims acts to prevent overreaction, by making evident the limits of the claimant's objectives. The Soviet response to our insistence that missiles be taken out of Cuba might have been far less accommodating had they supposed that the United States also contemplated the forcible overthrow of Castro. The communication of claims discourages miscalculation and tends to produce a reconciliation of opposing interests by compromise and nonviolent means; in addition, it avoids putting a nation in the situation of choosing between surrender and forcible resistance. The proposed installation of a "hot line" between Washington and Moscow is a further recognition of the connection between authoritative communication and the regulation of international conflict.

Why is this claiming procedure drawn into the province of law? An answer to this question requires a brief reconsideration of the distinctive needs of a horizontal legal order. Without the availability of normal legislative procedures for the reform and extension of existing rights, reasonable claims by nations to act are themselves equivalent to legislative facts. An excellent way to demonstrate the reasonableness or unreasonableness of a controverted novel claim—that is, a claim that is not provided for by precedents—is to show that it is authorized or prohibited by policies embraced in legal doctrines acceptable to contesting parties. Law provides rhetoric, analogies, and some standards to help with the determination of whether a particular claim is reasonable. This serves to civilize the process of conflict by revealing a concern with community approval. It is a legal proceeding partly because its outcome is precedential, affecting greatly future appraisals of reasonableness. A second quarantine on shipping carrying missile equipment to a nuclear-free zone, formally opposed as a region to the shipment, would appear to have a provisional validity as a result of the outcome of the 1962 quarantine claim.

Nuclear Weapons and the Doctrine of Nonintervention

The development of nuclear and rocket technology has such an important influence upon the tasks set for world law that it deserves separate mention. For one thing, this new military technology acts to reinforce legal norms prohibiting the use of force by one nation against another in open warfare between states. The organized response of the world community to the use of force in Korea and the Suez has further strengthened the status of this prohibition, although Goa, Tibet, and the Sino-Indian border dispute suggest that violence remains a relevant means to settle certain kinds of international disputes, especially if the victim of the coercion does not possess international personality or if the stakes of conflict are relatively limited. The mutual disadvantage of warfare on the nuclear level also discourages lesser forms of warfare and provocation which contain a significant perceived danger of escalation. This suggests that an effect of nuclear weapons has been to establish agreement in norm and interest among important nations about the need to eliminate force from major international arenas of conflict. Legal technique can reinforce this political disposition by clarifying the content of the prohibition, perhaps by developing an authoritative definition of aggression, which will thereafter be available for the guidance of officials in national and supranational institutions.

A related consequence of nuclear weaponry has been to shift aggressive political energies into modes of conflict that are relatively unlikely to initiate an escalation process. The cold war struggle for dominance in the underdeveloped portions of the world is far enough removed —although the Chinese and Russians disagree about how far removed— from vital centers of power to make a nuclear response, even on the level of threat, implausible. However, whether this implausibility will remain after China acquires a nuclear capability is uncertain. Modernization, the vestiges of decolonialization, and a miscellany of domestic strifes create many revolutionary opportunities in the Afro-Asian countries. These opportunities are well adapted to Sino-Soviet capability, ambition, and ideology. The attempts to extend the orbit of communist influence has induced strong Western countermoves, and has especially encouraged military and economic aid to incumbent regimes. The result has been to produce a series of internal wars fought between rival domestic factions, supported and directed to varying degrees by either the United States or the Soviet Union. The participation of external rivals in internal war has not been effectively regulated by traditional international law. Civil strife had been regarded by international law as a matter within the domestic jurisdiction of the state and not as an appropriate subject for international concern, except to the extent of fixing certain standards for the relationships between the insurgent faction and external states. The traditional system allowed foreign states to help the incumbent suppress minor or short-term challenges to its governmental supremacy (rebellion, insurgency) favoring, to this extent, the stability of the *status quo,* whereas it prescribed neutrality toward the warring factions if the challenge was protracted and substantially sustained in scope and duration (belligerency). Such a scheme, never overly persuasive nor conspicuously observed, has collapsed under the pressure of the cold war conflict: the revolutionary orientation of communism, its national party organization on a global scale, and its tactics of subversion and indirect aggression that seem to constitute such a pervasive challenge to the stability of noncommunist governments throughout the newly developing portion of the world (Falk, 1964). This challenge has often led the West, and especially the United States, to defend the incumbent by fairly visible participation in the struggle for domestic power. In reaction to the futility of noninterventionism (as demonstrated to the Western democracies by the course and outcome of the Spanish Civil War) whenever the incumbent has significant support abroad, coming from an international rival, it is prevalent, although not invariable, United States policy to resort to counterintervention (Halpern, 1963).

The United Nations and Regional Organizations

The growth of supranational institutions is, like the advent of nuclear missiles, so important for the shape and prospect of world law that it, too, warrants some separate consideration. The evaluation of the role of these institutions cannot be isolated from the significant fact that major wars *between* nations are now most characteristically fought *within* a single nation. This new pattern is facilitated and sustained by the many revolutionary situations created by the modernization process that is going on and will continue to go on for decades to come throughout the ex-colonial world. The recurrence of protracted political violence has become a threat to *international* peace even if the fighting is confined to the territory of one nation, and as such, has been increasingly treated as a matter of supranational concern that legitimates the assumption of jurisdiction by regional and global institutions.

It is artificial to separate the study of international norms from a consideration of the role of supranational institutions. This is especially true with respect to the regulation of conflict in the contemporary world. The character of world legal order is partly created by the expectation that the United Nations has a considerable capability to regulate violent conflict, whether in the traditional form of a war between states or in its more modern form of rival sponsorship of factions in a war within a third state. United Nations contributions are usefully divided into three categories: First, the United Nations can organize the community against an aggressor, authorizing or undertaking countermeasures, for example, Korea or Suez. If the realities of power prevent an effective response, it can, provided the political support is forthcoming, at least censure an aggressor: Hungary in 1956. Second, the United Nations is available to intervene in a situation of civil strife to restore peace if foreign participation is present or threatened; the alternative to United Nations intervention is often a competition between national interventions on the side of rival domestic factions. The Congo was a setting in which United Nations intervention was chosen as preferable to the danger of big-power interventions. Third, and as yet untried (the United Nations can use its authority and the support of its members to prevent national interventions, thereby allowing a domestic conflict to reach a "natural" outcome. This was the original idea of a policy of nonintervention with respect to foreign civil strife; the role of the United Nations would be to assure mutual compliance with duties to refrain from intervention. This might re-establish contact between the principle of self-determination and the doctrine of nonintervention that has been broken by the tendency of aggressors since the Spanish Civil War, especially Hitler and the Soviet bloc, to expand the domain of national influence by helping a sympathetic elite to win control of a foreign government (Huntington, 1962). As yet, except in exhortatory fashion, the United Nations has not yet tried to make itself an effective instrument of noninterventionism. These same three functions can be performed by regional organizations, subject only to over-all United Nations supervision to prevent the commission of "regional aggression" in the guise of a regional security operation. The further emergence of a world law system will depend heavily, it is felt, upon how effectively and justly the security organs of the United Nations and regional organizations are able to carry out these three functions.

The Functions of Law in the Contemporary World

This section tries to identify some of the less evident functions performed by law in acute conflict situations. As this undertaking is not within the repertory of the traditional concerns of lawyers, it will be offered in a very hazarding and tentative way.

If we conclude that the persistent violation of nonintervention norms have temporarily suspended their application in international relations, law, as rule and as technique, nevertheless provides or emphasizes certain limiting rules for participation in internal war. The basic character of law is to make a common standard of behavior explicit and to establish certain expectations on the part of international actors, the disappointment of which will produce destabilizing escalation. Two kinds of limits illustrate this conception of law. First, the failure to use or threaten nuclear weapons to influence the outcome of an internal war. Second, the failure to expand the arena of violence across boundaries except perhaps to provide sanctuary for insurgent groups. These two horizontal norms serve to limit the conflict in method and space. A legal character can be attributed to these norms because a departure from them would be discernible and it would be viewed as a wrongful act contrary to community expectations that justifies censure and retaliatory action. It is the provision of common standards for conduct, and not the method by which these standards are generated, that establishes the horizontal content of international law. Thus, despite the failure of rules of nonintervention to govern the behavior of nations, law continues to be relevant to national participation in the internal affairs of foreign states by contributing minimum stability to the prevailing patterns of interventionary politics. It is the task of the jurist to make this function of law more operative by clarifying the role of these norms in the maintenance of minimum international stability. A failure of national officials to adopt a policy that conforms with these limits could precipitate dangerous breakdowns of order, imperiling seriously the state of nuclear peace. Cold war participation in internal struggles for power, as a relatively safe but effective way to promote expansionist politics, has limited ends, the attainment of which is worth only limited risks. Just as the dangers of pursuing unlimited political objectives in Europe shifted the main arenas of conflict to overseas colonial wars in the eighteenth and nineteenth centuries, now after nuclear technology and the devastation of two world wars, there again seems to be an increasing disposition to avoid a violent encounter at the European center of conflict; this disposition is difficult to implement, however, because each side seeks to assure stability within its own domain, an end that can be gained only by giving Berlin, a symbol in the over-all struggle for world dominance, completely to one side or the other. The main control functions of law in relation to international conflict in the existing world are to reinforce the renunciation of force across international boundaries expressed in the phrase of the strategists—"nuclear stalemate"—and to identify the limits of permissible participation in intrastate conflict. These two endeavors are linked because a refusal to abide by intrastate limits endangers the stability of the interstate prohibition; thus the introduction of nuclear weapons into the war in South Vietnam would be a significant step in the direction of general nuclear war.

There are additional roles played by law in contemporary conflict patterns. For one thing, if one nation violates clear norms of international law, then it strengthens the appeal of the victim to the organized community for protection of its rights; if this protection is not forthcoming, then recourse to self-help, even of a violent variety, is perceived as less unreasonable. For example, in the first paragraph of its note of protest to Haiti charging a violation of the immunity of its embassy, the Dominican Republic typically characterized the events as "glaring violations of the rules of international law, universally consecrated and especially recognized by the inter-American system" (*New York Times*, April 29, 1963, p. 1). Defense Minister Malinowski increasingly invokes international law as one basis upon which to castigate United States policy toward Castro's Cuba and to urge adoption of a militant Soviet counterpolicy. This is partly self-justifying rhetoric, but it is also an appeal to that portion of the conscience of the world community that expects states to abide by the common standards set by international law. Furthermore, evidence of a serious violation of law by one state helps to vindicate a neutralizing coercive response by another state. This consequence, which is especially prominent when the violation of a generally accepted norm is patent—as when Haitian police violated the Dominican embassy—acts by itself to deter conduct that is readily demonstrated to be illegal. Most nations seem sensitive about their reputations and eschew illegal conduct except when under great pressure. It is this determination to behave in accord with community expectations, as specified in part by the acknowledged content of international law, that also acts to discourage nations from adopting extreme positions. In the context of domestic decision-making there is some pressure that can be created to bring national conduct into as close conformity with international law as the pursuit of necessary policy permits. The illegality of an act is itself a provocative challenge directed at another state stimulating it to make a major response, if only to uphold its pride and prestige. The effort of the United States, even if not entirely persuasive, to assert its demand, in a manner that accorded with law, that the Soviet Union remove nuclear-capable missiles from Cuba by limiting its interference with the freedom of the seas to a minimum and by securing the authorization and participation of the regional security organ, the Organization of American States, may have not only restrained United States behavior (precluding invasion or bombardment of the missile bases) but, as well, restrained the Soviet and Cuban responses. Law permitted the claim to be conveyed in narrow terms, guarding against the possibility of a Soviet interpretation of United States conduct as a demand for unacceptable action and limiting the affront to Soviet and Cuban dignity. Thus in a crisis situation there are several considerations that allow law to perform moderating functions, even though some applicable norms may be extended sufficiently beyond their normal meaning or accepted usage to make the conduct "a violation": first, there is a motive to avoid a clear violation of law so as to interfere with community responses in favor of the victim; second, censure of the lawbreaker at home and in international forums encourages the domestic adoption of those policy alternatives that are in accord with, or at least adhere as closely as possible to, applicable norms of law; and third, there is a greater likelihood of eliciting an accommodating response to hostile demands if these demands are restrained by the display of general respect for relevant legal boundaries. These restraining functions of law are peculiarly applicable in crisis confrontations, that is, at just those times when it is popularly supposed that international law has nothing to contribute, nothing at least until it has developed a regular police force capable of instantaneous and nonpolitical responses to illegal behavior. In noncrisis or precrisis situations, there is, of course, even more pressure to behave within the limits of law; the pressure is generated by the bureaucratic administration of the modern state to act in accord with applicable rules of law. A bureaucracy does not depart from applicable rules, even international rules, unless it has been authorized to do so by the top political leadership; and as leaders do not participate in the formulation of noncrisis policy, such departure is administratively difficult to arrange. This leads to a basic pattern of automatic compliance.

Notes on the Frontiers of World Law

There is also an emerging role for law with respect to the participation of organs of the United Nations or regional institutions in the control of domestic conflict that threatens the peace. Authorization for action is based upon the United Nations Charter, an international agreement serving as the institution's basic constitutional document. The general mandate to uphold peace has been used to legitimate claims by the United Nations both to defend victims of violence in an international conflict (Korea, Suez) and to restore domestic order in the event that civil strife (Lebanon 1958; Congo 1960) threatens world peace. The right to resist aggression has been claimed as a basis to legitimate (by reference to principles of collective security and self-defense) claims by regional organizations to resolve conflicts in accordance with the will and capability of the consensus; it is on this basis that the United States officially justifies the quarantine action against Cuba in 1962. The extent to which regional discretion is subject to United Nations control is an inevitable, but troublesome consequence of the development of law on several levels without adequate coordination between them. In general, Article 53 (1) of the United Nations Charter claims that ". . . no enforcement action shall be taken without the authorization of the Security Council." No content has been given, as yet, to this custodial responsibility over regional action that has been apparently entrusted to the United Nations; if we shift the focus from Cuba versus the O.A.S. to Israel versus an Arab regional organization, or Formosa versus an Asian one, a clearer sense of the potential dangers implicit in the subjection of a nation to regional consensus may emerge.

The relation between the domestic suppression of human rights and the use of international intervention as a technique of liberation is also a matter that lies along the frontier of a developing world-law system. If a consensus transcending the cold war can be developed in support of a consistent interventionary policy based on fixed objectives and restraints, then it is quite probable that the United Nations will be increasingly entrusted with a role in the promotion of human rights regardless of whether or not the incumbent government gives its consent; the Republic of South Africa is likely to provide the first important test of the limits and effectiveness of this form of community intervention under United Nations auspices. Such an interventionary claim is a radical denial of traditional notions of territorial sovereignty and domestic jurisdiction; these norms that hallowed the doctrine of sovereignty allowed, despite occasional instances of so-called *humanitarian interventions* (as when the Turks were persecuting Christian minorities), a government to determine conclusively the rights of its nationals, even if national administration resulted in shocking suppression. The notion of "crimes against humanity" expressed in the Nuremberg Judgment established for the first time restraints upon the extent of supranational deference to the sanctity of the social policies promoted by national elites. The expression of public opinion on the world level and the relative openness of most of the noncommunist world generate powerful political pressures that curtail national discretion in the area of human rights. Increasingly, national boundaries are being subordinated to the claims of racial affinity in the human-rights area. This is not an altogether progressive development, but it does undermine the reactionary dogma of sovereign prerogative with respect to human rights, creating thereby the basis for the imposition of certain minimum community standards. This development is linked to the central concern here; the prevention of international violence. For the prolonged suppression of human rights in secondary states will produce in the contemporary world an eventual protest movement, often abetted by interventionary support from abroad. This support, given the pervasity of the bipolar struggle, is likely to acquire a cold war tone, perhaps inducing competing interventions, generating crises, increasing tensions, and enlarging the scale and costs of conflict. An overwhelming preventive intervention by community institutions emphasizes an axiological, rather than a political (or cold war), mode of conflict resolution. World law is just beginning to devise procedures and norms by which to carry out such stabilizing operations, although no formal legal commitments have been made as yet.

A POLICY ORIENTATION

Should nations be expected to obey "the law" under all circumstances? It is difficult to find out just what such a question means. For if legal rules are necessarily susceptible to interpretation in light of the policy they serve, and if a legal system provides complementary rules and policies (McDougal, 1962), then there is always available a legal argument to justify a course of national behavior. But if law is to be *guide* to behavior, rather than a mere *rationalization* of it, then to obey the law must mean something more than finding a legal argument to support a particular national position. There is a difference between invoking law to justify action already taken and invoking law to identify in advance the limits of permissible action.

In the context of conflict the predominant directive of world law is to require states to refrain from the threat or use of force except in situations of self-defense. This limiting principle, so vital if we seek to guard against the outbreak of war, is corroded if major nations remain free to interpret self-defense. There is a need for objective limits, discernible by all actors, upon the concept of self-defense. Article 51 of the United Nations Charter could provide these limits, but only if the requirement of a prior armed attack is taken quite literally, that is, a nation is not entitled to claim self-defense unless it has been the victim of an armed attack across an international frontier. But can a nation anticipating a nuclear surprise attack be expected to wait until the enemy missiles have been delivered? I think that the answer even here is properly given in the affirmative; this conclusion is based upon the stabilizing advantage of an invulnerable second-strike capability and its consequence of making a nuclear surprise attack an act of suicide.

But limited force may be used to prevent the risks of major uses of force thereafter. Does a region have the legal discretion to use force to maintain regional security? To keep nuclear weapons out? Do regional organizations possess a broader competence to use force than does a single state? No authoritative answers are contained in the current law. However, the dangers of escalation require the effort of law to prevent, to the extent possible, international force, even if backed up by a supranational claim. Assuredly interregional force should not be employed more readily than international force. The more difficult questions are raised by the need to limit intraregional force. Here there is an ill-defined analogy to the status of intrastate force, the regional organization possessing some of the attributes of the incumbent government in a civil strife. Regardless of the context, reliance on force should be minimized. This is the central effort of law. But it is not the only effort. Otherwise there would be no right of self-defense whatsoever. Therefore, there is an attempt by law to balance interests in peace and survival. Particular rules are developed: for example, the norms of nonintervention in the internal affairs of sovereign states. Intervention, especially if in the form of coercive force, would appear to be an illegal use of force. But is not a military intervention an "armed attack" within the meaning of Article 51? Is there anything in law that corresponds to self-defense that can protect a state from minor coercion, perhaps applied in the form of support for or suppression of an insurgency? These questions are rarely analyzed from a legal point of view. A brief response is to suggest that norms of law in a horizontal legal order are valid only so long as there is a pattern of mutual adherence. The intervention by X in Y entitles Z to counterintervene to a proportional extent; or the facts of intervention justify the counterintervention of a regional or global international institution.

In addition to the avoidance of force, obedience to world law requires deference to community procedures and decisions. How much deference? Suppose the General Assembly passes a resolution that recommends a prohibition on subsequent nuclear testing. What is the legal status of the resolution? What conditions should prompt the United States to disregard the resolution? Here, the role of reasonableness in the assessment of legality is crucial. If a state disregards the resolution without giving an adequate account of its reasons for doing so, then it sets a precedent for self-reliance that is most damaging to the status and future of law. The minimum demand of horizontal law is that a nation, when its action is seriously challenged by other significant actors in the system, provides reasons. This is the notion of minimum reasonableness: (the giving of reasons is less burdensome than is optimal reasonableness) an impartial balancing of the reasons for and against the contested conduct in argument and in behavior. A refusal to satisfy the demands of minimum reasonableness discloses an unwillingness of a nation to acknowledge that the will and welfare of the world community is an important determinant of national policy.

Suppose, however, that an unambiguous decision adverse to national interests is rendered by an international institution. At this stage some flexibility of national response must be retained in form because it will be manifest in fact. Therefore, a rigid commitment to deference or submission is unrealistic. A legal claim is just one of several sources of guidance. But its significance may be lost. A nation that refuses to accept the adverseness of a *particular* supranational determination, especially if it is a nation that is exercising the kind of leadership that determines patterns, creates a *general* atmosphere of response to adverse judgments, thereby conditioning the expectations of other members and of the community as a whole and affecting the support that can be mobilized to coerce compliance. Therefore, the acceptance, even if awkward and frustrating, of an adverse international judgment or an adherence to a legal rule that interferes with immediate national aspiration, may often serve the national interest of the state to a greater extent than would lawless behavior. For there must be some weight accorded now to the longer-term interests of states in transforming the world to achieve more reliably national interests measured out over decades and centuries of survival rather than over months or years of temporary advantage; the transformation of the world must gradually come to be an instrumental element in present behavior. Otherwise the gap between facts and goals is necessarily made permanent. Realism for the nuclear age resembles idealism in early centuries, but this remark is encouraging only to the extent that governing elites and publics can be made to perceive and behave accordingly. To make this orientation operational—that is, to strengthen the law orientation of major actors in world affairs—requires a convinced sense of the relevance of the goal of a warless world to the conception and execution of present policy, and this enlivened awareness encourages, in turn, a new and essential juridical concern with "the transition problem" to inventory the means available to transform the existing system of world affairs from a threat system into a genuine peace system.

REFERENCES

Cardozo, Benjamin H., *The Nature of the Judicial Process*. New Haven: Yale University Press, 1921.

Case of the S.S. *Lotus*, PCIJ, Ser. A, No. 10 (1927).

Corbett, Percy E., *Law in Diplomacy*. Princeton, N.J.: Princeton University Press, 1959.

Falk, Richard A., "Toward a Theory of the Participation of Domestic Courts in the International Legal Order: A Critique of Banco Nacional de Cuba v. Sabbatino," *Rutgers Law Review*, XVI (Fall 1961), 1-41.

———, *Law, Morality, and War in the Contemporary World*. New York: Frederick A. Praeger, Inc., 1963.

———, "Janus Tormented: The International Law of Internal War," *International Aspects of Civil Strife*, James N. Rosenau, ed. To be published 1964.

Halpern, Manfred, "The Morality and Politics of Intervention." Pamphlet published by the Council on Religion and International Affairs, 1963.

Hartmann, Frederick H., *The Relation of Nations*, 2nd ed. New York: The Macmillan Company, 1962.

Huntington, Samuel P., "Patterns of Violence in World Politics," *Changing Patterns of Military Politics*, Samuel P. Huntington, ed., pp. 17-50. New York: Free Press of Glencoe, Inc., 1962.

Kennedy, John F., *Law Day, U.S.A.—1963, Federal Register*, XXVIII (January 1963), 817.

Korovin, Y., "International Law Through the Pentagon's Prism," *International Affairs*, VIII (December 1962), 3-7.

Larsen, Arthur, *When Nations Disagree*. Baton Rouge, La.: Louisiana State University Press, 1961.

McDougal, Myres S., "International Law, Power, and Policy: A Contemporary Conception," *Hague Recueil des Cours*, LXXXII (1953), 137-259.

———, "Some Basic Theoretical Concepts About International Law: A Policy-oriented Framework of Inquiry," *Journal of Conflict Resolution*, IV (1960), 407-431.

———, "The Ethics of Applying Systems of Authority: The Balanced Opposites of a Legal System," *The Ethics of Power*, Harold D. Lasswell and Harlan Cleveland, ed., pp. 221-240. New York: Harper & Row, Publishers, 1962.

McDougal, Myres S. *et al., Studies in World Public Order.* New Haven: Yale University Press, 1960.

Morgenthau, Hans, *The Decline of Democratic Politics.* Chicago: University of Chicago Press, 1962.

O'Brien, William V., "Nuclear Warfare and the Law of Nations," *Morality and Modern Warfare,* William J. Nagle, ed., pp. 126-149. Baltimore: Helicon Press, Inc., 1960.

Report of the Secretary General, "Question of Defining Aggression," A/2211, 3 October 1952.

Schwarzenberger, Georg, *The Legality of Nuclear Weapons.* London: Stevens & Sons, Ltd., 1958.

Scott, James Brown, ed., *Texts of the Peace Conferences at the Hague, 1899 and 1907.* Boston and London: Ginn & Company, 1908.

Singh, Nagendra, *Nuclear Weapons and International Law.* New York: Frederick A. Praeger, Inc., 1959.

Stoessinger, John G., *The Might of Nations.* New York: Random House, 1961.

Stone, Julius, *Aggression and World Order.* Berkeley and Los Angeles: University of California Press, 1958.

Tucker, Robert W., *The Just War—A Study in Contemporary American Doctrine.* Baltimore, Md.: The Johns Hopkins Press, 1960.

CHAPTER

12

Systems Theory and Human Conflict

CHARLES A.
McCLELLAND

After so many centuries of historical experience, it would seem very unlikely that many of the important *facts* about public conflicts in human societies would have gone unobserved and unrecorded. And, it is hard to believe that any large number of the possible *ideas* about the causes and the cures of such conflicts would have gone unrecognized. What insight, what pertinent meaning about the nature of conflicts or about ways to prevent or attenuate them must not have been entirely familiar at some time and place?

Since we have no basis for assuming that our ancestors were less intelligent than we are, why is it possible for us to imagine, short of impudence or intellectual arrogance, that we can now study the phenomena of public conflicts between groups, between organizations, or between whole states and societies, with the expectation of arriving at fresh results? Against the numerous kin of the present age who quite loudly and insistently argue that social research, at its best, only furnishes us with complicated and unworkable solutions (given in unreadable language and improbable equations) to problems for which the store of past knowledge is good enough, anyway, for practical people, I should like to base a case for the probability of finding out something new and useful about conflict.

It should be noted here that general systems, by any means, is not the whole of the subject. In fact, it is a remarkably restricted portion of the new outlook on the world although it is in full harmony with the new philosophy of science. How then, does one define general systems? General systems is but a name of an approach to the investigations of several families of complex problems. Perhaps in due course, some more resonant title will be found for it, but the particular state of mind—or orientation —to which reference is being made will be unchanged by the label. A number of attempts have been made to describe succinctly what general-systems research is about (Ackoff, 1961; von Bertalanffy, 1955; Boulding, 1956, McClelland, 1962b) and to specify its various possible applications. The reader is referred to these writings since, in this essay, the ambition is no more than to extract some approximations to what the general-systems approach will contribute to the increase of knowledge and control over social conflict and, particularly, over international conflict. The procedure to be followed here is to examine first a number of general problem situations which, if taken one at a time and considered in isolation and then together, will illustrate the process of moving from the simple into the complex of the real world. Second, having considered a generalized setting of complexity, we shall be in a position to judge the applicability of general-systems inquiries to the subject of conflicts of social systems. Some patience may be needed to reach the connection between the two.

PROBLEM-SOLVING
IN COMPLEX AND DYNAMIC SITUATIONS

Take first, as an illustration, the extremely common testing procedure that even the less technologically inclined among us have learned to use. Suppose a floor lamp will not work. If the lamp will not light, three things are done and then, possibly, a fourth: (a) push the plug more firmly into the outlet on the wall, (b) wiggle the switch, and (c) try another lamp bulb. Success with any step forestalls the use of the others still to be tried. If none of these tests is successful, we may use the fourth procedure which is to check to see if the electricity is on elsewhere in the building. A different kind of problem situation, but one having the same general *form*, is that of coping with the problem of getting home in the suburbs from work in the city. When the commuter finds out that a 4:30 P.M. departure time from the office leads to stop-and-go driving on the road home, he may try several expedients, one set of which is to arrange his hours so that he leaves at 3:30 P.M. before the rush or at 6:00 P.M. after it.

The point is that we can find large numbers of commonly experienced situations in which some problem or difficulty is recognized and a general form of testing is used, the rules for which are: (*a*) ignore all the complications in the "middle" of the situation, (*b*) do something at one end of the problem, (*c*) observe to see if a desired result occurs at the other end. And, fourth, if nothing works, begin considering "outside" factor-and-solution possibilities (as in the first case, check the electricity supply and, in the second, begin considering moving to town, finding a job in the country, commuting by train, and so on). Not the specific illustrations but the type of the approach to problem-solving may be called *input-output analysis.* To state it again, the approach is to apply an input (then vary it, if need be) to a system and evaluate the resulting output.

Before anyone can object that input-output analysis is a fancy term for simple experimentalism or just plain horse sense, let it be said that the operations of defining the system according to the interest there is in a problem, of deliberately excluding the concern with the internal complexities of the system ("blackboxing" it), and of determining the procedures for selecting the right inputs and for relating these to outputs are not invariably technically simple and, even in mildly complex systems, call for some conceptual sophistication. There are, in fact, many matters in each of these operations that still await exploration, both formally and empirically. To call attention to input-output analysis is to refer to the concept of systems. It is also to emphasize the importance of recognizing common features in the forms of problems and the forms of problem-solving. What we want to do to increase knowledge is to convert such common features to formal statements—either mathematical or verbal —about relationships which, when experienced, may seem to be as diverse as the terms *electronic, biological,* and *sociological* suggest. Yet, for all that, the homely illustrations given at first reflect the fundamentals of one sector of the general-systems approach. Note that facts *are* acts: that the investigation of the defective floor-lamp problem is part of the "system" of light-not-working-man-intervening-to-solve-the-problem. Note that cause-effect relationships tend to blend into a single comparative operation and that here, as in the "blackbox" approach and in the matter of identifying a system apart from its relevant environment in which it is "actually imbedded," a significant simplification takes place. The simplification in coping with complex problems can become enormous, but it is an established fact that the input-output analysis techniques have worked well without any need to identify every variable or to factor out every characteristic of the system.

Let us move ahead another stage to consider something else quite familiar. Systems are often coupled to each other in such a way that there is a kind of colony of them in which some outputs from two systems must work in pairs or one system must have an output that travels to another system to serve as the latter's input. There are many combinations that a reasonably observant person can see all about him. When the ladies at the church decide to hold a cake sale, the kind of meshing together of "acts" of committee meeting, telephoning, baking, delivering, selling, and so on is all commonplace and requires no description. A serious failure anywhere in the sequence creates a "problem," however, and the ordinary means of coping with such problems are numerous ("supervision," "emergency standbys," "duplications of effort," "contingency planning," and so forth).

As long as the sequence of related "acts" is not too long, as long as the coupled "systems" (i.e., lady-baking-cake-selling-at-the-church) are not too numerous, too unfamiliar, too complexly interlocked, and too finely adjusted, one to the other, there will be no strong requirement for a specialist to integrate the systems in the whole process (or, if we prefer, we can call the whole process *the system* and each of the *unit-acts* being integrated subsystems or components). But, what of the situation where there are several levels of subsystems so that, while in one part of the system-as-a-whole some subsystems are pouring their outputs directly into the main process, elsewhere and at the same time, sub-subsystems feed subsystems which feed the system in sequence? The possibilities of further complexity are obvious: subsystem outputs descend to sub-subsystems as inputs; these are converted to outputs to other sub-subsystems before the products of these ascend to other tiers to complete a sequence, and so on, in what becomes a dazzlingly complex situation.

When phenomena like this appear, we understand that we are no longer dealing with things like cake sales. We come face to face, instead, with factories making complicated products, large business enterprises, the ebb and flow of many forms of interdependent plant and animal life on a hillside or in the sea, government bureaucracies, and with a variety of system complexes that require, very interestingly, that man-sequences mesh in and work with machine-sequences. What kinds of problem-solvers are needed to chcek and control processes and to get jobs done when there is a large amount of dovetailing and phasing of sequences of system operations?

The answer is in the want-ad columns of any big-city newspaper because the supply of competent "systems engineers," "systems designers," "operations analysts," and "management consultants" runs far behind the demands of industry and government. Largely (but not entirely) because of the increase of the intricate and intermeshed problems in the operations of subsystems of the kind mentioned above, a new and important occupation has developed since World War II in the work of planning, controlling, and trouble-shooting complex systems. The space programs, in particular, have stimulated the growth of expertness in these lines just because they are so expensive, so intricate, so unexplored, and so extended in time through the research, development, and testing phases. A good many operations specialists or systems analysts are quick to deny that they are "scientists" or that they are doing "research." Their posture is that they are problem-solvers who take on specific jobs that involve complexity, costs, timing, and organization and that they apply systematic techniques to find practical answers. Scientific or not, many of the methods that have been worked out and used for examining and integrating possible relationships and functions (Stanford Research Institute, 1959) and for analyzing networks of operations under complicated scheduling demands such as PERT (Bigelow, 1962) suggest applications in many different fields and for many different types of problems.

If we look in a journal such as *Operations Research*, we discover the links with theory. Much attention is given to the explications of properties of complex systems with respect to how they work and to the spelling out of characteristic forms of their relationships. We encounter frequent repetitions of phrases that, although unfamiliar to the lay public, refer to these traits: poisson functions, stochastic problems, and Markov processes. All of this development is in the spirit of the general-systems approach.

A third step that should be taken toward building a conceptualization of how problems of complexity in systems come about is to take note of limits and boundaries. The root of this phenomenon is spread widely in common affairs. We might start with the question: When does enough cease being enough and turn into too much, or, when does not enough definitely become too little? Ordinary instances of deciding this question often become so routine—so "automated"—that they go unnoticed. A traffic problem offers one good illustration: when has a driver acted correctly with respect to the amber light of the traffic signal? Obviously, if he brakes hard at the instant that the light turns yellow, and at that moment is close to the entrance of the intersection, he may easily come to a stop in the middle, blocking traffic in all directions, or he may be inviting a collision with the car behind. The thing to do is to go on through. But, the issue is, how late is the time that he can safely and correctly (not risk getting a traffic citation) react to the yellow light by moving on through? There is some kind of invisible limit at work with which every driver must cope. By trying to play it too safe, the driver can exceed another boundary at the other extreme: by trying to anticipate when the yellow light will appear and by stopping when the green one is still on.

To generalize, we can say that the traffic lights, the intersection, and the traffic of automobiles and pedestrians moving across the intersection area are, altogether, a system having fairly definite boundaries. Staying within the limits is the driver's responsibility, but he is subjected to training, conditioning, and coercion to make him keep the system "working." What drivers actually do has been investigated, incidentally (Gazis, Herman, and Maradudin, 1960; Olson and Rothery, 1961). Note in connection with this familiar example that a solution is not a foolproof or perfect arrangement but something just good enough to keep down accidents and to avert serious complaints. The amber warning light which tells the driver either to stop or to go is ambiguous and, for people who insist on perfect safety, it is inadequate.

Another boundary-maintaining problem, typical of many others encountered daily, is that found in modern homes with radiant heating. Invariably, these heating "systems" are controlled by thermostats (which, themselves, are very familiar control systems that adjust outputs to variations in the input). Householders are usually well satisfied with the cleanliness and the sense of comfort and freshness offered by radiant heating, except on some days. These are the times when the outside temperature has dropped so quickly that the heating of the interior, which is a relatively slow process, falls behind and the home gets uncomfortably cool. Not much can be done about this except to have some auxiliary heating device as a standby. But, where is the boundary problem? The answer is, of course, in the reactions of the householders who, at some point during a narrow range of temperature lowering, should change their usual attitude of ignoring the temperature by beginning to give it persistent attention. It is at this point (at a "subjective moment") that the radiant heating system is overpowered by the change in the outer environment; its boundary of usual performance has been crossed to the discomfort of the human beings involved.

The notion that operating systems of various kinds behave within bounds, and that situations that bring about approaches to or violations of these bounds create problems, is very simple. It is astonishing, however, to realize how many different ways there are to bring about a boundary threat. Population growth and population decline are two of these ways. Bunching and queuing of people, products, prices, processes, and many other such "operators" are another. How things are timed is an important variable in many instances. Studies of diverse phenomena have led to generalizations about the process. The investigations of the spread of diseases, the multiplication of fruit flies, and the balancing and imbalancing of competing plant and animal populations have provided helpful tools for analyzing boundary maintenance and boundary violation.

Some further observations about system boundaries are worthy of special notice. In human and biological systems, boundary zones often shift about so that even the systems, themselves, may be changed or transformed. Adaptation to change is best observed at the boundaries of systems in many cases. Sometimes, the overriding of a boundary by some series of actions is reversible and sometimes it is not. Cataclysmic breakthrough, gradual infiltrations, and an even slower and less perceptible process than infiltration—evolution—are various means of restructuring systems and system boundaries.

Another general point to be noted in particular has to do with the strategy of change. Most of this brief discussion of system boundaries has emphasized *maintaining* a system through some unspecified kind of self-organization or control which keeps the operations of a system within limits. If a problem-solver who is dealing with a complex system wishes to change that system, he will seek either to introduce from the environment into the system an "outside" input of such character as to override its usual limits and start up an unusual sequence of events in it or to modify subsystems in order to induce new input-output chains of events within the system. Of course, the make-up of the system, with respect to the numbers and kinds of components and the numbers and kinds of intrasystem relationships, will determine the more likely procedures for overriding the boundaries of the system to cause it to change.

If this were an extended account, here would be an appropriate place to discuss several varieties and patterns of the general-systems property of stability. It would have to do in considerable part with boundary maintenance and boundary change (Ashby, 1960). Much is known about the subject in the mechanical and electronic fields, but there is also much that is not yet understood. While we might think that in an age almost always called *revolutionary* there would be a vast amount of detailed research on the processes of change in complex social systems, there is, in fact, very little of it.

A picture of how complexity occurs in the workings of systems takes form when we begin to reflect on the character of the sequences of "linked acts" of subsystems operating in normal performance ranges. This basic trait of complexity appears in commonplace circumstances as the preceding illustrations have sought to show. It prevails in enterprises and inquiries such as developing a new weapon system, conducting a foreign-aid program, campaigning for election to public office, finding the causes of cancer, or planning how to get to the moon and back. There is nothing very remarkable in noting this: human societies in all ages have slowly worked out methods for intervening in the complex cycles of nature in order to control them for their own purposes. Peasant agriculture practiced in traditional societies and economies is a good example of the deep-rooted skill of intervention and control. The noteworthy fact that we have been attempting to emphasize is the very recent advent of greatly improved techniques of general problem-solving for control over the complex interplay of the myriads of "acts" of systems.

Where "tangibles" are involved—the paramount example of the present time is in space exploration—we understand very quickly both the broad nature of the problem and the need for the advanced methods of "systems design" and "systems control." When it comes to more purely human affairs in the functioning of big organizations or in the relations between peoples, however, we are much slower to admit that simple wisdom and common sense are insufficient to manage our problems. After all, we say, men have not changed very much during the last century or the last millennium. We understand human nature in its main manifestations—in spite of all the material and mechanical innovations of recent times—so that there is little need for new concepts or for new governing practices. This point of view seems to take into account too little another source of system complexity, however. An example or two should make this clear.

The iron puddler carried out the work of controlling the carbon content in the making of iron. He did not change or lose the skills of his system of work when his techniques became outdated. *He* stayed the same but a change in his environment—the advent of the Bessemer process—changed him from an essential worker into an unemployed man.

Over many centuries, the Chinese developed an international system to govern their relationships with foreigners. Its long existence and the persistence of its form over time testify to its effectiveness. Yet, a change in the international environment in the shape of powerful intrusions of the Western state system in the middle of the nineteenth century undermined it, destroyed its viability, and threw the officials responsible for its maintenance into confusion (Hsu, 1960). We might say generally that the Chinese officials, presiding over the inputs and the outputs of the traditional system, did things that always worked before, but, after the middle of the nineteenth century, were perplexed, discouraged, and finally unsuccessful because, without their fully realizing it, the steady factors of their environment had been altered fundamentally (neither they nor their system of procedures had changed very much).

It is the post-1900 scientific revolution and, in particular, its philosophical offshoots such as the attitude behind the general-systems approach that bolster confidence in the faith that it is *possible* to learn how and where to intervene to bring about control over the dynamics of the complexes of systems and their environments—even of social systems. In the latter, we must take into account another major source of added complications by recognizing that there can be—and usually is—more than one party trying to play the game of control over system processes. A corporation that builds a successful business by ordering a sector of a market regularly encounters the additional complex operation of fending off (or sharing with) others that move into that sector. Countermeasure research and development (the problem of solving the antimissile missile problem, for example) also illustrate the point. Planning and building a common market in Europe are reordering processes in a very complex situation, but, as everyone now knows, the prospect of the change of enlarging the size and the "input-output ability" of the European economies has acted as a trigger to set off further complicating sequences of responses on the part of the Soviet Union, Great Britain, and the United States. New methods of attacking this family of problems have been developing (Rapoport, 1960; Schelling, 1960).

APPLICATIONS OF GENERAL SYSTEMS IN THE STUDY OF SOCIAL SYSTEMS AND INTERNATIONAL CONFLICT

Perhaps enough has been stated by now to illustrate that general-systems research is not simply a pretentious naming of a perfectly familiar methodology or a popular frame of reference. Only two claims have been made for it: (*a*) that it is one manifestation of the new scientific outlook and (*b*) that it is a general guide to where and how to go about looking for answers to problems where complexity of actions and responses is the rule. The strategy, first of all, of conceiving of many kinds of phenomena in terms of working relations among their parts and then of labeling them *systems* according to a definition of what part of the "problem" is most relevant is the key to the approach. Then, the procedures of by-passing many complexities in order to investigate relationships between input and output, of systematically moving to different levels of analysis by recognizing the links of subsystems to systems, of being alert to "boundary phenomena" and the ranges of normal operations of subsystems and systems, and of taking into account both "parameters" and "perturbations" in the environments of systems are other major parts of the general systems apparatus. We have, at the last, emphasized the special gamelike relationships that are prevalent in the interactions of controllers of social systems. It is clear that there are no behavioral theories—as such—in the general-systems framework, but it is also clear that specific theories about regularities and relationships of one and another kind of complex system can grow on this ground. We may tend to approve the systems analyst who disclaims the title of theorist or scientist and who, in effect, understates that he is only a problem-solver with a recipe book. It is a healthful attitude if it is not accepted at full face value. It follows, too, that the general-systems outlook has nothing in particular to do with the subject of conflict. Only *applications* of the outlook to such a subject are made.

In fact, a set of sociological concepts such as conflict, competition, cooperation, accommodation, and isolation does not mesh automatically with the systems perspective. Translations and rough equivalencies have to be considered between the two. To give one example, it may not be just soft talk to call a certain conflict an instance of oscillation behavior about a boundary point.

It is probably necessary to decide first to focus only on "social systems" and to define conflict as one of the system-states that societies *can* be in. But, what is a society or a social system? Are we to make the identification on "strictly empirical grounds" or according to a "construct" made up from the idea of certain sequences of related events that, if we looked around for similar ones in the real world, might be recognized? The approach would instruct that we follow the procedure of defining "the system" according to the need we have—and that means, accepting the alternative of the construct.

The answer to a current question, "Is there an international system or several of them, including the Soviet international system, the neutralist international system, the Atlantic-community international system, and several others?" is that there is one international system if we have reason to consider some particular series of actions and responses in that frame of reference. Then, it might well be considered that a number of identified subsystems such as the Soviet bloc, the NATO alliance, the Latin American countries, and others "feed" the one big system. On the other hand, the advantageous choice for some interests and some problems will be to view the Soviet bloc as *the* system operating with its particular subsystems (Albanian actions as one, perhaps) and in an environment from which come influencing responses, from de Gaulle's France, for instance.

Another common beginning problem is in the reaction, "If you are going to identify systems that way, what, then, is *not* a system?" Beyond the rule, if there are no transactions between some subsystems, there cannot be a system, there is no answer to this complaint other than the Humean advice of skepticism tempered by common sense. As we have noted before, the system approach is close to the ground: *if* you have a real-life problem, attack it by conceiving a system relevant to it and look for what has been going on in the way of process—in the actions and subsequent responses and in the levels of coupled input-output activity. If there is no success, cast about, once again, for an idea with operations connected with it of the kind roughly comparable to "check the plug, wiggle the switch, change the light bulb, inspect the supply of electricity in the house."

Although concerted research efforts self-consciously following the systems approach are still at the beginning, an interim report on some of these starts is now possible. Much of the activity has channeled into conceptual and programmatic statements. It is critical to decide which bodies of fact are needed for the research, which systems are to be identified, and which hypotheses concerning the processes of the systems will be tested. Faithful to the "practical" orientation, the applications of general systems to conflict have clustered about the subjects of international conflict, cold war diplomacy and strategy, and the conditions for forestalling major wars. Where the conceptual problems have been settled momentarily, the quest has turned to how to collect and analyze pertinent data. The dilemma seems to be that there is a superabundance of reports on some aspects of international conflict which creates a problem of collecting, sorting, and categorizing, while other matters that the conceptual scheme make important are reported on very little or not at all.

EXAMPLES OF SYSTEMS RESEARCH
ON INTERNATIONAL CONFLICT

One program of research has been proceeding according to the general idea that conflict is, primarily, a property of those systems that have an inadequate internal organization or "integration." Robert North, who directs this program, is following a long-term research plan to investigate the possibility that an effective decline of conflict—at least of that conflict that endangers the system itself—accompanies the rise of more closely functioning and more interdependently connected subsystems. A loosely articulated system—the old Western state system especially—in which the latitude of variation in the actions of the subsystems is very wide, will experience sporadic instabilities during which the officials charged with maintaining such a system will be hard pressed to keep it going. Such occasions are acute international crises and are considered to be particularly intense manifestations of international conflict, sometimes leading to breakdowns and system transformations (that is, the overthrow of governments, wars, and other violent or disruptive effects).

The Stanford Studies in International Conflict and Integration program presently is concentrating on ways to measure the presence and the patterns of tensions affecting the controllers of poorly integrated international systems by analyzing the verbal behavior of officials during periods of international crises. This is to show the various mechanisms and effects of tension that arise with threats to the security of the system and to its "normal" operations (Stanford Studies in International Conflict and Integration, 1963). Of particular interest are those psychological situations that tend to reduce the decision-makers' perceptions of possible restoring actions that would encourage the system to return to its more usual range of operations. Integration is thought of as a system organization that facilitates the working out of effective methods and rules for directing conflicts toward resolution without a resort to violence. The history of the gradual linking together of local and provincial organizations—political, economic, and social—into the greater articulated whole that we know as the national state provides both a model and the belief that international systems made up of national subsystems can achieve similar integrations. Which inputs applied under what conditions to subsystems will do the most to encourage integration is considered to be both a research question and a practical concern in abating destructive conflict. The Stanford project is one of the few in being that is oriented specifically by the general systems concept and approach.

If one wishes to find out in the most complete available detail the applications of the general-systems approach to the subject of conflict—and, in each instance, with ultimate reference to international conflict —one should *study* Kenneth E. Boulding's *Conflict and Defense* (1962), and, along with that, two other works, *Fights, Games, and Debates* (Rapoport, 1960) and *The Strategy of Conflict* (Schelling, 1960). For most people, a rapid, casual reading will not do because most are unaccustomed to sustained attention to the analysis of movements in dynamic situations. In the second place, most of us weary quickly of mental constructions and problems that concentrate on the characteristics of the *whole* form that actions may take in one kind of a setting and then another. As the basic structure of the language we use encourages, we are habituated to become impatient to find out the specific "who does what to whom." There is insufficient space here for anything like a propositional inventory of the contents of these three books (as Coser [1956] provided for Simmel's writing, for example). A brief listing of ideas would be certain to blunt or foreshorten an understanding of the theoretical relevancies. What we shall do is to consider very quickly a few of the matters that the conceptual detail in the works of Boulding, Rapoport, and Schelling has enriched.

It would appear that the most important single emphasis in these works is in the rule "to understand what we do, understand what they do." A succession of states resulting from the interactions of one system with another is the fundamental conception. Boulding writes, "These are processes in which a movement on the part of one party so changes the field of the other that it forces a movement of this party, which in turn changes the field of the first, forcing another move of the second, and so on" (Boulding, 1962, p. 25). The sweeping aside of the illusions of purely egocentric perspectives on personal and social phenomena he characterizes as a dawning "Copernican revolution." It is the interplay that is important and not merely a matter of seeing the other fellow's situation. Of course, this view is not entirely new but it has a good many implications that are. Long ago, in 1932, David Low, the cartoonist, put the common touch on this insight in the famous cartoon showing a lifeboat (labeled *World Money Problem*) in distress in high seas. In the bow sat resting figures of Britain, France, and the United States; in the stern, awash, were smaller figures titled *Middle Europe* bailing furiously with buckets. The caption read, "Phew! That's a nasty leak. Thank goodness it's not at our end of the boat" (Low, 1957, p. 243).

Not to be insistent about it but in order merely to relate the concept to the earlier discussion, this Copernican view does put in the fore the singular importance of recognizing the coupled input-output sequences inside and between systems that not only simply make these systems interdependent, but also constrain them to share a history of movements in a field. It is the property of complex conjointedness that counts.

A further fundamental in the three major works on the systems approach to conflict is the emphasis on the mix or co-presence of those qualities (or, perhaps, we should call them *system-states*) that in our human-centeredness we are obliged to call conflict and cooperation, mutuality and exclusiveness, trust and suspicion, and so on. In the layout of different conditions of his static model of conflict, Boulding attempts to show how there are several basic situations in a field that two or more parties seek to occupy so that some conditions permit trading and bargaining, while others reduce the alternatives to the single one of conflict. Thomas C. Schelling has explored carefully the varieties of circumstance in which parties that may see themselves in total conflict nevertheless create cooperative arrangements, particularly for communicating their intentions and, in concealed ways, cause their "system operations" to dovetail or coordinate. "System transforms" from conflict to bargaining or from bargaining to conflict also interest Schelling. Although it is easy to ridicule the seeming futility in the situation, it is also important to realize (and analyze) the reality of the "barber-shop mirror effect" in which the first party needs to perceive the intentions of the second party while, at the same time, the second needs to perceive how the first is perceiving the perceptions of the second, and so on. Perhaps we laugh when we see the outcroppings of such intricacies because we *must* believe that things are simpler; simpler than evidence shows them to be when we begin to examine closely and intently such things as interacting perceptions. Anatol Rapoport mines another vein by describing, systematically separating, and then relating the distinctive forms that conflict may take —fights, games, and debates. He, like Boulding and Schelling, follows the new path of being preoccupied with moving relationships and the alternative forms in which they may be identified. His facts, too, turn into acts.

The concerns over the boundaries of dynamic systems are not neglected. As Boulding stresses, boundary crossing means a change of the state of the system—a transformation. Even if "the system" is not "real" in corresponding at every main point with what observers report is "really going on," when analysts can show which boundary is crossed, which system change occurs as a result, and whether or not there can be a crossing back, that model of a system becomes immensely interesting and also of practical importance. Boulding notes that it is the action or upset at or close to boundaries that ought to attract our attentions. A central theme in *Conflict and Defense* is that conditions in the world are now such that national states have in hand the abilities that allow several of them to decide at any time whether or not to permit the others to continue to exist. In more general form, this is to say that sub-systems of the over-all international system have interpenetrated the boundaries of one another so that all are coming into the circumstance of "conditional viability" (Boulding, 1962, chap. 4). Earlier, John H. Herz (1957) had grasped the meaning of this development and had represented clearly that the change processes were strong, numerous, and well rooted in the recent past. Certainly, the shift from unconditional to conditional viability (or from balance of power to deterrence; from national security under sovereign guarantee to contingent security) is not within any traditional conceptualization. Is it not likely that the change is as drastic for all nations now as was that revolution imposed on the Chinese when their international system of dealing with barbarians changed from viable to nonviable?

With new systems emerging and old systems working in new environments, we need to know more about the boundaries. Boundaries usually have been thought of as lines on territory. Note that in international politics, such lines have also been called *frontiers*. In other contexts in the English language, frontiers denote moving locations between the known and the explored to the unknown and the unexplored. The latter meaning may be just the concept we need to attach presently to the term *system boundaries*. Earlier in the discussion, a system boundary was described with reference to limits of usual operations. In Boulding's writing, one finds this strategic idea elaborated in several ways: in the delineation of "Richardson processes," in the discussions of the pressures that fill up systems to create boundary tensions, of the changing and rising response sensitivities to actions that occur close to boundaries, and in the consideration of the "drift" and slow change in boundary conditions as sub-systems (both biological and social) are used up, age, and get replaced. Above all, it is in the central idea of intelligent *control* that men can impose deliberately when they know what the boundary conditions are and how the regularities and the trends of system activities occur. Schelling is much preoccupied by boundary matters especially as they yield information and clarify meaning in tacit and indirect communications. Rapoport, in an extremely provocative passage at the close of his book, explores what may be the most frightening and dangerous boundary experience of all—the transactions at the boundary when values and beliefs that are held to be mutually incompatible by opposing parties are exposed in the conflict form that Rapoport calls *the debate*.

It is in the setting of the understanding of the complex activities of system change and boundary crossing that the recent inquiries into the subject of the dynamics of trust and suspicion achieve great significance. The common-sense view has been, probably, that a person either does or does not feel trust toward other persons, groups, or objects and that somebody who is trusted or suspected pretty well deserves the response according to his past record. The new studies show, however, that there is much more to this phenomenon. The theory on the logics of trust-suspicion situations—particularly concerning certain dilemmas—and research on the dynamics of behavior in the dimensions of trust and suspicion are fresh approaches which seem to be very fundamental for understanding conflict and learning new measures for its control (Rapoport, 1962; Deutsch, 1958, 1960; Deutsch and Krauss, 1962; Ratoosh, Scodel, and Minas, 1960; Scodel and Minas, 1960; and Scodel, Minas, Ratoosh, and Lippetz, 1959).

In recent years, a distinction has gradually emerged that is proving useful in the study of international relations. It is that there is a main division of labor in the cultivation of knowledge in this field: one division focuses on the processes that converge in a society and state in the making of decisions about what to do in foreign relations while the other concentrates on the interplay between two or several streams of actions emanating from these decision sources. Richard C. Snyder, H. W. Bruck, and Burton M. Sapin 1962) did a great deal toward establishing this framework while emphasizing the first perspective on decision-making and the formulation of foreign policy within governments. Morton Kaplan (1957) directed attention to several forms that the interactions of "national actors" might take and helped to bring the term *international system* into common use. In particular, Kaplan demonstrated how differences in the performances of international systems came from different patterns of organization of their constituting parts (the structures) and from different processes taking place in the structures. *System and Process in International Politics* helped to generate a new awareness of the "Copernican view" that Boulding has emphasized and that is the essential idea in the scheme of complex relationships of subsystems to systems discussed in the first part of this essay. In the perspective that has been developed here, it is hoped that the reader will see at once that the decision-making approach and the international-system approach are directed at different analytical levels but that they are contained and related in a general-system framework.

The dividing of the study of international relations into two broad areas with one concentrating on subsystem phenomena and the other on the organization and action-patterning in the international system has achieved status and substantial acceptance (Rosenau, 1961a). Snyder (1962) has reported on the more recent developments. These trends do not all relate directly to conflict research, it is true, but they provide a basis for many fresh approaches to the study of international relations and international conflict. They undergird, for example, new conceptions in the study of acute international crises.

The interest in crises is oriented to the study of conflict processes, of course. The systems orientation suggests hypotheses about the crisis form of conflict in the existing international system. Both chronic and acute conflicts are characteristic of that system and a conception of the fit of these traits in the structures and processes of the international system would seem, then, to be requisite to any satisfactory explanation of international conflict. It would be a matter of general consensus to state that hostile interactions are persistent among pairs of states and that their intermeshed behaviors keep them in a boundary zone where the presence of organized force is constant and breakovers at the boundary from non-violent to violent conflict are ready possibilities. The oscillations around an unsteady equilibrium point have dominated the relations of the United States and the Soviet Union for more than a decade and a half. The international history of this period is, in large measure, the record of the fluctuations of that conflict. An observer can see that there are two "system-states" in the cold war: one of relative inaction and relaxation in the pattern of relations and the other one of intensification of actions and the heightening of psychological tensions. Acute crises—of Berlin, Cuba, the Congo, Vietnam, Suez, Quemoy, and others—belong in the latter category.

In the perspective of the international-system approach (but not of foreign policy and decision-making) an investigation of the phenomena of alternating phases of the system's performance will direct attention to the outputs of the involved parties without any undue attention to all details of the intricate internal networks of the subsystems of the national states. It is unnecessary, in other words, to assume that everything must be explained in order to get reliable results. The simplification is in looking only at the traits and the recurring configurations of the responses of the antagonists to each other (one must study the nonrecurring in order to differentiate the recurring, it should be noted). Interaction or response analysis is a naming of the approach.

This writer was led into the effort to study the response patterns of acute crises both by the desire to develop a method of analysis in terms of system dynamics and by the puzzle presented in the writing of Joseph Schumpeter (1951). Schumpeter argued from a series of historical findings that modernizing nations ought to be expected to show a marked decline in their propensities to engage in heroic confrontations and showdowns such as crises and international wars. His case was quite convincing, but, as he himself recognized, it was not an explanation that fitted recent facts. Why was Schumpeter wrong—or was he? A set of propositions was set forth concerning the character of acute international crises and their functioning in modernizing social systems and in the international system (McClelland, 1961).

The fundamental proposition is that the problems and demands in keeping a complex modern society, economy, and policy in viable operation are so difficult and preoccupying that carrying on relations with other countries, however unavoidable, actually "runs against the grain" of the intentions and aspirations of these highly modernized, industrialized, urbanized, and rationalized national states. The long-term tendency is to cut down the costs and the distractions of international relations and to reduce them to administrative routines. Yet, crises and wars continue to occur or threaten among the "advanced moderns" as well as among the "transitionals" where the phenomena are more to be expected. The facts of the cold war seem to fly in the face of this theory; the argument is simply that the behavior is vectored between the push of international conflict and the pull of domestic values. An acute crisis is a cost-cutting substitute for war and the challenge-response aspects of crises become "routinized" and fall into a relatively small number of patterns. The analysis of the growth of routines and the tracing of patterns are thought to be matters for empirical research.

It is still possible that Schumpeter was right in thinking that old conceptions and old practices wear away very slowly. That one particular social class persists in propping up outmoded thoughts and practices (as Schumpeter thought about the aristocrats, and the communists still believe about the "finance capitalists") seems to be increasingly untrue, however, at least in the view of the writer. As modern societies move ahead in development, the distributions of preferences and values seem more and more to cut across class and occupational lines and to become pervasive in national populations. Or, it may be simply that social values, already dominant in advanced modernizing societies, do not support and reinforce violent adventuring in foreign affairs but that the leaders are enmeshed in complex networks of challenge-response relations in international politics and do not know how to extricate themselves and to draw back far enough from the boundaries of danger. The answers begin to come, not from the conception, but from historical analyses and comparisons (McClelland, 1962a).

In any case, a secondary or engineering prospect has developed from the inquiry. If we can find the appropriate methods for identifying the large numbers of short sequences of action response that appear in antagonistic relationships during acute crises and, then, by drawing out the recent histories of the combinations of such "trajectories" for comparison with the events of the moment, we may be able to develop a kind of prediction. There is no hope of predicting when a crisis will occur or what initial act will start it, but, once a crisis begins, its development may be amenable to tracking and analysis so that predictions can be made from the past patterns of move and countermove. Knowing the path the crisis is taking is to invite policies and measures to control that path. Boulding (1962) gives a clue to what to watch for in his chapter on the static model of conflict.

A time may come when a decision-maker on one side or the other may want to move from a crisis situation into a nuclear war. The ability to predict the development up to and over the system boundary would be of no help in forbidding such an act of will; indeed, it might assist the decision-maker to bring about the effect that he wants. On the other hand, if knowledge and skill can be developed by means of theory and empirical research to make less probable the blundering and the stumbling in the dark from crisis into war, that increase in security is of about the order of magnitude that we might realistically expect. If ever the intent to disarm should become full-fledged, a technique similar to that conceived as possible for crisis control might well assist in analyzing the situation and finding a successful path through the maze of negotiations that, in all likelihood, would have to precede disarmament steps.

THE WORK AHEAD
IN THE STUDY OF THE CONTROL OF CONFLICT

There are dozens of significant research projects on international conflict and the problems of its management that the systems approach suggests. By no means are all of these forced to follow the lines laid down in operations research or by mathematically oriented systems analysis. Many of the channels and linkages between different levels of national subsystems that lead finally into the influences on decision-makers have never been explored and await straightforward descriptions. Only a few studies have been made to probe these depths (Cohen, 1957; Rosenau, 1961b, for example). We sometimes suspect that "warmongers" and "peacemongers" wield more influence on foreign affairs than either their numbers or their ideas warrant, but research on their actual operations, their effectiveness, and the situations that sometimes give them opportunities to be very influential is scant.

From communication research we learn that there are men in roles called *gatekeepers* who let through some kinds of information but not others. Many criticisms are leveled against the conflict proneness in the reporting of the mass media. Try to find in the library, however, any considerable number of careful descriptive accounts of exactly what these gatekeepers do, who they are and who influences *them*, and how and why the selection and emphasis are on the side of conflict. It will be discovered that precious little is known about them, although they look very important. In other sectors of society, our knowledge about sentinels, alarm sounders, pacifiers, agitators, mediators, and innovators on issues of foreign affairs is extremely thin. We do not know who the United States foreign-policy "influentials" outside official circles are, how many there are, or how they operate. It is understandable, therefore, that we also know little about their counterparts in Great Britain, the Soviet Union, Japan, Mexico, India, and any number of other countries. Simple research techniques applied to many of the subjects mentioned and to others of similar type could move knowledge about subsystem phenomena forward to a considerable extent.

Two further hypotheses about the generation of conflict are not beyond investigation. One is that the large-scale organizations that are prevalent in modern society—in education, business, government, the professions, and even in research—are so unwieldy and so unresponsive to changes in their environments and also so insensitive to the needs for flexibility and variation deep in their supporting subsystems that, in the first instance, they lumber unwittingly into social collisions at home and abroad, and, in the second instance, breed frustrated and angry men who maintain the subsystems. Alienation and apathy may be the familiar results for many "organization men" but, within and without, do the big organizations—a relatively recent development (Boulding, 1943)—feed streams of hostility and aggressiveness into both domestic and international affairs and supply recruits for all manner of social conflicts?

The second possibility relates more specifically to the international system. Even the surface evidence of the last two decades is that multiple changes of immense importance have reverberated through the international system: the sudden rise to superpower status of the United States and the Soviet Union and the relative eclipse of the Western European states, temporarily at least, the collapse of colonialism and the rise of nationalist independence movements in Africa and Asia, the increasing pressure of population growth in many lands, the rise and spread of communist regimes since World War II, the transformations in the means of travel and communication, and, of not least importance, the vast revolution in military technology. The result by now must be considered to be a thoroughgoing disturbance of the international system and a mixing of old and new elements. Is it not likely that the turmoil, the confusion, the very clash of the old with the new, and the uncertainty of it all would stimulate aggressive social behaviors and would be a prime cause of conflicts, particularly between peoples, races, and nations? There are no doctrines that will explain and simplify multiple changes of such magnitude. The speculative proposition is that men will be tempted to "fight their way to coherence" unless other alternatives for living with change are found.

More social research on the phenomena of the mixing of old and new systems would not harm the situation and it might help. There is not available enough information on what the old international system was like before the great change began. Sometimes, we hear that history and historians are now useless because they can offer no guide whatever to the future. Perhaps that is only the retort of those who become indignant with the complacent souls who believe things have not really changed, either nationally or internationally. One would think, however, that historians could help greatly by looking back past the massive changes of the last two decades, but with the perspective of that revolution in mind, to the earlier part of this century in order to reconstruct in more vivid detail the conditions that then prevailed—the systems and other operating properties, so to speak—before the take-off. The simple thesis is that we cannot see the ramifications and the consequences of the new complexities without having a clear view of what the old order was and of which part of it has tumbled down and which of it still stands. Historical scholarship should be capable of providing the estimates and approximations that are needed now for the understanding of where we came from and, hence, where we may be going.

Seldom before has there been such a great need for normative inquiries. The United States may not be the best place for meeting that need because of our prevailing norm of always holding to the pragmatic and the practical. But elsewhere, perhaps, there may develop new comprehensive views of a desirable future. We have had in the modern world what has been called a *subsystem-dominant international order*. It may be an accurate appraisal to say that the product of the massive change of recent years has not been the destruction of subsystem dominance but that the consequence of further international change will bear hard on *all* subsystems—hard enough, in fact, to force them into new shapes and to make them vulnerable to new environmental conditions. Whatever international stability now obtains cannot be expected to last for long. The image of the steel ball poised on the end of an egg may be too vivid; It is not easy to conceive of a soft and gradual transition into a condition comparable to that of the steel ball rolling about gently in a teacup, however.

In the anticipation of what is coming, we need pictures of Utopias. One of the "metatasks" of great importance is to work out sets of ideas of what international systems and national subsystems should become. How should they fit together and how should the many tiers of related subsystems be ordered to serve themselves and the international order as well? Where are the best control points for safeguarding the stability of boundaries and what means for the self-correction of many levels of system operations should be devised? Which networks in which setting would be likely to diminish or amplify our favorite aspirations for the human race? What social systems are going to have the property of winning values for some but losing them for others and are there any systems that impel gains for some but no losses for all others?

Above all, what are the speculations and imaginative projections that would ride with system dynamics and, thereby, put out the faint tracings of a route for getting from where we are to a preferred future? Perhaps, if we are thoughtful about it, we may realize that being Utopian is not sinful or wrong-headed when even one step toward an idealized future can be visualized and taken. The fascination in machines is that the one-step-at-a-time method is leading toward such wonders as devices that will someday take in pages written in Arabic and print out the text in English or any other language as good as the original. In 1885, practical men would have called *that* idea, Utopian dreaming.

This essay cannot be brought to a close without repeating the initial argument that common sense and customary knowledge have become inadequate to cope with current social complexity and current social change. Those who reject the legitimacy and the potential contribution of organized social research are urged to reconsider their stand in the light of the many evidences of a great unfolding of social, political, psychological, and economic transformations. This does not seem to be a time for mandarins.

Practical applications of physical and biological science are the sources of many of the changes. But, as we have noted at the beginning, a new philosophy of science came with the package of twentieth-century scientific discovery. Not mere techniques, but a basic point of view of how to go about solving complex problems has appeared with the problems themselves. The general-systems approach is already the foundation of a successful practice in analyzing, planning, and guiding systems where complexity is the most prominent characteristic. This is happening in industry, in business management, in government operations, and in research and development of military man-machine technology.

Although we are still at the beginning, general-systems, being *general*, being specific to any wanted degree in application, and being indifferent with respect to the dividers usually set up to keep subject matters apart, appears to have good prospects for the study of social systems and such dangerous properties as conflict within and between social systems. Yet, for all that promise, it should be kept in mind that the general-systems approach is neither a formula nor a doctrine, but a cluster of strategies of inquiry; not a theory, but an organized space within which many theories may be developed and related.

REFERENCES

Ackoff, R. L., "Systems, Organizations, and Interdisciplinary Research," *Systems: Research and Design,* Donald P. Eckman, ed. New York: John Wiley & Sons, Inc., 1961.

Ashby, W. Ross, *Design for a Brain; The Origin of Adaptive Behavior.* New York: John Wiley & Sons, Inc., 1960.

Bigelow, Clifford George, "Bibliography on Project Planning and Control by Network Analysis: 1959–1961," *Operations Research,* X (September–October 1962), 728-731.

Boulding, Kenneth E., *The Organizational Revolution.* New York: Harper & Row, Publishers, 1943.

————, "General Systems Theory—The Skeleton of Science," *Management Science,* II (1956), 197-208. Reprinted in *General Systems Yearbook,* I (1956), 11-17.

————, *Conflict and Defense: A General Theory.* New York: Harper & Row, Publishers, 1962.

Coser, Lewis, *The Functions of Social Conflict.* New York: Free Press of Glencoe, Inc., 1956.

Deutsch, Morton, "Trust and Suspicion," *Journal of Conflict Resolution,* II (1958), 265-279.

————, "The Effect of Motivational Orientation Upon Trust and Suspicion," *Human Relations,* XIII (1960), 123-140.

Deutsch, Morton and Robert M. Krauss, "Studies of Interpersonal Bargaining," *Journal of Conflict Resolution,* VI (March 1962), 52-76.

Gazis, D. C., R. Herman, and A. A. Maradudin, "The Problem of the Amber Signal Light in Traffic Flow," *Operations Research,* VIII (1960), 112-132.

Herz, John H., "The Rise and Demise of the Territorial State," *World Politics,* IX (1957), 473-493.

Hsu, Immanuel C. Y., *China's Entrance into the Family of Nations; The Diplomatic Phase, 1858–1880.* Cambridge, Mass.: Harvard University Press, 1960.

Kaplan, Morton, *System and Process in International Politics.* New York: John Wiley & Sons, Inc., 1957.

Low, David, *Low's Autobiography.* New York: Simon and Schuster, Inc., 1957.

McClelland, Charles A., "The Acute International Crisis," *World Politics,* XIV (October 1961), 182-204.

————, "Decisional Opportunity and Political Controversy: The Quemoy Case," *Journal of Conflict Resolution,* VI (September 1962a), 201-213.

————, "General Systems and the Social Sciences," *ETC: A Review of General Semantics,* XVIII (February 1962b), 449-468.

Olson, Paul L. and Richard W. Rothery, "Driver Response to the Amber Phase of Traffic Signals," *Operations Research,* IX (September–October 1961), 650-663.

Rapoport, Anatol, *Fights, Games, and Debates.* Ann Arbor: University of Michigan Press, 1960.

————, "Formal Games as Probing Tools for Investigating Behavior Motivated by Trust and Suspicion." Preprint 98, Mental Health Research Institute of the University of Michigan, December 1962.

Ratoosh, Philburn, A. Scodel, and J. Minas, "Some Experimental Two-person Nonzero Sum Games," *Proceedings of the Sixth International Meeting of the Institute of Management Science.* London: Pergamon Press, 1960.

Rosenau, James N., ed., *International Politics and Foreign Policy.* New York: Free Press of Glencoe, Inc., 1961a.

————, *Public Opinion and Foreign Policy.* New York: Random House, 1961b.

Schelling, Thomas C., *The Strategy of Conflict.* Cambridge, Mass.: Harvard University Press, 1960.

Schumpeter, Joseph, *Imperialism and Social Classes.* New York: Augustus M. Kelley, 1951.

Scodel, A. and J. Minas, "The Behavior of Prisoners in a 'Prisoner's Dilemma' Game," *Journal of Psychology,* I (July 1960), 133-138.

Scodel, A., J. Minas, P. Ratoosh, and M. Lippetz, "Some Descriptive Aspects of Two-Person, Nonzero Sum Games," *Journal of Conflict Resolution,* III (1959), 114-119.

Snyder, Richard C., "Some Recent Trends in International Relations Theory and Research," *Essays on the Behavioral Study of Politics,* Autin Ranney, ed. Urbana: University of Illinois Press, 1962.

Snyder, Richard C., H. W. Bruck, and Burton M. Sapin, *Decision-making as an Approach to the Study of International Politics.* Princeton: Foreign

Policy Analysis Project, 195. Rev. ed., New York: Free Press of Glencoe, Inc., 1962.

Stanford Research Institute, "Notes on System Matrix Methodology." Appendix A, Quarterly Progress Report, No. 3, Project No. 1U-2568 (June 1959).

Stanford Studies in International Conflict and Integration, "Crisis and Crises," *Stanford Today,* Ser. 1, No. 4 (March 1963).

von Bertalanffy, Ludwig, "General System Theory," *Main Currents of Modern Thought,* XI (March 1955).

Decision-making Theory and Human Conflict

CHADWICK F. ALGER

When Emperor Haile Selassie of Ethiopia addressed the General Assembly of the United Nations in October 1963, it was a moving occasion for all present. Recalling his personal appeal before the League of Nations thirty years earlier and the League's inability to defend his nation against aggression, he noted that the United Nations peace-keeping operations in the Middle East and the Congo are indicators that some progress has been made in developing methods for handling international conflict. But those in attendance were not given long to muse over these achievements. As soon as Haile Selassie had been ushered from the room, a delegate from Indonesia strode to the rostrum and launched into an attack on certain statements made earlier by a delegate from Malaysia regarding Indonesian opposition to the establishment of the Malaysian nation. At this point a journalist in the press gallery sighed, "There they go fighting again. I thought this was the *United* Nations!" Similar comments are often heard, revealing widespread failure to understand that the United Nations has an important role to play not only in resolving conflicts, but also in providing an arena for the waging of nonviolent conflict. Indeed, one of the major challenges for our age is to devise techniques for getting conflicts into arenas such as the United Nations where they are waged according to agreed rules.

The United Nations, and other international organizations, may also have less dramatic—and not so easily observed—actual and potential effects on international conflict because we are only beginning to comprehend the developing knowledge about social conflict. Repeated failures to eliminate violent conflict have to a large degree been caused by the application of erroneous notions about what makes social order possible within nations to problems of international order. There is still widespread belief that order, or what is often called *rule of law*, is chiefly brought into being through laws and police. However, the failure of this simplified view of the causes of social order in handling other problems, in addition to international relations, is stimulating a more sophisticated approach. In our own neighborhoods, police and laws have not been adequate for the control of juvenile delinquency and other crime. It has been found necessary to alter the social and physical environment in which those who break social norms live and also to alter the environment in which crimes are committed. Failure to export Western democratic institutions to other parts of the world has also deepened our understanding of the relationship between social organization and political institutions. A recent study of seventy-five political systems in Latin America, Africa, and Asia does not give major emphasis to the executive, legislative, and judicial functions of government, but instead focuses on factors outside formal governmental structure: political socialization and recruitment, interest articulation and aggregation, and political communication (Almond and Coleman, 1960, pp. 3-64). Applying knowledge of social conflict to international relations, Robert C. Angell makes a similar emphasis when he concludes that ". . . what is clearly needed is a more inclusive set of relations that will bring the contending elements into a single social system" (1957, p. 204).

Therefore, our developing knowledge of social conflict and of political systems suggests that international organizations cannot resolve conflicts, nor provide less violent substitutes for violent conflict, unless they are established in an appropriate international social system. We would also expect that the United Nations, with only limited success in controlling extreme forms of conflict, could have achieved this degree of success only in the context of a certain degree of development of an international social system. Since the United Nations is an intergovernmental organization, the intergovernmental sector of international society would appear to be of crucial, although not exclusive, importance to the development of United Nations effectiveness in dealing with international conflict. This chapter will be concerned with the impact of international organizations on intergovernmental social systems, primarily based on an examination of the United Nations.

Activity at the United Nations has usually been characterized as multilateral diplomacy in contrast to traditional bilateral diplomacy in national capitals. It is also described as public diplomacy in contrast to the more private diplomacy at national capital sites. Both of these images highlight differences between the two kinds of diplomatic sites; however, the customary usage of these terms suggests only aspects of the diplomatic revolution that is taking place in our generation. Diplomacy at the sites of international organizations is multilateral in the sense that meetings take place in which a number of nations participate. But it is important to note that much bilateral diplomacy also takes place at these diplomatic sites. Likewise, public meetings of councils and assemblies are important activities at international organizations. But much of the work done on items on the agendas of these bodies is done in private; and private diplomacy is conducted on many problems that never get on the agendas of councils and assemblies.

It is useful to look at diplomacy in international organizations in the context of the historical development of diplomacy. This development reveals a gradual evolution toward the establishment and extension of permanent face-to-face links between national governments. The development of missions to international organizations can be regarded as a second important step toward this permanency. The first step took place in the fifteenth century when permanent diplomatic missions in foreign nations began to develop out of temporary missions that had been dispatched for special tasks (Numelin, 1950, pp. 306-307). The second step saw the development of permanent international conferences, or international organizations, out of *ad hoc* international conferences. Dag Hammarskjold wrote that the establishment of permanent diplomatic missions in New York by most of the members of the United Nations ". . . and the growing diplomatic contribution of the permanent delegations outside the public meetings . . . may well come to be regarded as the most important 'common law' development which has taken place so far within the framework of the Charter" (Hammarskjold, 1959, p. 10).

The establishment of international organizations has thus not only added "public" and "multilateral" diplomacy to international relations, but has brought the addition of fundamentally different kinds of diplomatic sites to social systems that link national governments. At these sites, where virtually all the nations of an international system or subsystem are represented, each nation does not represent itself to one other nation but to all other nations represented. There are regularly scheduled meetings through which an agenda is established for the entire system. Meetings are organized in a parliamentary-like format and take place on international territory. This chapter will consider six effects that the creation of international organizations has on intergovernmental social systems: (*a*) continual access of officials of more nations to each other, (*b*) access of more kinds of officials of each nation to officials from other nations, (*c*) diminished restraints on day-to-day intergovernmental contact, (*d*) creation of new roles with concern for the total system, (*e*) extended contact between intergovernmental social systems and the outside world, and (*f*) learning experiences of participants. In each case an effort will be made to indicate the significance of these effects for international conflict.

CONTINUAL ACCESS OF MORE NATIONS TO EACH OTHER

The traditional pattern of national-capital diplomatic relations is not one in which all nations are represented in all capitals. There are a few large nations that have representation in virtually all independent nations and in whose capitals are to be found representatives from most other nations. But most nations only have representatives in a part of the world. A variety of factors may be taken into consideration in deciding where the limited personnel and money available for diplomatic representation should be utilized. Nations are more likely to have diplomatic representatives in nations that are geographically closer, that have a similar general posture on international politics, and with whom they have important commercial relationships. Quite noticeable in the traditional pattern are the great number of smaller nations who do not exchange diplomatic relationships or who have minimal contact because one foreign mission is accredited to many nations. Thus, a small European nation may have an ambassador resident in Mexico City who occasionally visits half or even all of the nations of Latin America. Some small nations may also find it difficult to maintain bilateral relations with all of the nations in its region. Thomas Hovet, Jr., in his study on *Africa in the United Nations*, reports:

> Many of the newly independent African states would find it financially burdensome to maintain embassies or legations in all the other African capitals, and the various UN representatives provide an obvious source of communication among all the African states. New York City, then, more than any African capital, is the place where inter-African contacts can be made and maintained with the greatest facility and the least expense (1963, p. 80).

The United Nations provides a diplomatic site where virtually all nations are represented. There are some major capitals where most nations are also represented and that occasionally serve as places for the carrying on of diplomatic relations between nations who do not exchange resident representatives. The United Nations offers a different kind of site of universal representation, however, because a representative at the United Nations represents his nation to the other 112 nations on a continuing basis. Furthermore, this kind of diplomatic site is different than the traditional site because it has a common agenda of concerns in which all nations participate—concerns which may span the entire system. In the course of a continual round of meetings of councils, Assembly, and their subsidiary bodies, all nations represented are continually thrown together in the discussion, lobbying, negotiation, and debate of the common agenda. During this activity each nation has opportunity for contact with all others, in contrast to the limited choices available elsewhere.

In most subsidiary bodies, as well as in a multitude of *ad hoc* negotiating and working groups, an effort is usually made to obtain membership that reflects the major geographical areas and viewpoints of the entire system. This kind of selectivity constantly throws together representatives of nations that would not have any diplomatic contact at all under the more traditional system. An example would be the Special Committee on Policies of Apartheid of the Government of the Republic of South Africa, a subsidiary of the General Assembly, with the following membership: Algeria, Costa Rica, Federation of Malaya, Ghana, Guinea, Haiti, Hungary, Nepal, Nigeria, Philippines, and Somalia. This committee reviews the racial policies of the government of South Africa when the General Assembly is not in session and reports to the General Assembly or the Security Council when appropriate. The officers of the committee are from Guinea, chairman; Costa Rica, vice-chairman; and Nepal, rapporteur. It is improbable that these nations would engage in any joint effort under the traditional system of diplomatic representation.

Therefore, we observe at the United Nations tendencies for contact and cooperation that cut across more traditional patterns of interaction and joint activity. One example is the opportunity that the United Nations provides for world cooperation between the less developed nations whatever their location or political alignment. Another example is the development of a world-wide lobby of small nations for disarmament. These nations were largely responsible for keeping the issue on General Assembly agendas in the last decade. In 1962, eight of these nations were added to the ten-nation disarmament committee, previously composed only of Warsaw Pact and NATO nations, which had been meeting in Geneva. Those added were Brazil, Burma, Ethiopia, India, Mexico, Nigeria, Sweden, and the United Arab Republic. These nations have taken a number of joint initiatives since being added to the committee. Though small nations on the committee from the two military blocs are required to play a different kind of role, nations such as Canada and Poland have also been active in behalf of disarmament.

The development of new contacts, cooperative activity, and interest groups that cut across older interest groups and regional groupings is of particular interest when examined in the context of literature on overlapping group membership. Max Gluckman, an anthropologist, has found that even a relatively small population cannot form a cohesive unit without what he calls *cross-cutting memberships:*

> Thus a thousand people on an island in the South Seas, or a couple of thousand in a Plains Red Indian tribe harried by constant attack, seemed unable to hold together as a political unit unless they were involved in cross-cutting systems of alliance, so that a man's opponents in one system were his friends in another (1955, p. 85).

Gluckman considers "cross-cutting memberships" to be so crucial to "political institutions" that he asserts that "all the various ties of friendship linking one small group with another have political functions and are political institutions" (1955, p. 68). Two other anthropologists, M. Fortes and E. E. Evans-Pritchard, write about societies in which "the stabilizing factor is not a superordinate juridical or military organization, but is simply a sum total of intersegment relations" (1940 and 1961, p. 14).

Sociologists have also been concerned with this phenomenon. Lewis Coser, in *The Functions of Social Conflict* (1955, pp. 75-80), draws our attention to the work of Edward A. Ross and Robin Williams. Writing in 1920, Ross provides a classic description:

> Every species of social conflict interferes with every other species in society . . . save only when lines of cleavage coincide; in which case they reinforce one another. . . . A society, therefore, which is ridden by a dozen oppositions along lines running in every direction may actually be in less danger of being torn with violence or falling to pieces than one split just along one line. For each cleavage contributes to narrow the cross clefts, so that one might say that *society is sewn together* by its inner conflicts (pp. 164-165).

Robin Williams, in his study of *American Society*, uses similar terminology when he writes that "American society is simply riddled with cleavages. The remarkable phenomenon is the extent to which the various differences 'cancel out'—are noncumulative in their incidence" (1951, p. 531).

The cross-cutting memberships, also referred to as *multiple-group affiliations*, stimulated by involvement in United Nations politics have not, to my knowledge, been deliberately planned, nor their potential contribution to the integration of international society widely understood. Representatives do express concern, however, when certain delegates from other nations do not vote with them on some issues, whereas they do on most others. There is also widespread concern about the increasing number of items on the agenda of the General Assembly. The literature on cross-cutting memberships puts a new perspective on these concerns by indicating that the United Nations is likely to be more effective in handling conflicts as the number of nations with which each nation occasionally votes increases. A new agenda item may add cement to the intergovernmental society at the United Nations as it adds not only a new conflict cleavage, but perhaps also a new cooperative coalition.

Multiple-group affiliations also help us to think about the role that regional organizations can play in international relations. It is often asked whether regional integration aids or hinders the integration of the entire system or the likelihood of world peace. Quincy Wright asserts that more powerful regional groupings in Western Europe, the British Commonwealth, the Middle East, the Far East, Latin America, and Central Europe could serve "as offsets to the power of the United States and the Soviet Union" and thereby contribute to peace (1955, pp. 59-60). The multiple-group-affiliation literature suggests that the greater the overlapping memberships in regional groups, the more they will contribute to the lessening of violence. Rensis Likert has discovered the importance of "the overlapping group form of organization" to effective performance of business organizations. He uses the term *linking pin* to refer to those who link together separate units through multiple membership (1961, pp. 113-115). In the international system, a nation such as Iran could serve as a "linking pin" because of its membership in the Western security system while at the same time sharing the economic development aspirations of other Asian nations. Hovet points out that the Commonwealth group in the United Nations "plays a harmonizing role because its members belong to other groups" (1963, p. 6).

DIRECT ACCESS OF MORE OFFICIALS OF EACH NATION
TO OFFICIALS FROM OTHER NATIONS

It is not only the establishment of many new international organizations that has brought an increase in the number of national officials in direct contact with their counterparts from other nations; greater speed in transportation and the development of bilateral economic and military programs have also been factors. Nevertheless, international organizations have both added to the quantity of face-to-face confrontations between officials from different nations and have provided opportunities for different kinds of contacts than occur elsewhere. The findings of Karl Deutsch, Richard W. VanWagenen, and their colleagues (1957) in the study of ten instances of political integration in the North Atlantic area encourage us to give close attention to the movement of national officials that accompanies participation in international organizations. They found that "present in all [their] cases of successful amalgamation was the mobility of persons among the main units, at least in the politically relevant strata." They make this further observation:

> Taken together with our finding that the free mobility of commodities and money, like other economic ties, was not essential for political amalgamation, our finding of the importance of the mobility of persons suggests that in this field of politics persons may be more important than either goods or money (1957, pp. 53-54).

The September to December meetings of the General Assembly are the occasion for the addition of other officials to the United Nations diplomatic community. Figures compiled for 1958, when the United Nations had 81 members, in contrast to the present 113, indicate that delegations to the Assembly included 1,436 persons. Only 543 of these were members of permanent missions to the United Nations. The remainder was made up of 358 from foreign offices (including 57 foreign ministers), 183 from overseas diplomatic posts other than the United Nations, 96 members of parliaments, 86 from government posts other than the foreign office, 63 private citizens, with 107 whose posts could not be classified on the basis of available information. This reveals a remarkable opportunity for national officials concerned with foreign affairs, and a few private citizens of high status, to make direct contact with a global group of similar persons from other nations. Thus, participation in the United Nations not only extends the number of face-to-face communication links to other nations, but also encourages the transfer of certain decisions to intergovernmental sites.

DIMINISHED RESTRAINTS
ON DAY-TO-DAY INTERGOVERNMENTAL CONTACT

A traditional national-capital diplomatic site consists primarily of separate foreign missions and a foreign office. Most of the business of a mission is with the foreign office, occasionally with other government agencies, and with citizens from the mission's own nation. Business is conducted either at the foreign office or the foreign mission, and in some cases by telephone. When located in small cities, members of diplomatic communities may become well acquainted, but in large cities, Hugh Wilson informs us, "The Corps is widely scattered, meets officially only once or twice a year and mingles more with the society of the city itself and less with its colleagues" (1938, p. 123).

The contrast between a traditional national-capital diplomatic site and the United Nations has a provocative analog in two kinds of Israeli communities studied by Richard Schwartz in his article, "Social Factors in the Development of Legal Control" (1953–1954). He compared two Israeli communities, both having a population of approximately 500 persons (the population of national officials in permanent missions to the United Nations is approximately 675). One (*kvutza*) was a large primary group whose members engaged in continuous face-to-face interaction as a result of the cooperative organization of their settlement, requiring that they work together, eat together, and share a variety of common facilities. The other (*moshav*) was a community in which families worked their own plot of ground and lived in separate bungalows. Both were orderly communities, but the *kvutza* developed no specialized legal institutions, whereas the *moshav* organized a judicial committee. Schwartz concluded, "Law has thus been seen to develop where disturbing behavior occurred which was not as adequately controlled informally as it could be with the aid of legal controls" (1953–1954, p. 491).

A most stimulating aspect of Schwartz's study is the indication that patterns of social relations can perform the same function in a society as formal legal mechanisms. The diplomatic community at the United Nations clearly does not have the degree of integration that the *kvutza* has, but it has more pronounced *kvutza* tendencies than national-capital diplomatic sites. The often voiced opinion that certain kinds of formal legal and governmental organizations must precede international order stimulates further consideration of the significance of these *kvutza* elements for intergovernmental relations. In his work on *The Human Group*, George C. Homans warns that the "student of social control will go hopelessly wrong if he thinks of it as always lying in the hands of policemen, district attorneys, judges, and their like" (1950, p. 284). He cites Bronislaw Malinowski's assertion in *Crime and Custom in Savage Society* that "Law and order arise out of the very processes which they govern" (1926, p. 123). Homans also draws our attention to Mary Parker Follett's essay on "The Psychology of Control" in which she states, "The interacting *is* the control, it does not set up a control, that fatal expression of some writers on government and also some writers on business administration. . . . We get control through effective integration. Authority should arise within the unifying process" (Metcalf and Urwick, 1942, pp. 202, 204).

Sufficient data is not available to permit an extensive assessment of the contribution of the *kvutza* tendencies of the United Nations diplomatic community to the handling of international problems at the site. There are data, however, that will enable us to move toward such an understanding. In 1960, Gary Best interviewed a randomly selected representative from each of the national missions to the United Nations and asked them to compare diplomacy at the United Nations with their national-capital diplomacy. He asked, "As compared with a post in a national capital, here at the U.N. do you personally have more contact or less contact with diplomats from countries other than your own?" Eighty-six per cent said that they had more contact. Best reports that a comment by an Eastern European delegate was typical of the majority of the delegates: "The contact that you have here with other diplomats is ten or twenty times more than that which you would have in a national capital" (1960, p. 121). Even when the General Assembly is not in session, 51 per cent said they go to a United Nations headquarters three or more times a week and 82 per cent go twice a week (1960, p. 98). Largely because of the parliamentary format for activity, which often requires hurried contacts in corridor and lounge, as well as the sharing of a variety of common facilities, 82 per cent responded that relations with other national representatives at the United Nations are less formal (1960, p. 134); 83 per cent said they would be more ". . . likely to communicate with another delegate without regard for diplomatic rank" (1960, p. 124).

One of the very significant aspects of the United Nations diplomatic community is the inclusion within the community of representatives from nations that may be unfriendly and have little opportunity for contact elsewhere. For example, within the walls of the United Nations headquarters it is possible for a South African representative to invite a group of African delegates to lunch without the event receiving public notice that might present difficulties at home. Perhaps the most important finding of Best's study was that 91 per cent of his respondents believed that they would ". . . be more likely to have contacts with delegates from an unfriendly country" at the United Nations than in a national capital (1960, p. 127). Some governments instruct their delegates to have contact with unfriendly countries in the United Nations while at the same time instructing their diplomats in national capitals to the contrary.

CREATION OF NEW ROLES
WITH CONCERN FOR THE TOTAL SYSTEM

The establishment of international organizations requires the creation of new roles that are concerned with the total system represented in the organization. These roles are played both by national officials and by members of international organization secretariats. Our discussion has already acknowledged the fact that national missions to international organizations are created which are composed of roles that are in many respects different from those in national-capital diplomatic sites. The need to maintain relations with missions from 112 other nations places a particularly onerous responsibility on the chief representative from a large nation that has a broad range of interests. The United States has responded most dramatically to the challenge by staffing its permanent mission with five men of ambassadorial rank. The United States has also acknowledged the peculiar significance of its United Nations Mission by appointing an influential political figure to the senior ambassadorial post and by giving him cabinet status.

Other new roles, *international* roles, must be created at the sites of international organizations in order to enable the bodies of parliamentary diplomacy to function. Bodies such as the General Assembly and the Security Council have presidents and numerous committees have a chairman, vice-chairman, and rapporteur. These roles are generally exercised with considerable detachment from national loyalties by diplomats from all regions of the world. The chairman of a committee, for example, normally satisfies even those from countries unfriendly to his own because he tries to give a fair hearing to all and has not steered debate in ways advantageous to his own nation. One reason a chairman finds it necessary to do this is that retaliation for unfair treatment could be quickly applied in other bodies where others have the chair. But it is also the case that unfairness might wreck committee proceedings by encouraging unnecessary argument and wrangling. This seems to be avoided because there is a desire on the part of chairmen and other elected officials to be recognized as good performers. As a result chairmen are concerned with such things as getting through the agenda on time, having a full list of speakers for each meeting, and getting resolutions in on time. Thus, the institutional norms for a "good" chairman cause diplomats to behave much differently from how they would if sitting at their country's seat. National officials assigned to United Nations missions are selected to fill other international roles such as participating in visiting missions to colonial territories. There is a tendency for national delegations to support reports and recommendations for which their own diplomats share some responsibility.

Some delegates play important international roles in facilitating the reaching of agreement within United Nations bodies. In this role they may mediate between two conflicting points of view or attempt to find common ground in a body that has such diverse tendencies that it appears unable to take any action at all. Sometimes delegates stand aloof from debate in the early stages so that they may be available for mediation later on. Some may work hard encouraging others to introduce resolutions and perhaps even writing resolutions for them to introduce, willing to accept anonymity with the public and perhaps even so far as some of their diplomatic colleagues are concerned. In performing this kind of role a diplomat may forego advancing the preferred policy of his own nation, although usually with the approval of his foreign office, in the interest of advancing what seems to be the most advantageous final outcome.

In their summary of the characteristics of seventy-five political systems in the "developing areas," Almond and Coleman (1960, pp. 38-45 and 551-556) found that less developed political systems have less capability of aggregating diverse interests behind specific governmental policies than more developed political systems. One of the methods whereby such aggregation takes place in developed systems is through political parties. The United Nations falls far short of this kind of aggregation; however, delegates who work at finding consensus and who negotiate in the name of groups of nations are, perhaps, in more embryonic form performing an aggregation function as well.

An important part of the role of any secretariat is the gathering of information on substantive issues for the use of the councils and assemblies that it services. Secretariats are a common information source for participating nations which tend to increase agreement on what the facts are and what the significant problems are. The documentary product of the secretariat is particularly important for small national missions who cannot afford research staffs. Not only through documents, but also in continual rounds of discussion, secretariats provide an anational pool of information that erodes away some of the more extreme information products of national governments. An example has been the information supplied by secretariat and national diplomats who have gone to colonial territories on visiting missions. Information provided by both nations administering territories and by nations attacking their colonial administrations has received effective challenge by information collected under United Nations auspices.

EXTENDED CONTACT BETWEEN INTERGOVERNMENTAL SOCIAL SYSTEMS AND THE OUTSIDE WORLD

The public sessions of bodies of international organizations provide a new element to intergovernmental relations whose merits have been much discussed. While only a part of the political process of an organization like the United Nations can be observed by the public, more is revealed, particularly during extemporaneous interchange, than would be the case without public sessions. Public debate probably extends public interest and knowledge. But, as Elmore Jackson points out, extended public debate may cause disputants to take extreme positions not previously taken which cannot be easily abandoned (1952, pp. 134-135). The need to publicly take positions on so many issues in the United Nations also affects the nature of policy. There is little doubt that the fact that administering nations have had to defend their colonial policies in the United Nations has had an effect on these policies. Public debate also often misleads observers who do not take into consideration the full range of United Nations political activity. Representatives who impress the folks back home with their eloquent phrases, or perhaps their severe castigation of enemies, are not always the most effective in achieving national objectives through the United Nations political process.

Because the United Nations is in the United States, and because United States correspondents form the largest national contingent in the United Nations press corps, the relations between United Nations officials and the press are highly influenced by United States practice. The press conference, with impromptu questions from correspondents, is accepted as part of the task of participating in the United Nations by all diplomats. Correspondents are on the invitation list of most large parties. The delegate's lounge is the most fertile hunting ground for the press, with the press sometimes outnumbering the diplomats at the bar. It is not uncommon to see correspondents maintaining a vigil outside a bloc meeting or smaller private negotiating sessions held in conference rooms in United Nations headquarters. Sometimes diplomats cannot resist the opportunity to get their side of the story to the press, resulting in the same kinds of difficulties for private negotiation that are so common in congressional politics in Washington.

Thus, the United Nations site has some of the same kind of effects on the press as it has on the diplomatic community. Sharing common facilities, with most operating from within its headquarters, it is a more integrated corps than is the case in a national capital. The global concerns of the diplomatic community provide a challenge to the press that is not offered elsewhere. It is possible for the press to get virtually any issue explained in the actual words of an official from any nation, rather than from secondhand sources. It is more difficult for a journalist to neglect the variety of global concerns while only concentrating on a few issues considered important in his nation. But it is not always possible for him to convince editors that the important concerns of the world are more numerous than his paper portrays. A wire-service bureau chief is quoted by Rubin as saying, "A sad part of the U.N. assignment is the amount of work it does that cannot be fully reported because newspapers are interested in what sells newspapers, and conflict sells newspapers. You don't sell newspapers with stories about UNICEF or WHO" (1963, p. 27).

While press, and nongovernmental-organization representatives as well, spend much time conveying information on United Nations activity to the outside world, they also help to give the diplomat a more varied intellectual diet than he is likely to obtain in many other places. Some diplomats spend considerable time in discussion with press and non-governmental-organization representatives in a mutual exchange of information and ideas. A United States correspondent commented, "Reporters are also asked for information by [diplomats]. . . . It's a process of trading information. Diplomats try to get many views about the same subject. For instance, a Russian diplomat here asked me what I thought of Khrushchev's speech. They put it together with everything else" (Rubin, 1963, p. 33). Milbrath wrote of Washington lobbyists, "Officials require lobbyists to be knowledgeable because they need information and want something in return for the time and attention they give" (1963, p. 222). The nongovernmental-organization representatives are the United Nations equivalent of the Washington lobbyists, and the most effective provide diplomats with information that they feel they need. The United Nations "lobbyist" can more often aid the diplomat whose nation has a small mission with his information needs than the diplomat from a large mission that is more likely to be able to collect its own information.

Though no studies are available on the development of new international interest groups as a result of the establishment of the United Nations, the effects of the United Nations have probably not been so dramatic as those reported by Haas in Europe. But the United Nations is providing a focal point for activity of international interest groups. There are ten international nongovernmental organizations—business, labor, agriculture, and veterans groups as well as the Inter-Parliamentary Union and the World Federation of U.N. Associations—who have a special consultative status with the Economic and Social Council. They may submit written statements for circulation as documents, present their views orally to the Council and its commissions, and propose items for inclusion in the Council's agenda. Over 100 other international nongovernmental organizations have all of these privileges, except the right to propose agenda items. Representatives of all of these organizations, and others as well, may attend public sessions of all United Nations bodies as observers and have access to United Nations delegates in the lounges and corridors of United Nations headquarters.

LEARNING EXPERIENCES OF PARTICIPANTS

Kenneth Boulding once wrote, "The growth of a system-attitude toward international relations will have profound consequences for the dynamics of the system itself, just as the growth of a systems-attitude in economics has profound consequences for the dynamics of the economic system" (1959, p. 131). It has already been indicated that the creation of an organization requires the creation of new roles in foreign offices, missions to the international organization, and international-organization secretariats that must contend with aspects of the entire system represented in the international organization. The existence of the organization also encourages members of the press, nongovernmental organizations, and interested members of the general public to look at the entire system as well.

For those actually working in or directly observing an international organization, the learning experience is probably the most profound. Reading about the foreign policies of many nations, and perhaps even reading United Nations debates, does not have the same impact on the reader as direct participation in the United Nations. A member of the United States Congress, who was a United States delegate to the General Assembly, once told me she was sitting through much of the time-consuming general debate because she thought she got something out of personal attendance that she couldn't get out of reading the record. Though the nations of the world are many, it is not easy to forget about many of them for long at the United Nations. If a delegate makes a proposal, the world talks back through live human beings who speak directly to his arguments. The experience may be unpleasant, since it is in many ways more comforting not to have to contend with such diversity of viewpoint as is sometimes found. However, those who have to contend with this kind of experience over long periods of time look at the world differently than they did before. Some supportive evidence comes from H. Daalder in his description of the impact of participation in international parliamentary bodies in Europe on Dutch parliamentarians:

> Sometimes there tends to grow a psychological rift between the ordinary member of parliament and those who go to the foreign assemblies. Both groups may develop a different sense of priorities: the "foreign" member gets a little irritated with the "provincial outlook" of the domestic members insisting as it is said on discussing secondary matters as if they were of world-wide importance; the "domestic" member, on the other hand, deplores a tendency on the part of the foreign experts to deal in *groszen Worten* (1960, p. 126).

After serving for several years in the missions of Canada and the Netherlands to the United Nations, two diplomats wrote that "there is no doubt that the personal and parliamentary experience which delegates get at the United Nations may have long run consequences of value to the international community" (Hadwen and Kaufmann, 1962, p. 54).

There is no reason to believe that diplomats from any part of the world are immune from the learning experiences of United Nations participation. Writing of the United Nations diplomats of the Soviet Union, Alexander Dallin notes, "Soviet personnel stationed at the United Nations—be it with the USSR mission or on the United Nations staff—tend to be more practical and pragmatic in outlook than those in the 'home office'; they at times seem less concerned with doctrine than with success. And while it is easy to exaggerate such nuances, there are occasional suggestions of different perceptions of reality" (1962, p. 96).

Chadwick Alger's interviews of twenty-five delegates to the General Assembly, soon after their arrival at the United Nations and again two months later, offer some idea of the learning that takes place at the United Nations (1963). After only two months at the United Nations participants were aware of an expanded number of issues and nations. An official from a Middle Eastern foreign office indicated that he had not previously heard of some of the African territories discussed in his committee. Some delegates were surprised at positions taken by some nations in United Nations debate. For example, a Far Eastern delegate who had served in his foreign office for twelve years was surprised to find that the older nations of the Commonwealth did not vote as a bloc in his committee. An African delegate was surprised to find that the United States voted with his nation on the South West Africa question.

To some who are accustomed to the routine of a foreign office or the traditional negotiation setting in a foreign embassy, the parliamentary milieu of the United Nations may be upsetting. For example, a British foreign office official stated, "The United Nations is a mob. . . . There are no negotiations carried on here at the United Nations. Oh, there is some in the corridor, but mostly it is just a matter of speeches. You have an expression, 'It's a hell of a way to run a railroad.'" But many who are assigned to permanent missions at the United Nations, or who return to the Assembly often, become adept at operating in the United Nations setting. Through United Nations experience diplomats are learning the political skills necessary to operate the political processes of international organizations. To a large degree this requires a merging of the skills normally expected of diplomats and those possessed by successful parliamentarians. Thus, the day-to-day activity in the United Nations has served as a laboratory where a world-wide intergovernmental community has developed its own techniques for intergovernmental relations. It is also a training ground where officials from 113 nations are trained in the utilization of these techniques.

CONCLUSION

In this chapter we have found that international organizations encourage a variety of changes in the pattern of intergovernmental relationships. They tend to integrate intergovernmental social systems in which they are established by placing more nations in direct contact with each other, putting more officials from individual nations in direct contact with their counterparts from other nations, and providing sites for intergovernmental contact that stimulate freer interaction. International organizations also tend to integrate these social systems through the creation of roles that operate in the context of the entire system represented in the organization and through the learning experiences that occupants of these roles acquire. There is some "spill-over" of integrative impetus to press and other nongovernmental organizations.

Examples have been utilized to show how the developing knowledge of human conflict is helping us to become more sensitive to the potential relevance of the characteristics of intergovernmental social systems to international conflict. These examples suggest that a broad knowledge of the social science of human conflict is as necessary in making governmental decisions related to international organizations as are knowledge of diplomatic history, of international law, and of the charter and issues of particular organizations. Should a particular nation seek admittance to or be admitted to an international organization? Should a nation include parliamentarians on General Assembly delegations? Should a new item be admitted to the agenda of an international organization? Should an effort be made to assign all foreign-service officers to a tour of duty in the United Nations? Though all of these questions may not at first glance appear to be related to the capability of international organizations to handle international conflict, they most certainly are. Over fifty years ago, in his *Fundamental Principles of the Sociology of Law*, Eugen Ehrlich provocatively wrote, "At the present as well as at any other time, the center of gravity of legal development lies not in legislation, nor in juristic science, nor in judicial decision, but in society itself" (1936, p. xv). Those of us who are concerned about international conflict, with the help of the developing larger discipline of human conflict, are only gradually becoming fully aware of the profound relevance of Ehrlich's insight.

REFERENCES

Alger, Chadwick F., "United Nations Participation as a Learning Experience," *Public Opinion Quarterly*, XXVII (1963), 411-426.

Almond, Gabriel and James Coleman, *Politics of the Developing Areas*. Princeton, N.J.: Princeton University Press, 1960.

Angell, Robert C., "Discovering Paths to Peace," *The Nature of International Conflict*, International Sociological Association. Paris: UNESCO, 1957.

Best, Gary, "Diplomacy in the United Nations." Ph.D. dissertation, Northwestern University, 1960.

Boulding, Kenneth, "National Images and International Systems," *Journal of Conflict Resolution*, III (1959), 120-131.

Coser, Lewis, *The Functions of Social Conflict*. New York: Free Press of Glencoe, Inc., 1955.

Daalder, H., "The Netherlands," *European Assemblies: The Experimental Period, 1949–1959*, Kenneth Lindsay, ed., pp. 115-132. New York: Frederick A. Praeger, Inc., 1960; London: Stevens and Sons, Ltd., 1960.

Dallin, Alexander, *The Soviet Union at the United Nations*. New York: Frederick A. Praeger, Inc., 1962.

Deutsch, Karl W. *et al.*, *Political Community and the North Atlantic Area: International Organization in the Light of Historical Experience*. Princeton, N.J.: Princeton University Press, 1957.

Ehrlich, Eugen, *Fundamental Principles of the Sociology of Law*, Walter L. Moll, trans. Cambridge, Mass.: Harvard University Press, 1936.

Fortes, M. and E. E. Evans-Pritchard, *African Political Systems*. London: Oxford University Press, H. Milford, 1940. Reprinted 1961.

Gluckman, Max, *Custom and Conflict in Africa*. New York: Free Press of Glencoe, Inc., 1955.

Hadwen, John and Johan Kaufmann, *How United Nations Decisions Are Made*. New York: Oceana Publications, Inc., 1962; Leyden: A. W. Sythoff, 1962.

Hammarskjold, Dag, "The Developing Role of the United Nations," *United Nations Review*, VI (September 1959), 8-18. Reprint of *Introduction to the Fourteenth Annual Report of the Secretary-General on the Work of the Organization*, 1959.

Homans, George C., *The Human Group*. New York: Harcourt, Brace & World, Inc., 1950.

Hovet, Thomas, Jr., "Political Parties in the United Nations." Paper prepared for the 1962 Annual Meeting of the American Political Science Association, Washington, D.C., September, 1962.

————, *Africa in the United Nations*. Evanston, Ill.: Northwestern University Press, 1963.

Jackson, Elmore, *Meeting of Minds*. New York: McGraw-Hill Book Company, 1952.

Likert, Rensis, *New Patterns of Management*. New York: McGraw-Hill Book Company, 1961.

Malinowski, Bronislaw, *Crime and Custom in Savage Society*. London: Routledge & Kegan Paul, Ltd., 1926; New York: Harcourt, Brace & World, Inc., 1926.

Metcalf, Henry C. and Lyndall Urwick, eds., *Dynamic Administration: The Collected Papers of Mary Parker Follett*. New York: Harper & Row, Publishers, 1942.

Milbrath, Lester, *The Washington Lobbyists*. Chicago: Rand McNally & Co., 1963.

Numelin, Ragnar, *The Beginnings of Diplomacy*. London: Oxford University Press, 1950.

Ross, Edward A., *The Principles of Sociology*. New York: Appleton-Century-Crofts, 1920.

Rubin, Ronald, "The UN Correspondent." Unpublished paper, Department of Government and International Relations, New York University, 1963.

Schwartz, Richard, "Social Factors in the Development of Legal Control: A Case Study of Two Israeli Settlements," *Yale Law Journal*, LXIII (1953–1954), 471-491.

Williams, Robin, *American Society*. New York: Alfred A. Knopf, Inc., 1951.

Wilson, Hugh, *The Education of a Diplomat*. New York: David McKay Co., Inc., 1938.

Wright, Quincy, *Contemporary International Law: A Balance Sheet*. Garden City, N.Y.: Doubleday & Company, Inc., 1955.

Part 4 The American Peace Movement

14

The American Peace Movement

DONALD F. KEYS

Is there an American peace movement? Not in the proper sense of the word. In fact, what exists is a general movement in the direction of peace, variously understood, by a number of groups and individuals. There is a wide uneasiness about the direction of the cold war, and an inchoate protest against its most dangerous aspects. But the groups are too diverse in their approaches and in their constituencies too small to constitute a movement.

On the scene in the Forties and Fifties were essentially two groups of organizations at the far ends of the policy spectrum. In the one wing were the general foreign-policy groups such as the Foreign Policy Association and the World Affairs Councils. There were the special-purpose groups—the American Association for the United Nations, in support of the U.N. and its diverse activities; and United World Federalists, in favor of giving the U.N. the powers of limited world government. Both of these organizations have nationwide membership and important educational programs. United World Federalists is a political-action organization as well. There was also the Americans for Democratic Action, an organization mainly of liberals from the Democratic party, concerned in part with foreign policy. On the other end of the spectrum, a second group of organizations includes the American Friends Service Committee, a Quaker agency, which in addition to its welfare work has agencies and departments concerned with world peace, centers in major US cities, and a large peace-education program. Another Quaker agency, the Friends Committee on National Legislation, was and is an effective Washington lobby on a number of legislative issues, including those dealing with the arms race.

The Women's International League for Peace and Freedom, which has its origins in World War I days, is a widely respected membership organization, nonpacifist in policy, but closer to the pacifist position than the U.N.-oriented groups. The Fellowship of Reconciliation is a religious pacifist organization, largely of Protestant clergy. The secular pacifist group is the War Resister's League. More recently the Committee for Non-Violent Action has emerged. This group practices civil disobedience. Together these organizations constitute the pacifist or pacifist-oriented wing of the peace-group spectrum.

In a rather different category is the Federation of American Scientists, more or less a professional group, lobbying from within a specific area of competence. Until recently the FAS and the "Bulletin of Atomic Scientists" group represented most of the science participation in action for peace. The pacifists among the scientists have been found, for the most part, in the Society for Social Responsibility in Science.

The National Committee for a Sane Nuclear Policy was created basically because neither of the groupings mentioned—the U.N.–world-law group or the pacifists—had placed themselves in a position of much political relevance to the major cold war issues and the arms race. SANE was a child of default—the default of the existing groups to take up the testing–arms-race-disarmament issues in a meaningful and relevant way. Theoretically, the U.N.-oriented groups could have done so with only minor modifications of their policies. There are however two contradictory factors which must be met if a "peace organization" is to be effective. It must balance its advocacy of ideas against their acceptability in the society. It runs the dual risks of advocating a bold and needed policy and thereby effectively alienating itself from society, or of becoming so respectable and conservative in order to reach society that its policy becomes meaningless in its dilution. The "hard-core" pacifists had, and have, effectively isolated themselves from the society in which they live. The less radical of the pacifists groups such as the American Friends Service Committee and Fellowship of Reconciliation have done exceedingly effective educational work but are not political-action groups, nor do they have a policy capable of wide acceptance. The U.N.-oriented groups had paid such a high price for respectability that they were severely limited with regard to the flexibility needed to meet changing needs and new challenges.

The founders of SANE hoped to create a center of gravity between the existing and polarized peace groups, to the left of the political parties. They sought by these means to give those within the parties who should wish to advocate more relevant policies, more room within which to maneuver. SANE tried to balance on that difficult knife edge where advocacy and acceptability become tangent. It tried to maintain another balance as well—that between a mass movement and an intellectual elite.

As the major antitesting movement to emerge in the US, SANE was launched in 1957 in a vacuum of effective dissent, and at a point of high but unvoiced public concern. Nuclear testing was, for the moment, the ripe political issue. The organization used rather radical means to press for a fairly conservative policy: a treaty to end nuclear-weapons tests, and a treaty on inspected and controlled world-wide disarmament.

The attitude toward efforts to achieve peaceful co-existence has changed considerably in the past several years. The former no-man's land is no longer a void: "peace groups" are popping up on every hand. Two important new groups are the Women Strike for Peace and the Student Peace Union. Many students left SANE for the Student Peace Union, when it was formed, because of their disagreement with SANE's policy of excluding communists. The students, having come to political consciousness during the McCarthy period, considered it a civil-liberties issue. Other students wanted to work on issues such as desegregation, which SANE's policy did not include.

Women Strike for Peace consists of three major elements: the first of these are the veterans of many years in women's struggle for peace. Much of the leadership has come from the Women's International League for Peace and Freedom. A second group are dissenters from SANE who disagreed with its communist-exclusion clause. Most important, there are a greater number of women who have never before been active in any social cause in their lives. Women Strike for Peace is the second important new antitesting and prodisarmament development in recent years. I say "development" because it is not quite a movement, and it claims not to be an organization. Their policy is as yet a little vague.

Looking now in the other direction, there have been substantial stirrings in the academic world. The Boston Area Faculty Group came forward on the civil-defense issue in a very effective way. Seeding the intellectual soil has been the Council of Correspondence (publishing a limited circulation newsletter) and some of the work being done by the Center for the Study of Democratic Institutions. Recently, the Universities Committee on the Problems of War and Peace has begun to organize on a number of campuses.

The Scientists on Survival, an effort to bridge the behavioral and physical sciences in work for peace, began in a confused and confusing conference, which, nevertheless, brought forward a surprising attendance. Two other newcomers are the Council for the Gradualist Way to Peace, begun by Amitai Etzioni, and the Council for a Livable World (formerly the Council for Abolishing War) established by Leo Szilard. There is little if anything to differentiate the policy of the Gradualists from that of SANE—any effort to achieve controlled disarmament and the preservation of American values will be gradual. Yet, the new group appears "safe" enough to enlist an echelon of the elite not previously involved. The Council for a Livable World also appears to be a highly individualistic effort, with attractiveness to some from the aforementioned "next echelon" and acceptable to status-conscious groups. Again, the goals and methods differ little from those of the political-action arm of SANE or the United World Federalists. The unique feature of the Council for a Livable World is the request to its supporters to "tithe" themselves to the amount of 1 or 2 per cent of their income for political-action objectives. Both these groups are elitist and hierarchical and will probably never achieve a large constituency.

I shall not attempt to unravel the other significant development of the past two or three years—the burgeoning interest and activity loosely categorized as peace research. I should like, however, to make one or two general comments. We who have been laboring long find this new development very welcome indeed. Peace research puts backbone, reality, authenticity, and acceptability into the race for peace. It creates a momentum of commitment, funds, and ideas; it provides information where information was lacking and only sentiment existed. This is legitimate peace research and serves legitimate purposes. But many times research can become a refuge from action, when a case is already clearly defined and action is required. Research is legitimate as long as it is not undertaken as an alternative to taking a stand when a stand is needed, as long as it is not begun to avoid crusading when crusading is required, as long as it does not provide merely an easy road of avoiding commitment when commitment is asked.

From time to time there are pressures for an ecumenical movement among the peace-interested groups. This has never been more true than at present. Over the past year, a new effort has been made to activate a framework in which the diverse groups we have discussed would be able, insofar as their policies and modes of action allow, to coordinate their efforts and exchange materials and information on a greatly increased scale. This effort is called Turn Toward Peace. Under the policy framework of Turn Toward Peace the constituent groups agree to differ—to take note of the fact that their policies contain points at wide variance with each other—but to recognize that they agree on certain fundamental necessities, such as general disarmament and initiatives away from war.

At the national level, Turn Toward Peace is to act as a clearinghouse, to accumulate advisory and informational resources of interest and help to the national groups, and to circulate widely the views of all of them. At the local level, Turn Toward Peace envisages the establishment of the same clearinghouse function through "peace centers," centralizing information and literature on each group and creating a reservoir of community resources such as mass-media contacts and a speaker's bureau.

It is hard to tell yet how this experiment may work out in practice. There have been so far debits as well as credits marked up for Turn Toward Peace. It was hoped that Turn Toward Peace would become effective in stimulating interest and activity regarding disarmament in the churches and labor unions. It has succeeded to some degree, but unless Turn Toward Peace can actively involve some of the groups to the "right," participation of groups in the middle will become increasingly difficult. At the local level, Turn Toward Peace must proceed with caution, for in establishing peace centers in a community where numerous groups are active, it creates one more vortex of activity which can be diversionary of both money and time. Whether this diversion will, on balance, be useful remains to be seen. If the peace center projects a "peace" image into the community, and becomes a hang-out for "peaceniks," then it will defeat its own purposes of greater community outreach and involvement. It also risks the alienation of its constituent groups and a behind-the-scenes struggle over resources.

In sum, because of their discrete doctrines and constituencies, there are finite limits to any ecumenical movement among the peace groups. Most groups, through the pressures to which they have subjected themselves and the series of choices they have made, have become specialized instruments for the reaching of a discrete constituency on a specific and limited policy which they will support. Only a few organizations have the dynamism and the policy framework which has potential for wide community participation. The peace groups cannot be dissolved into some sort of "peace-movement stew" without violating their reason for being and losing their constituency.

The picture at the world level is quite similar. A number of the groups mentioned are members of world-wide internationals. Among these are the Fellowship of Reconciliation, American Association for the United Nations, the United World Federalists, and Women's International League for Peace and Freedom. Particular interest is attached to the World Peace Council, a communist-dominated body, derived from the Stockholm Peace Appeal. This body has branches throughout most of the world, although none in the United States. By default, this organization has posed for a numbed of years as *the* world organization for peace and disarmament. Like the World Peace Council, the Japan A- and H-Bomb Council has played host at international conferences and is also communist dominated. There is a new independent group in Japan, but it is too early to tell whether it will become effective. Of particular importance are the Campaign for Nuclear Disarmament in the United Kingdom—the British counterpart of SANE—and the European Federation Against Nuclear Arms, which includes the Campaign for Nuclear Disarmament and similar movements on the Continent.

In January of 1962, the European Federation called a conference at Oxford, England to consider the establishment of a world-wide federation of all nonaligned or independent groups working for peace. Seventy-five delegates from pacifist and nonpacifist groups agreed to establish the International Confederation for Disarmament and Peace. Because of its broad diversity, the new organization will be limited to the role of sort of a world-level Turn Toward Peace, providing information, communication, and, occasionally, a platform for world-level discussion. It will, incidentally, create a condition of parity for discussion with the World Peace Council, the Soviet Peace Committee, and other communist-dominated groups, and it will undoubtedly shift the center of gravity away from them.

PEOPLE AND THE PEACE MOVEMENT

Let us move now to a brief analysis of the kinds of people found in the peace movement, and their philosophies and motivations, and try to define some of the groupings into which they fall. First, there is the matter of communists, noncommunists, and anticommunists. Any group which seeks seriously to attract a substantial following on a long-term basis in the US must be clearly and unequivocally noncommunist. This is easier to be than to prove. There is a less expedient and more fundamental reason which is equally pragmatic in its implications: an organization subject to communist influence cannot and does not deal fairly with the sins of commission and omission on both sides in the cold war. It not only lacks objectivity, but loses credibility within Western society, and rightly so. Many American peace organizations, such as United World Federalists and SANE, have a noncommunist membership policy. Others such as Women Strike for Peace do not.

Anticommunists are not a problem in the American peace effort. American anticommunists are found largely in the Birchite and isolationist wing in the US. But in the United Kingdom anticommunists do a great deal of damage in the peace movement. The British also have much more trouble with bona fide communists than US peace groups.

The radical wing of the US peace movement is plagued with another type—the congenital malcontent—a basically antisocial person who is usually "anti" whatever lies closest at hand. In matters of peace, it is the US government which incurs their rancor. A certain number of these persons are Soviet apologists, some are unreconstructed Stalinists but not Communist Party members—persons who are actually left of the Communist Party line. There are also a small number of other Marxists, Trotskyites of various shades, socialists and anarchists, most of whom sincerely believe that no real progress can be made toward peace without profound social change. The anarchists fall into two groups: an antisocial group composed of what one might call *temperamental anarchists,* and the philosophic anarchists. These people, small in number, tend to impart an antiauthority "tone" to peace activity much out of proportion with its real strength.

And of course there are the pacifists themselves. Perhaps as much as academia, professional pacifists have been a reservoir for new projects, new concepts, and new departures for the US peace groups. They have been well organized for a number of years and have worked valiantly to establish a Gandhian toe-hold in American society. From the pacifist intellectuals came the original impetus for SANE, for Women Strike for Peace, and for Turn Toward Peace. The pacifists again are of several kinds, including the religious pacifists and the humanistic pacifists. The first are pinning their hope on a moral revolution to save the world from war, and the second, like the Marxists, see no hope short of profound social, political, and economic change. There are also the nuclear pacifists, which in the US is an ill-defined group. Many members of SANE, for instance, if they were challenged, would probably say that they would consider it immoral to push the button and would not themselves do so. Many of them have never heard nuclear pacifism discussed and would not have thought of applying the term to themselves. They, like most of the clergy, are pinning their hopes on multilateral agreements and have not considered deeply other possibilities in the event of failure to achieve agreements.

The effects of the Marxists and pacifists, and for that matter their techniques and attitudes, are quite similar with regard to the peace effort. Both groups feel that they have the sacred light and the only long-term solution to the cold war. Both regard groups such as SANE as expedient compromisers. Both tend to look upon communication and dialogue with the Establishment, and particularly with its military branches, as treasonous and damaging. Both groups tend therefore to isolate themselves from society and to restrict their effect. The reaction of the public is predictable and healthy: the Marxists are distrusted because they are believed beholden to a foreign power or at least to a foreign ideology which does not respect American rights and freedoms. The pacifists are mistrusted because they seem to advocate a philosophy which might lead to settling for "peace at any price."

Both Marxists and pacifists, finding themselves effectively self-isolated, regard other organizations in the peace movement both with self-righteousness and, paradoxically, as a prime area of activity for themselves. The reason is, of course, that the adjacent groups are their only means of contact with society at large. As with the Marxists, so with the pacifists: both groups try to build or manipulate "fronts" for themselves in the peace area (I am not equating the morality of the two). They also attempt to establish popular fronts or alignments in which they will get a free ride out into society in conjunction with other groups. "We are all for peace," they say, "so why don't we all work together," failing to realize or conveniently overlooking that the word has as many meanings as the people who use it.

To a certain extent there has been a wise division of labor among the various groups, each with its particular constituency and each contributing a useful point to the dialogue. Each group has an appeal to a sector of society which is ready to accept its particular slant and policy. Thus a multiplicity of groups makes it possible to reach into, educate, and affect nearly all elements in the society, bringing them along to whatever is *for them* the next step in understanding and internationalism. The spectrum of peace groups has what might be called an *interlocking directorate* among its boards and officers; and indeed there is also considerable cross-membership at the local level.

Trouble in keeping the groups sorted out emerges, however, at the time of Easter Marches and similar activities, when the call for joint action is difficult to resist, and as a result, the lines and images tend to become jumbled, and to negate one another. When this occurs, an entire effort may be labeled *pacifist* by the press, and buttonholed and forgotten as being of no significance, inasmuch as, a priori, demonstrations are expected from pacifists. Demonstrations, therefore, to be effective and not just a public catharsis for the participants, must be too large to be ignored or labeled merely *pacifist*, and must be predicated on slogans and concepts which are not merely antiwar or anti-one bloc.

The pacifists and fellow-traveling types also have a similar effect on policy pronouncements and on the "tone" and image of public action. They tend to veer away from well-defined objectives and goals, from insistence on world authority and controls. They make common cause with "peacey" slogans of the antiwar, "ban-the-bomb" type. Unfortunately, the emotionally motivated, unthinking supporter of peace sees nothing wrong in this.

One of the most important and hopeful developments has been the fact that groups with a multilateral disarmament policy have succeeded in disrupting (not without causing pain and distress) the ingrown pattern of the organizations working for peace, enlisting many thousands of new people who have not been previously active. This has been accomplished by high visibility and communication with the community as opposed to the self-congratulatory and ingrown programming into which peace groups tend to fall. The renewed effort at outreach coincides with deepening concern among the wider public which has been subjected to the shock treatment of nuclear tests, civil-defense calls, the Berlin and Cuban crises. These events have constituted "teachable moments" in which rapid expansion has been possible. Increasing numbers of middle-class Americans are swelling the ranks of the prodisarmament groups as a result. There are not many signs of "mass" response. The peace organizations are not working-men's groups. SANE, for instance, might categorize its membership as upper middle class, professional and semiprofessional, white collar, Protestant and Jewish, and white. The reason for lack of Negro participation seems to be due to preoccupation with racial and living-standard problems, and consequent lack of interest in the arms-race crisis.

Also within the peace movement are increasingly found the disenchanted Stevenson liberals, and those who feel that their organization or party is too identified with the Establishment to exert any pressure on it. If we move far enough across the spectrum we find that under the World Law and Order banner semimilitarist types can be found, people who take as simplistic a view of the world problem as do the Marxists. They find it easy to be for a world federation because they believe in authority, and also because they see no chance of Russian acceptance. Incidentally, the pacifists tend to find common cause with anarchists and Marxists in being *against* world authority—suspicious of a strong U.N. and opposed, for example, to a U.N. with a police force, and in particular one with nuclear weapons.

These, then, are the obstacles to any real ecumenical movement within the peace effort, and are the very real reasons for the diversity which exists.

Are there any accomplishments that the peace groups can point to as adequate justification for their existence and for the money and effort which has poured through them? It is difficult to measure general contributions to an atmosphere of public opinion, which is what the work of the peace groups amounts to. One of the prime indications that the work has been meaningful is precisely the proliferation of groups which now exists. Peace is no longer quite so suspect; in a minor way, it has become "the thing."

Work for peace is a lot like punching a pillow, but occasionally there are concrete indications of effect. For instance, both Edward Teller and a representative of the U.N. Secretariat credited SANE with discouraging nuclear tests during the Eisenhower administration and of maintaining the conditions for the continuation of the dialogue. Of course this became impossible after the Russians resumed tests. The Arms Control and Disarmament Agency has had high praise for United World Federalists, SANE, and other organizations which played a role in the political representations leading to the establishment of the agency.

Approval of the U.N. bond issue depended heavily on the combined efforts of a number of groups. The fact that the mass media have found themselves a little less tongue-tied lately has been due in no small way to such things as SANE's ads featuring Dr. Spock, the women's and student marches, and similar activities.

What about the future? One can postulate that groups and organizations will continue to proliferate. One reason for this is that those who were cautious and refrained from early activity, finding it "safe" now, prefer not to support those organizations which made it safe for them but rather to start their own. Many want to be the head of their own group, others wish to avoid identification with the battle-scarred groups which have accumulated contentious images.

One can postulate that there will be some mergers: there is no reason, for instance, that Dr. Etzioni's group and the late Dr. Szilard's group should not find common cause. It might be possible and desirable for those action groups which have foresworn tax-exempt status in order to work politically for peace, and which have in common a multilateral disarmament position, to merge into one large centralist body.

In terms of policy, we can expect a continued evolution from protest to advocacy. The peace groups are realizing that they will have to do more than protest existing policies if they wish to garner support. They will also have to be able to show that they realize disarmament is not going to mean the end of international contention, which will perforce continue at other levels. What prescriptions do they have for this? Some groups are talking about "peace plus"—that "plus" being the defining of national goals outside of the military aspects of the cold war—continued striving for political and economic freedoms abroad and their preservation at home, making the point that only with the end of the arms race can we guarantee either effort.

Beneath the drive for world federation, for support of the U.N., and for the achievement of world peace lies a usually unexpressed groping toward world community, toward a world-level loyalty and identification with the human experiment per se. To the extent which this growing sense of world community is submerged in the considerations of the *modus*—the institutionalization of peace—the groups working in that direction have often failed to capitalize on the motive power inherent in this deep-seated intuition the race has received. It is beginning to occur to many people now that this fuel has been neglected, and it may be predicted that the peace groups will begin to search for the means to reinject and re-employ it. "We need," Arnold Toynbee stressed in a recent interview, "a pyramid of loyalties. The top of the pyramid," he said, "remains to be placed."

Is there, then, an American peace movement? Not in the sense usually implied. Nor is it likely that there will be. The peace groups will probably play out the role of a minority in a democratic society: they will take the responsibility for giving visibility to ideas whose time has come, and undertake to create a mandate for them. As was the case with the Socialist party in the US, when the need and the mandate became great enough, the policies advocated by the peace groups will be adopted and pressed by the parties in power. The peace groups will play a political role, but not as a party. They will seek the endorsement and support of those candidates who will take the strongest stands on the peace issues. The experience of running independents in 1962 was enough for most peace groups. They saw that their candidates received only 1 or 2 per cent of the vote, whereas in areas where volunteers worked actively for worthy candidates *within* the parties, they were often elected.

If there is hope for growth of a widespread "movement" in the US, it will undoubtedly have to develop along policy lines which are politically realistic, in terms which are ultimately acceptable by American society, and in terms which hold real hope of ending the arms race. The main elements of such a policy are certainly multilateral disarmament and peaceful economic competition with the Soviet bloc.

There are those who say often and loudly that what the peace movement needs is more intellectual content, more expertise, and that if we will prepare to deal as elites with elites we would meet with greater success. We should prepare as well as possible, but I would demur from the view that our major function is to deal directly with elites. Our major task is, and it seems to me should be, to do a more general job of public education on a dilute level as to what disarmament is and why we need it, and to build the kind of political support I have mentioned for these policies. All the expertise in the world will not press a bill through Congress if the Senator feels his constituency would not support him.

What are the major lacks in the effort to work successfully for world peace? Basically, I think, a design for the future, which can be enthusiastically supported. We do not really know what kind of world we want or how to secure commitment for it. "Survivalism" and even "peaceful competition" are not enough. The basic nature of the world crisis is not often touched on. As the wreckage of the old civilization comes tumbling down, the US blames the chaos on communist expansionism and the Soviet Union blames it on capitalist imperialism. Paradoxically, it is the end of an age for both of them equally, and they blame their discomfiture on each other. That the control of atomic energy should have emerged to sharpen this great joke is a touch of divine irony.

It is my own feeling that peace movements, peace research movements, and conflict-resolution studies are all only a prelude to this important task which is urgently before us.

Part 5   The Future of Human Conflict

CHAPTER

15

The
Future
of
Human
Conflict

ELTON B. McNEIL

The invention of plans for peace is undoubtedly as ancient as the first conflict and, probably, predates overt warfare. From his history man can select any of a number of workable solutions to hostility, yet each age seems to bear such individual characteristics and seemingly unique difficulties that the life span of peace plans is short indeed.

The last six centuries have been an era of alternating vicious war and uncomfortable peace in which there has been a piling-up of peace plans to a degree that clearly indicates that the nature of the plan is less relevant than the need of the combatants to seek an end to hostility. In the history of peace plans, we are indebted to the Greeks for early notions of federation (mostly religious) and the use of arbitration in settling disputes, to the Romans and Pax Romana as a brilliant example of an enforced national peace extending across vast territories, and to the papacy, during the Middle Ages, as the supreme and final arbiter of justice and right in the world. The Protestant revolt put an end to the existing hopes of world federation based on religion.

The early plans for peace bore two general characteristics: federation and arbitration. Pierre DuBois, for example, was an adviser to Philip le Bel, king of

France, and in this capacity suggested, early in the 1300's, that a federation of Christian sovereign states and a council of nations be established to arbitrate human disputes. His proposal of an international court armed with the weapons of boycott and concerted military action thus preceded the sanctions of the Covenant of the League of Nations by over six centuries. While the work of DuBois has been described as a mixture of equal parts of prophecy and program, he anticipated our current economic concerns when he suggested that the financial savings to be realized from the abolition of wars was to be spent on the establishment of international schools.

Some of the violent partisans of peace—Erasmus for one—maintained that the clergy ought to refuse burial in consecrated ground to all who died in battle and to insist that wars not be declared by leaders but by the full and unanimous consent of the whole people. These propositions were startling for the early 1500's, but they contained a flaw in the form of Erasmus' approval of what he described as "just, defensive wars."

Among the most celebrated of all peace plans was that attributed to Henry IV of France. It was a classic federation of states and it involved the grand design of dividing up Europe into equal parts to prevent territorial jealousy. In the early seventeenth century the air was full of schemes for conferences to end war. William Penn maintained in 1693 that "wars are the duels of Princes" and he proposed a peace plan to end them; Rousseau, in 1782, became one of the prophets of international peace; Jeremy Bentham was, in 1786, one of the first great men to stress disarmament; Immanuel Kant joined the ranks of those working for peace in 1795.

In Sylvester J. Hemleben's history of plans for world peace (1943) it was noted that World War I produced more peace plans than any war in history. There is little question that the opening of the thermonuclear age will soon surpass this record and establish a new one—hopefully the last time peace plans need be formed. Hemleben reports that, on the average, early peace plans leaned heavily on the side of unrealistic, simple panaceas for man's woes; plans always reflect the political order of the times and perhaps this is their fatal weakness.

It is traditional to approach the problem of human conflict by pointing out the scale of horror and incredibility it has attained. One of the most literate essayists on this topic is Norman Cousins—an observer who is fully aware that the horror appeals of 1919 and 1939 failed to reverse the rush to war. As Cousins so eloquently phrased it:

> It is not enough, therefore, to shudder over pictures of bloated bodies floating up on a beach, or of maggoted corpses piled up like cordwood. All the poetic fervor in the world against war will not abolish war if men do not understand how wars begin and how peace must be made (1960, p. 32).

I think it is clear that an inflation of violence has taken place. When it is estimated that in World War I about 126,000 Americans were killed, that the number rose to 397,000 in World War II, and that the speculations about World War III calculate a range of 10 to 160 million American corpses, we must begin to wonder what limit horror will eventually find. This statistical horror is an insufficiently effective construction, however. Human beings cannot long be frightened by cold facts or graphic descriptions. Fear is a more personal experience and one not easily aroused in the abstract. With the increasing sophistication of all societies and the growing ease of communication, simple atrocity piled atop atrocity seems unable to evoke the emotional response it once did. Nuclear holocaust has grown beyond the realm of comprehension and thus has lost its capacity to inspire a continuing terror. When man has moved beyond the limits of terror he becomes capable of assimilating fearlessly and undiscerningly the grossest distortions of simple rationality.

The social scientist who observes this critical situation strives to encompass all its dimensions at once in order to find a single solution to the problem, and in this effort he fails. He fails, in part, because in the intricate system of social weights and balances the problem cannot be solved until man first extricates himself from the impossible tangle into which he has fallen. Throughout history man has relied on military power to bring about change in international relations: he has used force to achieve what he fails to achieve by understanding his fellow man. Now, military diplomacy has overreached itself with technology and man must search for a new path of escape. Having unsuccessfully tried all other paths, man must search the recesses of his social behavior to find the way back. The citizens of this era have for so long faced each new day with anxiety that little energy was available to invest in the distant tomorrow. Yet, beyond the specter of sheer survival lay always the more vital question of the shape of the future. In an age of likely extermination it is not surprising that the prevailing view of what is yet to come is far from a cheery one.

A PATH FOR SOCIAL SCIENCE

Gunnar Myrdal describes the issue clearly when he observes that

> None of our individual disciplines has a broad enough research front to attack in a decisive and completely fruitful way the problem of how to bring about effective international cooperation. It is only when our resources are pooled together that we can hope for a real clarification of the issues and a forging of the powerful tools of social engineering which are so badly needed in this field where more than anywhere else the practitioner must at present work by rules of thumb (1952, p. 6).

We need urgently a new breed of scientist—one less tied to his discipline and dependent on its limited view of man's hostile international relations. Despite the fact that scientists in every discipline cry that they are unable to absorb even the literature in their own field, it still seems vital to me to have a new breed of scientist whose intellectual grasp is great enough to encompass knowledge and method across the range of political science, economics, history, psychology, social work, and the like. It would be regrettable if the pursuit of such an intellectual direction produced only shallow meddlers in man's international world, but I don't think that that is what will happen. It is not necessary to trade understanding and insight in order to get breadth. Every field is saturated with material that is less than relevant to its central aims, purposes, and principles, and I believe that it is possible to do an intelligent job of stripping away the fat from each of the important disciplines and to reassemble the lean remainders into a new and powerful pattern of intellectual armament. A new breed of generalists in human affairs is desperately needed and we continue daily to pay the price of their absence. It is apparent that civilization is overburdened with an increasing production of narrow specialists who can grasp well only a limited part of the problem of man's peaceful relations with his fellow man. It is equally apparent that attempts in the last few years to gather the various disciplines together for cooperative exchange have produced a great deal of conversation, but it has been what Ross Stagner labels *a dialogue of the deaf.*

When the multifaceted nature of the problem of international hostility began to be apparent to those responsible for exploring man's conflict with his fellow man, it was anticipated that the solution would be fairly simple. The assumption was that intelligent, dedicated men in all the sciences would simply gather together to pool their specialized knowledge and evolve a more comprehensive, realistic, and suitable approach to mankind's inability to halt his own destruction. As C. P. Snow was quick to point out, the various sciences no longer found themselves able to communicate with one another. The evolution of the separate sciences had been such that two distinct intellectual cultures had evolved—cultures that could no longer comprehend the orientation and values of the other. It is in this gulf that separates us from the physical and natural sciences that the tragedy lies, for we find ourselves at cross-purposes with those we wish to help and with those on whose shoulders the final decisions may ultimately rest. Our efforts to find common ground ought to continue with full vigor, but, in addition, we need to go further and develop a new direction for behavioral science.

Ideally, I think we should begin at once to make room in our educational institutions for the training of a new breed of scientist. This suggestion, while reasonable, presupposes that we will be granted time enough to wait for this evolution to occur. Since the crisis seems always to be now, something more immediate is called for. It has been said that you can't teach an old dog new tricks, but, today, we all know that's not true. The urgency of world affairs dictates that specialists in the behavioral and social sciences ought to begin now to retread themselves to form the prototype of this new breed. Having achieved depth in their own discipline, established scientists will bring a biased perception to the study of other fields, but it is the best we can do given our late start. The plan of action is exceedingly simple. It amounts to a kind of intellectual tithing for the sake of world peace. No complicated organizational structure is called for and no committee needed to give it direction.

The plea, simply, is for every interested social scientist to begin at once using the ultimate weapon—his brain. To read, study, discuss, write, and think, and act to solve some of the problems of international human relations. To do these things not just from the viewpoint of his own specialized training but from a broader viewpoint—one big enough realistically to encompass man in his total political, economic, historical, social, and personal environment. It is only by seeing man as a total unit that we can avoid solutions that fail or are derided for their narrowness and provinciality.

One handicap to be overcome is the matter of the visibility of the products of social science in action. When a capsule is fired into orbit or a space unit is sent to probe our planetary system, the breathtaking accomplishments of the physical sciences are at once evident to all mankind. The social scientists can offer nothing as comparably easy to perceive and understand in an instant. In this respect it is an uneven race because it is a meaningless comparison—it is a new version of the ancient attempt to compare apples and oranges. In addition, the social sciences have not yet been able to struggle free from the basic problem of demonstrating that their formal attempts to help others are all they are claimed to be.

An even greater task confronting the social scientist is to convince decision-makers of the need to use our methods and theory in asking some very fundamental questions *before* crises reach a critical stage. Decision-makers notoriously are driven relentlessly from crisis to crisis with no time to think ahead of the current emergency. They clearly need assistance in examining, with less haste, questions such as: "Why are things as they are in the world?" "How could they be different?" "How can we change them?" Without searching for answers to these questions, we will be forever steering a course no more distant than the end of our nose. These are times when this is a highly hazardous practice.

In all this we must be fully aware that a part of the necessary education of decision-makers must focus on creating realistic expectations of what the social sciences can accomplish and realistic anticipations of where best their efforts might be applied. It will avail us little if we manage to overcome resistance to social science only to discover that we cannot live up to the enthusiasms of those who feel we can solve the world's problems with some simple magic formula.

Finally, of all the challenges the social scientist must face, undoubtedly the most difficult is that of changing the perception of the decision-makers about the nature of the *real* problem to be solved. We are disadvantaged by the fact that since the time the United States lost its atomic monopoly the race between Eastern and Western cultures has been defined in terms of missile hardware, warheads, nuclear-delivery capacity, and military force. The notion that world dangers can be traced to human reactions among world leaders is never completely abandoned, but it is never really given much credence. In the scramble to stay abreast of the forward thrust of technology, the fundamental problem of the psychological nature of the human beings whose lives are at stake in this race has hardly been considered. For most of us it is apparent that the race can best be described as that of two runners who are so busy watching to see that the other does not gain that neither runner is aware that the race leads only down a blind alley—an alley from which there may be no return.

I think our fundamental problem, then, is to cast the emphasis in war and peace in terms distinct from those that have dominated the last fifteen years of negotiations and foreign policy. I think this can best be done by a concerted effort on the part of social scientists to become active in the search for the best ways and means of having an impact on policy at all levels of its determination.

If we, as a group of scientists, fail to meet this challenge in the near future it will unfortunately be true that we will have failed to contribute significantly to the prevention of World War III and may not have the opportunity to improve our performance in World War IV.

I have no plan that will sweep away the multitude of difficulties that lie ahead for the social sciences, but I have a vision of what might happen if the thousands upon thousands of us were each to devote a part of our professional lives to the task of thinking, planning, experimenting, exploring, and writing about our views of man's relation to his fellow man and about the means by which it might attain a less destructive character. I think the task can be accomplished by a grim determination on the part of each of us to make our presence felt in every way possible to us. It is time we each gave serious thought to the relative importance of our day-by-day activities when compared to the issue of the survival of mankind.

REFERENCES

Cousins, Norman, "Beyond Horror," *Saturday Review* (October 15, 1960).

Hemleben, Sylvester J., *Plans for World Peace Through Six Centuries*. Chicago: University of Chicago Press, 1943.

Myrdal, Gunnar, "Psychological Impediments to Effective International Co-operations," *Journal of Social Issues*, Supplement No. 6 (1952), pp. 1-31.